I0119182

Praise for PASSING the TRASH

This book provides an up-close, evidence-driven story of how school employee sexual predators operate and the ways that predators groom victims, colleagues, families, and communities while sexualizing an organizational climate. Every part of the sad and shocking practices and patterns of child sexual abuse by school employees can be found in this chronicle, each backed up with primary sources and documents: "passing the trash"; grooming students, parents, colleagues, and community members; intimidation and threats; failure to believe victims; and cowardice or indifference from those who are supposed to act. The only thing different from what happens to *10% of students* (that's *4.5 million children*) during their K-12 school years is that in this instance, a courageous and caring School Board member acted and the predator was arrested. This book provides a deep look at employee sexual abuse and why it continues in our nation's schools.

– Charol Shakeshaft, Ph.D.
Professor, Dept. of Educational Leadership
Virginia Commonwealth University
Leading expert on educator abuse

People often ask, *"But how do they get away with it for so long?"* **PASSING the TRASH** shows how one public school educator "gaslighted" his victims and groomed the whole community, literally for decades. The author has performed an invaluable public service with this meticulously documented case study.

– Jennifer Roback Morse, Ph.D.
Founder and President, The Ruth Institute

This horrifying story of a sexual predator – a Toledo-area school superintendent – should shock every parent in Ohio and throughout the country. The author's careful documentation of the man's heartless sexual narcissism at schools (in both Michigan and Ohio) will keep you on the edge of your seat. While those in authority failed to hold him accountable, his victims multiplied as he preyed upon both teen girls and women staff under his supervision. I highly recommend **PASSING the TRASH**, from which we can all learn valuable lessons about how to better protect our children – by exposing these abusers and throwing the book at them. My hope is that this book will spur the Ohio General Assembly to pass legislation with more stringent regulations requiring ethical educator behavior, and prompt reporting of any violations.

– Linda Harvey
MissionAmerica, Columbus, OH

Passing the Trash

Covering Up Educators' Sex Crimes ... and How a Superintendent Was Caught after Decades of Lies

Louisa Miller

With the exception of short excerpts used in critical review, no part of this work may be reproduced, transmitted, or stored in any form whatsoever without the prior written permission of the author and publisher. The book's organizational design, transcripts of testimonies or public comments, and curated screengrab images (from WLS School Board videos) are also subject to copyright protection, including their use in motion pictures, television productions, dramatic productions, or Internet videos.

Although every precaution has been taken to verify the accuracy of the information in this book, the author and publisher assume no responsibility for any unintentional errors or perceived omissions. No liability is assumed for damages that may result from others' use of the information contained herein.

Copyright © 2020 by Louisa Miller
Three Lakes Publishing
Kalispell, Montana
All rights reserved.

Email the publisher: PassingTrash@gmail.com

ISBN: 978-0-578-63187-5
Library of Congress Control Number: 2020900933

DEDICATION

Cindy Louise Perry

Cindy Perry was President of the support staff union at Washington Local Schools (OAPSE 279) in Toledo, Ohio.

A selfless advocate for workers, labor activist, mother, grandmother, and friend, Cindy fought for truth, justice, and equality in the labor community. Cindy was one of the first labor leaders to see beyond Superintendent Patrick Hickey's carefully crafted persona. Along with several others in the community, she heralded the call for change and transparency in the Washington Local Schools administration.

While Cindy may have shunned the spotlight even during her campaigns for the School Board, her leadership of OAPSE during Washington Local Schools' dark days remained firm and unwavering.

Her lifetime of dedicated service took its toll on Cindy and she left us too soon in February 2019. She can be at peace knowing that her convictions and endurance helped bring a bad actor to justice.

This book is dedicated to her memory.

– *Jim Langenderfer*, former member, Washington Local Schools Board of Education (1990-1994 & 2014-2018), Toledo, Ohio

CONTENTS

INTRODUCTION

Malpractice is rampant in America's schools. This book is not, however, about the abandonment of the three R's. It is not about the latest fad curriculum, or falling test scores, or explicit sex education, or ever-growing school budgets.

This book addresses the worst malpractice of all: the sexual abuse of a child by an educator. It also focuses on sexual exploitation of subordinates in the school workplace. In both cases, school environments are sexualized, authority figures lose respect, and children are harmed.

There are multiple victims in this true story: First, the individuals (whether child or adult) who were seduced and sexually used by a narcissistic con artist. Then, the people *beyond* those involved in the sexual misconduct: the victims' families, the seducer's family, the school districts where he was employed, and the communities who fell for his deceptions.

This is a case study in how a predator operates. There is detail going back thirty years: how he groomed and abused his victim; why his victim succumbed; how he later covered his tracks; how those in authority failed to stop him; and how he was finally brought to justice.

The story is told in the voices of the parties involved: retrieved emails, Facebook posts, statements at School Board meetings, school district documents, witness statements, police interviews, and court proceedings. It is a documentary history of abuse, seduction, deception, and gullibility.

Context of the scandal

This decades-long scandal did not happen in a vacuum. There were larger social forces at work that set the stage and allowed it to roll on.

The saga of former school Superintendent Patrick Hickey can be seen as an example of fallout from the "sexual revolution" that took hold in the 1960s.

The messages of this revolution have permeated our culture over the last half century. Sexual freedom came to be seen as *modern, enlightened* behavior. Many eagerly adopted the new ideology since it liberated them to act out without constraints or guilt.

A prime theorist of the sexual revolution was Alfred Kinsey. The Indiana University entomology researcher published two pseudo-science volumes on human sexual behavior (in 1948 and 1953). The American media promoted Kinsey's ideas that sexual promiscuity was normal and shameless, and that freeing oneself from traditional sexual morality would bring individual fulfillment.

One influential Kinsey myth is that children are sexual from birth and that youths' uncommitted, pre-marital sexual experimentation is healthy. Kinsey's co-author, Wardell Pomeroy, clearly stated this in his advice books for teens (from the late 60s on). "Sex ed" in the schools has conveyed this same attitude, undermining traditional restraints and parental authority.

Young abuse victims were thus targeted twice, first by their morality-free education, then by their adult seducers.

A notorious advocate of sexual freedom, *Playboy*'s Hugh Hefner, called himself "Kinsey's pamphleteer." Hefner said, "I believe embracing sexuality is a part of what it means to be free." *Playboy* made pornography acceptable and readily available at the corner drugstore.

Radical feminists joined the sexual revolution, telling girls and women they could engage in free sex just as men did. The birth-control pill and legal abortion further encouraged females to get in on the act. *Cosmopolitan* and *Seventeen* magazines popularized the sexual autonomy message at grocery store checkouts.

Soap operas showcased sexual freedom. Movies and popular music consummated the assault on protective traditional standards of sexual behavior.

Our courts and legislators adopted the new attitudes and refused to recognize the harm pornographic magazines or movies did to women, girls, families, and society as a whole. Banning "obscenity" was a thing of the past. State legislatures bought into the Kinsey myths and reformed laws on sexual crimes, easing sentencing guidelines. The new no-fault divorce laws contributed to the free-wheeling.

Since the 1950s then, selfish individuals were given a green light to get their pleasure wherever they could wrangle it.

While libertines have always existed, their numbers clearly multiplied recently in our sexual-free-for-all culture. *"If it feels good, do it!"* That mantra has encouraged people to sexually engage while ignoring any cautionary messages. Concern for one's sexual partner became optional. Many have suffered as a result.

Otherwise responsible adults engaged in "liberated" sexuality and reaped the consequences, whether sexually-transmitted disease, unwanted pregnancy, emotional trauma, depression, or dysfunctional family life.

A community torn apart

And so, we arrive at the true story of the malfeasance of one Patrick Carl Hickey, former Superintendent of the Washington Local Schools district in Toledo, Ohio.

A typical American community in northwest Ohio was terribly divided and shamed by their school Superintendent's sexual escapades and associated lies – which were finally exposed after decades of deception.

In 2018, following thirty years of rumors, Patrick Hickey was forced to confess his decades-past, multi-year sexual relationship with his teenage student which began when she was underage. There is evidence of his violation of another girl at that time. His later seduction and exploitation of female teachers under his authority – which triggered his final undoing – rounded out his catalog of sexual misconduct.

Could any reason for scandal *other than sex* tear apart a community as did the Hickey revelations? Would the conflict have been so acrimonious had the Superintendent been an embezzler of school funds, rather than an embezzler of the sexual and emotional well-being of others?

What we see in this chronicle is a gut-wrenching example of the long-term destructive effects of the sexual revolution.

Children are the victims

It takes only a few sexually licentious people to turn a community upside-down. Patrick Hickey's harm to children didn't end with his early violation of a teen girl in the Addison, Michigan high school. The chaos that broke out in the Washington Local Schools decades later also horribly impacted children.

How sincere were the district's vaunted "core values" of *dignity, honesty, respect, trust, excellence*? Or statements like, *"It's all about the kids."*

This chronicle is a warning to parents and community members: If your gut tells you something is off with a particular educator, monitor him closely and expose him if necessary.

Thankfully, there were watchmen on the walls for the Washington Local Schools. Two brave School Board members, a private investigator, several teachers, school union leaders, community members, and Hickey's early victim finally called him out. *The Toledo Blade*, northwest Ohio's premier newspaper, went beyond the sensational aspect of the scandal and emphasized the failure of our schools to ensure ethical leadership.

Yet many in the Washington Local School district have continued to believe in Hickey. His devotees have controlled the School Board even *after his conviction* for a sexual crime against a minor and his stint in jail. How is that possible?

"Passing the trash"

This isn't the story of just one man or one school district. Sadly, similar scenarios are happening in districts around the country. Sexual crimes perpetrated by an educator, coach, or school employee against a student have been in the news all too often in the last several decades. These cases may be on the increase. Many abusers get away with their crimes.

The key nationwide study on this problem (from 2004) estimated that about 7% of students had received unwanted physical sexual contact by teachers, coaches, or other school employees. And about 10% of students reported misconduct not including touching, such as sexual talk, sharing pornography, or sexual exhibitionism. The fact that no more recent reliable study exists underscores that this issue is not being adequately addressed.

Recent data from the Ohio Department of Education show that *educator misconduct charges have steadily increased in the last decade,* with about *a thousand credible charges* each year. (This is in just one state.) Misconduct can include unethical behavior of all sorts. Investigations can drag on for years before a finding of guilt and license revocation, *leaving the suspect educator in his job for years.*

Due process is, of course, a bedrock requirement. Rumors and unsubstantiated stories don't count. Solid evidence is needed. But even when it exists, such crimes often still go unreported.

Too commonly, school boards and administrators refuse to properly deal with a sex offender when first identified. They choose to overlook the misconduct, just wanting to get the perpetrator out of *their* district. (Other unprofessional or unethical conduct may get a pass, as well.) They will fail to notify law enforcement. They will take the easy way out and *"pass the trash"* (the errant employee) to some other unsuspecting school system. Sadly, their institution's reputation is more important to them than students' (or employees') welfare.

Educators are all aware of this problem – but most don't want to deal with it. Some of the likely perpetrators are their friends, after all! And who wants to risk being the whistleblower? Even when an abused student or employee comes forward – and many hold back – the perpetrator may still escape justice.

School employees and their communities should be on guard. Parents and children need to watch out for each other and be unafraid to speak up. Adults must have the courage to step in and corral offenders.

Cover-ups just encourage more bad behavior. When the Addison, Michigan schools **"passed the trash,"** Patrick Hickey saw that he could escape punishment for a criminal act. He went on to refine his skills of seduction and evasion over the years. He finally went too far, tripped up, and had to pay for his early crime.

"Passing the trash" in our schools is an abhorrent violation of the public trust and will always bring disastrous consequences. Ask the Catholic Church.

People and Places

We have changed the names of Patrick Hickey's admitted student victim and alleged student victim (late 1980s-1990), and the Washington Local Schools teachers who had relationships with Hickey (2012-2016), to protect their privacy.

WLS = Washington Local Schools, independent school district in Toledo, Ohio

MSP = Michigan State Police

Patrick Carl Hickey – Former Superintendent of Washington Local Schools in Toledo, Ohio. After covering up his crime for three decades, he was convicted in 2018 of criminal sexual conduct with a minor ("Dawn") in the late 1980s when he was her teacher and basketball coach in Addison High School (Michigan). In 2015, he was at the center of a scandal when a wife and husband teaching couple at the WLS high school filed a complaint against him over his relationship with the wife. He was then reprimanded by the School Board in September 2015. After subsequent unprofessional conduct and rumors about his past reaching the Board, Hickey was forced to resign as Superintendent in December 2015. His community supporters remained faithful to him despite an ongoing police investigation (regarding Addison), and elected him to the WLS School Board in November 2017. His hopes to control the Board were foiled as the MSP investigation proceeded and he was indicted for his Addison crime in March 2018. After his conviction in June 2018, he served ten months in Lenawee County Jail in Michigan. After his release, he faces five years on probation and 25 years on the Ohio Sex Offender Registry.

Jim Langenderfer – Long-time resident of the WLS district and retired school administrator, he served on the WLS Board for four years, 2014-2017 (as well as earlier in the 1990s). In late 2015 after Supt. Hickey's unethical behavior with WLS teacher "Anna" was revealed to the School Board, Langenderfer heard stories of criminal conduct in Hickey's past at Addison High School in Michigan. Acting on his own and with personal funds, he hired private investigator Chris Gill to look into the rumors. Hickey's supporters accused Langenderfer of attempting a coup, surveilled him, sent him death threats, vandalized his property, harassed his family members, accused him of ethical violations, and repeatedly called for his resignation. But Langenderfer's intuition about Hickey's seriously flawed character proved correct and brought Hickey to justice.

Chris Gill – Private investigator (and former Lucas County, Ohio Sheriff's Detective) hired by School Board member Langenderfer to look into rumors of Hickey's sexual violation of his female students and basketball players in Addison High School (Michigan). Once Gill sensed Hickey was a bad operator, he continued his work *pro bono*. Over two years, he spoke with Hickey's victim "Dawn" and helped convince her to come forward. He turned over his initial findings to the Michigan State Police in 2016 and continued to consult with them as their investigation progressed.

Addison High School, Addison, Michigan – A small town in southern Michigan near the Ohio border where Patrick Hickey had his first job after graduating from college. He taught English and coached girls' basketball (1986-1990). It was there that he seduced his underage student "Dawn" and continued a sexual relationship with her for three years.

Introduction

MSP cite evidence that he had an inappropriate relationship with a second high school girl there, "Julie," and there were rumors of others. The school administrators failed to deal properly with his ethical violation, allowing Hickey to resign without reporting the situation to the authorities and failing to inform future employers of the circumstances behind his resignation. They "passed the trash."

"Dawn" – Student and basketball player at Addison High School in the late 1980s. She is Hickey's admitted victim. She confessed her sexual relationship with him (beginning when she was underage) to Addison Schools authorities in November 1990. That led to Hickey's abrupt resignation. She eventually came forward in 2018 when she learned he was still in education and read of his ongoing predatory behavior involving subordinate women in the Washington Local Schools. She said then that she wanted to get him out of education and have him placed on the Sex Offender Registry.

"Julie" – Second Addison High School student and basketball player suspected to have had a sexual relationship with Patrick Hickey (beginning when she was underage), but who did not confirm it either to the Addison administrators in 1990 or to the MSP during their 2016-2018 investigation.

"Mark" – Dawn's older brother who contacted WLS Board member Langenderfer in the fall of 2015 after learning of Hickey's scandalous behavior with a WLS teacher. That prompted Gill's investigation which eventually led to the involvement of the MSP. Mark had earlier warned the WLS Board about Hickey in 2007 (as he was promoted to Superintendent), but they ignored his information.

Detective Sgt. Larry Rothman – With the Michigan State Police. He began investigating Patrick Hickey in 2016 after receiving private investigator Gill's initial findings. In 2018, he completed the investigation with Dawn's cooperation, leading to Hickey's criminal charges, guilty plea, and sentencing.

Teacher "Anna" – Whitmer High School (WLS district) teacher who had a several-years-long inappropriate relationship with Patrick Hickey. She and her husband filed their informal complaint against Hickey with the WLS Human Resources Office in the spring-summer of 2015 when Hickey would not respect their request to cease contact with Anna. The

7

couple's complaint is detailed in this book. This scandal triggered events (including a formal reprimand of Hickey) that led to a re-examination of Hickey's history at Addison High School.

Husband – Teacher Anna's husband, also a teacher at Whitmer High School, who joined his wife in the complaint against Hickey in 2015. His emails with Hickey appear in this book.

Teacher "Becca" – Young married teacher at Whitmer High School and one-time friend of Anna. She at first complained about Hickey's "aggressive flirtation" with her in 2014 but went on to conduct an inappropriate relationship with him. Revealing emails between Becca and Hickey (retrieved from the WLS email system via public records request) appear in this book.

Patricia Carmean – WLS Board member, 2014-2017, at the time of the Hickey scandal. She is a retired WLS teacher and widow of the previous Superintendent. She was allied with Langenderfer on the effort to uncover Hickey's malfeasance. She became a prime target of Hickey's (and his fans') harassment.

Thomas Ilstrup – Local attorney and WLS Board President at the time of the 2015 blow-up and Hickey's resignation, and again in 2018 when Hickey was briefly seated on the Board.

David Hunter – WLS Board member; President 2016-2017. He was a member of the Board that selected Hickey as both Asst. Superintendent and Superintendent of WLS. He repeatedly praised or defended Hickey even after scandalous facts were known.

Eric Kiser – WLS Board member at the height of the Hickey scandal and parent of children in the district. He courageously stood with Langenderfer and Carmean in late 2017 to foil Hickey's plan to control the School Board.

Jeremy Baumhower – Toledo blogger and former local radio producer who was the premier pro-Hickey *provocateur* from September 2015 on. He stated in his iBook that he was having an affair with teacher Anna coinciding with her involvement with Hickey. In that book, he assailed a community member who he believed was behind several anti-Hickey websites. He passed away in 2019.

Introduction

The Toledo Blade – The newspaper that covered the Hickey scandals in detail. *The Blade* published the emails between Hickey, Anna, and her husband; the initial 2016 MSP investigation reports; other revealing documents; and closely followed Hickey's disruption of the WLS community through his conviction in June 2018. The newspaper called attention to the foul practice of "passing the trash" in the country's education system.

Map of NW Ohio and SE Michigan

Addison, Michigan (at marker) in relation to Toledo, Ohio. Patrick Hickey's first teaching position was in Addison High School. Washington Local Schools, where Hickey was Superintendent, is on the north side of Toledo, Ohio. The Lenawee County Court and jail which saw Hickey's investigation, court proceedings, and imprisonment are in Adrian, Michigan.

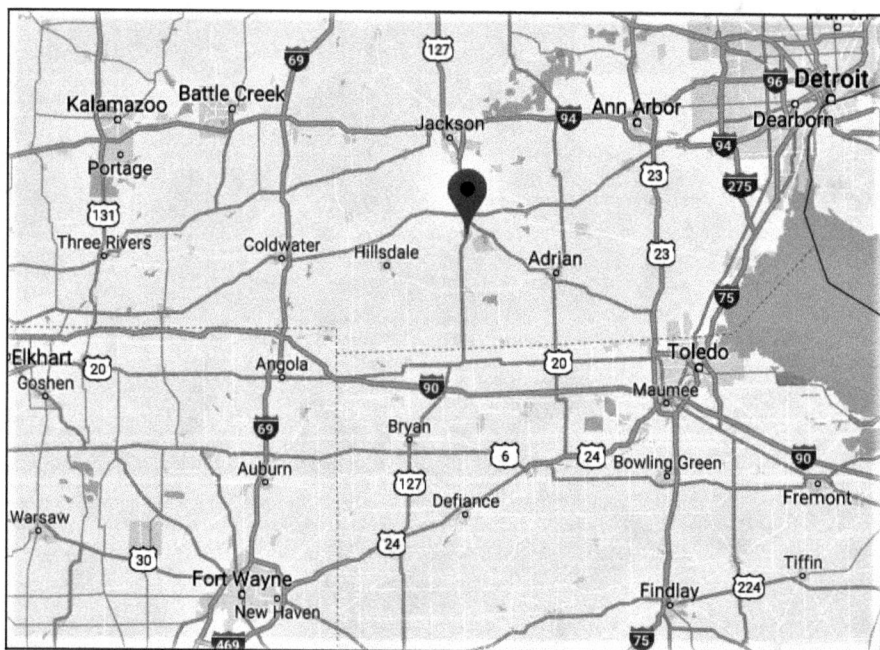

Note on documents

The Kindle edition of this book contains digital images of the Michigan State Police reports and various other documents related to Patrick Hickey's career. Anyone wanting visual confirmation of the quotations or summaries of such material in this paperback edition can refer to the Kindle edition.

CHAPTER 1
Patrick Hickey's Sentencing Hearing
Lenawee County Court, Michigan
– June 28, 2018 –

"I knew then he was a predator and
I finally had to say something..."
– Dawn, Patrick Hickey's victim

Patrick Hickey's sentencing hearing [1] on June 28, 2018 contains both the inception and end point of this chronicle.

His victim "Dawn" tells the Court the story of her three years at Addison High School in Michigan in the late 1980s, when she was held under Hickey's spell. This fatherless young teen girl was overwhelmed beginning at age 14 by a relationship with her charming teacher and coach, which quickly became sexual. He kept the sexual relationship with her going until she graduated – even after he got married. And then he reportedly moved on to another high school girl.

Thirty years intervene between that time in Addison and Hickey's crime catching up with him. Dawn was able to recover from her experience, which she thought at the time was true love but later come to understand as the abuse it was.

Hickey, however, went on to live a lie, prevaricating about his past while feeding his ambition. He continued to develop his skills in seduction, and the Washington Local Schools district in Toledo, Ohio became his latest victim.

But his Addison past came back to haunt him and finally did him in when a School Board member, Jim Langenderfer, found him out.

And so, the Patrick Hickey saga also ends at this hearing with his guilty plea and sentencing to a year in the Lenawee County Jail in Adrian, Michigan. After his release, he faces 500 hours of community service, five years on probation, and 25 years on Ohio's Sex Offender Registry.

The statements in this chapter are taken directly from the official transcript of the Lenawee County Circuit Court proceedings on June 28, 2018. The speakers at the hearing are, in order:

- **"Dawn"** – Hickey's victim when she was a student at Addison High School (her name is changed to protect her privacy)
- **Dawn's Husband**
- **Patrick Carl Hickey**, defendant
- **Lorin Zaner**, Hickey's attorney
- **Angela J. Borders**, Lenawee County Senior Trial Prosecutor
- **Honorable Anna Marie Anzalone**, Judge, Lenawee County Circuit Court

Dawn

Patrick Hickey conducted a sexual relationship with Dawn for three years while she was a student at Addison High School in Michigan, beginning her sophomore year when she was underage. He was her English teacher and sometime basketball coach. Dawn tells her story at Patrick Hickey's sentencing. She did not want to put herself and her family through a long trial, so a plea deal had been worked out: Hickey pleaded guilty to a charge of criminal sexual conduct just short of sexual intercourse with a minor.

My name is Dawn … I'm here as the victim in this case. Thank you for the opportunity for allowing me to speak to clarify some things and to let you know how this man has affected my life.

I'd like to begin by answering the question that so many have asked me: Why now, after nearly 30 years? When I graduated from high school, I told Mr. Hickey that I would never expose our relationship as long as he promised he'd never do what he did to me to another student.

Needless to say, my sophomore year of college I was called out of my class to my basketball coach's office for an emergency phone call. When I arrived and took the call, it was my high school basketball coach, second father, and mentor, Tom Britsch. I knew immediately that the phone call was going to be an unpleasant one for me. He asked me about my relationship with Mr. Hickey and if we had had sexual intercourse. He mentioned that there was another student that Mr. Hickey was allegedly having sex with at Addison.

At this time there are many emotions going through me. I was scared, I was humiliated, I was angry that Mr. Hickey had put me in this position, and I was hurt to find out what he had moved on to another student.

Patrick Hickey's Sentencing Hearing

As embarrassing as it was, I did tell Mr. Britsch the truth that Mr. Hickey and did indeed have a relationship that began when I was 14 until I graduated and moved away to college at age 17. Mr. Britsch took what I told him to the Superintendent at the time, Jeff Kersh. I heard and was under the impression that the school was obligated to report his behavior regardless of whether I would press charges or not, which would mean that he would not be allowed to continue teaching. I found out late November of 2017 that Jeff Kersh had swept everything under the rug and let Mr. Hickey resign without prejudice. I was shocked and I was angry.

When I heard that he was teaching again in Ohio, it was my understanding that it was an all boys school. I can't remember where I heard that, but apparently it wasn't true. I didn't hear anything for quite a while so I believed he was still there.

Then all the phone calls, the voice mails, and letters started. I received calls from detectives, private investigator, reporters, school board members, and attorneys threatening to have me subpoenaed if I didn't talk to them. It was a constant interruption in my life. Other classmates began sharing their stories with me about what Mr. Hickey did to them while they were in high school. I knew about the girl he had sexual intercourse with after I left for college, but not the others. I knew then that he was a predator and I finally had to say something to put this to rest. Then he had the audacity to send me a Facebook message to try to intimidate me to stay quiet, similar to when he drove to my college to find me in order to keep me from telling Mr. Britsch the truth about our relationship.

I'm tired of the interruptions and frustrations this is causing me, my family, and friends. I also can't continue to look my daughters and son in the face and expect them to make good moral decisions when I didn't. I have thought many times over the years when my girls were in school and had a male teacher if anything could possibly be going on. Thank goodness, the male teachers in their lives were stand-up human beings and not predators.

During our few years together, Mr. Hickey and I had sexual intercourse on many occasions. It started when he would rub up against me and touch me in places that I knew were inappropriate. But at the time, it was exciting and flattering to me that a very cute teacher and coach was interested in me. I could feel his erection when playing one-on-one basketball as he rubbed up against me. I was still 14 at the time in

September of 1986. We didn't actually have sexual intercourse until the February 1987 timeframe when I was 15. He was not only my teacher in the classroom and on the basketball court, but also in the bedroom as I was not experienced and many times found myself embarrassed not knowing how to do certain things.

I remember him being very patient and loving. We would call each other in the morning at 6 a.m. to say "good morning" and tell each other "I love you." The night before his wedding, when he was with me for the last time as an unmarried man, I remember him telling me he loved me and wanted to be with me, but that Sue – that he and Sue were obviously too far along in the wedding plans for him to change anything. I went to the wedding for one reason, hoping that he wouldn't be able to go through with it. After all, we loved each other, right? Well, so I thought. I was wrong. Looking back, I believe it excited him that I was there to watch. It was one of the most painful moments of my life.

When I met with the prosecuting attorney, Ms. Borders, she asked me what I wanted out of this case as far as punishment for Mr. Hickey. At the time I told her the most important thing was that he was exposed; for him to have to register as a sex offender, and he must plead guilty and fully admit to our relationship.

People have asked me why I would even entertain a plea deal for him. My answer to that was simple: I didn't want to put my 74-year-old mother, the rest my family and my friends, and of course myself through a long, drawn-out trial.

With that, however, I am completely insulted with his lack of admission of guilt. His admitting to only touching my butt for his own sexual gratification was, once again, him trying to make people believe he did nothing that bad. Wanting people to potentially feel sorry for him that a woman brought charges against him 30 years later for only touching her butt. That is absolutely ridiculous.

Your Honor, I'd like to request that the full jail time be added to my wish list of punishments for him. It appears he needs to take the time to take responsibility for his actions and stop blaming other people for his decisions. I'm not sure what he teaches his kids, but I teach mine accountability; to understand their actions have consequences and they need to own those actions regardless of the embarrassment or the negative publicity it may cause.

For me to have to sit my children down and tell them about my past with Mr. Hickey was humiliating and embarrassing. But when I looked them in the eyes, I knew I was doing the right thing not just for me, but also as a mom and a role model for them. All I've seen Mr. Hickey do is deny, laugh at the accusations with his blogger friend, Jeremy [Baumhower], and continuously blame everyone else by playing the victim. He is an undeniable narcissist who has time after time gotten away with crimes by resigning instead of having to own his actions.

I beg you: Please do not let him take the easy way out of this plea deal with no jail time. He needs to have time to reflect on the human being that he wants his kids to call proudly Dad, someone who owns his actions and accepts the consequences for those actions. I want – I hope that after he has time to reflect, he comes to the conclusion that what he did was beyond wrong.

I want to forgive him, but I cannot do that until he believes that he was not the victim in this and takes accountability. It takes way too much energy to hate someone, and I've already given him way too much of my life to give him any more.

Mr. Hickey, this is the last thing I ever wanted to happen. I don't want to be here right now in this situation. I loved you, but you just couldn't stop. You hurt me to points where I thought I could die. And to add to the hurt during all of this, I heard you deny and laugh about our relationship. Not to mention your latest stall tactics. Watching you try to make a mockery of this court so you can delay taking responsibility once again. You continued to drag this out, putting me and my family through even more stress when all I want to do was get it behind us and move on.

I thank God for giving me the strength to pull through it, and I'm so grateful for my loving family and friends that have been so supportive. I've watched you always fighting to have the last word with excuse after excuse. But now in this instance Judge Anna Marie Anzalone has the last word. I pray you get the rehabilitation you need. Thank you.

Dawn's Husband

… I'm the husband of the victim, Dawn. I won't take much of this Court's time, but I feel compelled to articulate what my wife has gone through the past year.

My wife is a very strong and successful woman. However, this court case has caused her and our family great anguish. For example, over the past year I've had to wake my wife up almost every night from a bad nightmare. It's the same -- it's generally the same nightmare where you,

Mr. Hickey, are on top of her forcing yourself on her or trying to hurt her or trying to shut her up. The nightmare's generally between 2:30 and 4:00 in the morning, and I have to wake her up and hold her down so she calms down. It can take her hours to get back to sleep and this has caused her to be very tired and very lethargic. As she is an account executive who travels a lot, not getting enough sleep has made her job a lot tougher and a lot more stressful.

The stress of this court case has had a negative physical impact on her as well. Dawn has beautiful long blond hair and during this time she had called me into the bathroom on many occasions to show me clumps of her hair that had fallen out and that became very stressful to her as her hair was getting more and more thin. She tried everything that she could, every remedy, but nothing worked. Again, she would come to me crying and get emotional because of this. I felt helpless and all I could do was hold her. Mr. Hickey, that's just simply not acceptable.

My wife told her story very well. Emotionally this has been very difficult for her. She's just starting to get back to her old self. She's starting to have fun again and is beginning to put this behind her. His continued attempts to hold – to back up and hold up these court dates, however, is beginning to make this more and more difficult.

I do want to reiterate that Mr. Hickey is not the only one culpable here. Jeff Kersh, the former superintendent, and the entire Addison administration owns accountability in what occurred to my wife and my family. If he would have done his job, this would not have had to happen and my wife would not have had to suffer the way she has. Let's hope the new administration truly has created a process whereby other young women will be protected and other predators like Mr. Hickey will be exposed and not allowed to continue to work and be in leadership positions as Mr. Hickey was allowed.

In conclusion, Your Honor, as my wife has requested, I too request that Mr. Hickey is given the maximum jail time allowed so that he can think about what he has done to my wife and our family. He frankly deserves far more than the maximum allowable under this plea deal. Mr. Hickey, you have a history of getting your way and laughing at your victims and opponents and not taking responsibility for your actions. That stops today. My wife stood up to you and clearly showed the world the predator that you are. For you, I hope you can finally take that responsibility and apologize to all that you have wronged. As my wife has stated, you do that and we certainly will forgive you. As of today, we can now thankfully put this behind us and move forward. Thank you, Your Honor.

Patrick Carl Hickey

Patrick Hickey watched Dawn as she spoke before the Court. He then makes his own statement. He emphasizes his own childhood traumas and discloses that he underwent years of psychological counseling after he was forced to resign from Addison High School.

THE COURT [Judge Anna Marie Anzalone]: Before the Court passes [sentence] – first, I'll start out with saying the Court is contemplating giving you a sentence that is in excess of the sentencing guidelines. Before the Court passes sentence, do you wish to say anything on behalf of your client?

MR. ZANER [Hickey's attorney]: Your Honor, first of all, if the Court would approve, my client would like to say something and then I would say something afterwards.

THE COURT: That's fine. Mr. Hickey.

HICKEY: My sexual relationship with Dawn was horribly wrong, [Hickey faces accuser:] and I want to apologize to her, your childhood family, and your current family. I am so sorry and my words can never give you back what I took, but know that I'm deeply sorry for the pain and confusion that I caused you. I find some relief if you have overcome my actions with a great family and career. I deeply regret and I cringe at my behavior in 1987.

[Addresses the Court:] Upon leaving Addison 31 years ago, my wife and I agreed that I needed severe psychological help. I was a 23-year-old [when he began teaching in 1986], and untreated psychologically for childhood sexual abuse and the devastating death of my 15-year-old sister when I was 11. I voluntarily and instantly entered into psychotherapy and group psychotherapy. I attended therapy sessions every week for three years in the hope that I would never hurt anyone in the way that I did Dawn.

After three years of therapy, my wife and I wanted an additional two years before we had children to be sure that I was truly changed and not a danger to anyone. In the intervening decades, my wife and I have raised four kids and I have worked with thousands of kids. I wanted to right the wrong by advocating for all kids.

In your field, Your Honor, you hear remorse but you must hope for action. In my case, I hope you see that my remorse for my errors in 1987 did lead to action insuring that my behavior never repeated itself.

[Hickey turns toward Dawn.] And I also want to say to Dawn that I did not delay these hearings on purpose.

THE COURT: Sir, if you could please address me.

HICKEY: Okay. And that wasn't – I'm probably getting in trouble with my attorney, but I wanted her to know that wasn't –

THE COURT: I understand.

HICKEY: Okay. Thank you. And I appreciate the time.

Lorin Zaner, Hickey's attorney

Hickey's attorney, Lorin Zaner, seems to blame others for Hickey's crime and later cover-up, citing an older sibling who sexually abused him as a child, a drunk driver who killed his sister, and a therapist who used poor counseling strategies. Zaner also discredits people in the Washington Local Schools community who wrote to the Court (and who were aware that Hickey's inappropriate sexual behavior didn't end at Addison). Zaner persists with the false story that Hickey left Addison Schools "for job opportunities." He references a simpler time 30 years ago when punishments for sex offenders were less severe. In closing, he faults Dawn for changing her mind about what an appropriate punishment would be.

May it please the Court. Your Honor, I've been practicing law a long time and I don't recall ever sitting down and writing out a sentencing memorandum and a speech for this Court. Normally I just speak off the top of my head. But there's been so much miscommunication, misinterpretation, and everything that's happened with this whole case, I want to – hopefully I want to make sure that what I'm saying to the Court is accurate based on the facts and circumstances in this case.

So, Your Honor, Patrick admits that he had an inappropriate sexual relationship with a student over 30 years ago while he was a teacher and coach at Addison High School. He admits that relationship was wrong and he sincerely apologizes for his action as you have already heard. What occurred was totally his fault and not the student's.

As he's already indicated, he was molested as a child by an older sibling. He lost his 15-year-old sister to a drunk driver. And all of these events led him to do inappropriate actions as a 23-year-old. He's no longer 23 years old, he's in his 50s, who has taken steps to confront the issues and the things that occurred in his life that led him to have this inappropriate sexual relationship with the student. As he's indicated to you, he entered into counseling for three years with Jacob Elliott and Associates. We've provided documents to the Court for that. He went through almost three years of counseling to try to deal with his past, to try to save his marriage, and also the inappropriate sexual relationship he had with the victim in this case.

One of the problems with the counseling, he was taught something which, in retrospect, was a mistake. He was taught to move forward and not live in the past. And I believe that was a mistake and part of the reason why we're here today as opposed to 30-some years ago to have taken care of it. He's truly sorry he listened to his counselor, which is when you're in counseling that's one of the things you do. He should have admitted this relationship 31 years ago. And he truly apologizes for that and not doing so.

He realizes he has put the victim in this case through a lot as a result of his actions. He's not seeking forgiveness, he knows he's not entitled to forgiveness. But the point is he's no longer a 23-year-old. He's no longer that teacher who took advantage of a child. He's tried to be a positive force to accomplish things and to help society.

Even though he has numerous people that don't like him, the number of letters the Court has received are obviously enormous. Many of them are unfavorable and many of them are favorable. We know when he was the superintendent of Washington Local Schools, there was a writing campaign where people were writing letters as if it was coming from numerous individuals when it was really coming from only two or three. I can't tell you whether that's accurate here or not, but that's the kind of impact that he's had with people. You love him or you don't love him. And the Court's obviously seen numerous letters.

I think it's important for the Court to know some of the things that he's accomplished. He's been married over 30 years. He has four children, including a special needs child. And all of the children are doing well. The special needs child has found a job and is only able to get to work through the work of his father by taking him back and forth because his mother is employed full-time.

And there's also a letter that we have submitted to the Court that I'd like to point out a few of the things in this, and this is from a Sharon Giles, who was his executive secretary while he was the superintendent of the Washington Local Schools, and she spells out some of the things that Mr. Hickey – positive things Mr. Hickey has done and I think it's important to spell those out.

"It was" – and I'm quoting what she says – "It was common for staff and students to ask Patrick for prayers and for him to lead a prayer for a special event. He was a goal-driven and energetic leader for the Washington Local Schools who was named the number one leader into 2014 by Workplace Dynamics. Under Patrick's leadership, Washington Local Schools thrived and became a highly sought-after district for families.

"He was a proponent of Challenge Day, where every 10th grade student participated in a day-long program designed to break down barriers, learn compassion, and be the change. At times of the death of a student or staff member, Patrick always reached out to the family personally to offer support and condolences.

For special needs children, his comment was he always says that God made each person exactly the way they are supposed to be. He sponsored a program, "Falling as Equals, The Journey to Find Courage," which showed him jumping out of a plane with a disabled child.

"Every year Patrick spoke to the seniors the week of prom to share the heartache he and his family experienced when his sister was killed by a drunk driver.

"He was often asked to speak to community groups such as the Board of Realtors, Toledo Symphony League, and others."

So there's numerous things that Patrick has done to try to rectify what he did in the past, which obviously cannot be rectified, but to try to be a better person and to help society.

And it's frightening all the rumors that have happened in this case about Mr. Hickey, including one we just heard today, he's coming in [into] court in a wheelchair. The rumors he was out jogging recently, he made a disturbance at a hospital, that he was not living at home. All of those are absolutely preposterous, none of them are true.

Jill and I were at his home, which you can see the border of Michigan from his home, and we saw the difficulties he was having as a result of injuries to his back and all the medication that he was on.

In my opinion, a lot of these letters are from Washington Township do-gooders that have no place in this case. And, in fact, Jill and I both being graduates from Whitmer [High School in Washington Local district], it's embarrassing to be part of that system considering all of these letters that have come forth.

And obviously this case is about Patrick Hickey and the victim and what occurred to her over 30 years ago and what's the appropriate punishment. I think it's important to know that he didn't leave Michigan to avoid prosecution. Nothing had been filed. No one ever said anything about prosecution. He left for job opportunities. If he had stayed in Michigan, the statute of limitations would long ago have run, we wouldn't have – we wouldn't be here. His punishment would not be as harsh back then as it is today because it's my understanding back then there was [sic] no registration requirements, which clearly he now is going to have to register as a sex offender, which would not have happened at that time.

And the other effect this is having on him, he will no longer be able to travel out of the country. And having a cottage out of the country, he will no longer be able to get there.

The Court is aware that the victim originally was only looking for a few certain things: A short period of incarceration, registration, and a period of probation. And she's changed her position as a result of what was said at the time of the plea.

Well, I would indicate it's my understanding she was aware of what Mr. Hickey was going to say. I sat down with the prosecutor so the statements that Mr. Hickey made would satisfy the requirements of the statute. And so what he said was essentially based on the advice of counsel. But as we sit here today, he is accepting full responsibility for everything that he has done with the victim in this case.

Your Honor, the Court is well aware that there's a lot of punishment he's already been handed to him with all the media attention. Certainly [it has] taken a toll on him, his family. But I'm not here to minimize what has occurred to the victim and her family, but I do find it interesting in reviewing her husband's statement prior to court and I'd like to quote something that he said:

"My wife is a very strong and successful woman. However, this court case has caused her and her family great anguish."

The media harassment, the constant phone calls the family received from others to push her to do things is unconscionable. This should have been up to the victim, her family, the prosecutor. And all these other people trying to get involved and get in the middle of this, in my opinion, have no place.

The Court is aware from documentation we've provided to the Court that he does have back problems, he's on a lot of different medications, and we – I'm not here asking the Court for probation. Obviously that's not going to happen. We discussed with Mr. Hickey at least some thoughts that the Court discussed with us. And if we're talking going to prison or being incarcerated locally, it's greater punishment to be incarcerated locally and then be put on a period of probation, the Court will have more control over Mr. Hickey to make sure he follows all of the guidelines that he needs to follow. And he's aware that the Court's likely to hear all kinds of things from people, whether it's true, which hopefully it's not, and those are things, you know, I've advised him of some things he needs to do to try to protect himself from future false comments and rumors and that kind of stuff.

So, Your Honor, we're asking this Court when it comes to sentencing that the Court impose local incarceration, as I've indicated previously from what the victim originally wanted, the 10 to 15 days we feel is sufficient. Likely the Court's going to do a lot longer than that. But we're asking that it be local incarceration and not prison. The Court's aware Mr. Hickey has no previous record, no contacts. He's had a difficult childhood with things that happened to him, doesn't excuse what he did, but he took steps to try to rectify it by going through counseling and all the good things that he has done.

There's lots of rumors about him doing other things that are bad. Whether they're true or not true, there's no charges or anything else. And he's prepared for his sentencing. If it's local incarceration, I'd ask the Court to allow him to be able to have his medication while he's in custody for the back issues that he has. Thank you.

Angela Borders, Assistant Prosecuting Attorney, Lenawee County

THE COURT [Judge]: All right. Thank you, Mr. Zaner. Anything further? Ms. Borders?

MS. BORDERS: Your Honor, I'm – I don't plan to say much other than to defend the victim because she's not able to stand back up here and defend herself. She did not know exactly what he was going to say at the time of the plea. He knew. And all she really cared about was that he would admit the relationship, but not to the amount that he minimized that relationship. She did not have that insight or that information.

Otherwise, as far as anybody – Mr. Zaner's statement that you either love him or you don't love him, it's actually been made pretty clear to me that if you know him, you either love him or you hate him. It's not that you just don't love him. There's definitely two sides, and I think that that needed to be cleared up.

Otherwise, I support the victim. I've always supported the victim in this case. She's been my primary focus and that's what has driven me through this and into this day. So I want the Court to think about her words and her husband's words and not mine. So I have nothing further to say to this Court.

Judge Anna Marie Anzalone ("The Court")

*Note that while Hickey admitted to and was convicted for a lesser crime (basically "groping" Dawn's buttocks), the Judge states that Dawn "was 14 when [Hickey] started grooming her and 15 at the time that [he] **had sexual penetration**. She was a minor."*

THE COURT: [Addressing Hickey:] Could you step back up to the podium, please?

As I said earlier, the Court is contemplating giving you a sentence that is in excess of the sentencing guidelines of 0 to 9 months. I have spent several days reviewing every single letter that I have received, paying closer attention obviously to people who witnessed events that occurred both for and against you. So I have this pile on your behalf and this pile obviously against you. But I wanted to make clear that I did review and respect every letter that I received from everyone.

I also reviewed the sentencing memorandum that was provided to me by Mr. Zaner.

The Court is contemplating giving you a sentence that is in excess of the sentencing guidelines for several reasons. One, I read your description of the offense and I was very bothered by your statement that the victim accepted what you were doing and consented to allowing you to do it. She was 14 when you started grooming her and 15 at the time that you had sexual penetration. She was a minor. There's no consent at all for a minor.

In determining the appropriate sentence in this case, the Court has considered the seriousness of the offense, your history, the principle of proportionality, the statutory penalty, the cost of confinement, the sentencing guidelines, the report and recommendation of the probation department, and what has been said upon the record at this hearing.

The criteria and reasons for the sentence are the nature and gravity of the offense, the discipline appropriate to its commission, deterrence against repetition by you and by others, the potential for reformation, vindication for the law, and the protection of society.

I was a former teacher and one of the biggest things that I knew is when my students walked in, their parents sent them to school knowing that their children would be cared for and be safe. And that is a vow that you – almost a vow that you take as a teacher to make sure that you do no harm, and in this case harm was done.

Also male teachers across the United States suffer because of people like you. So my daughter plays basketball, she has a male coach. And as a parent you end up questioning male teachers of female students because of behavior like this. And that is a shame.

Unfortunately, this did not come back up – come out back in the '80s because you should have never been allowed to continue to work in a school environment with minor children.

So I have thought what sentence would be more proportionate to the offense that occurred and the things that you have done. Because of the age of the victim, because of the position as a teacher, you should be punished. So I don't think jail – no jail and probation is appropriate in this matter. If I send you to prison, you will serve 16 months with the Michigan Department of Corrections and maybe get a few months of parole and then you'd be done and there would be no further sanctions or no further control of this court and no further monitoring of your behavior. In this case I don't think that's appropriate. I think that you would be getting off very lightly if I did that.

Therefore, it is the sentence of the Court that you will serve one year in the Lenawee County Jail with zero credit served. And you will be placed on probation for a period of five years.

I understand that you reside in Ohio and that probation will be transferred to the parole department in the state of Ohio. Understand that if you violate probation by even jaywalking, I can send you to prison. Do you understand?

HICKEY: Yes.

THE COURT: You will register as a sex offender and I believe that is for 25 years.

You are not to have any contact with the victim ["Dawn"] or her family. You're not to have any contact with minor children under the age of 17 with the exception of your own biological children. You are not to go on any school grounds where minor children attend.

You must perform community service of 500 hours, which you must complete within the five years. It has to be preapproved by the probation department before credit will be given and supervised by an adult when doing so.

You must not live, work, or loiter within a school safety zone described – which we define as 1,000 feet – within 1,000 feet of a school property. That's private schools, developmental kindergartens, after-school programs, and summer camps unless you meet a statutory exception.

During that five-year period you are not to have any social media accounts.

You must not be within 500 feet of parks, municipal swimming pools, playgrounds, child care centers, preschools, arcades, or other places primarily used by individuals 17 or under within prior written approval by your field agent.

You must not use or possess alcoholic beverages or any other intoxicants. You must not enter bars or any place where the primary purpose is to serve alcoholic beverages for drinking on site unless you're given permission by the field agent.

You must comply with the requirements of alcohol testing as directed as well as drug testing. You must not use any controlled substances or drug paraphernalia unless prescribed to you by a licensed physician.

And you must, as I said earlier, perform 500 hours of community service. And you must not use or possess any object as a weapon.

There is also a clause you must allow the field agent into your residence, your home, or access to your phone and computer at any time upon request.

Now, you do have the right – there will be $130 crime victim rights fee, $68 in state costs, $12.50 per month supervision fee, $750 in court costs, $60 DNA fee.

Now, you do have the right to appeal this sentence. My bailiff is going to hand down to you your notice of right to appellate review. Please sign the top copy for our records. The other copy is for your records. If you wish to appeal the sentence, you would fill out the information on the form and mail it to the address listed on the form within 42 days.

Mr. Jones, is there anything further?

MR. JONES: I believe that's it, Your Honor.

THE COURT: All right. Very good. I've received back a signed copy of the notice of right to appellate review. Thank you.

MS. BORDERS: Thank you, Your Honor.

MR. ZANER: Thank you, Judge.

CHAPTER 2
No-Nonsense Langenderfer

Though few in the Washington Local Schools district realized it at the time, they were fortunate that Jim Langenderfer was elected to their School Board for a four-year term beginning in January 2014. He and Board member Patricia Carmean would prove effective watchdogs during a turbulent time for the school district.

If Jim had not been on the Board, it is likely that Patrick Hickey would have skated and never have to pay for his early crime. It was Jim who moved forward, without Board authorization, and hired a private investigator to check out the rumors from Hickey's time at Addison High School. He paid for this out of his own pocket.

As we will see, over many years the Board leadership had lacked courage to take the hard look at Hickey that was needed. Jim changed all that.

Educator and WLS district resident

Jim is an old-school kind of guy. Gruff and to the point, he mercilessly cuts through nonsense.

Jim has over 38 years of experience in education. He was a school administrator for 28 of those years. His expertise is Special Education. In recent years, Jim has worked at the University of Toledo as a consultant in Special Education for school districts around the Midwest.

Raised in a middle-class family, his hard-working parents imbued Jim with respect for honest labor. After graduating high school in 1968, he went on to college, earning a B.Ed. and M.Ed. from the University of Toledo. He did post-graduate work in Special Education Administration at Eastern Michigan University, Youngstown State University, and Grand Valley State University.

Jim spent over 20 years as a referee for football, basketball, and lacrosse at the college and high school levels. During the 1980s, he was Football Commissioner for the Tri-County League in southeastern Michigan.

Jim has lived in the Washington Local School District (WLS) for over 40 years. Both his children graduated from the district schools. They are now managers in major American corporations.

His connection to the WLS community runs deep. Jim served a four-year term on the WLS School Board starting in 1990, including two years as President. He served again from January 2014 through December 2017.

Seated: Board President **Thomas Ilstrup**, Superintendent **Patrick Hickey**, Board Vice President **David Hunter**. Standing: Treasurer **Jeff Fouke**; Board members James **Langenderfer**, **Patricia Pedro Carmean**, and **Steve Zuber**; Assistant Superintendent **Cherie Mourlam**.

2014 Board of Education, Washington Local Schools, Toledo, Ohio [1]

Elected to WLS Board of Education, Nov. 2013

In 2013, Cindy Perry was President of the Washington Local Schools support staff union (OAPSE). She had watched Patrick Hickey's shenanigans over the years since 2002 – first when he was Assistant Superintendent, then Superintendent (starting 2007) – and she wanted him out. For some time, the Board had apparently looked the other way while suspecting unethical behavior by Hickey. The union leader was looking for an honest broker on the Board who would address the support staff's concerns. They were looking for someone unaffected by the local power plays.

So in 2013, Perry and several others urged Jim to run for the School Board. As a long-time district resident, comfortably semi-retired, he had nothing to gain or lose from his service on the Board. He agreed to run.

He had no idea what a ride was in store for him!

Perry managed Jim's low-key campaign for the School Board. He spent only his own money – and very little of that – on his run. Also taking a seat on the Board in January 2014 was OAPSE-endorsed Patricia Carmean, retired WLS elementary teacher and widow of Hickey's predecessor as WLS Superintendent. Along with Jim, Carmean became Hickey's other prime critic on the Board.

Jim the Disrupter

Jim knew something was off when he first saw Patrick Hickey in action. He detected a sincerity deficit. Jim nicknamed the showman Superintendent "Hollywood Hickey."

Hickey and his fans intensely disliked Jim, whom they called a "carpetbagger." Though Jim had lived in the district for decades, he had worked in Michigan school systems so was relatively unknown to many in the WLS district.

His critics pointed to what they called his "disrespectful" body language at School Board meetings. Any slander would do to take Jim down. *No one would dare challenge or doubt their community cheerleader, Patrick Hickey!*

In an angry outburst at a public, recorded School Board meeting, one mother falsely accused Jim of slamming into her wheelchair-bound daughter and then marching off without apologizing. But how obviously out of character that was for an educator whose career was helping special-needs children! (A review of security footage at the school proved the accusation false.)

On numerous occasions, there were angry calls at School Board meetings for Jim's (and Patricia Carmean's) resignation.

But by late 2015, Jim (along with Carmean) had inside knowledge and solid grounds to suspect wrongdoing by Hickey that the public didn't know. Jim had seen inappropriate communications between Hickey and a female teacher he supervised. Furthermore, he had received a tip about Hickey's early years that seemed serious enough that he decided to hire a private investigator. *Jim personally funded the initial investigation that would prove key to Hickey's downfall.*

Daring to question Supt. Hickey

The Superintendent's over-the-top showmanship just didn't sit right with former administrator Jim. How appropriate was Hickey's favorite line about students – that he wanted to *"love them and lift them up"*? Then there was Hickey's "overly familiar" physical style with staff, students, parents, and community members. Hugs were frequent – and not just a light touch on a shoulder, but chest-to-chest, arms-encircling hugs. Hickey even professed his "love" for individual students at public School Board meetings. And then there were the rumors of inappropriate relationships with school district staffers under his supervision.

Jim also saw problems with Hickey's arrogance in bulldozing through his pet projects. One such incident that got the end drama rolling was Hickey's advertising pact with Brondes Ford, a dealership in the district. The Superintendent had gone so far as to have the field house floor repainted with the company's logo before the Board had been properly informed or approved any deal with the company.

Another issue was the support staff contract negotiations, when the OAPSE union leaders felt he had dealt in bad faith and generally undervalued them. Supt. Hickey sometimes even skipped required monthly meetings with the union leaders. Furthermore, OAPSE asked why $70,000 was set aside for teachers' "professional development" in what they saw as a boondoggle to a corporate-funded private school in Atlanta, Georgia. Meanwhile, the support staff hourly wages hung in between $8 to $15 an hour.

Jim, being a public-school advocate, agreed with their concerns and championed the OAPSE viewpoint. He objected to school moneys going for the teachers' trip. He saw no practicality to dreams of remaking WLS – in an economically depressed area of a rust-belt city – after the model of a swank private school. Furthermore, there was then no proven track record for student achievement at that Atlanta school, so how could the argument be made that its teaching style was effective?

For this sort of dedication to fiscal oversight, transparency, honesty, and open discussion, Jim was targeted by Hickey's supporters. He was slandered at public Board meetings. His house was under surveillance. He got nuisance phone calls, including death threats. His tires were slit. His mail went missing. His adult children were harassed. For Jim, it felt like something out of organized crime was coming at him.

Typical exchange between Hickey and Langenderfer

Below is a characteristic public exchange between Jim Langenderfer and Patrick Hickey at a School Board meeting. [2] (Their conversations out of the public eye were not so jovial.)

No-Nonsense Langenderfer

The Whitmer High School girls' basketball team was honored at the April 22, 2015 Board meeting for having the highest GPA of a high school sports team in Ohio. [3] The entire Board congratulates them. Langenderfer notes how unusual this achievement is and that he had previously advocated setting higher GPA requirements for WLS athletes.

Note that Jim (a former high school and college athlete himself) sticks to business. But Superintendent Hickey is focused on the girls' good looks.

Hickey says to the girls' team, "What a *good-looking* group of humans you are, too!"

Jim jokingly says: "Quit brown-nosing, Patrick." Hickey and others laugh. Jim continues, "See, we could have football, basketball – *everything* could be like that. You could be nationally known, Patrick!"

Hickey responds, "I am!" Jim chuckles.

Jim stuck to the issue: Raising GPA requirements for school athletes.

Hickey watches the girls' basketball team leave after complimenting them on their good looks.

CHAPTER 3
Hickey at Addison High School
– 1986-1990 –

Patrick Hickey's early years

Patrick Hickey was born in 1963, grew up in Toledo, and graduated from St. John's Jesuit High School in that city. He recounted two childhood traumatic experiences at his 2018 sentencing hearing: He was sexually abused as a child by an older sibling, and his teenage sister was killed by a drunk driver when he was 11.

Hickey was a devoted athlete during his high school and college years.

In 2015, he told this story about himself to then Washington Local Schools Board President, Thomas Ilstrup, advocating second chances for young people who have committed offenses:

> There once was a Superintendent who, for a variety of reasons, made very poor choices in high school. I am indebted to my Principal for giving me a second chance whereby I earned 1st honors at St. John's my senior year, did not have any referrals, and was given a special award at our Baccalauerate [sic] Mass for improvement (discipline letter attached). I have kept it in my desk for many years to remind myself that kids who need the most love and discipline will ask for it in the most unloving ways. Maybe I am clouded by my own experience.

In a letter sent to Hickey's parents at the end of his junior year, the Associate Principal of St. John's High School hoped that young Pat would learn to "assume responsibility for his actions" and noted that the Deans agreed he needed to be sent a warning letter.

> I am writing to you to suggest that you and your son, Pat, look over the record for this year and make some appropriate resolutions for senior year.... In particular, I note [his] being asked to leave class **five** times, three other referrals, sixteen (16) morning lates to school, plus the Maumee bus incident.... We have talked in the past about Pat's need to assume responsibility for his actions. I know that he is more than capable of being much more cooperative

than he has been this past year. The school does expect considerable improvement from Pat during his senior year.

Hickey graduated from St. John's High School in 1981. Five years later in 1986, he received his B.A. in English from Siena Heights University in Adrian, Michigan. The only "D" grade on his college transcript was in a course called "Values I." He had a cumulative undergraduate GPA of 2.90. He listed his college honors as "Athlete of the Year" in 1983 and "Student Teacher of the Year" in 1986.

Hickey does not explain why he took five years (rather than four) to earn his B.A. degree. His transcript shows his fifth year devoted to a light load of education credentialing courses (methods and student teaching). His résumé (dated 1986) notes that worked as a "bus person" at college and "heavy equipment operator" in Toledo during the five summers of 1981-1985.

Hickey at Addison High School, 1986-1990

Fresh out of college in the fall of 1986 at age 23, Patrick Hickey began teaching English at Addison High School in southern Michigan. He also coached the girls' JV basketball team, assisted girls' varsity coach Tom Britsch, and coached girls' varsity teams at state tournaments. He claims he was "Lenawee County Basketball Coach of the Year" in 1989.

Addison High School Principal Donald Dieck wrote an *undated* letter of reference for Hickey after knowing him for "two years." Since Hickey started at Addison in the fall of 1986, the letter would have been written sometime in late 1988 or possibly early 1989, but certainly before the scandalous fall of 1990 when Hickey was forced to resign.

The letter stated that Hickey:

> ... has exhibited the qualities one would want in a teacher, a coach and a friend. Patrick is sincere in his dedication to students and the teaching profession. During the time I have know [sic] Patrick he has always been and continues to be a credit to our school and community.
>
> Patrick's loyalty and judgement can be counted on in all situations. He is one who leads by example and his enthusiasm for life is contagious.
>
> Patrick is an excellent teacher and he relates well to his students. He is well accepted by both students and staff.
>
> I can wholeheartedly recommend Patrick as a desirable candidate for your consideration.

In April 1988 during Hickey's second year teaching, Dieck wrote a letter recommending him for tenure. He noted that Hickey willingly spent time with students after normal school hours:

> In addition to his teaching, Patrick coaches girls' junior varsity basketball and 8th grade boys' basketball. Patrick is an excellent English teacher. He is creative and projects a positive attitude in his class. His students are involved and active in class. Patrick also is a willing worker. He is always ready to help after school and on weekends. We need more teachers who are as willing to work as Patrick.

These early letters by Principal Dieck were written before the scandal erupted in November 1990. Hickey could later use them to cover up the circumstances of his resignation from Addison Schools.

Many photos in the Addison HS yearbooks show Hickey alongside Coach Tom Britsch at girls' basketball events or standing with the JV girls' basketball team in their official portraits.

Hickey's relationship with student Dawn

From 1986-1989, Hickey had an ongoing relationship with "Dawn," a student on the basketball team. She also had Hickey as her English teacher in her junior year.

Hickey began his sexual grooming of Dawn when she was 14. She was 15 (legally underage) when they first had sexual intercourse at his home (according to the Michigan State Police investigation).

After Dawn graduated in 1989, Hickey was rumored to be engaged in a sexual relationship with another basketball player on the high school girls' team, "Julie." He was seen with this second girl in a rocking car in the local cemetery in the fall of 1990. The witness, mother of another high school student, reported this to the Addison administrators and circulated a petition to have Hickey fired. Dawn was then contacted by her trusted old coach, Tom Britsch, and confessed her earlier relationship with Hickey. This led to Hickey's sudden forced resignation from Addison High School in November 1990.

In addition to the witness statements in later chapters, the high school yearbooks provide evidence that Hickey had an inappropriate relationship with Dawn.

Hickey left the note below in her 1987 yearbook at the end of her sophomore year. It lends credence to her later testimony about the two of them playing one-on-one basketball, plus the significant happenings the night of the Pittsford away game when their sexual relations began. (Hickey would later claim Dawn was lying about the Pittsford incident in his interview with the Michigan State Police.) His inscription was all written in upper-case:

> IT SURE HAS BEEN FUN BECOMING YOUR FRIEND. KEEP PRACTICING HOOPS & STUDYING AND YOU CAN ACCOMPLISH <u>ANYTHING</u> YOU WANT. REMEMBER ONE ON ONE HOOPS, WATER FIGHTS, 1ˢᵗ PERIOD (INCLUDING TOP GUN FLYING), SHOOTING HOOPS IN MY ROOM, THE PITTSFORD BASKETBALL GAME, AND ALL THE OTHER GREAT TIMES.
>
> IWABYBF   <u>ME</u>

Dawn explained that Hickey's tag "IWABYBF" meant, "I will always be your best friend." Hickey signed it "ME" so others wouldn't easily identify the writer, she told the MSP Detective. It reads like a note from a high school boyfriend, not her teacher.

Hickey's note to Dawn in her 1988 yearbook (her junior year) was less personal and he signed formally with his last name, "Mr. Hickey." He writes this in script and enumerates the ways she will succeed. It reads:

> Always remember that you have a great deal to offer your many friends. Your personality & warmth are cherished by many people. You will be a success in life, marriage, kids, career. I wish you all the best.
>
> BE GOOD   Mr. Hickey

His note in Dawn's 1989 yearbook (her senior year) includes the phrase, "Somewhere out there." She told the MSP Detective that Hickey was referring to a favorite song and made her "think that they would be together someday." (Like the 1987 inscription, it was all written in upper-case; ellipses are in the original.)

> WHAT CAN I SAY? OUR FRIENDSHIP WILL ALWAYS BE A CHERISHED POSSESSION. SOMEWHERE OUT THERE.... YOU WILL BE A SUCCESS IN ALL THAT YOU DO ... & IN ALL THAT YOU WANT TO ACCOMPLISH. YOU ARE VERY SPECIAL.
>
> FRIENDS ALWAYS   ME

Hickey was unmarried during his first year and a half teaching, then married Sue in April 1988. (That was in the spring of Dawn's junior year.) Dawn would later state that he invited her to the wedding and she attended – calling it the worst day of her life. Hickey would later deny to the Michigan State Police that this happened, or that his wife even remembered Dawn. (However, a yearbook photo shows Dawn sitting next to Hickey's wife at a school event.) He also entirely denied his sexual relationship with Dawn to the MSP, though it continued even after he was married, Dawn said.

Many contemporaries back up Dawn's story of the sexual relationship. And, of course, Hickey finally confessed to it in 2018 (though to a lesser charge of criminal sexual conduct, thanks to a plea bargain).

Witness statements about Hickey's time at Addison and his violation of Dawn comprise Chapters 4-6.

Two complaints and Hickey's two days off

Hickey's rumored second underage conquest at Addison, "Julie," was on the girls' basketball team after Dawn had graduated. Julie has never admitted to the relationship, either to school authorities at the time or to investigators in recent years.

However, the Michigan State Police reports do note that there is "evidence" of the relationship, without noting what that evidence is. (Those MSP reports from 2016 and 2018 are in Chapters 18 and 22.)

But it was what two people reported seeing Julie do in a cemetery one night with Hickey that began a chain of events ending with Hickey's abrupt resignation from Addison High School on November 5, 1990.

An Addison mother, Mrs. Judith Brooks, and her daughter Brooke (who was on the basketball team) witnessed Hickey and Julie departing school in their separate cars after basketball practice one night. Both Hickey and Julie drove off in the same direction – which was odd since they lived in opposite directions from the school. So, Mrs. Brooks and her daughter (who already had their suspicions) followed the cars to a dark and isolated cemetery. From a distance they saw one person join the other in one of the cars which began rocking from the activity inside. When Mrs. Brooks turned on her headlights aimed at the cars, both Hickey and Julie fled the scene.

That sighting, plus the "common knowledge" that the relationship was ongoing, led Mrs. Brooks to complain to Addison School administrators and start a petition to have Hickey fired. This stirred up division among the girls on the basketball team, resulting in a locker room fight over Hickey.

Mrs. Brooks' complaint to the school administration happened sometime in October 1990. The school then conducted a brief internal investigation. Tom Britsch, head coach of the girls' basketball team, was asked to contact Dawn (then a sophomore in college) about the rumors that Hickey had earlier had a sexual relationship with her. At first Dawn denied it because she was ashamed to admit the affair to her old coach and "father figure" Britsch.

Hickey apparently got wind of the school's investigation and he took a few days off as things heated up. His personnel file reveals that on October 31, 1990 he took a day off for "family illness," and on November 1 he took another day off for "personal business." On one of those days, Hickey drove to Dawn's college to try to get her to keep quiet.

Dawn's roommate ran interference, so Hickey did not get to speak with Dawn that day. She later told the Michigan State Police Detective (in 2018), that the surprise visit from Hickey so upset her – along with hearing that he was having sex with another student – that she called Coach Britsch back and told him the truth about the sexual relationship she'd had with Hickey.

In this same period, Hickey made another feeble attempt to protect himself. Just days before the administrators booted him from Addison High School on November 5, he filed a complaint (#1990-00011578 dated November 1) with the Lenawee County Sheriff's Office against Mrs. Brooks (who had spotted him in the cemetery with Julie). The police record reads:

> [Complainant Hickey] advised over last three weeks a subject by the name of Judith Brooks, W/F, approximately 40 years old has made some statements to Addison school where [he] works, accusing him of having sex with some girls and making threats to have [him] fired. [He] also says suspect Brooks is following [him] around. [He] does not [want] offender contacted, but just something on record. Disposition: Comp. [complainant] has contacted an attorney and will try to stop offender…

Mrs. Brooks' complaint, along with what Coach Britsch learned from Dawn, quickly led to Hickey's abrupt resignation on November 5. That morning, he was confronted by Principal Donald Dieck and Coach Britsch and was gone before the end of the day. He chose not to dispute the charges or ask his union to defend him, clearly implying his guilt.

Addison Schools Superintendent's report on Hickey's resignation

The documents below come from the Michigan State Police investigation (2016-2018).

In the immediate aftermath of Hickey's dismissal, the following document was placed in his personnel file by the Superintendent. Addressed "To Whom It May Concern," it vaguely states, "the sequence is something like the following."

Superintendent Kersh wrote that the investigation by Addison Schools was "immediately halted" after Hickey left the school.

This internal report was apparently not shared with anyone on the outside. As far as can be determined, *no future or potential employers would be informed of the real reasons Hickey was forced to resign.*

Why did the Addison School system then simply drop their investigation? Why didn't the Addison School system report Hickey to law enforcement for a proper investigation? Neither the Michigan State Police nor the Lenawee County Sheriff's Office was ever notified about Hickey's transgressions until 2016 – and that contact was by private investigator Chris Gill.

No records have been found during the recent investigations indicating that a child welfare agency was ever notified. Hickey would later claim that there was an investigation by both law enforcement and the Department of Human Services, and that he was cleared of any wrongdoing. Julie likewise claimed she was interviewed. But Dawn later told the Michigan State Police that she was never contacted in 1990 by either law enforcement or child welfare workers.

Apparently, those in charge there believed the reputation of their district was more important than protecting students from abuse.

Hickey was free to apply for employment elsewhere, including schools, with no criminal record or even a formal reprimand by the school on file.

Addison Community Schools
Addison, Michigan 49220

BOARD OF EDUCATION
Kerby Fandin, President
John Opel, V. President
Nicholas Thomas, Treasurer
Joel Hassanzahi, Secretary
Phillip Ferris-Smith, Trustee
Melinda Perez, Trustee
Steven Southard, Trustee

SUPERINTENDENT
Jeffrey M. Kersh
517-547-6123
SECONDARY PRINCIPAL
Donald E. Dieck
517-547-6121
MIDDLE SCHOOL
PRINCIPAL
Bradley Hamilton
517-547-6125
ELEMENTARY PRINCIPAL
Robert Tabo
517-547-6124

SUPERINTENDENT KERSH REPORTS ON PATRICK HICKEY'S RESIGNATION

NOVEMBER 1990

TO WHOM IT MAY CONCERN:

Jim Kersh, Supt.
November 1990

AS YOU REVIEW THIS PERSONNEL FILE OF MR. HICKEY YOU NEED TO KNOW THE CIRCUMSTANCES SURROUNDING HIS SUDDEN RESIGNATION. THE SEQUENCE IS SOMETHING LIKE THE FOLLOWING:

1. ONE OF THE MOTHERS OF THE GIRLS ON THE BASKETBALL TEAM SUBMITTED A WRITTEN ALLEGATION THAT MR. HICKEY HAS ENGAGED IN INAPPROPRIATE BEHAVIOR WITH ONE OF THE MEMBERS OF THE GIRL'S BASKETBALL TEAM. SHE CLAIMED TO HAVE WITNESSED AN AFTER GAME MEETING BETWEEN THE TWO IN A COUNTRY CEMETERY. SHE DEMANDED AN INVESTIGATION. NOTE: RUMORS ABOUT A RELATIONSHIP BETWEEN MR. HICKEY AND THIS BASKETBALL PLAYER HAD BEEN CIRCULATING FOR ABOUT ONE YEAR.

2. AN INVESTIGATION INTO THE CHARGES MADE AGAINST MR. HICKEY WAS INITIATED IMMEDIATELY. ABOUT TWO WEEKS INTO THE INVESTIGATION I RECEIVED WORD THAT A PAST GRADUATE FEMALE BASKETBALL PLAYER WANTED TO MAKE A STATEMENT ABOUT HER RELATIONSHIP WITH MR. HICKEY WHILE SHE WAS A STUDENT AT ADDISON.
NOTE: THERE WERE MANY RUMORS ABOUT THIS STUDENT AND MR. HICKEY AT THE TIME OF HER ATTENDANCE IN SCHOOL, BUT NOTHING WAS EVER SUBSTANTIATED.

3. ABOUT ONE HOUR AFTER MR. HICKEY WAS TOLD ABOUT THE FORMER STUDENT WILLINGNESS TO MAKE A STATEMENT, HE RESIGNED. HE LEFT THE SCHOOL GROUNDS EVEN BEFORE THE END OF THE SCHOOL DAY.

4. LATER IN THE SAME WEEK, THE REGIONAL UNION REPRESENTATIVE WANTED DETAILS, OF HIS RESIGNATION, I WAS WILLING TO COOPERATE. I WAS THEN INFORMED, BY THE UNION REPRESENTATIVE, THAT MR. HICKEY DECLINED ANY REPRESENTATION WITH REGARD TO HIS RESIGNATION.

5. THE INVESTIGATION WAS IMMEDIATELY HALTED.

14-0056-18

PASSING the TRASH

There is no mention of the circumstances of Hickey's resignation in Addison Schools' brief letter to potential employers (below), retrieved from his Addison personnel records. It states only, "Mr. Patrick C. Hickey resigned from the Addison Community Schools on November 5, 1990. He did so without prejudice of any sort. If you have further questions please contact me." It was signed by Superintendent Kersh.

As noted above, Hickey could have used the undated letter from Addison High School Principal Donald Dieck – written before his forced resignation – for his Addison reference.

Also in his Addison personnel file, an "Employee Status Change" form dated 11/5/90 says simply that Hickey "resigned – personal reasons." Hickey asked Addison Schools to fax him a copy of this form in 2010.

Former Addison educator's memory of circumstances of Hickey's resignation

In a May 2019 letter to the editor of *The Toledo Blade*, former Addison educator Jim Driskill (currently on the Addison School Board) gave his recollection of the circumstances surrounding Hickey's resignation and the several years after. He laid the blame for Hickey's escape from justice at the feet of Supt. Kersh.

> ... the sex-offender "trash" [Patrick Hickey] was allowed to skate because of one individual, the Addison superintendent [Jeffrey Kersh], not [other school] officials.
>
> The *Exponent* and *Telegram* [Brooklyn and Adrian, Michigan] papers in the early 2000s, chronicled his [Kersh's] superintendency and detailed how he spent educational funds for personal benefit and his resignation.
>
> Fortunately, several did not remain silent [about Hickey's deeds].
>
> First, sisters [Terri Kern and her sister who live in the Washington Local district] who were told about Hickey in the late 1980s sounded the first alarm. Second, the Washington Local School Board members [Langenderfer and Carmean], who when informed — and despite much criticism and denial by Hickey — maintained their dogged determination to see justice by not being silent and by throwing him out at personal expense.
>
> Third, one private and one public investigator [Chris Gill and MSP Detective Rothman] put the facts together with a prosecutor [Angela Borders] who took on the 30-year-old case. Fourth, the courageous career women [sic], wife, and mother ["Dawn"] stepped forward in November, 2017, and again on June 28, 2018. Don't forget the mother and daughter [Mrs. Brooks and Brooke] who were vilified in 1990 in Addison for first revealing Hickey.
>
> But, sadly other women, for whatever reason or reasons, still to this day remain silent, and that is truly sad.
>
> Please note that those sisters, students at Whitmer, as teenagers in the 1980s knew the Addison high school secretary's son and were informed about Hickey.
>
> Please note the gap of public school employment, from November 1990 to 1996. [Hickey was employed at St. Anthony Villa – not a public school – from 1991-1995.] That [Addison] secretary did not remain silent. She would dutifully fill out the references per a

signed agreement of Hickey and the superintendent. Then she went home and, at great personal risk, called prospective employers. She did not remain silent. [1]

What Hickey said he learned from his Addison experience

Patrick Hickey's later ally, Jeremy Baumhower, published his iBook (*Socked*, 2017) on the social media wars surrounding the Hickey scandal at Washington Local Schools. [2] In the brief Foreword Hickey wrote for the book, he denied wrongdoing at Addison and portrayed his resignation as a learning experience:

> I left Addison 26 years ago amidst rumors that I had sex with students... these allegations were investigated by the State Police and Children's Services three decades ago with the outcome that the claims were unsubstantiated. I gave this information to the former Superintendent of Washington Local Schools Michael Carmean when he hired me. In true transparency I divulged it to every board I served under. I left Addison with written assurance that I was in good standing with the school district.

> The Addison situation made me a better educator and leader in the three decades that followed. It made me be more aware and more responsible. While I was embarrassed, I awoke every day with the goal of responsibly serving kids and families.

CHAPTER 4
Witness Statements on Patrick Hickey's Time in Addison

Dawn graduated from Addison High School in June 1989. Patrick Hickey's abuse of her ended when she went off to college. She did her best to move on with her life.

Many contemporaneous Addison witnesses would remember what had happened to Dawn. Below are statements by her brother and others from Addison, as recorded by private investigator Chris Gill from late 2015 through 2017. Gill's interviews later became part of the Michigan State Police investigation of Hickey.

Mark – Dawn's brother

Dawn's older brother "Mark" understandably could not get over Hickey's violation of his younger sister.

Sometime in 2006 or 2007, Mark told Dawn's story to Jonathan Walsh, an investigative reporter at WTOL TV-11 in Toledo. (See Chapter 9.) Mark also tried to warn the Washington Local Schools Board of Education in 2007 – around the time Hickey was promoted from WLS Assistant Superintendent to Superintendent – but he said the Board member he called would not listen to him.

Sometime in October 2015, Mark contacted School Board member Jim Langenderfer after seeing newspaper reports on Hickey's scandalous behavior with a female teacher at WLS. He later met in person with Langenderfer and Board member Patricia Carmean and told them about Hickey's past offense. He gave them the handwritten letter (below), dated November 4, 2015.

> To Whom It May Concern:
>
> I am writing this letter on the matter of Patrick Hickey. Mr. Hickey was my little sister's assistant basketball coach and a teacher at Addison High School in Addison, Mich.
>
> I did not live at my mother's house during the late 80's, but I would stop by and see my mom and my sister Dawn.

Mr. Hickey would be there on a weekly basis. I questioned his presence to my mom and sister. I was told he was a mentor and father figure to her.

Later, my sister admitted that they had sexual relations. I found out and I went to Addison High School and was told that he resigned that day.

My mom and sister did not want to press charges against him.

My sister knows of his recent actions, but does not want to have her children know about this.

But I will do anything I can to make sure this does not happen to anyone ever again.

Sincerely,
Mark
11-4-15

Langenderfer found Mark credible, so then personally hired private investigator Chris Gill to look into Hickey's past.

Mark spoke in person with Gill and his partner Jay Schramm in Adrian, Michigan on November 6, 2015. Here are their notes from that interview (included in the MSP investigation):

Mark wished to speak with these investigators regarding an ongoing incident involving his sister Dawn and her high school basketball coach. Mark identified the basketball coach as Mr. Patrick Hickey, and indicated that the incidents occurred in or about 1988 to 1990/91.

Mark stated that he recently read about Mr. Hickey being involved in similar incidents in Toledo, Ohio where Mr. Hickey works as Superintendent of Washington Local Schools. Mark had knowledge of instances between his sister and Mr. Hickey, who was her coach back in 1988 or 1989. Mr. Hickey would drive Dawn home and the two would swim in Round Lake together.

Mark was 27 years old at the time and became suspicious of this incident and surmised the relationship might be improper. Mark then brought it to the attention of his mother and the mother talked with her daughter who confided in her regarding "a sexual relationship" with Mr. Hickey. The mother then forwarded the incidents to Addison Coach Thomas Britsch, along with his wife Judith. Thomas Britsch then took the matter immediately to School Superintendent [sic; HS Principal] Mr. Donald Dieck. Mr. Dieck informed Mark that Patrick Hickey would never work in the education system again.

Apparently Dawn did not wish to pursue the incident either due to embarrassment, feeling that the matter was handled to her satisfaction, or feelings toward Mr. Hickey. Mark had tried to persuade his sister to follow through with authorities but she didn't wish to and still does not wish to.

Once the matter was brought to Addison School officials ... [they] escorted Mr. Hickey from his classroom on Nov. 5, 1990. Mark then heard that Patrick Hickey was elected [sic] as superintendent of Washington Local Schools in 2006 [sic; 2007] and [Mark] called a School board official from Washington Local, who didn't take his complaint seriously. Mark then became more upset that Hickey got back into the school system.

No mention of the incident is in Mr. Hickey's personnel file from Addison High School. To further complicate matters another incident came to the attention of Mark. He informed us that Hickey had been caught in a cemetery with a young female student [not his sister] having sex.

Now in 2015 more matters of a peculiar nature have surfaced [at Washington Local Schools] and he feels more compelled to have his sister come forward. Mark had acted as a father figure for his sister since their dad was never in the picture. He felt he may have not done what was necessary to protect her.

Mark indicated he would continue to encourage his sister to contact us to further investigate this matter.

Tom Britsch, Girls' Basketball Head Coach, Addison High School

The next day, Gill and Schramm interviewed Tom Britsch, retired staff member and head coach of the girls' basketball at Addison High School. (Their notes were included in the MSP investigation report.)

Mr. Britsch worked at the school during the years 1988 thru 1992 and thereafter and had hired Mr. Patrick Hickey as Girl's Assistant [Basketball] Coach.

Mr. Britsch stated that he had been informed of some inappropriate actions towards the female players by Patrick Hickey but would not elaborate. He would not say who informed him but that once he became aware of these incidents he reported them promptly to the school board. These allegations must have been of a serious nature since two school officials escorted Patrick Hickey from the school office off the property on Nov. 5, 1990. This is the date that Patrick Hickey was dismissed from his position at Addison School.

Mr. Britsch went [on] to say that Patrick Hickey was a great salesman and could relate well to the players as a coach. We asked Tom Britsch if it was an acceptable practice for a coach to take a player home after practice in their personal car. He emphatically stated no, that it was not an acceptable thing to do.

We believe that Mark's sister, Dawn, was victimized and had come forward to Thomas Britsch's wife Judith, who was a staff member for the school system at the time. Judith then let her husband know of the allegations and Thomas in turn went to the school administration.

Brooke Brooks Kelly

Brooke Brooks Kelly was contacted by Gill and Schramm in late November 2015. She is a military veteran (military police investigator) and is now a violent crimes investigator with the Richmond County Sheriff's Office in Augusta, Georgia. Her email response on December 1, 2015 is included in the preliminary MSP report (Feb. 2016).

> I am writing this letter to describe my personal experiences [and] observations of inappropriate behavior of Mr. Patrick Hickey. I was a student at Addison High School in Addison Michigan from 1989-1992. Mr. Hickey was my basketball coach from 1989-1990 and also my English teacher in 1990. During that time there was much talk of Mr. Hickey having a sexual relationship with two female high school students. From these well traveled rumors, other school districts became aware. After one of our away games in Hanover Horton, friends and family who attended this game relayed to us players that people in the audience from Hanover Horton were trying to guess as to which one of us girls our coach, Mr. Hickey, was sleeping with.

> The second incident I observed, along with my mother Judith Brooks, was after one of our home basketball games. As we were driving out of the parking lot, I observed one of my teammates exit the school grounds in the direction of her home. Mr. Hickey left the grounds immediately behind her and followed her. This caught my attention due to the fact that Mr. Hickey lived in the opposite direction and with it being approximately 10:30 pm there were no businesses open and therefore no legitimate reason for him to take that route. My mother and I proceeded to follow Mr. Hickey and my teammate. We followed them until they turned into a remote

cemetery where they turned off their headlights and parked in the far left corner. My mother and I stopped on the road outside of the cemetery and shut off our head lights so as not to alert them to our presence. Once they were parked one of them exited their vehicle and got into the other's vehicle. Very shortly after they were in the same vehicle that vehicle began rocking and bouncing up and down. My mother and I watched this for several minutes before we turned our headlights back on, which were directly pointed at their vehicles. The rocking and bouncing ceased almost immediately. A couple minutes later the person got back into their own vehicle again and they both exited the cemetery traveling at very high rates of speed in opposite directions, my teammate towards her residence and Mr. Hickey in the direction of his residence.

After witnessing this incident, my mother contacted a member of the school board to report what we witnessed. At our next game my mother brought a petition asking for Mr. Hickey to be fired for what was obviously inappropriate behavior for a high school teacher/coach. Shortly thereafter, Mr. Hickey filed a report with the Sheriff's Office citing my mother for harassment. Also, my mother received a cease-and-desist letter from Mr. Hickey's attorney in Lansing, MI telling her to stop her harassment of Mr. Hickey. Shortly after all this transpired, Mr. Hickey left Addison high school, never to return again.

My mother is happy to provide her own statement but has been unable to at this time to a recent illness... Due to my living in GA, meeting in person would prove to be difficult but I am more than happy to speak with you via phone if you have any questions. Thank you for your time and attention.

Brooke added that she heard that Dawn suffered emotional and psychological trauma and was considered suicidal at the time due to her relationship with Hickey.

As things heated up for Hickey in late 2017 and early 2018 at Washington Local Schools, Brooke traveled from Georgia to give her testimony before public meetings of the WLS School Board and on Toledo talk radio WSPD. She emphasized that "the only investigation that has ever taken place" of Hickey's time at Addison started in 2016, prompted by Jim Langenderfer's hiring of investigator Gill and later taken up by the Michigan State Police.

PASSING the TRASH

"Jackie" – classmate of Dawn

Gill received the following email from former Addison High student "Jackie" on November 14, 2017 which was incorporated in the MSP investigation:

> I graduated from Addison High School in 1990. What follows are my recollections and encounters with Patrick Hickey. He was my basketball coach for my Freshman year and I was in at least one English class he taught.
>
> Basketball: I remember two different times he walked into the girls' locker room while we were showering & changing clothes. (I witnessed this because I was in there.) He used the excuse that he was used to coaching the boys' team. On another occasion he did the same thing but I was outside the locker room already changed for practice. I remember hearing the screams of the girls and looking over to see Hickey coming out of the locker room red-faced.
>
> Patrick Hickey's advice on how to make a free-throw: He told us to imagine the net was full of naked photos of whoever we wanted & the only way to get the photos down was to make the shot. Someone pointed out that wasn't quite right & he said the likes of "OK, so the photos are only half-naked. You choose which half." Someone then said they wanted the photos to be of his butt; I don't think it was said with the intent of him hearing it but he did hear it. Hickey then stood under the basket with his backside toward us and wiggled his butt. I would say that half of the girls were offended with this whole event and the other half were enthralled and laughing about it.
>
> There was also an incident after practice where Patrick Hickey was caught making out with someone upstairs on the wrestling mats. I remember starting to go up the steps (I had my head down watching my steps because they weren't standard size steps) when someone from the team came running down the steps saying, "You don't want to go up there! Hickey's up there making out." I looked up quickly and saw a woman going down the stairs on the other side. I quickly turned and went back down. As I reached the bottom the same woman was going out the exit door at the opposite end of the gym. I never saw her face, just her backside. Hickey came down shortly after that with a beet-red face & smirking. Several of the girls were teasing him & saying, "Awe, someone's busted!"

Witness Statements on Hickey at Addison H.S.

It is difficult for me to say this, but he was making out or even more because he still had an obvious erection. He also had a clothing item inside-out, I honestly can't remember if it was his shorts or shirt, I just remember some girls pointing it out, saying the like of "If you don't want to get busted, make sure your clothes aren't inside-out."

There was also a time when I was waiting outside for my ride home after practice along with a few other teammates who were smoking when Hickey came up to us, chatted for a minute or two and then left. He never said one word about them smoking even though it was against school policy. This may not be considered inappropriate, but I did and was dumbfounded on how a coach could let his athletes smoke.

I will also point out that by the end of the basketball season it was considered "common knowledge" among the team and fellow students that Patrick Hickey was sleeping with Dawn. I personally didn't witness anything happen between them and cannot testify that there was, just that it was considered "common knowledge" and not necessarily what adults would have called a "rumor."

CHAPTER 5
More Witness Statements on Patrick Hickey's Time in Addison

Once investigator Chris Gill was convinced there was substance to the rumors about Patrick Hickey's crime at Addison High School, he took his information to the Michigan State Police (MSP) in early 2016. But the MSP put their preliminary investigation on hold because Dawn chose not to come forward to charge Hickey. She then changed her mind in late 2017, so the MSP renewed their investigation and spoke with more Addison people in early 2018. The interviewer for the witness statements below was MSP Detective Sgt. Larry Rothman.

Though no one caught the couple *in flagrante*, witnesses stated that it was "common knowledge" that Hickey and Dawn were involved in a sexual relationship.

Kristina Hassenzahl

Investigator Gill met with Kris (Elston) Hassenzahl in late 2015 but she was not then ready to go on record. Two years later, on January 4, 2018, MSP Detective Rothman interviewed her. That was the day after her emotional testimony at the WLS Board meeting, when she emphatically pleaded with them not to seat Patrick Hickey as a School Board member. (See Chapter 20.)

Kris was a student and basketball player at Addison High School during Hickey's time there (1986-1990). Hickey was both her coach and English teacher. She was his student aide for three years. She kept her experiences secret until telling Brooke Brooks Kelley in late 2015 or early 2016, as the Hickey scandal erupted at Washington Local Schools.

She said she was never attracted to Hickey as a teenager. In retrospect, she sees "how he was trying to break her down." She helped Hickey with the boys' team, and he always made her sit with him on the bus to and from all the away games. Once during her freshman year, Hickey had her up against the wall in the gym and told her that her boyfriend couldn't do anything for her because he was not a real man.

He said, "If only I was a little bit younger and if you were a little bit older it would be such a different ball game."

Hickey would also brush up against her all the time very intentionally. Once his relationship with Dawn started, he'd leave her alone. She watched what was going on with them. She said that "one time, Dawn had a nervous breakdown during school." This was around the time Hickey's wedding happened. Later, she knew Hickey was having a relationship with another girl on the team, "Julie," and saw him at Julie's house when she (Kris) was there. (Kris was then dating Julie's brother.)

Starting in her sophomore year, she would "always see Mr. Hickey and Dawn together in the hall talking and just hanging out." Their head coach, Tom Britsch, encouraged the athletes to "hang out after school for team building reasons." All the girls on the team knew about Hickey's and Dawn's relationship. Kris also mentioned that Julie and Hickey were found in a cemetery together after borrowing a friend's car.

Kris remembered getting a phone call from a reporter at *The Toledo Blade* in 2013 about the Addison rumors. But she denied everything then. She has felt overwhelming guilt for not saying anything for 30 years and not helping Dawn at the time.

Kris's later interview on WSPD Toledo radio and testimony before the WLS School Board in January 2018 are consistent with what she told Detective Rothman.

Brooke Brooks Kelly

The account Brooke gave Detective Rothman lined up with what she had told investigator Gill in late 2015. (See Chapter 4.) Brooke also testified before the WLS School Board in early January 2018 and gave several interviews on WSPD radio.

She was a student at Addison High School from 1988-1992. Hickey was her coach on the freshman girls' JV basketball team. She and her mother followed Hickey (in his car) and Julie (in her car) to a local cemetery at night where they saw the two get into the same car which began bouncing and rocking. Her mother informed a School Board member and demanded an investigation of Hickey. That ultimately led to Hickey's resignation in November 1990.

Classmates of Dawn

Jackie

"Jackie" graduated from Addison High School in 1990. She had Hickey as her coach for JV basketball in 1987 and her English teacher in one or more classes. She gave a statement in November 2017 to investigator Gill (in Chapter 4), which the Michigan State Police added to their investigation. She gave this further statement to MSP Detective Rothman in late January 2018:

> I remember in English class Hickey bragging that he discovered his key was a janitor's master key... I remember him jumping out of the janitor's closet a few times while we were outside waiting for him to let us in the room. On more than one occasion he would jump out to scare us. I remember [a female student] jumping out with him once. I asked her if that was the case. She said yes...

> I also remember Hickey having an anger tantrum in class about students telling on him, that he was a person we could trust and shouldn't abuse that privilege. It left a lot of students confused, but most of the athletes knew he was referring to being told on for buying booze for students. I remember it because it was odd that he went from the whole trusting BS line to students should not spread rumors. It was like he was trying to guilt us into not saying anything about his buying booze or sleeping with students.

> I can't remember which male student told (bragged) to me that he and his friends used to go over to Hickey's trailer to drink (when Hickey lived in the trailer park by Devils Lake). That Hickey would invite a lot of the male athletes over to party. For some reason, I recall one of the guys saying that they would smoke pot there too...

> Julie's older sister was sleeping with a teacher, [named]. I know this for a fact because (one day during softball season) he was absent and [she] was bragging that she was going to call him at home. I told her I didn't believe her, she then told me she was sleeping with him, I said "Bullshit." She then felt the need to prove it to me and had me listen while she called him from the special ed classroom phone. I heard [the teacher] tell her that his wife was gone and she should come over... I never asked her about the rumors of her sister [Julie] and Hickey. Although it seemed obvious to me and a few others because about an hour after school was let out and the majority of teachers had left, you could walk down the hallway and [RS's] and Hickey's door were the only two

doors shut with the lights off. It was standard for teachers to leave the doors open for the janitors to clean.

I quit the softball team because I heard from my godfather ... who was on the school board that [a teacher/coach] was taking bribes from parents... Later [the assistant coach] pulled me aside and said he knew it wasn't easy, was proud of me and wished his own daughter could have done the same. The parents that were supposedly making bribes were Julie's and ...

In answer to questions from Detective Rothman, Jackie filled out the story about Hickey walking into the girls' locker room unannounced on three different occasions while they were changing. The girls would scream. "She stated he would apologize and use the excuse that he was used to coaching the boys. She said the first time she could understand it but not the second time... after the third time ... they posted a girl on the outside of the locker room."

She told the Detective that it was considered rumors or common knowledge that Hickey and Dawn were having sex. She also said, "she has heard that Mr. Hickey and Julie's family were close and she has seen his car at their house before." When he asked what her opinion was of Mr. Hickey, "she stated that he needs to be locked up."

Abigail

"Abigail" was on both junior varsity and varsity girls' basketball teams. She remembers both Hickey and Tom Britsch coaching her. She also had Hickey for speech class. She said her good friend Brooke Brooks Kelly encouraged her to come forward.

She stated that her job during study hall was to go and wash the towels and the uniforms. She stated after each game she would have to take the uniforms to the laundry room... She remembered one time when she was in the room Patrick Hickey came into the room and was all over her. She stated at one point he tried to put his hands down her pants. She stated that happened on two or three occasions... It got to the point that she quit doing the laundry... it was [during] her 10th grade year. She stated the following year Patrick Hickey cut her from the basketball team... he would come into the room and ask her, "what color panties do you have on today"... he would just ask inappropriate things. [She] has tried to block things out over the years but believes he tried to touch her about three times...

She added that it wasn't just rumors that Hickey had a sexual relationship with Julie.

> She was pretty good friends with Julie at the time and she remembered Julie telling her that she and Patrick Hickey were seeing each other and that she loved and cared about him. Abigail stated that Julie would say that she would go to his house when his wife was not around. [MSP Detective Rothman] asked Abigail if Julie told her it was a sexual relationship and she stated yes.

Abigail said Hickey was "very good looking and all the girls thought he was cute." He "always flirted with people" and girls were arguing about him "all the time and even girls from other schools would talk about it." Hickey came to the 1992 Addison High School graduation, she recalled – one and a half years after he was forced to resign.

Abigail thought Julie would not come forward because she has young children in the Addison schools.

Constance

From the MSP report:

> "Constance" graduated from Addison High School in 1989. She lived in the same trailer park as Patrick Hickey and "has firsthand knowledge of the relationship" between Dawn and Hickey. She was not on the basketball team but was good friends with Dawn and they would often sleep over at each other's homes.

> She stated that Patrick Hickey's trailer was closer to the road than hers so Dawn would park her car in her [Constance's] driveway when she wanted to go spend time with Hickey... She would cover for Dawn numerous times when Dawn was over to Patrick's house... She remembered Dawn telling her that she and Patrick were having sex. (It should be noted that she [Constance] called him Patrick. She stated she just can't call him Mr. Hickey.) ... She even said that she thinks Patrick prevented Dawn from having a boyfriend that was her own age... she remembered Dawn telling her that Patrick would teach her how to perform oral sex. Constance witnessed Patrick and Dawn kissing each other and also saw Patrick grab Dawn's butt before. She stated that they would touch each other just like a normal boyfriend and girlfriend situation... she does remember seeing Dawn and Patrick out on a pontoon boat ... from her house... She stated that [Hickey] was more like a part of the group of friends rather than a teacher or coach.

More Witness Statements

Trisha

"Trisha" was in the Addison High School Class of 1989 along with Dawn. She had Hickey as her basketball coach sophomore year. She told Detective Rothman that when she was in high school, Hickey provided her and other girls with alcohol and he bought alcohol for her separately as well.

She said she was in Hickey's house and saw him go into the other room with Dawn. She "stated she was fully aware that Dawn and Patrick Hickey were in a sexual relationship."

She told the Detective that "Hickey was more of a friend than a coach" and that "it was clear that Patrick Hickey was having sex with Dawn [and] her circle of friends were all aware of it, were a part of it, and all of them knew about it. She stated that Mr. Hickey was OK with all of them knowing about the relationship." She recalled being in the same house when Hickey and Dawn were having sex in the bedroom.

The girls would go to Hickey's house "from time to time" when Hickey's wife Sue was there. She said "she was surprised that Sue didn't know" about Hickey and Dawn having sex. "She stated that Mr. Hickey would ask Dawn to go to the games and sit with Sue so she [Sue] would feel like part of the group." (There is photo evidence supporting this claim in an Addison HS yearbook.)

Hickey would invite the high school girls to his trailer to "drink and play cards." He provided them with wine coolers. "He would always have some there for them." There weren't guys there too, just girls. Trisha said that "Sue knew that Mr. Hickey would occasionally give them [the girls] alcohol."

Dawn shared with Trisha and her close friends that she was having sex with Hickey.

From Detective Rothman's report:

> She stated at the time the girls really didn't think anything was wrong with it and thought it was kind of cool to be sleeping with a teacher [and] Mr. Hickey was pretty open with them about it... prior to him getting married he would have his arms around Dawn. She stated sometime during her junior year is when Patrick Hickey became engaged to Sue and that kind of messed everyone up.
>
> I asked Trisha what would she say if Patrick Hickey denied having a sexual relationship with Dawn and she laughed and stated that would be impossible... She stated that Mr. Hickey was kind of interested in knowing that she [Trisha] was dating a guy that was

no longer in high school... [then Hickey] came right out and asked her if she was still a virgin. [Trisha said she was and] Hickey found that shocking. [He] proceeded to teach them (she and her friends) how to give a blowjob... there was more than just a couple of girls there... it happened in the gym...

It was Mr. Hickey who taught her how to sneak out of the house and she remembered ... that he also told them that the first time they have sex they may bleed and it may be painful. She stated that Patrick Hickey was like their "Mr. Robinson"... She stated that he told them about the size of a man's penis and how the width is more important than the length.

Trisha said the girls "tried to keep Dawn and Mr. Hickey's relationship a secret from people but mostly from her [Trisha's] father because he was already not happy with Mr. Hickey's behavior." Her father would pick her up at school after her practices. She knows her father and mother went to the School Board about Hickey's inappropriate behaviors, and her father also spoke to the principal, Mr. Dieck. But a lot of parents liked Hickey and "things cooled down once Mr. Hickey got married."

Hickey would help Trisha with her free-throw practice after school. She remembered that she got in a big fight with her parents over his coaching style. "Mr. Hickey would stand behind her and kind of put his hands on her hips and sort of reach around and help her hold the ball. ... Her dad was so mad that she was not allowed to ride with Coach Hickey to the basketball camp the next summer." Hickey made it clear that he liked that she had to wear a larger uniform because of her big breasts. He would often put his hands on her legs. But he never tried anything sexual with her. He was very flirtatious and had a favorite phrase: "Oh, if you girls were a little older!"

She would see Hickey with his arm around Dawn, and the two of them holding hands. She knew Dawn was hurt by the relationship by the time they were in college and found out that Hickey had "just moved on from her... Dawn thought there was more to their relationship."

Trisha told Detective Rothman, "there are probably 100 people in Addison that knew they had a relationship."

Karol

"Karol" spoke with Detective Rothman in early 2018. She graduated from Addison High School in 1989, the same year as Dawn. She played basketball all four years but never had Hickey as her coach since she was in varsity starting her freshman year. (Hickey would assist Coach Britsch with the varsity team but was officially the girls' JV coach.) She did have Hickey as her English teacher one year.

> Karol stated that she was not one of his victims and that he was with Dawn at the time. She stated at the time they were all 14 or 15-year-old girls and the thought of having a teacher or coach being attracted to you was kind of cool. She stated he was telling Dawn what she wanted to hear at the time. I asked [her] if she knew that Dawn and Patrick Hickey were having a relationship and she stated absolutely [and that] she has a real hard time believing none of the teachers knew about it because all of the kids knew at the time. [She] stated she was close to Dawn and they hung out a lot. She stated that she was never over to his house because she knew he was with Dawn and didn't want to step on any toes. She stated after high school she really felt bad for not ever coming forward but back then they were all pretty popular and Dawn was really popular so if she would have said anything back then Dawn would have hated her… She stated that Patrick Hickey was a big flirt and charming at the time.

She said he was always friendly and smiling.

"She remembered Mr. Hickey telling her that she would look good in a bikini and that he wanted to take her on a trip so she could wear a bikini all the time but then stopped and would say, 'well, not the whole time'." Hickey included flirtatious lines about beach destinations in her yearbooks : "See you in Australia" and "Looking forward to the Bahamas."

From her yearbooks shown to Detective Rothman:

> Karol – I wish they wouldn't have taken my picture before I shaved. Seriously … I think you are a great kid. Your personality & smile are very contagious. Your improvement in basketball has been great. Shoot 10,000 shots this summer & you will be All-League – I promise. – Mr. Hickey
>
> *P.S.* See you in Australia   [ellipsis in original]

Hickey's second yearbook inscription:

> Karol – You can accomplish anything you want. I hope you always remember the success you had in B-ball because of hard work. I hope you have all the success you want. You are the greatest aid [aide] of all time. – P. Hickey

P.S. LOOKING FORWARD TO THE BAHAMAS. [upper case in original]

Lindsey

"Lindsey" graduated the same year as Dawn (1989). She told Detective Rothman that she was "best friends" with her. When asked what she knew about any possible relationship between Dawn and Patrick Hickey, she answered "they absolutely had a relationship." She said Dawn first started "seeing Mr. Hickey" while she was still dating her boyfriend in sophomore year.

> She remembered that Dawn was having a hard time when Mr. Hickey became engaged. She stated when Hickey did get married she went with Dawn to the wedding … and the reception… She stated that she asked Dawn why she wanted to be there and … Dawn told her that she was just hoping he would not go through with it. She stated that Dawn was with Mr. Hickey the night before his wedding. Lindsey stated they didn't stay long at the reception and when she was driving Dawn home she was a mess.

> [She] stated that Dawn thought her relationship with Mr. Hickey was a long term thing. She stated that their relationship didn't stop however when Mr. Hickey got married… Lindsey doesn't remember when the relationship ended because she ended up leaving Addison after her junior year.

> I asked [her] if she ever personally witnessed Dawn and Mr. Hickey together and she stated not sexually but she does remember seeing them touching each other. She stated he would touch her in a way that was way more than a teacher should be touching a student…

> I asked [her] if she remembered how many times she dropped Dawn off at Mr. Hickey's trailer and she said around 6 or 7 times. She stated she got her driver's license before Dawn so she would drive her there.

> … [She] stated [Hickey] was a very good looking man, younger, and everyone thought he was handsome. He was very outgoing and personable. She stated that he was very close to Mr. Britsch and even though he was not her coach he was around the [varsity] team. She stated looking back she can see now how manipulative Mr. Hickey was back then. She stated she also heard rumors of Hickey with other girls at the school as well.

More Witness Statements

Esther

"Esther" graduated from Addison High School in 1989 along with Dawn. She was on the basketball team with her all four years. She says she was one of Dawn's best friends in a group of about five during high school and they all knew about Dawn's relationship with Hickey. It "was common knowledge at the time." She never witnessed sexual intercourse between them but would catch them being affectionate in the hallways sometimes, "standing really close together," and they were "very flirty with each other." She said, "looking back it seemed odd and was inappropriate... [but] Dawn really didn't confide in her about the relationship because at the time she really didn't approve of it." At the same time, all of the girls "thought that Mr. Hickey was really good looking and they were all attracted to him."

In her sophomore year, Hickey coached her. He would use "hand gestures and mimicked with his mouth and tongue how to have oral sex or give someone a blowjob."

> ... she remembered hearing that Dawn and Patrick Hickey had sex out on the boat ... and she was pretty sure that Hickey was married at the time. I asked Esther if she believed Dawn when she says that she had a sexual relationship with Mr. Hickey and [she] stated absolutely 100 percent! ... I asked ... [her] opinion what [head coach] Tom Britsch was like ... and she stated that Mr. Britsch was amazing and that he was like a dad to them. She stated he really cared about the girls. She stated looking back she can't believe he didn't know about what was going on ... she thinks that people just looked [sic] a blind eye to some of the things back then. She stated that Patrick Hickey moved on to Julie after Dawn.

Ronna

"Ronna" spoke with Detective Rothman in March 2018. She graduated from Addison High School in 1988, a year ahead of Dawn. She was friends with Dawn but was not on the basketball team and never had Hickey as a teacher or coach. "She stated that all Dawn's immediate friends knew about Dawn's relationship with Pat Hickey."

Ronna told of going to Hickey's house with Dawn. They "were there talking about an hour or a little longer... Dawn sat next to Pat on the couch and she sat on a chair." When Hickey's wife came home, Dawn felt uncomfortable so they left. Ronna added that Hickey also "had an affair" with another girl ("Julie").

Nadine

"Nadine" graduated from Addison High School in 1989. She identified herself as a distant cousin of Patrick Hickey but said she has no contact with him. She said she was friends with Dawn, but "really didn't see anything going on between Dawn and Patrick Hickey but heard the rumors and thought it was pretty much general knowledge that there was something going on." She said she was surprised that Sue actually married him and stayed with him for so long. "She remembers Dawn as a pretty good person … honest and upfront and doesn't have anything bad to say about her."

Hannah

"Hannah" was Dawn's roommate at their Michigan college. She remembered the day in the fall of 1990 when Hickey drove to Dawn's college, hoping to keep her from telling the truth to the Addison administrators. Detective Rothman wrote:

> Hannah remembered the day when Patrick Hickey arrived at their college campus [and] remembered Dawn freaking out that Patrick was there… several of her teammates took Dawn across the hall to another room. Hannah stated that she made contact with Patrick Hickey [and] remembered Patrick being upset and crying. She stated he wanted to talk to Dawn and they would not let him… he stayed for a while wanting to talk to Dawn and then she [Hannah] told him he had to go… She remembered that Dawn was in a panic about him showing up. She stated that Dawn had told her that she had been in a long term sexual relationship with Patrick Hickey. I asked Hannah if she believed Dawn and she stated absolutely. She stated that was the only time she ever met Patrick Hickey but can remember it because it was a big deal.

CHAPTER 6
Statements by Addison Schools Staff

In early 2018, MSP Detective Larry Rothman interviewed former Addison Schools staff: Superintendent Jeffrey Kersh, basketball coach Tom Britsch, and athletic director Ken Mullin. All three were at Addison High School at the time of Hickey's resignation in November 1990.

Addison Supt. Jeffrey Kersh – Interview #1

On January 16, 2018 Detective Rothman spoke with Jeffrey Kersh, Superintendent of Addison Schools from 1984 to 2002. Kersh said that the High School Principal at the time, Donald Dieck (now deceased), recommended hiring Patrick Hickey because he could serve as an athletic coach as well as teach English.

Kersh said he remembered hearing rumors about Hickey having a relationship with a female student (Julie). He said he asked Principal Dieck to look into this. Dieck told Kersh that none of the girls on the basketball team would say anything about it. Dieck suggested enrolling girls' varsity basketball coach Tom Britsch in the investigation since he was "very close with Hickey and a mentor to him" and was "grooming him to be his replacement." Kersh said he then heard back from Dieck that Britsch had talked with Hickey and that "Hickey was going to resign and agreed not to be in teaching again."

Detective Rothman showed Kersh the memo he had written in November 1990 regarding Hickey's resignation. It noted Hickey's relationship with a former student (Dawn), as well as the rumored relationship with another (Julie). Kersh said that he had drafted the document and remembered parts, but not the part about Dawn's willingness to make a statement.

Kersh said he didn't remember any other rumors about Patrick Hickey and students. He recognized a picture of Dawn in an old yearbook.

He said he was not present at the meeting with Hickey when he resigned. Kersh also said he thought Dieck was *not* in that meeting, only Britsch and Hickey.

> Mr. Kersh said he was not sad to see Patrick Hickey go because he was a "hot dog". When asked what he meant by that he stated Hickey would always brag about things like living in Michigan and registering his vehicles in Ohio so he would not have to pay as much for insurance.

> I then provided Mr. Kersh with a few letters of recommendation for Mr. Hickey that was [sic] signed by him. Mr. Kersh stated that was part of the agreement Hickey had as part of his resignation. Mr. Kersh stated he was never told what Hickey did or to whom. He stated if any of the girls on the team would have come forward the situation would have been completely different but no one ever came forward.

Kersh also said he had never spoken with Julie or any of the girls on the basketball team. Kersh thought that "Hickey resigned before any evidence could be found."

Kersh confirmed to Rothman via phone two weeks later that he was "pretty sure" he was not in the meeting when Hickey resigned.

Tom Britsch, Girls' Varsity Basketball Coach

Tom Britsch was the girls' varsity basketball coach at Addison High School during Hickey's time there. He also taught economics and accounting. Britsch was a "father figure" to Dawn, she said. (Dawn's brother Mark noted that "their dad was never in the picture" at their home.) She confessed her relationship with Hickey to Britsch in the fall of 1990 during the school's internal investigation.

Britsch spoke with the private investigators in November 2015. (See Chapter 4.) On January 28, 2018, Detective Rothman spoke with Britsch in person. Mrs. Britsch was also present and added a few comments.

Britsch remembered Dawn as a great basketball player and student and thought she would have had a full scholarship to Western Michigan University but for tearing her ACL (knee ligament) during her senior year. He wrote in her senior yearbook:

> I will miss your smiling face in school, your cooperative spirit & your intensity in basketball. But most of all & most importantly for life I'll miss you as a person. Genuine, quality "what you see is that you get" person. You are always welcome in my home. I couldn't

be more proud of you if you were my daughter. You are the type of person that makes coaching & teaching a rewarding experience. I will be disappointed if you don't stay in touch with me. Best wishes, Mr. Britsch   Matt. 6:33

He recalled being very impressed with Patrick Hickey as an outstanding teacher and said he "knew what he was doing" as a basketball coach. High School Principal Donald Dieck had assigned Hickey to be Britsch's assistant coach for the high school girls' JV and junior high boys' basketball teams. He didn't remember Hickey being involved in any of his girls' varsity practices.

Britsch said he'd never heard any rumors about Hickey having inappropriate relationships with students and said, "if he had heard the rumors things would never have gotten to where they were." The last time he spoke with Hickey was "a few minutes before Hickey was told to leave the school in the Superintendent's Office."

Principal Dieck had heard from student Brooke Brooks' mother about the cemetery incident (where Hickey was seen with Julie in a "rocking" car). Dieck then asked Britsch to look into the other rumors about recent graduate Dawn since he had a good relationship with her. That is when Britsch contacted Dawn at her college, and she confirmed her long sexual relationship with Hickey. He said "there is no doubt in his mind that Dawn was telling him the truth. He stated Dawn would not lie to him."

Dawn also told Britsch she didn't want to pursue charges, and he told her he would still try to "get rid of Mr. Hickey at all costs." Britsch then confirmed to Dieck what he had found out and Dieck sent him on to Superintendent Kersh. Kersh agreed "there was no doubt that Dawn was telling the truth and Mr. Hickey needed to go."

> Britsch stated that Mr. Kersh said they were going to put something together and he would be gone. Mr. Britsch stated he didn't know what that meant at the time but looking back he thinks there was a deal made that if Mr. Hickey were to pack his stuff and leave, then nothing would be put in his records that would lead to prosecution... he believed that Hickey had promised never to get a job around Addison again... he thought Mr. Hickey was out of education and that was the best they could have done because Dawn didn't want to do anything at the time. Mr. Britsch stated on the day Mr. Hickey resigned he called Mr. Hickey in the office, explained the situation to him... he doesn't remember any dialogue between he [sic] and Mr. Hickey other than he looked at him and

said, "you know what you did." ... the other thing he remembers from the meeting is Mr. Hickey got up and left and he was gone.

Detective Rothman told Britsch that Kersh denied being in the meeting with him and Hickey, or even in the building. Britsch said that was a lie. He is confident in that memory. He recalled that Hickey "had no desire to fight it" and did not request representation from the teachers' union.

Britsch never "dug deeper" after Hickey left. He didn't talk to his girls' basketball team about it. He had heard the rumors about Julie. He said "the people above him should have dug deeper to see just how deep things went but they didn't... It was also unheard of that someone would quit with no questions asked in the middle of the school day if the allegations were not true."

Detective Rothman told Britsch that there was a document signed by Kersh in Hickey's file which stated there had been a two-week investigation. That does not sync with Britsch's involvement. Britsch said, "He was asked by Principal Dieck to look into things in the morning, contacted Dawn that same morning, was in Kersh's office later that morning, and Hickey was gone before lunch. He stated he doesn't remember if Dawn's name was brought up in the meeting but thought that because he was in the room, Hickey should have known that it involved Dawn."

Addison Supt. Jeffrey Kersh - Interview #2

The day after he interviewed Coach Britsch, Detective Rothman spoke a second time with former Superintendent Kersh. He told Kersh that he had spoken with Britsch who:

> ... was adamant that he [Kersh] was in the meeting when Patrick Hickey resigned. Mr. Kersh laughed and stated, "I don't recall it whatsoever." I asked Mr. Kersh if he didn't remember being in the meeting or was he certain he was not in the meeting. Mr. Kersh stated that he can't remember and that would be something that he should remember... he remembered getting the results that Patrick Hickey had admitted to being in the wrong and resigning but again stated he does not remember being in the meeting... He had very little contact with Patrick Hickey the whole time he was employed at Addison.

> I asked Mr. Kersh if anyone ever made contact with him and advised him that Patrick Hickey was involved in inappropriate

behavior with female basketball players. Mr. Kersh stated no one ever came to him and said that "Mr. Hickey did this to me." He stated he remembered the process being difficult to pin him (Hickey) down to get him to admit he was in the wrong. Mr. Kersh stated he doesn't recall ever being told what he may have done and the focus at that time was on a student named Julie. Mr. Kersh stated the other girl (Dawn) was not mentioned until I mentioned her [to him].

Kersh remembered Principal Dieck telling him that Coach Britsch had gotten Hickey to agree to resign. He "doesn't recall Hickey signing anything but he should have signed something saying he was resigning. He stated the only thing he knows is that he was told that Hickey resigned and promised not to be in K-12 education."

Ken Mullin, Addison Schools Athletic Director

Ken Mullin was Athletic Director and a sixth-grade teacher at Addison Public Schools while Hickey was employed there. Detective Rothman spoke with him on January 30, 2018. This was several weeks after Mullin had made a public statement at the WLS Board meeting, advising them against seating Hickey as a Board member. (See Chapter 20.)

Rothman wrote:

> Mr. Mullin stated that he had heard the rumors about Mr. Hickey and even told Mr. Kersh the Superintendent at the time that he thought the rumors were false ... until after one of the girls' basketball games [in 1990] when he remembered being in the teacher's lounge relaxing. He stated when he walked out of the room he noticed that Patrick was engaged in what he described as a "lovers' spat" with a student named Julie. Mr. Mullin stated as soon as they noticed him they split and took off [and] the next day he went and spoke to Mr. Kersh and told him about what he had witnessed.

> [He] told Mr. Kersh that he now believed the rumors about Pat Hickey were true based on what he had seen... he remembered that several parents were concerned about Mr. Hickey's behavior so he would travel to all the away games to keep an eye on him.

Mullin told of a female student (whose name he can't recall) telling him she had dropped Julie off at the local cemetery, and while she didn't see Hickey, she did see his motorbike there. The student agreed to speak out and he then took her to Superintendent Kersh's office.

On the day Hickey resigned, Mullin was on the school grounds. Principal Dieck informed him that Hickey had been confronted earlier that day and had been given two options: "One was to resign and the other was to be turned over to be prosecuted. Mr. Mullin stated that Mr. Dieck said that Mr. Hickey started to argue and was told that there was no argument and Pat [Hickey] signed and left."

> Mr. Mullin stated he told the custodians at the time that when they see Mr. Hickey come in to clean his room out to come and get him [which they did]... Pat Hickey, his wife and an older couple were in his classroom. Mr. Mullin assumed it was either his parents or his wife's parents. Mr. Mullin said he asked Pat if he could talk to him. He stated Mr. Hickey came out in the hallway and he asked him if he was OK because he never considered Pat Hickey a stable guy and didn't want him to do something rash like suicide.

Detective Rothman noted that "Hickey made a comment that Mullin stated proved to him that the rumors were true":

> Mr. Mullin said the last words he heard from Pat Hickey face to face was when Mr. Hickey said, "I just want you to know that it was not all my fault." Mr. Mullin said he didn't know at that point [whether] to punch him or walk away so he walked away and went into his office.

> Mr. Mullin stated that he didn't think Mr. Kersh was in the meeting [with Hickey] but it was under his direction. I advised Mr. Mullin that [Kersh said] that he didn't know anything first hand that things were going on. Mr. Mullin stated that was a lie. [He] remembered walking the girl [who saw Hickey's motorbike at the cemetery] down to Mr. Kersh's office and introduced them and she sat down and he … left.

Some years later, Mullin was in Kersh's office once when he overheard a call from Findlay, Ohio where Hickey was to start working in 1996 as high school Assistant Principal. Kersh told whomever was calling, "Yes, Patrick Hickey worked at Addison" but that was all he could say. Mullin thought it was strange so went to his office and made a note of it. Later Kersh came into his office to ask if he had heard the conversation and Mullin said that he had. Kersh then explained that Hickey said he would sue him because he gave him a bad reference.

Kersh asked Mullin to hang on to the notes he'd taken of what he overheard him say in case Hickey did try to sue him.

Mullin told Detective Rothman that "the Superintendent had 'zero balls'."

Mullin's understanding was that Hickey was let go for his "affair" with Dawn, not his relationship with Julie. He said Dawn "is the nicest kid you'd ever want to meet" and both "are great girls." He added that Julie "and her family will never talk about what happened." He knew that her family "even invited Mr. Hickey to her graduation open house" and everyone wondered how that could be.

Mullin believes the rumors about Hickey's time at Addison are "absolutely true; there's no doubt in my mind."

He suspects Hickey must have someone in Toledo protecting him. "He has to, to get away with what he does."

CHAPTER 7
The Intervening Years
– 1990-2002 –

Hickey continues to work in educational institutions

In January 1990, Jim Langenderfer – resident of the Washington Local Schools district and school administrator elsewhere – began a four-year term on the WLS Board of Education (including two years as President). His younger child was then attending Whitmer High School in the district. Decades later, Jim would be instrumental in exposing Hickey's misdeeds.

In November 1990, English teacher and basketball coach Patrick Hickey was abruptly expelled from the Addison, Michigan school system after reports he'd had sexual relationships with one (and possibly another) of his students.

This chapter recaps the twelve years after Patrick Hickey's sudden departure from Addison High School. *Notably, he continued working with children in educational institutions.*

Because the Addison School administrators had kept their truncated investigation internal and the Superintendent was afraid of being sued by Hickey, the delinquent teacher was free to present himself as an unblemished educator who had moved from Michigan to accommodate his wife's new job. He could pull out the early letters from the Addison High School Principal to prove what a wonderful teacher and role model he was.

Since neither the Addison Schools nor the victims reported Hickey's abuse to the Michigan State Police, the Lenawee County Sheriff, or a child welfare agency, there was no complaint or criminal record on file for Hickey.

The missing year

In Hickey's statement before the Court the day he was sentenced in 2018, he made an interesting confession:

> Upon leaving Addison 31 years ago, my wife and I agreed that I
> needed severe psychological help. I was 23 years old [when he

began teaching in Addison Schools], and untreated psychologically for childhood sexual abuse and the devastating death of my 15-year-old sister when I was 11. I voluntarily and instantly entered into psychotherapy and group psychotherapy. I attended therapy sessions every week for three years in the hope that I would never hurt anyone in the way that I hurt Dawn. After three years of therapy, my wife and I wanted an additional two years before we had children to be sure that I was truly changed and not a danger to anyone.

Note that Mrs. Hickey was a party to her husband's psychotherapy in the years after he left Addison, and she was aware of his misdeeds there. This period of his admitted psychological distress coincides with almost a year of unemployment for Hickey.

The strange circumstances of Hickey's dismissal from Addison would lead him to prevaricate on his later employment applications. How would he cover over his lack of a reference from Addison Schools and the "missing year" in his employment history?

There is a nine- to ten-month gap between Hickey leaving Addison (early November 1990) and his stated beginning date his next job at St. Anthony Villa (SAV) in Toledo (August 1991). What did he tell SAV he was doing during that missing time, and how did he explain his reasons for leaving a comfortable teaching job?

Hickey's five years at St. Anthony Villa, residential center for troubled teens

Hickey worked for five years at St. Anthony Villa, from 1991 to 1996. It was a state-licensed residential center for teens with behavioral problems – both girls and boys. SAV was at that time connected to the Catholic Church. In this job, Hickey would have "full and total access to the kids" in the facility, according to a fellow employee.

At this time, most of the youth were there for drug and alcohol dependency treatment, according to *The Toledo Blade*. [1] SAV closed in August 2001 due to "the high cost of running the programs and the lack of need for them in the Toledo area," says that report.

The spokesman at SAV's later parent company then (Boysville of Michigan) told *The Blade* "the agency's five-year history of problems [prior to 2001], including complaints about abuse by staff, problems with the physical facility, and incomplete paperwork, had nothing to do with the announcement" of its closing in 2001. But in September 2000, "the Ohio Department of Job and Family Services issued a proposed adjudication order informing the Villa of intent to revoke its certification after years of sporadic complaints." Improvements to the physical plant, "new staff," and other changes earned a reprieve with its license renewed, but only through January 2002.

The *Blade* report does not specify what sort of "abuse" by staff might have occurred. Well-adjusted teens are sometimes targets of predators. But troubled teens could be even more vulnerable. Meticulous background checks for staff should be the rule at this sort of facility.

Apparently, SAV had no problem with Hickey's résumé. Did he use the undated letter from Addison High School Principal Don Dieck, written in the year-plus before his forced resignation? Was the brief note from Superintendent Kersh considered an adequate reference?

Both of Hickey's WLS applications give his four job titles at SAV as Executive Director, Principal, Division Manager, and Educational Coordinator. In his 2007 WLS application, he wrote that he "oversaw 100 staff, and the treatment of 75 abused and neglected children [who] received treatment and were educated on campus." He listed some of his responsibilities at SAV: "overseeing foster care, independent living, sex offender treatment, chemical dependency, volunteers, day care, latch key for at-risk kids."

The Michigan State Police did not look into Hickey's time at SAV (whether through the Catholic Diocese of Toledo or its later manager, Boysville of Michigan). But a reliable source cast doubt on Hickey's stated job titles and responsibilities there.

His old colleague from Addison Schools, David Driskill (now an Addison School Board member and Lenawee County Commissioner), read a letter he had emailed to the Washington Local School Board at their public meeting on February 21, 2018. He urged them to vote newly elected member Hickey off the WLS Board. He pointed to the "six pages of lies" on Hickey's 2002 and 2007 WLS job applications. He said:

> I write this with the utmost sincerity as a fellow Board member, albeit in a rather small Michigan district. I wish to express two observations and concerns, with the express interest of the Washington Local School district at heart... I just happened to remember who worked at Boysville and St. Anthony's Villa ... And I called [his friend] Timmy up – and Timmy is as big as that gentleman over there in uniform – OK? And I said, "Hey, do you remember Pat Hickey who worked at Boysville St. Anthony's Villa?" "Yeah." "Was he Executive Director and Principal?" "Heck no! He was a Treatment Specialist just like I was. And I was there

for 16 years, and the five years that he was there, and then he left."
That's the kind of Board member you have.

Driskill was asserting that Hickey inflated his job responsibilities at SAV.

Hickey attempts to alter his Addison personnel file

The Michigan State Police investigation of Patrick Hickey (2016-2018) yielded this information from his Addison personnel file:

In 1995, just before he left SAV and likely in preparation for job applications, Hickey attempted to alter what was in his Addison personnel file. On September 5, 1995 he sent a memo (photo below) to Superintendent Kersh instructing him what to say in conversations with potential employers. He dictated this altered wording for his future letters of reference, adding that he left "in good standing with the district":

> Patrick C. Hickey was employed as a teacher and a coach with the Addison Community Schools commencing May 12, 1986 and ending November 5, 1990. He resigned from the Addison Community School without prejudice of any kind and in good standing with the district.

Hickey's memo continues with his demand:

> All future calls in regards to my employment will be met with "I will send you a letter of reference." Any persistence on the part of the caller will be simply met with the same response and the letter will be sent forthwith.

Hickey also states in his letter to Kersh that there was an agreement between High School Principal Dieck, Coach Tom Britsch, and himself on November 5, 1990 that "all future letters of reference would be positive in nature." Mr. Hickey then requests that Kersh sign the letter as he dictated it, then fax the signed letter and agreement back to him that same day.

Kersh perhaps feared a lawsuit from Hickey, according to Addison Schools Athletic Director, Ken Mullin. (See Chapter 6). So, he complied with part of Hickey's request and added the start date of his employment to the letter on file in Addison. Kersh also signed Hickey's suggested "compromise" agreement. But Kersh's referral letter dated two days later dated Sept. 7, 1995 continued to state only that he "resigned without prejudice of any sort" – without adding "in good standing with the district."

Memorandum

To: Jeff Kersh
From: Patrick Hickey
Date: 9-5-95
Re: References

This memo is in response to our phone conversation today. I am including text that I feel should be included in all future letters of reference.

Patrick C. Hickey was employed as a teacher and a coach with the Addison Community Schools commencing May 12, 1986 and ending November 5, 1990.

He resigned from the Addison Community Schools without prejudice of any kind and in good standing with the district.

Sincerely,

J.M. Kersh

All future calls in regards to my employment will be met with "I will send you a letter of reference." Any persistence on the part of the caller will be simply met with the same response and the letter will be sent forthwith.

This wording is in compliance with the meeting held between Mr. Don Dieck, Mr. Tom Britsch and myself held on November 5th 1990. At that meeting it was agreed that all future letters of reference would be positive in nature.

This wording is also in compliance with our conversation of September 14th 1993 at which time you stated that all calls for reference would be responded with, "that he resigned without prejudice of any sort". You followed that agreement up with a letter to me that states same.

Please fax me a copy of the letter on ACS letterhead. Please sign at the bottom and fax back to me at 419-473-0806 if you are in agreement with this compromise.

I the undersigned agree and will abide by the procedure for reference calls, and reference checks for Patrick C. Hickey as set forth in this letter:

Jeff Kersh, Superintendent, Addison Community Schools

X _____

Patrick C. Hickey
X _____
xc: Joe Cooper, J.D.

Kersh retired as Addison Superintendent in 2002 under curious circumstances, according to *The Toledo Blade*. [2] (See further detail critical of Kersh in Chapter 3, provided by former Addison educator Jim Driskill.)

Kersh's referral letter did not include the phrase
"in good standing" as Hickey had requested.

Hickey: Asst. Principal at Findlay High School, 1996-2002

After leaving Saint Anthony Villa, Patrick Hickey became Assistant Principal of Findlay High School (Findlay, Ohio) from August 1996 to August 2002.

His Addison file contains a copy of the form sent on May 9, 1996 by Addison Schools to Findlay Schools. It verified Hickey's dates of employment at Addison Schools (ending November 5, 1990).

Former Addison Athletic Director, Ken Mullin, told investigator Gill that he overheard a brief phone conversation between Addison Supt. Kersh and someone in Findlay. Kersh told Mullin he was worried Hickey would sue him for giving him a bad reference. (See Chapter 6.) That implies that Findlay Schools did not get much detail from Addison. Did that make them question Hickey's résumé? What did Hickey tell Findlay Schools about his curious end date (a few months into the school year) at Addison High School, and his nine to ten months of unemployment? Findlay Schools proceeded to hire Hickey anyway.

Little is known about Hickey's record as Assistant Principal at Findlay High School. The Michigan State Police did not look at his time there. No one in the Findlay Schools would go on record with private investigator Gill concerning Hickey.

The Toledo Blade reported in May 2018:

> Along with Addison and Washington Local, Hickey worked for about six years in the Findlay school district. In response to *Blade* questions about whether the district plans to investigate whether Hickey may have engaged in inappropriate acts while in the district, [Findlay] Superintendent Edward Kurt said in a statement that Findlay schools would cooperate with law enforcement in any investigation. "We have no information of any situations regarding misconduct while under our employment," Mr. Kurt said. [3]

In Hickey's 2007 application for Superintendent of Washington Local Schools, he gave this Findlay experience as one of his qualifications: "Extremely strong in building security and oversaw security planning in the Findlay City School District."

CHAPTER 8
Hickey Hired as WLS Asst. Supt.,
then Superintendent
His Problematic Job Applications
2002 & 2007

Hickey's applications to Washington Local Schools

Things started getting sticky for Patrick Hickey as his ambition took hold. He had to figure out how to represent his time in the Addison Schools as he climbed the school administration ladders.

- **2002 Application**: Hickey's prevarication is clear in his first application for employment at Washington Local Schools (WLS) in 2002. He applied for two openings: Assistant Superintendent and High School Associate Principal. He listed his employment dates at Addison Schools as "August 1986 to 1990" – *with no end month given* – and his starting date at his next job (St. Anthony Villa) as August 1991.

- **2007 Application**: Hickey was one of 22 applicants in 2007 for the position of WLS Superintendent. Somehow, he rose to the top. In his 2007 application he misrepresented his employment end date at Addison as "8/90" – though he was there through his forced resignation on November 5, 1990.

- Hickey's personnel file in the Addison Schools included the letter from Superintendent Kersh dated Sept. 7, 1995 that gave Hickey's end date for employment as November 5, 1990. (See Chapter 7.) Did the WLS Board see this? Did no one notice the discrepancy with Hickey's stated end date? Or did WLS simply fail to verify his dates of employment at Addison Schools?

- Hickey did not name anyone at Addison Schools as a "professional reference" in either his 2002 or 2007 WLS application, though he was employed there for over four years. Did he use the early letters by Addison High School Principal Donald Dieck? (See Chapter 3.) He did name Dieck as his immediate supervisor who could be contacted in his 2002 application.

- Both WLS applications dishonestly state his reason for leaving Addison Schools as "Relocation of Wife."

- As noted in the previous chapter, Hickey's applications may have misrepresented his job titles at St. Anthony Villa/Boysville.

- The handwriting on both applications is totally different than that seen in Hickey's yearbook inscriptions and communication with Supt. Kersh. Did he not personally fill out his application forms?

It is striking that WLS hired him *both times*, perhaps without questioning these oddities. Beyond Hickey's vagueness and misrepresentations, there is also the *long gap* (at least seven months, possibly as long as ten months) in his employment history according to his own given dates.

Hickey's lies in his WLS applications were later included in the "37 Charges" document prepared by the School Board's attorney (though not formally leveled) against Hickey in December 2015 when he resigned as WLS Superintendent. (See Chapter 17.)

Hickey claimed the WLS Board who hired and supervised him, along with his predecessor Superintendent Michael Carmean, were fully aware of what had happened in Addison – at least *his version* of it. (See the quote from Hickey's Foreword to Jeremy Baumhower's iBook, *Socked*, at the end of Chapter 3.) If true, why did he fudge his end dates and reason for leaving Addison in his two applications?

(Images of the complete applications from 2002 and 2007 are available in the Kindle version of this book.)

2002 application

In 2002, Washington Local Schools at first offered Hickey the position of Associate Principal of Whitmer High School, but the person first offered the position of Assistant Superintendent dropped out of consideration. So, Hickey was in luck and in 2002 became the WLS Assistant Superintendent. He must have felt confident that his criminal past was adequately hidden.

The School Board makes the final decision on hiring of the Assistant Superintendent. The WLS Board that chose Patrick Hickey in 2002 included Frank Erme (served 1991-1999 & 2006-2013; now deceased),

John Adler (served 1997-2014; now deceased), Steve Zuber (1996-2014), David Hunter (1994-2019), and Lisa Canales (2000-2007 & 2016-2019).

Here is the crucial page 3 of Hickey's 2002 application:

Hickey promoted to WLS Superintendent, 2007

Patrick Hickey served as Asst. Superintendent under Superintendent Michael Carmean from 2002 on. Since he was not in the spotlight then, there is not much public information on Hickey's record as Assistant Superintendent.

Due to failing health, Superintendent Carmean submitted his resignation in early 2007. Then Hickey got his big chance. He felt ready to supervise 800+ employees, the $82 million budget, and thousands of students at the high school, two middle schools, and nine elementary schools.

Hickey named as references WLS Superintendent Michael Carmean and Treasurer Jeff Fouke, but no one at Addison. Superintendent Carmean, however, played no role in Hickey's selection. Mr. Carmean was *not* consulted by the Board and did *not* recommend Hickey for the position, according to his widow Patricia Carmean. Mrs. Carmean has also stated that Hickey was sometimes hard to locate during school hours, which frustrated her husband. Mr. Carmean did not have a high opinion of Hickey, she has recently stated.

It is the Board of Education that conducts the search, screening, and selection of a Superintendent. *The Toledo Blade* reported that the WLS Board paid the Ohio School Boards Association (OSBA) $5,500 to perform the preliminary vetting and shorten the applicant list from 22 to 9. [1] Hickey made that first cut.

Sources explain that OSBA conducts a superficial review of submitted applications without any deeper background checks. Nevertheless, it is hard to imagine they failed to pick up on the date discrepancies, comparing Hickey's Addison personnel file (end date "November 5, 1990" in Supt. Kersh's 1995 letter) and what Hickey wrote on his application ("8/90"). Apparently, OSBA did not verify his basic claims with the Addison Schools. Did they also miss his long period of apparent unemployment after Addison?

The WLS Board interviewed the nine candidates from the OSBA's short list. Hickey was then unanimously chosen as the new Superintendent.

The buck stops with the 2007 Board members, all of whom voted for Hickey: Lisa Canales (then President; served 2000-2007 & 2016-2019), Frank Erme (then V.P.; served 1991-1999 & 2006-2013), John Adler (1997-2014), David Hunter (1994-2018), and Steve Zuber (1996-2014).

Both Erme and Adler are now deceased. Will the other three members ever speak about what they knew and when they knew it? Did they miss the long gap in Hickey's employment history? Did they accept the mealy-mouthed "reference" by Supt. Kersh? Were they given the early letters by Principal Dieck (one being undated)? Or did they never even ask for anything from Addison? Did they miss the end date discrepancies and the missing year? Did they notice something was off in Hickey's résumé, but choose to ignore it?

Hickey wrote in his application, "There is no greater calling and no better place to work than in the public school system where we educate all who come to our doors as dictated by the founding fathers and the Constitution of this great country." (He noted History as one of his majors at college.) He claimed, "I have turned down many opportunities to stay with this awesome district."

Here is the crucial second page of his 2007 application:

Educational History:

School name	Location (city, state)	Major course or subject	Dates attended From	To	Graduated Yes	No	Degree
High school St. John's Jesuit	Toledo, Ohio	College Prep	9/77	5/81	X		H.S. Diploma
College (list all attended)							
Siena Heights College	Adrian, Michigan	English/History	8/81	5/86	X		Bachelor of Arts
University of Toledo	Toledo, Ohio	Educational Administration	8/87	4/94	X		Master of Education
University of Toledo	Toledo, Ohio	Educational Administration	4/94	8/97	X		Education Specialist
University of Findlay	Findlay, Ohio	Professional Development	8/97	6/02			ongoing Professional Development
Lourdes College	Sylvania, Ohio	Professional Development	8/02	Present			ongoing Professional Development

Professional Experience:

Starting with present or most recent, list all previous employers. If more space is required, please continue on a separate sheet. You may attach resume, but complete application as well.

No. of Years	Dates From	To	Position Title	School District/ Organization, Address	Reason for Leaving
5	8/02	Present	Assistant Superintendent	Washington Local Schools 3505 W. Lincolnshire, Toledo, OH	Presently Employed
6	8/96	8/02	Assistant Principal	Findlay City Schools 1200 Broad Ave, Findlay, OH	Professional Growth-to work for Washington Local Schools
5	8/91	8/96	Executive Director Principal Division Manager Educational Coordinator	Lucas County Educational Service Center Jobsville of Michigan St. Anthony Villa/Holy Cross Children Services 2740 W. Central Ave. Toledo, OH 43606	Professional Growth-to work in the public schools
4	8/86	8/90	English Teacher/Coach	Addison Community Schools 311 Comstock St. Addison, MI 49220	Relocation of Wife
5	summers 81+86		Heavy Equipment Operator	City of Toledo-Parks and Recreation	Teaching Career

Other Work Experience and Achievements Valuable to Your Career:

See Attached

Outside Activities:

See Attached

CHAPTER 9
Aborted Investigations of Hickey
– 2007-2013 –

Unpublished WTOL investigative report, 2007

In 2006 or 2007, WTOL News (Toledo) investigative reporter Jonathan Walsh received an anonymous tip about Patrick Hickey's time at the Addison, Michigan schools.

Private investigator Chris Gill (working for Board member Jim Langenderfer) interviewed Walsh over the phone on November 29, 2015. That interview and Walsh's written statement below became part of the Michigan State Police investigation.

Walsh said his investigation took place in "2006-2007." But since Walsh refers to Hickey being Superintendent at the time, it would likely have been sometime in 2007.

Walsh traveled to Addison that year and spoke with people in the community. Eventually, he tracked down Dawn's older brother, Mark. Mark then put Walsh in touch with Dawn and she agreed to do a taped phone interview. Walsh said he also recorded his interview with Mark. But the tape(s) could not be located.

On December 1, 2015, Walsh gave this written statement on his 2007 findings to investigator Gill:

Statement by Jonathan Walsh, former reporter with WTOL News

Dec. 1, 2015

While working for WTOL News 11 in Toledo, Ohio, I, Jonathan Walsh, received an anonymous tip about possible questionable behavior surrounding Washington Local Superintendent Patrick Hickey and his time as a teacher and coach at Addison High School. As I followed up on that tip, I spoke to many people in the Addison community who corroborated what the anonymous tip had indicated.

My first stop in Addison was at a local corner store where I asked the clerk if she had heard anything about inappropriate relationships concerning Patrick Hickey. The young woman told me that she had gone to school during the time that Patrick Hickey was a coach for the girls basketball team. She remembered there were talks around the school about Patrick Hickey and "Dawn" having a sexual relationship while Dawn was a student and athlete on the girls' basketball team. From there, I started searching for family members of Dawn and any teachers or administration that worked at Addison High School during the time of Patrick Hickey's employment there.

I found several confidential informants who I verified did work at the high school at the time in question. As a journalist, I must keep my word and allow them their anonymity but they too told me stories about questionable behavior of Patrick Hickey with Dawn. Based on their information, I was able to track down the principal of the Addison High School Dan Dieck during the time in question. I called him and he verified that he was the principal and that he did have a meeting with Patrick Hickey. My informant told me that during that meeting Don Dieck told Patrick Hickey that Don Dieck had reason to believe that Patrick Hickey had a sexual relationship with Dawn and that Patrick Hickey had two choices: Patrick Hickey could deny the allegations and there would be a formal and public investigation or Patrick Hickey could resign that day. My informant told me Hickey decided to resign that day in November of 1990.

During a public records request, I obtained the paperwork surrounding Patrick Hickey's time at Addison High School. Patrick Hickey's abrupt resignation letter in November of 1990 was in that paperwork. Once I had that information, I made another public records request for Patrick Hickey's application to be the Washington Locals' Superintendent. I then noticed that in his application he wrote that the reason he resigned from Addison High School was because his wife had accepted a new job.

I was able to track down Dawn's brother Mark. On the phone, he told me that he observed questionable behavior between Patrick Hickey and his sister. Mark told me he always thought a sexual relationship was happening and that his sister finally told him there was, in fact, an inappropriate relationship that had happened between she [sic] and Patrick Hickey. Mark even agreed to an on-camera interview and he described all of the visits that Patrick Hickey would make to their house and how Dawn was spending time at Patrick Hickey's home.

I was able to then obtain the phone number of Dawn. She agreed to do a taped phone conversation with me about her time as a basketball player and student at Addison High School. She told me she had sexual intercourse with Patrick Hickey on numerous occasions while Patrick Hickey was her coach. She told me of times that she would stay after practice and the two would have sex in the equipment room of the high school. She told me Patrick Hickey and she would meet secretly to have sexual encounters including at the local Addison cemetery. She also told me that Patrick Hickey would invite her to dinner at his home and, while Patrick Hickey's wife was there, they all had dinner together and the wife didn't know Patrick Hickey and Dawn were having an affair.

Dawn also informed me that after she graduated from high school and went to college, Patrick Hickey visited her at college. One time Patrick Hickey called Dawn from the parking lot outside her dorm/apartment asking her to come down to see him. Dawn told me it was during that same time that she found out about another student Patrick Hickey was having an inappropriate relationship with. Her name was "Julie."

During our phone interview, Dawn told me that the reason she was doing the interview was because she was afraid that Patrick Hickey would prey on other students. She told me that she was a mother now and she would want another parent that was in her shoes to come forward if it meant that he/she would be protecting Dawn's children in a similar situation.

I was able to track down the mother of Julie. I called the mother and she was emphatic and, in my opinion, quite defensive about the claims that her daughter had a sexual relationship with Patrick Hickey. She told me "it was proven that nothing had ever happened" between her daughter and Patrick Hickey and she immediately hung up the phone.

Because we didn't have a second victim or her family willing to go on camera or do a taped interview, over the years two of my news directors and my general manager decided it was Dawn's word against Patrick Hickey's word and it was not enough to air on WTOL.

This is my statement made on December 1, 2015.

– Jonathan Walsh

In Walsh's phone interview with Gill on November 29, 2015 (a few days before his written statement), he said that Addison High School Principal, Donald Dieck, "called Hickey into his office on Nov. 5, 1990 and pretty much told him 'The jig is up, I know what you're doing'."

According to Walsh, Dawn's dinners in the Hickey home with Mrs. Hickey present were

> ... very awkward for her at the young age of 15-16 years old. Once Dawn had graduated and went on to college, Hickey would show up there and call her to come down to his car from her dorm room. Dawn states she has had years of emotional stress over this and he told her he would leave his wife for her in order to keep having sex with her, but he never intended to leave his wife. Jonathan also learned of another student Hickey was having an inappropriate sexual relationship with and she was only 14-15 years old at the time and her name was "Julie." Jonathan contacted her mother and it appeared to him that [her] parents were okay with Hickey being with their underage daughter. [Julie's] mother promptly hung up on Jonathan.

WTOL spiked Walsh's report as an unverified he-said/she-said story. Had WTOL gone further with a more in-depth investigation in 2007, Patrick Hickey might not have continued as WLS Superintendent. Further police investigations could have followed and Hickey might have been convicted then.

More aborted investigations of Hickey, 2010-2013

There were several more aborted investigations into Patrick Hickey's time at Addison during his tenure as Superintendent – and he was likely aware some of these. (The detail below comes from the Michigan State Police investigation files.)

In August 2010, Hickey had his attorney contact the Addison Schools administrators, asking them to alter the contents of his personnel file. The attorney requested they remove the 1990 memo by Supt. Kersh and add Kersh's brief letters from 1993 and 1995. The attorney wrote:

> Mr. Hickey has reason to believe that certain persons are pursuing his work history with the specific intent of finding damaging information. As you would certainly know, the reputation of an educator is a fragile thing, particularly for those serving in the most conspicuous capacity of school district superintendent. It goes without saying that even the mere suggestion of wrongdoing by an educator – though false – can have a devastating impact on lives, careers, and professional opportunities...

> The document requested for removal is a two-page typewritten memo to the Addison Board of Education, dated November 1990, from its then superintendent, Jeffrey Kersh... It relates allegations

of a parent that were found to be unsubstantiated. It is also inaccurate in that it suggests that Mr. Hickey resigned out of fear of a student's testimony against him, when in fact he had no knowledge of any such impending statement or testimony. The documents requested for addition to Mr. Hickey's file are two signed letters from Mr. Kersh from 1993 and 1995, indicating that Mr. Hickey's separation from employment was "without prejudice..."

Why was Hickey concerned? In September 2010, WTOL was again checking in with Addison Schools. The TV station contacted Tom Britsch – Dawn's basketball coach at Addison – and asked him to comment on several "leading" questions. Around the same time, former Addison teacher Jim Driskill (there at the time of Hickey's resignation) requested Hickey's personnel records. The Addison Schools' attorney noted at the time, "Clearly, something is 'brewing'." But nothing came to fruition that year.

In September 2011, Fox News Toledo submitted a public records request to Addison Schools for "any and all personnel records for Patrick Hickey" while he was a teacher at Addison Schools, "including any honors or reprimands he may have received, dismissal notices, complaints, resignation letters, etc." But no story appeared at Fox.

In April 2012, a sports reporter for *The Toledo Blade* submitted a public records request to Addison Schools for "all employment, disciplinary, and personnel records pertaining to former Addison teacher Patrick Hickey." This was perhaps related to possible "ethics violations" by WLS. (The administration later admitted to allowing ineligible out-of-district athletes to play for the school. See Chapter 12.) It appears Addison Schools refused to release any of Hickey's personnel records to the reporter, and no report mentioning Hickey's Addison past followed.

Former Hickey student at Addison, Kris Hassenzahl, told the Michigan State Police (in 2018) that she was contacted by *The Toledo Blade* sometime in 2013 concerning Hickey's time there. She did not want to come forward then. Later, she would speak to investigator Gill (in late 2015) and go on record with the MSP and the WLS Board (in early 2018).

So ... Patrick Hickey would manage to hang on for several more years.

CHAPTER 10
The Cult of Hickey

Hickey boosts the WLS Community

As Superintendent of Washington Local Schools, Patrick Hickey was an idol to many in the community. He had built up a powerful fan base in the district.

Perhaps he was pre-emptively maximizing goodwill in the community in case the truth about his misdeeds finally caught up with him. (That is a theory held by several WLS teachers.) But would his devotees be able to save him then?

The district citizens well knew that they lived in perhaps the poorest district within a very poor urban area. Toledo, a "rust-belt" city closely tied to the auto and glass industry, suffered greatly during the recent recession. The Ohio Department of Education [1] designated Washington Local Schools a Category 7 district, meaning "Urban – High Student Poverty & Average Student Population." [2]

Hickey praying at a school football game.

So, the WLS community needed a boost, and Hickey knew how to pump them up with "Panther" spirit. He was a talented salesman and cheerleader who made people feel good about their school district. And they loved him for it. One prominent teacher said, "Hickey was a larger-than-life figure and very good in the art of negotiating."

The pabulum that Hickey served up appealed to many. He often trotted out the WLS "core values" – the 12 character traits all should aspire to: *courage, dedication, dignity, excellence, gratitude, honesty, loyalty, respect, responsibility, service, teamwork, trust.* He added his list of WLS "non-negotiables" for successful schools: *high quality instruction, collaboration, data-based decision making,* and *technology as a learning accelerator.*

So, the community trusted that thoughtful adults were running the show, led by their vibrant Superintendent.

Here are some excerpts from his official biography (posted through late 2015):

> In 2014, Patrick was named the #1 Leader in the region and the district was named the #1 Workplace in the region based on an independent survey conducted by Workplace Dynamics. His leadership philosophy encompasses site-based management, collaboration and empowering others. Upon being hired as Superintendent, Mr. Hickey made a commitment to accomplish "76 goals in 1,000 days," and followed that with 62 Goals for a 50-Year-Old Superintendent.

> Superintendent Hickey encouraged input from staff members to help identify standards that would guide all decisions made in the district. Through collaborative effort, twelve core values were adopted by the board of education...

> Under [his] guidance, Washington Local Schools moved from a "Continuous Improvement" status to achieving an "Excellent" rating and having two buildings achieve an "Excellent with Distinction" rating...

> Superintendent Hickey's leadership has led the district to five consecutive new money levies passed by the [WLS] community. The 2011 and 2014 levies assisted the district's budget deficit – a deficit due to declining revenue, unconstitutional funding [sic] of schools, and reduced property tax revenue. In 2008, Hickey led not only a successful levy campaign, but acquiring [sic] the most "yes" votes ever at Washington Local....

He is an enthusiastic participant in student programs.... Where Superintendent Hickey is, you will find kids.

He portrayed his routine leadership responsibilities as praiseworthy accomplishments, for example; overseeing repairs to the older school buildings, organizing veterans' recognition events, implementing new business-educational partnerships, and promoting new university scholarship grants for Whitmer High School graduates.

Hickey often reverted to boilerplate educrat lingo. But he added his own twist: that he loved that he loved every child, every parent, every community member. He was honored to serve them. He wanted to "lift up kids" and "lead them to their destiny of infinite possibilities." He wanted to "make their dreams come true."

The Board of Education played along. Rainbow colors and a butterfly-shaped logo would make up for any delivery shortfall. Apparently, a happy façade will deter some people from looking more closely at what's happening inside.

washington local schools

Making dreams come true...

2011 WASHINGTON LOCAL BOARD OF EDUCATION

STEVE ZUBER
President

DAVID HUNTER
Vice President

JOHN ADLER

FRANK ERME

THOMAS ILSTRUP

The school district's motto, *Individual Attention – Infinite Opportunities*, included an unrealistic promise. But people wanted to believe it.

Besides his over-the-top clichés, Hickey showboated his dedication through exuberant physicality. However, his prodigal hugs for community members, teachers, staff, and students did concern some.

Hickey was everywhere! There were Hickey videos, Hickey photos, Hickey statements, Hickey proclamations. While he would constantly repeat "It's all about the kids," it often seemed it was all about the Superintendent. The photo below [3] is just one example. Students won the art awards, but Hickey inserted himself into the photo with them.

He appeared at athletic games, spelling bees, awards ceremonies, fundraisers, community service events. He walked the halls and dropped in on classrooms. He accompanied teachers on professional development trips. He slept in cabins with sixth-grade boys at a school overnight camp. He posted photos of himself shirtless at the beach on his public Facebook. His image dominated the WLS online news pages.

2013 Focus Art Show
Whitmer Artists Sweep Show, Take Top

Mad Ratter
Ceramic Teapot
Superintendent's Award

Whitmer swept the 2013 Focus Art Show. Of the 270 pieces selected for exhibition from over 1,300 entries, 87 pieces were created by Whitmer students.

Whitmer artists also received five of the prestigious Juror Awards -- more than any other school in NW Ohio or SE Michigan.

The Washington Local Superintendent's Award was presented by Patrick Hickey (far right) to

(not pictured).

Having a son with a disability made Hickey sensitive to the needs of students requiring extra attention, and he made the most of this issue. He promoted the "Infinite Opportunity" Olympics event at WLS. [4] He went skydiving with a special-needs boy (and made sure the video was posted). He celebrated a Homecoming Queen with Down syndrome (and posted his photo with her).

At the same time, School Board member Jim Langenderfer – whose career expertise was Special Education – noted that Hickey often did not come down hard on student bullies and malefactors. As Superintendent, his policy was to show them more "love." When the WLS campus was vandalized by students shortly before graduation in May 2015, Langenderfer was the sole voice on the Board advocating that the vandal students should be barred from participating in the graduation ceremony. But Hickey advocated forgiveness and a "second chance."

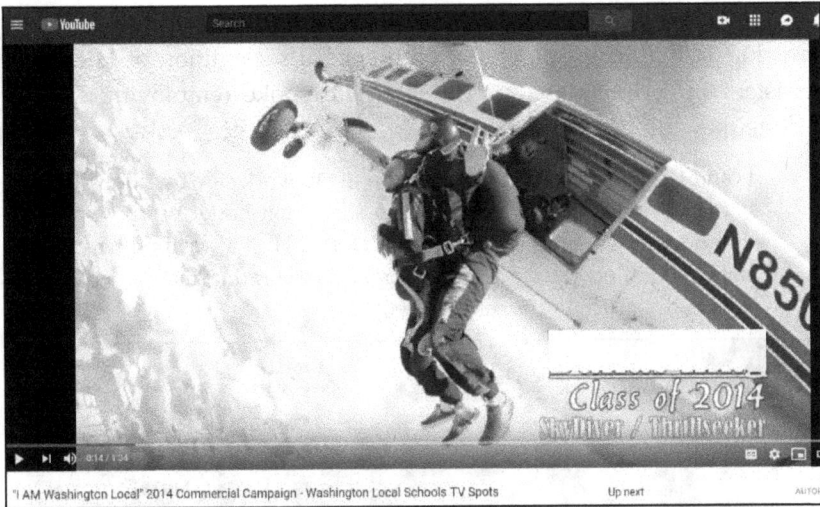

2014 WLS promotional video. [5] Hickey made a big deal of arranging this skydiving adventure for a special-needs student. Hickey also got to skydive that day (and asked to be reimbursed by WLS).

Hickey's 2013 Holiday message (in a video no longer online) gives a good sense of his style. He tells a story of how WLS is simply *not* normal; *great things* happen there. Throughout the video, though, his smile and happy talk seem forced. His acting was not always convincing.

Ever the promoter, Hickey engineered WLS's recognition by Workplace Dynamics and *The Toledo Blade* as the "top workplace in Northwest Ohio" for 2013. [6] In early 2014, he had his WLS production crew make a promotional video entitled "Happy" [7] to celebrate the award. Teachers dance inappropriately throughout the school buildings. One scene glorifies *"the #1 boss in the region – Patrick Hickey!"* A group of teachers sway back and forth to the music, holding up "Hickey masks" that cover their faces. Apparently, teachers were "happy" to lose their individual identities and be swallowed up in the cult of Hickey.

The February 19, 2014 School Board meeting held a celebratory showing of the "Happy" video, with special recognition of Hickey. [8] Assistant Superintendent Cherie Mourlam spoke (employing Hickey's "lifting them up" verbiage):

> I can't tell you how much it means to me to work side by side with Patrick every day and to be able to share that honor of knowing that he is so well thought of by our staff... He's always lifting up staff and lifting up students and really celebrating us... Tonight, Patrick, we are going to celebrate you.

Screengrab from WLS promotional video "Happy" where teachers don Hickey masks (2014).

At the same meeting, three junior high teachers performed a joke routine at the podium, quizzing Hickey (who formerly taught English) on literature terms. He failed to properly identify the first example: *Patrick is a pleasingly popular professional whose proud, persistent, and positively perky personality permeates his personnel.* He answered *limerick* (instead of alliteration). He got the next answer – *simile* – correct: *Patrick is like a fart in a windstorm. Once it's out there, you just can't control it.* Then the teachers read quotes expressing, "How we feel about our number one leader!" Here are a few:

> "A true leader always keeps an element of surprise up his sleeve which others cannot grasp but with which he keeps his public excited and absolutely breathless." The Greeks have a saying, "When a man dies, it is important that he lived his life with passion." Your passion for our children and our district is truly inspiring!

The Cult of Hickey

"If your actions inspire others to dream more, learn more, do more, and become more, then you are a true leader." *You, Patrick Hickey, are our number-one leader!*

During the first five years of his tenure as Superintendent, the district earned good grades from the Ohio Department of Education. [9] (Scores had been going up under the previous Superintendent as well.) While this was likely due primarily to hard-working teachers, the state grades helped secure local funding.

Hickey took credit for the five school levies passed during his tenure (an anomaly, especially in a poor district). And he got companies to advertise on the stadium scoreboard and donate needed items to the schools.

But even some of those efforts were tainted. He was accused of illegally [10] using school district resources to lobby citizens to support levies or contact their state legislators. [11] And his rogue negotiations with the local Ford dealer angered the School Board.

UPDATE - LEVY CAMPAIGN - ISSUE 14 - THANK YOU

VOTE FOR KIDS
WASHINGTON LOCAL SCHOOLS

Superintendent Patrick Hickey and Assistant Superintendent Cherie Mouriam, dressed as Pete and Penelope, encouraged those driving through the busy Wernert's Corners intersection to "Vote For Kids."

VOTE FOR KIDS
WASHINGTON LOCAL SCHOOLS

The Superintendent thanked the staff, students, families, and community for working together to pass Issue 14. Mr. Hickey said the levy success was due to a lot of people rowing together with "one heart, one voice, one message." He said he was sharing with the Board a list of 320 activities that were done to help promote the levy (210 district items, the others by schools or individuals). Only 27 items cost money; the rest were grassroots and partnerships with TAWLS, OAPSE, and the community.

Levy Thank-You - Audio: http://www.wls4kids.org/superintendent/monthlyreports/20112012/upload/Levy-thank-you-Supt-Report-2011-11-16.mp3

Hickey continued to make grandiose claims that WLS was the best school district in Ohio. But state measurements showed the district had actually been struggling academically from 2012 on (in his later years as Superintendent), according to the review by later WLS Superintendent Susan Hayward (hired in June 2016). By 2015-2016, the State Report Card gave WLS overall grades of mostly D and F. [12]

Despite any negatives that bubbled up over the happy talk, Hickey maintained his dominance of the WLS district. He had built up a cult following which allowed him to survive as Superintendent – until late 2015.

Hickey as Narcissist

Patrick Hickey wrote in 2011 that a plaque on his office wall displayed this quote: *"Mediocre minds will violently oppose great spirits."* And he added, "When you are striving to be great, you will be attacked." [13]

He apparently believed that Washington Local Schools were in the hands of a "great spirit" (himself) who was "striving" for the schools. And he continually told the district they were "great." He made them feel good and they showered him with affection in return. And they hoped to earn his loving personal recognition.

If an attack on Hickey were to come, it would only be because he was a "great spirit" working so hard for the community – and it would come from lesser people possessing "mediocre minds." If there were attacks on the district, those likewise would come from "mediocre" (and jealous) outsiders.

Patrick Hickey clearly exhibits at least some narcissistic traits. And he admitted at his 2018 sentencing hearing that he needed "severe psychological help" and underwent three years of psychotherapy after leaving the Addison Schools.

The concepts below may help make sense of the Hickey scandal that erupted in Washington Local Schools.

Narcissism defined

Mental health professionals distinguish between narcissistic personality traits and narcissistic personality disorder. [14]

Full-blown narcissism (a personality disorder) can be described as:

> ... the pursuit of gratification from vanity or egotistic admiration of one's idealized self image and attributes... Narcissism is also

considered a social or cultural problem... narcissism is usually considered a problem in a person's or group's relationships with self and others. [15]

From *Psychology Today*:

> The hallmarks of narcissistic personality disorder (NPD) are grandiosity, a lack of empathy for other people, and a need for admiration. People with this condition are frequently described as arrogant, self-centered, manipulative, and demanding. They may also have grandiose fantasies and may be convinced that they deserve special treatment. These characteristics typically begin in early adulthood and must be consistently evident in multiple contexts, such as at work and in relationships. People with NPD often try to associate with other people they believe are unique or gifted in some way, which can enhance their own self-esteem. They tend to seek excessive admiration and attention and have difficulty tolerating criticism or defeat. [16]

Prominent psychiatrists list "seven deadly sins" of the narcissist: shamelessness (he still sees himself as good despite wrong actions); magical thinking (he is perfect); arrogance; envy; entitlement; exploitation (of people under his authority); and poor boundaries (other people are just extensions of himself and his desires). [17]

Hickey might also fit the mold of a "sexual narcissist":

> Sexual narcissism has been described as an egocentric pattern of sexual behavior that involves an inflated sense of sexual ability and sexual entitlement. In addition, sexual narcissism is the erotic preoccupation with oneself as a superb lover through a desire to merge sexually with a mirror image of oneself. Sexual narcissism is an intimacy dysfunction in which sexual exploits are pursued, generally in the form of extramarital affairs, to overcompensate for low self-esteem and an inability to experience true intimacy. [18]

Another way to view Hickey may be as a "communal narcissist." An article in *Psychology Today* describes "communal narcissists" as:

> ... people who continuously seek to validate their self-perceived grandiosity, esteem, entitlement, and power – this type focuses on promoting him or herself through commitment to others, communal goals, and the supposed ability to listen and connect... They're people who talk about having a "mission" or are "committed to a cause," and they make it clear that while your life and concerns are petty and shallow, theirs are possessed of deep meaning and intent. You may have run into them on the PTA or at

a charity event, booster club, or fundraiser. You may have been surprised when one showed his or her true colors by becoming hugely territorial and much more concerned with personal aggrandizement and appreciation than the communal goal you thought you were all working toward. And then there's some terrible politicized brouhaha: Bingo! [19]

A "communal narcissist" makes grandiose statements; he "promises to fix whatever no one else has been able to."

Keep in mind that this is how the narcissist likes to think of him or herself. The reality is that he or she lacks the ability to empathize, is still a game-player, and carries all the other traits generally associated with narcissism. He or she is involved in community *only* as a validation of self.

Understanding communal narcissism explains why sometimes women and men who are largely viewed as "pillars of the community" and known for their devotion to charities and other causes can be highly destructive and unloving in their personal roles as friends, husbands, wives, fathers, and mothers. [20]

WLS community narcissism

The Hickey scandal that enveloped the district (from late 2015 on) can also be understood in the context of WLS collective (group) narcissism:

Collective narcissism (or group narcissism) extends the concept of individual narcissism onto the social level of self. It is a tendency to exaggerate the positive image and importance of a group the individual belongs to – i.e. the ingroup. [21]

WLS group narcissism grew out of Hickey's narcissism and charismatic leadership. (Of course, this doesn't apply to every citizen in the district, just his very vocal fan club.) Here is a psychologist's explanation:

An important characteristic of the leader-follower relationship are the manifestations of narcissism by both the leader and follower of a group. Within this relationship there are two categories of narcissists: the mirror-hungry narcissist, and the ideal-hungry narcissist – the leader and the followers respectively. The mirror-hungry personality typically seeks a continuous flow of admiration and respect from his followers. Conversely, the ideal-hungry narcissist [community member] takes comfort in the charisma and confidence of his mirror-hungry leader. The relationship is somewhat symbiotic; for while the followers provide the continuous admiration needed by the mirror-hungry leader, the leader's charisma provides the followers with the sense of security and purpose that their ideal-hungry narcissism seeks. Fundamentally both the leader and the followers exhibit strong collectively narcissistic sentiments – both parties are seeking greater justification and reason to love their group as much as possible. [22]

From an article at the British Psychological Society website:

Where does collective narcissism come from? ... collective narcissism may act as a compensation for low individual confidence and low self-worth. Lacking confidence in themselves, people can find comfort in aligning closely with a larger grouping, and seeing this group as somehow special and great. In turn, they are then highly defensive of their chosen group's status, ultra-sensitive to possible slights, and keen to derogate any threatening groups...

The new findings suggest that any politician [or school super-intendent] who ferments in their followers a grandiose belief in the in-group, combined with encouraging them to believe the in-group is being insulted or slighted by others, is arguably fostering collective narcissism and sowing the seeds for future conflict and hostility.... [23]

Rabble rousers – including students – wore T-shirts reading #IStandWithMrHickey at the Sept. 16, 2015 School Board meeting. [24]

Hickey, their leader, promoted the idea of WLS "excellence" and followers in the community ate it up. As residents of one of the poorest school districts in Ohio, they needed this boost to their self-esteem. In turn, Hickey's promotion of community self-esteem contributed to their cultish devotion to him as their *irreproachable* leader. *He was key to their feeling good about the WLS community and themselves.*

They saw their school system as "best" because their leader (who took so much of the credit) was the "best." Even Workplace Dynamics and *The Toledo Blade* said so! [25] Attacks on their leader were attacks on them. If their leader went down, they would go down. Those who dared question or criticize their leader were simply *"mediocre minds"* who couldn't recognize greatness – and those critics *deserved no respect.* So, his followers must directly attack anyone challenging him.

> Collective narcissism is characterized by the members of a group holding an inflated view of their ingroup which requires external validation. Collective narcissism predicts retaliatory hostility to past, present, actual and imagined offences to the ingroup and negative attitudes towards groups perceived as threatening. [26]

This group psychology may help explain the ferocity of Hickey's defenders when serious challenges to his record began in 2015.

Twitter #IStandWithMrHickey from 2015. [27]

CHAPTER 11
Violating Appropriate Boundaries

In Patrick Hickey's early career, he violated sexual boundaries between educator and student. In more recent years as Superintendent, he had inappropriate relationships with female employees under his authority. Eventually (in 2015), the Washington Local School Board reprimanded him for his "overly personal" style with several particular staff members.

But his "overly personal" style was also on full display in his interactions with other staff, students, parents, and community members. Why was that inappropriate behavior accepted so long by the Board?

From the slideshow posted by WLS teachers after their 2013 "professional development" trip to Ron Clark Academy in Atlanta. Teachers adopted Hickey's vocabulary: "We'll love em up and lift em up!" [1]

Hickey's "radical goals"

In the Foreword to the iBook *Socked* by his ally Jeremy Baumhower [2], Hickey stated that he advocated "radical goals." He cited his "new mission" when he became Superintendent "that included loving kids and families unconditionally." He said he initiated "hundreds of activities which allowed staff to love and foster students and families." He wanted his "staff to do what they do best: love and lift up kids."

What did all that really mean? Were Hickey's words just empty verbiage? Or did his approach open the door to inappropriate relations between educators and students? All his talk of "love" made some observers uneasy.

For a teacher or administrator to intrude on the family's realm ("to love and foster children and families") is indeed radical.

Many in the community wanted to stick with more traditional educational goals: academic achievement and skill acquisition. But Superintendent Hickey was in charge and wanted to put *his* mark on the district.

Grooming individuals and the community

Patrick Hickey had groomed the WLS community to adore him. But would their devotion shield him from accusations of inappropriate behavior in the present – or a past crime?

He eventually confessed to his crime in Addison. But recall what a popular teacher and coach Hickey was in that community. The head basketball coach and high school principal there never suspected him of wrongdoing and saw lots of talent and promise in the young man. They were pleased with his eagerness to devote extra time to his students.

An authority on educator sexual abuse, Professor Charol Shakeshaft, explains how a community is groomed by a predator, how he softens them up through charm and flattery, and so prevents them from accusing or identifying him as an offender.

> While there are no screening tools to help determine who is an active or potential sexual predator, school leaders can learn to read the warning signs and patterns that identify risk and boundary behavior.
>
> Anna Salter, an internationally known expert on sexual predators, recently reminded us that fixated abusers [those who slowly build up trust] work hard to be likeable. Popularity and likability are often confused with trustworthiness. When a fixated abuser is accused, victims protect them, parents refuse to believe the accusations, authorities discount the reports, communities support the predator, and juries acquit.
>
> School faculty and staff often rally around a teacher accused of sexual misconduct while shunning and shaming the victim. Even when the accused admits the crime, colleagues have been charmed and groomed to such a degree that some conclude the predator

confessed to spare family and friends the embarrassment of a public trial. [3]

The U.S. Department of Education includes this description in a 2017 report on "Adult Sexual Misconduct in the School Setting":

> At the same time [as he is grooming the individual victim], the perpetrator is also testing the adults surrounding the child or school, including those who work at school, individuals in the school community, and the child's family or guardian(s). It is not uncommon for the behaviors to be done publicly so that the perpetrator can gauge reactions; share information (true or false) to manipulate how the behavior is interpreted by the adults; and further control the child victim. For example, a teacher may lead their colleagues to believe the parent has provided consent for them to drive a student home because the parent needs help. In response, the perpetrator receives accolades and gratitude from their colleagues, and has begun the process of grooming peers as well... [4]

This could apply not only to Hickey's early career, but to his "overly personal" style with co-workers, parents, and children in the WLS community. If he could get away with giving everyone hugs and telling them he "loved them," he may have hoped he could get away with inappropriate behaviors with individual staffers. And the community might not want to believe any rumors about his past.

When people were enjoying his violations of proper interpersonal boundaries (hugs and *personal* compliments) vis-à-vis themselves, how would they ever speak against him? Many *wanted* love and attention from the powerful Superintendent.

Too much playfulness, too many hugs

To some, Hickey's brazen *public* behavior seemed violation enough to trigger his dismissal.

The Superintendent was setting a bad example for his employees.

Patricia Carmean, former WLS Board member and elementary teacher, described Hickey's behavior at an elementary school event which she found highly inappropriate. As a Board member, she attended a luncheon for students in grades 4-8:

> It was a great day. The kids were having a scavenger hunt. The Principals were there... I know some of these kids because they're from my building... And he wants the children to come up and

sing a song ... and he said he'd give an example of what a song would be. So, he starts the ABC song. He's standing on a table. And he goes, "A, B, C..." and all the way until you get to the letter P and ... he leaves that letter out. And he says, ... "Why do you think I left that letter out? ... It's running down my leg!" ... This is the Superintendent of our district! [5]

Hickey responded to Carmean when she told him his vulgar joke was out of line: "It was appropriate for this age level," he said. She explained that the Principals and teachers who were there "could not say anything because they would lose their jobs."

There are many photos showing Hickey standing on tables, jumping, and acting crazy or goofy around students. It's his *fun-and-games* philosophy of education, which seems to have been refined on his trips to the Ron Clark Academy in Atlanta where the headmaster models this style.

Hickey proudly posted photos like these on his personal Facebook.

He grabbed opportunities to share in others' achievements and used school news events for some physical contact – especially with women. There are numerous photos in the WLS "Across the Board" online newsletters showing Hickey with his arm around female staffers and even some students.

Familiar behavior with students

Patrick Hickey's sons and daughter attended Washington Local Schools. This meant that WLS students were often at the Hickey home.

That made it hard to maintain appropriate boundaries between administrator and student.

A comment by Hickey at the September 16, 2015 School Board meeting [6] seems to confirm this sort of thing happened at his home. A teenage friend of his daughter rose to speak. She said she was happy Hickey wasn't fired. He broke in: "I want to caution before 'M' speaks. She has spent the night at my house many times and anything that happens in that house is not for public consumption here. Now go!" (meaning "speak!"). That took place as the School Board had just formally reprimanded Hickey for being overly familiar with staff.

SPECIAL RECOGNITION - ANTI-BULLYING WEEK STUDENT ORGANIZERS

There is currently a push in the state and the country to focus on Anti-Bullying, but Washington Local has been working on cultivating a positive school climate for many years, because it is the right thing to do and because we care about our kids.

Two DECA/marketing students at Whitmer planned a whole week of events to address bullying and some of the activities blew Superintendent Hickey away.

To stop bullying, you have to stop the culture which allows any person to believe they are better than another.

The work of ███████████████ will have ripple effects and we thank them for all of their efforts. Special thanks are also extended to DECA teacher **Laura Ulrich** and Student Services Director **Neil Rochotte**.

Superintendent **Patrick Hickey** (*center*) recognized ███████ and ███████ for organizing an Anti-Bullying Week at Whitmer.

Note Hickey's arm around girl's back. From a 2012 WLS online newsletter. [7]

Several male students spoke at Board meetings and stated they "love" Mr. Hickey – and he said he "loves" them back. (See Chapter 14.)

In a characteristic Twitter exchange [8] between a high school student and Hickey, a boy says: "It always makes my day when @SuptHickey comes into work and I get to hug him. Such a good and caring man." Hickey responds @SuptHickey: "B — you are a great kid with a huge heart! You make my day. It is kids like you that make this job rewarding."

Professional boundaries crossed with staff

Hickey played favorites in the faculty which made for bad morale, according to various WLS sources.

Hickey often socialized with teachers outside of school. This is apparent in the emails between Hickey and high school teachers Anna (Chapter 13) and Becca (Chapter 15). He went with his "insider group" on skydiving adventures, to paintball games, and to athletic events (not connected to WLS). He apparently included Becca in highly personal events (family dinners, birthday celebrations), let her know what hotel he was staying at on trips, and was seen with her at a local fitness center.

Professional boundaries were not observed.

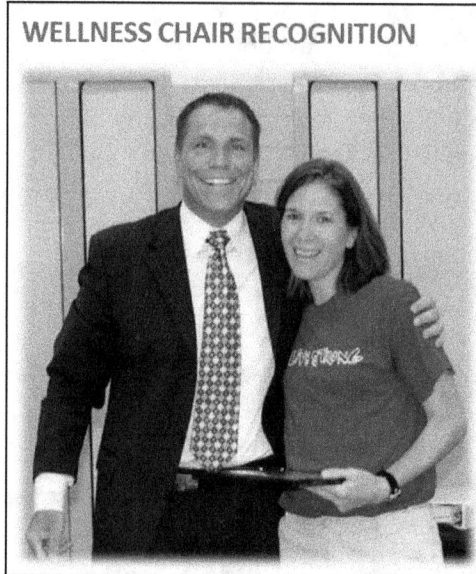

WELLNESS CHAIR RECOGNITION

There are many photos like this in the WLS online newsletters showing Hickey with his arm around women teachers. [9]

Eventually (in 2015), violations of proper boundaries with employees was what tripped Hickey up, when high school teacher Anna filed her complaint and he was seen publicly engaging in flirtatious behavior with another teacher, Becca.

WLS Employee Code of Conduct

The standards set forth in the official WLS Policies [10] are important for future chapters, as Hickey's behavior with female teachers became a concern and the School Board finally had to publicly reprimand him, then force his resignation.

WLS posted a video [11] in November 2016 (a year after Hickey's resignation) acknowledging that information on proper employee conduct had not been clearly conveyed in the past. The Interim Superintendent talks of the need to "reflect on our past practices and make adjustments."

The Human Resources Director and Interim Superintendent and explain the message of the Code of Conduct in the video:

> **Educators are held to a higher ethical standard by the community it serves.** [Employees must] Comply with justifiable directives issued by established lines of authority... **Demonstrate respect and integrity** when interacting with students, parents, staff, community members, and other stakeholders... Comply with federal laws, state statutes, and Board policies and District administrative procedures that prohibit coercive, harassing, threatening, retaliating, or discriminating conduct... **Refrain from any unethical activity that may reasonably interfere with either one's ability to effectively perform one's duties as assigned, or the legitimate operational interests of the District.** [Emphasis added.]

Sexual harassment of an employee

The Washington Local Schools district follows the 1964 federal Civil Rights Act on sexual harassment in the workplace [12] as part of their code of conduct. Some of the phrases from the posted policies (below) seem to apply to Superintendent Hickey's relations with two female teachers – though the School Board did not officially pursue this charge against Hickey. Note also that "favoritism of a subordinate employee with whom the superior is sexually involved" was a factor during Hickey's tenure as Superintendent which *affected other employees* and possibly resulted in a "hostile work environment." Excerpts:

> Prohibited acts that constitute sexual harassment may take a variety of forms. Examples of the kinds of conduct that may constitute sexual harassment include, but are not limited to:
>
> A. Unwelcome sexual propositions, invitations, solicitations, and flirtations.
>
> B. Unwanted physical and/or sexual contact.
>
> C. Threats or insinuations that a person's employment, wages, academic grade, promotion, classroom work or assignments, academic status, participation in athletics or extra-curricular programs or events, or other conditions of employment or education may be adversely affected by not submitting to sexual advances.
>
> D. Unwelcome verbal expressions of a sexual nature... [etc.]
>
> I. **In the context of employees, consensual sexual relationships where such relationship leads to favoritism of a subordinate**

employee with whom the superior is sexually involved and where such favoritism adversely affects other employees or otherwise creates a hostile work environment... – WLS, po1662, po3362 [Emphasis added.]

Appropriate boundaries between educator and student

Below are excerpts (with emphasis added) from the current and earlier WLS policies regarding appropriate boundaries between educator and student. The harassment definition (po1662, po3362) currently includes this:

> Inappropriate boundary invasions by a District employee or other adult member of the School District community into a student's personal space and personal life.

> A professional staff member shall not associate with students at any time in a manner which gives the **appearance of impropriety, including, but not limited to, the creation or participation in any situation or activity** which could be considered abusive or **sexually suggestive** or involve illegal substances such as tobacco, alcohol, or drugs. Any sexual conduct with a student by a professional staff member or other person in authority in the school subjects the offender to criminal liability and discipline up to and including termination of employment. [Emphasis added.]

An older version of section po3362 of the WLS policies (dated 8/10/2015, as seen in documents [13] given to *The Toledo Blade* in September 2015) included the list below. (It is curious that this list no longer appears in the WLS policies.)

> Examples of inappropriate boundary invasions include, but are not limited to the following:
>
> - hugging, kissing, or other physical contact with a student
> - telling sexual jokes to students
> - engaging in talk containing sexual innuendo or banter with students
> - talking about sexual topics that are not related to curriculum
> - showing pornography to a student
> - taking an undue interest in a student (i.e. having a "special friend" or a "special relationship")
> - initiating or extending contact with students beyond the school day for personal purposes
> - using e-mail, text-messaging, websites or other social media services to discuss personal topics or interests with students

Violating Appropriate Boundaries

- giving students rides in the staff member's personal vehicle or taking students on personal outings without administrative approval
- invading a student's privacy (e.g. walking in on the student in the bathroom, locker-room, asking about bra sizes or previous sexual experiences)
- going to a student's home for non-educational purposes
- inviting students to the staff member's home without proper chaperones (i.e. another staff member or parent of student)
- giving gifts or money to a student for no legitimate educational purpose
- accepting gifts or money from a student for no legitimate educational purpose
- being overly "touchy" with students
- favoring certain students by inviting them to come to the classroom at non-class times
- getting a student out of class to visit with the staff member
- providing advice to or counseling a student regarding a personal problem (i.e. problems related to sexual behavior, substance abuse, mental or physical health, and/or family relationships, etc.), unless properly licensed and authorized to do so
- talking to a student about problems that would normally be discussed with adults (i.e. marital issues)
- being alone with a student behind closed doors without a legitimate educational purpose
- telling a student "secrets" and having "secrets" with a student
- other similar activities or behavior

Supt. Hickey with high school cheerleaders in 2013. [14]

CHAPTER 12
WLS Core Values, Hypocrisy, Scandal

Patrick Hickey's legacy as Superintendent includes scandalous episodes that will forever tarnish the reputation of Washington Local Schools. His showboating and "overly personal" style as Superintendent set a terrible example and may have encouraged other educators to challenge appropriate boundaries.

This chapter documents hypocrisy at the top of WLS, some questionable administrative decisions, the sometime ineffective oversight by the Board, and examples of inappropriate content in official school video productions.

Core values

The WLS administration proclaimed virtuous standards under Superintendent Hickey's leadership. Hickey wrote in the district's online newsletter (2010):

> The Washington Local School District values and embraces diversity. We value and embrace families. We value and embrace all of the kids of this community. Our core values are our soul, and they guide us... We judge people – all people – on the content of their character. We also judge people on years of service, on years of behavior and attitude, rather than on days, much like a family makes decisions and judges their own on those same values. We value face-to-face communication as the only dignified, respectful, and courageous way to solve problems and disagreements.
>
> **The kids we serve look to us all of the time – they watch us, they see us, and they look at the way we behave. It is unbelievably important that we are role models to them – in our words, in our actions, and in our deeds...** It's unimportant that we have core values. It's unimportant that we have non-negotiables. It's unimportant that we have a living, breathing mission statement. But what is all-important is that we live them. [1] [Emphasis added.]

WLS Core Values, Hypocrisy, Scandal

Hickey said he spent a lot of time on the district's mission statement which "was five years in the works," reaching perfection in 2013. [2] Here it is accompanied by the district's rainbow butterfly logo:

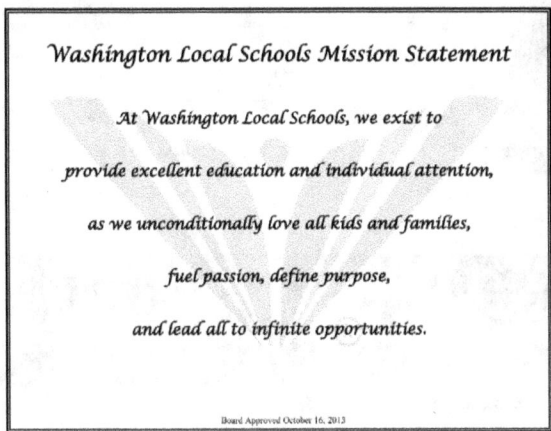

> *Washington Local Schools Mission Statement*
>
> *At Washington Local Schools, we exist to*
>
> *provide excellent education and individual attention,*
>
> *as we unconditionally love all kids and families,*
>
> *fuel passion, define purpose,*
>
> *and lead all to infinite opportunities.*
>
> Board Approved October 16, 2013

In early 2014, *The Toledo Blade* broadcast WLS's principles when the district was designated "#1 WORKPLACE in REGION" and Superintendent Hickey "#1 LEADER in REGION" for 2013.

> Like many organizations, the district has a list of core values and a mission statement, but Mr. Hickey says they aren't just words. **Administrators, teachers, support staff – even one of the 6,900 students – will call somebody out if he or she seems to be straying from those values.** That includes the portion of the mission statement that says district employees will "unconditionally love all kids and families." [3] [Emphasis added.]

Supt. Hickey's online report below is from December 2010. [4] In it, he described the new, colorful graphics designed for the School Board room that emphasize the district's core values:

> **courage – dedication – dignity – excellence – gratitude – honesty loyalty – respect – responsibility – service – teamwork – trust**

Were they just empty words?

But Hickey – along with several School Board members who initially failed to properly vet him, or those who later hesitated to discipline him – exposed the hypocrisy at the very top. Likewise, many in the community mocked these standards when they viciously turned on Board members Langenderfer and Carmean (who were simply taking their responsibility of oversight seriously).

Superintendent's Report & Communications

Graphics – On the side walls you see our core values; behind me are our non-negotiables and tagline. As you come into the building you see our promise to provide individual attention and infinite opportunities. As you enter this room, you see some of our graduates. As you look around this room, you see our diversity celebrated and the depth of what we're doing every day.

The graphics have warmed up the room, and we tried to really tag the core value with the picture. Obviously nothing would be complete without Pete and Penelope. We've had students coming back and taking pictures of their pictures on the wall. It will be here for a long, long time. I'm very happy with the way it looks and the story that it tells for all of our visitors who come in here.

Patrick Hickey
Superintendent

The graphics in the Board room celebrate the district's 12 core values – courage, dedication, dignity, excellence, gratitude, honesty, loyalty, respect, responsibility, service, teamwork, trust.

The room also displays our tagline (individual attention, infinite opportunities.) and our four non-negotiables:

• high quality instruction
• collaboration
• data-based decision making
• technology as a learning accelerator

washington local schools

welcome to washington local schools

our promise to you: individual attention, infinite opportunities

While surely *most WLS teachers and staff have lived up to high standards,* others in the system may have felt they could get away with inappropriate behaviors. After all, for years many had suspected their Superintendent's transgressions with staff he supervised. And they all observed his over-the-top physicality. Plus, there were rumors about his time in the Addison schools.

The Superintendent set the tone: Boundaries between supervisor and subordinate staff were blurred. Boundaries between educator and student were blurred. Misbehavior was in the air they all breathed at WLS.

If Hickey continued to fly high, why couldn't others push boundaries, too?

Some who misbehaved were caught, disciplined, or exposed.

This chapter describes scandalous incidents involving Washington Local Schools or WLS-commissioned videos from the Hickey era.

WLS "Passed the Trash"

The following is based on a 2013 report in *The Toledo Blade*. [5]

Patrick Hickey was WLS Superintendent in 2008 when the Monroe, Michigan school district requested information on a former WLS teacher under consideration for Monroe High School Asst. Principal. But the Monroe schools were not told then that the teacher's dismissal from WLS in 2001 had followed accusations of inappropriate relations with his high school students.

The back story: Teacher Scott Tucker resigned from WLS's Whitmer High School in January 2001 after accusations of sexual relations with high school girls. From January to June that year, he was "assigned to curriculum-review duties at home, according to an unsigned copy of an agreement he reached with the district." It was unclear whether sexual improprieties occurred when the girls were underage.

From 2004 on, Tucker was employed as a teacher in the Monroe schools. In 2008 he was promoted to Assistant Principal of their high school. In December 2012 he agreed to resign once Monroe officials found out about his checkered record at WLS.

This is a classic case of "passing the trash." No signed separation agreement with this errant teacher was put in his WLS personnel file, and later schools hired him without knowing why he left WLS. *The Blade* reported:

> Monroe officials say Mr. Tucker lied about his past and withheld information about the allegations to get his job in their district. Had Washington Local not concealed its separation agreement with Mr. Tucker, they say, he would not have been hired.
>
> "I would not even consider not allowing that information to be passed on," Monroe Superintendent Randy Monday said of the separation agreement. "That to me is common sense of ethics."

Current [2013] Washington Local administrators [Hickey was Superintendent then] said they knew nothing of the agreement Mr. Tucker reached with the district in 2001, and they would have provided any information they had about his time in Washington Local if Monroe had asked.

Washington Local officials dispute Monroe's contention that they were asked about Mr. Tucker in 2008 and denied knowledge of the [2001] agreement. They point out that when asked in August, 2012, district officials were upfront about the agreement and provided it and other records to Monroe. Washington Local Superintendent Patrick Hickey also said his administration has released four employees over similar allegations.

"If the same situation were presented [as in 2001]," Mr. Hickey said, "we wouldn't be making an agreement and having it stored at our attorney's office." …

Agreements allowing teachers to quietly resign when misconduct was alleged, washing a district's hands of a problem but allowing the teachers to seek work elsewhere, were common in the 1970s and 1980s, Ms. Brenton [WLS Human Resources Director] said, a practice called "pass the trash."…

"I will tell you, Nancy Brenton was fantastic to work with," he [Monroe Schools official] said. "But beyond that, [interactions with Washington Local] just didn't seem right."

The Toledo Blade account of WLS administrators' follow-up on the teacher smells of a cover-up.

Note that Hickey told The Blade that WLS had "released" four employees for allegations of inappropriate relations with students. Were they passed on to other school systems without revealing the truth, or were their cases handled with proper follow-up?

What went through Hickey's mind when he dealt with these cases, or when he spoke with The Blade about teacher misconduct?

Two WLS high school teachers resigned in 2008

WTOL reported on two Whitmer High School teachers who resigned in 2008 during Hickey's second year as Superintendent:

Two Whitmer teachers accused of sexual activity with former students have resigned. Their resignations were accepted by the Washington Local School Board, which held a meeting Wednesday evening. Mat Brueggemann and John Shook are accused of providing alcohol to students and of having sex with female students following graduation. Board members made no comment following the meeting… Brueggemann is one of the freshman football coaches and a social studies teacher. Shook teaches WWII to seniors and Government to juniors. News 11 spoke with a former student who says she had the opportunity to take classes taught by both teachers and opted out because of what she calls their "bad reputation." [6]

A WLS teacher familiar with the case said that Brueggemann and Shook (both coaches as well as teachers) would write notes and have one of the "pretty girls" in their class deliver it to the other teacher. They worked as a team. Notes would say things like "What about this one?" One girl was often alone with Brueggemann in his classroom, even preparing snacks for him. "Once girls had graduated and were 18, then the teachers would pursue them." After this burst into the media, the teachers resigned before their cases were fully investigated.

The Toledo Blade noted:

Mr. Brueggemann has been suspended without pay twice before for inappropriate contact with students.

In August, 2006, he was suspended for three days for allowing a student to visit him in his home where the two of them were alone, providing transportation in his private vehicle on at least two occasions without parental permission, and providing personal details to a student regarding his marital separation.

In February, 2007, Mr. Brueggemann was suspended for five days for disregarding instruction not to have contact with the student he was disciplined for interacting with the year before and allowing members of the girls basketball team to keep items in his classroom and personal desk drawers. [7]

Athletic Department ethics violations

In April 2012, a sports reporter at *The Toledo Blade* filed a public records request for Patrick Hickey's personnel file at Addison Schools. (See Chapter 9.) He was rebuffed. Possibly, the request was related to this scandal:

In December 2012, the Ohio High School Athletic Association ruled that WLS knowingly allowed an ineligible athlete to play for Whitmer High School in the 2011-2012 year. WLS was fined $50,000 for the cost of the investigation and had to vacate all their wins from the 2011 football season and 2011-2012 boys' basketball season for using an ineligible player.

Hickey's response: "We disagree, but we will comply. I believe a fine indicates wrongdoing. There's no wrongdoing. There has been a lack of full due diligence, which we have corrected." [8]

Professional development trips to Ron Clark Academy in Atlanta

A contentious item in the WLS budget was the professional development junket to the Ron Clark Academy (RCA) in Atlanta, Georgia. [9] For several years, WLS had sent teachers via chartered bus to costly seminars at this trendy private school funded by corporate donations. [10] (RCA is neither a public school nor a charter school.) It's a stretch to think that what is done there could be replicated in a poor public school district in the rust belt. Furthermore, RCA was then a fairly new venture without a long track record on student achievement.

But the RCA glitz was enticing. Hickey even admitted to a female teacher, Becca (in an email to her on the school system) that he had a "man crush" on the Headmaster of RCA!

Supt. Hickey and Asst. Supt. Cherie Mourlam were behind recommending RCA for WLS teachers' professional development. The two school leaders pushed for funds to be set aside for the teacher trips, costing $60,000-$70,000 for each group trip. (Any expenditure over $25,000 had to be approved by the School Board.)

Hickey accompanied teachers on these field trips. He would fly to Atlanta, while the teachers took a chartered bus. Several Board members had gone on the junket and rated it worth supporting. Board member Jim Langenderfer had visited the school on his own dollar (while visiting family in the area).

Teachers were fairly evenly divided on the value of this trip. The leadership of the local teachers' union, TAWLS, took a neutral stand on the trainings. One former TAWLS leader personally believes that the RCA trainings were *not* useful because most of what the teachers observed at this well-funded private school was not applicable to a poor, urban public school.

Hickey encouraged the TAWLS union leadership to go, with all expenses paid (including airfare instead of bus travel) to win their approval. But the union's president, Christopher Hodnicki, declined the offer. He understood it would be inappropriate for the union leader to be on the school's expense account as he was about to negotiate a new contract.

In 2014, this pet project of Hickey's was questioned by Board members Jim Langenderfer and Patricia Carmean, along with OAPSE (support staff union) President Cindy Perry. [11]

Hickey himself noted that the Board questioned the positive results of his survey of teachers who had gone on the trip. They worried the results may have been flawed because people felt coerced into answering in a positive way.

Several teachers stood up at Board meetings in 2014 and 2015, stating their visit to RCA inspired them to be better teachers. Their comments were absent of specifics.

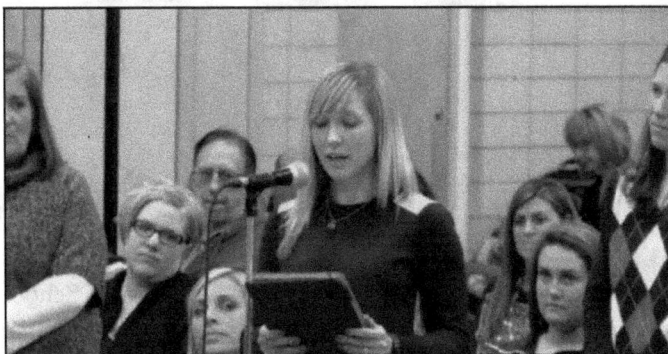

WLS teacher praising the trip to Ron Clark Academy at the April 22, 2015 School Board meeting. [12]

The teachers were apparently wowed by RCA's flashy façade. Photos from RCA show flashy, colorful, pop art everywhere in the school, including bathrooms. The four "houses" are a take-off on *Harry Potter*. A twisting tunnel slide connects floors in the central lobby area. There's a trampoline in the lobby, too. Looks like fun-and-games education, Hickey style.

The idea of making WLS buildings un-prisonlike is commendable, but it would only be possible with enormous funding. RCA spends $30,000+ per student and does *not* have to provide student transportation. But for WLS, student transportation is a huge part of the budget. And where were the data on student academic performance at RCA? Langenderfer brought up those concerns.

Was the trip really about learning effective teaching strategies? Or was it a boondoggle, an occasion for partying? For sure, a lot of fun was had on the bus trips, at the dinners out, and in the comfy hotels.

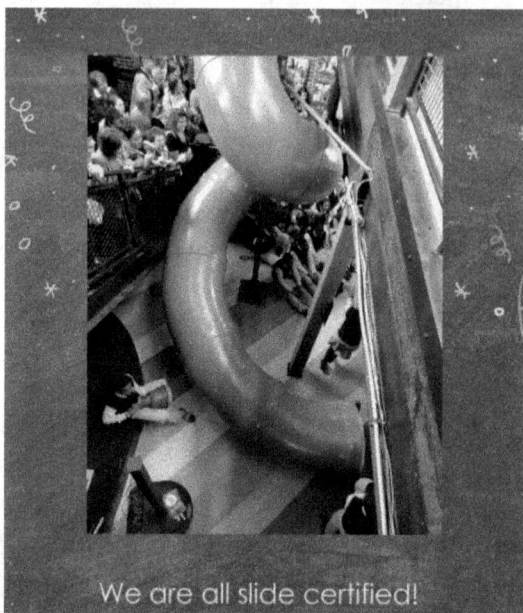

We are all slide certified!

From WLS 2013 trip to Ron Clark Academy. It's not clear how going down the slide contributes to a teacher's professional development. [13]

One obvious concern (not openly stated at the School Board meetings) is that public funds were being used to enable inappropriate behavior by *some* who went on the trip. The WLS community heard the scuttlebutt: Certain attendees wouldn't make it back to their shared hotel rooms at night.

Some WLS high school female *students* reportedly went on one trip as well. It is unclear why high school girls would attend a professional development training meant for experienced teachers.

In April 2015, the Board authorized $70,000 for "certified staff members" ($1,166 each) to go to RCA for a two-day training session later in 2015. Board members Langenderfer and Carmean voted "No." [14]

What did WLS have to show for this "professional development" training at RCA? Where are the specific examples of how teaching techniques or materials changed? One source said teachers who went were able to "enhance the rigor of our district and *make the school a home for students*." [15] Several junior high school bathrooms got facelifts [16] inspired by RCA. WLS posted promotional videos about these bathrooms, but no videos about how teaching was improved.

WLS meets RCA
November 2013

Above: Supt. Hickey (back row on right by gate) accompanied teachers on their visits to Ron Clark Academy in Atlanta. Below: Hickey on the trampoline.

Mr. Hickey gets ready to soar!

Board Member resigns over vulgar emails to staff

In April 2014, WLS School Board member (and former Board President) Steve Zuber abruptly resigned. The WLS website announced a vacancy on the School Board without explaining how it came up. [17]

The reason? For years Zuber had sent emails and texts with vulgar sexual content to WLS staffers and community members (both women and men). Even the WLS Human Resources Director (a woman) had received the off-color communications from Zuber. One example of his soft-core porn humor was a photo of a patient in the chair at a dentist's office with a naked female dental assistant standing alongside.

Apparently, Supt. Hickey was aware of these for some time but never objected. Complaints from community members and staffers eventually reached the Board. The Board finally confronted Zuber and told him he needed to resign.

STEVE ZUBER - BOARD LEADERSHIP AS PRESIDENT

Superintendent **Patrick Hickey** thanked **Steve Zuber** for his leadership on the Washington Local Board of Education. Mr. Zuber has served as President or Vice-President for nine years and is beginning his 15th year on the Board. At the 2012 Organizational Meeting, **David Hunter** was elected President and **John Adler** was elected Vice-President.

Supt. Hickey with Steve Zuber in 2012. [18]

The Toledo Blade report implies that WLS wanted to protect its image:

> After serving for 17 years on the Washington Board of Education, plus 30 years as a firefighter, Steve Zuber has resigned from the board, saying it is time to step away from public service.

WLS Core Values, Hypocrisy, Scandal

"There comes a time in a person's life when you have got to do for yourself," he said, and doing for himself means, for instance, going on vacation, such as to California, Arizona, and Florida where he has friends who are retired and enjoying life. "I want to plan some vacations. I am not getting any younger." He is 66 years old.

He devoted much time attending school activities, as do other school board members because they are dedicated to their elected positions, he said... The board, and the administration under the leadership of Superintendent Patrick Hickey, has accomplished much, Mr. Zuber said. [19]

Board President Thomas Ilstrup remarked as Zuber stepped down, "It can certainly be said that Mr. Zuber is a person who enjoys life, and living it on his own terms... Please join us in extending sincere thanks to Mr. Zuber for his lifelong dedication to Washington Local Schools."

"Happy" video celebrates Hickey & WLS with suggestive dancing

In January 2014, *The Toledo Blade* declared WLS the "#1 Workplace in the region" (Northwest Ohio) for 2013 after a Workplace Dynamic survey of employees in nominated organizations. [20]

The headline proclaimed, the "District operates as extended family." Superintendent Hickey was said to be the "#1 Leader in the Region."

"Happy" Washington Local Schools Voted TOP WORKPLACE in NW Ohio- OFFICIAL VIDEO - HD

52,495 views   499   19   SHARE   SAVE   ...

Punsalan Productions
Published on Feb 19, 2014   SUBSCRIBE 3.9K

WLS celebrated at a School Board meeting with a screening of a WLS video produced for the occasion. "Happy" showcased teachers dancing to Pharrell Williams' song. [21]

In one scene, teachers sway back and forth holding Hickey masks over their faces in cult-like obeisance to their leader. (See the photo in Chapter 10.)

The video may seem cute at first glance, but on reflection, it's not so innocent. It fosters inappropriate familiarity between educator and student, and open expression of teachers' sexuality in the schools.

The impact of a posted out-take from the production [22] is confirmed in its description: *"Here's the most famous out-take from our 'Happy' video production. Mr. M, English teacher-extraordinaire, lets loose."* ("Let's loose" what?) In the clip, a young male teacher shakes his rear at a group of giggling high school girls as he leads the dancing. This is an example of a school-produced video sexualizing the school (and workplace).

Happy Mullan - Outtake #2 - Mr Mullan Happy Washington Local Schools

High school girls giggling and dancing with male teacher in the WLS video.

The video includes children dancing with their teachers in some scenes. It was certainly watched by many students. How would young children think about their teachers after seeing them dance like this (with the "booty" emphasis) and making "come-on" faces?

What is the significance of "booty" dancing? Watch Jennifer Lopez's music video "Booty." [23] It's all about being "sexy." People will want to "meet" and "touch" you after you dance like this, the lyrics declare.

Below are several more screengrabs from the video.

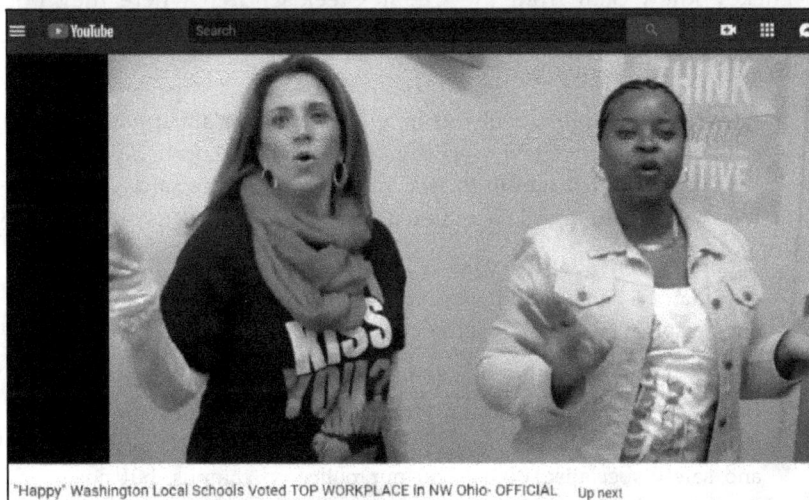

Happy Washington Local Schools Voted TOP WORKPLACE in NW Ohio- OFFICIAL   Up next

Teacher's T-shirt reads: "Can I kiss you?" [24]

Meanwhile, posted WLS policies [25] stated at the time:

> Conduct constituting sexual harassment may take different forms, including ... Causing the placement of offensive **sexually suggestive objects, pictures, or graphic commentaries in the school environment** or the making of offensive, **sexually suggestive** or insulting **gestures**, sounds, leering, whistling, and the like to or by a fellow staff member, student, or other person associated with the District, or third parties. – Administrative Guidelines, Section 3362

> A professional staff member shall not associate with students at any time in a manner which gives **the appearance of impropriety**,

including, but not limited to, the creation or participation in any situation or activity which could be considered abusive or **sexually suggestive** or involve illegal substances such as tobacco, alcohol, or drugs... – WLS Policy Manual, Student Supervision, Section 3213 [Emphasis added.]

The "Happy" video was still posted in 2020.

Hickey's handpicked Security Officer resigns in disgrace

Superintendent Patrick Hickey handpicked Randy Sehl to be security officer for WLS in 2013. Just over a year later, Sehl had to resign. In the school system where he had worked previously, Sehl had let a high school student into the school after hours to access exam questions. But was there more to the story?

Hickey knew Sehl from the Cedar Creek Church where they both attended. *The Toledo Blade* quoted Hickey, [26] who admitted the district didn't advertise the job opening:

> In August [2013], Mr. Sehl was hired as the district's first director of police, safety, and security. Washington Local officials [unnamed] invited him in to hear his ideas on school safety, and they were so impressed they offered him the $71,464-a-year job.
>
> Superintendent Patrick Hickey said Mr. Sehl was the only candidate he had in mind when consideration was given to putting one person in charge of the growing district's security programs.
>
> "We probably wouldn't have done this if we hadn't targeted Randy," Mr. Hickey explained. "It had to be the perfect person. We didn't advertise. We're not just hiring a cop. He's a school security and safety specialist. We've had our police on campus, but now they're headed by an officer with arresting power, if it's needed."

Sehl had formerly worked as a sheriff's deputy in Michigan, then as resource officer at the Dundee, Michigan schools and Bedford High School in Temperance, Michigan. He had kept a key to Bedford High School after his employment ended there and he had begun working at WLS.

His tenure at WLS was short-lived. He was forced to resign in February 2015 (but was paid for unused sick time and personal leave, plus given health coverage through July).

What led to his dismissal? Sehl was "seen on surveillance cameras entering the [Bedford] high school with a 15-year-old boy on six occasions between Dec. 24 and Jan. 5. The times of those visits varied between 8 p.m. and 11 p.m." [27]

The Toledo Blade reported that Sehl "worked out" with the boy in the weight room at night.

A Monroe County sheriff's report from Jan. 7 accused Mr. Sehl of enabling a ninth grader to enter Bedford High classrooms at night by turning off the school's alarm system using a pass key for the building that he retained after having worked there as a security officer. On Jan. 6, a teacher discovered "25 to 30 photographs of tests, answer keys, and the class work of other students" in the boy's smart phone.

Investigators determined the boy entered the classrooms several times between Dec. 24 and Jan. 5 on nights when he and Mr. Sehl also worked out in the school's weight room, the report stated. Mr. Sehl's pass keys were seized once the investigation started.

Washington Local officials emphasized that none of Mr. Sehl's alleged wrong-doing occurred in their district and expressed their "appreciation to Mr. Sehl for his service to the district and its students, and his cooperation in addressing issues of common concern." [28]

*Randy Sehl dances and laughs about handcuffing
a student in the WLS 2014 "Happy" video. [29]*

Note that despite the glaring irregularity of Sehl's behavior, WLS Supt. Hickey publicly thanked Sehl for his service to the district.

The Monroe County Prosecutor declined to charge Sehl. [27]

Hickey's paramours fight over him in Whitmer HS cafeteria

On November 17, 2015 – as the Hickey scandals were dominating local social media and *Toledo Blade* reports – the two women teachers involved in inappropriate relationships with Hickey loudly argued over him in the Whitmer High School cafeteria *packed with students*. The incident was witnessed by faculty as well. Teachers "Anna" and "Becca" were previously good friends, but now were falling out over the Superintendent and the social media storm. Anna's husband (also a teacher) got involved in the argument, too. The likely spark for the "cat fight" was the School Board's announcement of a meeting to discuss disciplinary action against Hickey. (See Chapter 16.)

Anna had been involved in a close relationship with Hickey for several years. (See Chapter 13.) The School Board had gotten confirmation of this intimacy when Anna and her husband filed an informal complaint with the Human Resources Office at the end of August 2015. Around this same time, Hickey and the other teacher, Becca, were engaging in highly personal communications (on the school email system) and were seen together publicly exhibiting too familiar behaviors. (See Chapter 15.)

Following the ruckus in the cafeteria, Anna, her husband, and Becca were suspended for several days, but no disciplinary action was to be noted in their personnel files.

Certainly, everyone knew what was behind their very public fight. It was their relationships with Superintendent Hickey and the very public scandal that had erupted.

A school is not a workspace populated by adults only; children were very much involved in this nasty scene. Sources report that students afterwards gossiped about what was going on between their teachers and their Superintendent: *"Who is the bigger whore?"* they were asking.

What did students learn from this very public cat fight? These adults were their authority figures. *So much for Hickey's grandiose statements about "core values" and staff leading by example.*

This incident was very upsetting to the other teachers. Their work environment had been grossly sexualized. Gossip ran rampant and distracted good teachers from their work. Instead of discussing curriculum or teaching techniques, they were gossiping about the Superintendent's inappropriate relationships.

This is a prime example of how Hickey's "too personal, inappropriate, forward, or flirtatious" behavior had a direct negative impact on students, teachers, staff, and the morale of the entire community. (See the School Board's formal reprimand of Hickey in Sept. 2015, Chapter 14.)

Flash mob at HS pep rally, teachers dance suggestively to "Uptown Funk"

Why does it matter what kinds of music and dancing adults recommend to children? William Kilpatrick, former Professor of Education at Boston College, explained it this way:

> Plato .. was much concerned with the moral effects of music – so much so that in the ideal society he describes, many kinds of music would be censored... Plato's argument is that certain kinds of music can foster a spirit of lawlessness which can creep in unnoticed, "since it's considered to be a kind of play," and therefore harmless. Despite the innocent appearance, however, some kinds of music are capable of subverting the social order... He was more concerned with music of a sensual or romantic type that would undermine discipline, moderation, and other civic virtues. The most obvious modern analogy ... is to the role rock music plays in prompting young people to throw off cultural and sexual restraints. [30]

The WLS "Happy" video of 2014 (see above in this chapter) was a warm-up to a more overtly sexualized WLS video production. Once again, appropriate boundaries between students and teachers would be erased as teachers danced in a sexually suggestive style before the packed gymnasium.

In February 2017, a flash mob of WLS teachers swarmed the Whitmer High School homecoming pep rally, dancing to the titillating pop tune, "Uptown Funk." [31] This was a major production, obviously requiring approval of the administration. Lots of planning went into it: hours of rehearsal time, various camera angles, and snappy editing.

The *InspireMore* website (its stated mission: to "brighten the world & spread hope") featured the WLS event with the headline, *"Gymnasium Goes Nuts When Teachers Storm Court with Epic 'Uptown Funk' Flash Mob."* The article states that when high school English teacher Katie Peters (who helped organize the performance) "first approached her colleagues about putting on a dance at the rally, they were probably a little hesitant." But what did she say they were worried about? The racy content of the song and dance style required? *No.* It was that "the students would probably make fun of them." [32]

Although the video was produced after Hickey had resigned as Superintendent (in December 2015), his influence was still hanging over the WLS community – and he was known to be planning a run for School Board in the fall of 2017. He still had a strong fan base in the district.

To understand the context of the WLS performance, the original video by Mark Ronson is essential viewing. [33] (By early 2020, the Bruno Mars music video has about 3.8 *billion* views.) *It is what the school is endorsing.*

The video begins with scantily clad young women strutting past the singer who says he is *"too hot (hot damn)!"* As for the vocabulary, *funk* can be defined as *groovy* or an *earthy sexual vibe.* (Of course, it intentionally comes close to *f*ck.) The lyrics clearly reference drugs, sex, acting wild, and living it up in big-city pop culture.

"If you sexy then flaunt it!"

That's what the teachers were doing: flaunting their sexuality. (The video even throws in a little "gender" confusion as the men sit under dryers in a beauty salon with curlers in their hair.)

Why would a school district approve such a production *after what it had just experienced with the Hickey scandal*?

Everyone in the community was still gossiping about the inappropriate antics of their former Superintendent, the teachers who argued in the cafeteria – and the whispered rumors about Addison, Michigan. Now *this*?

Blowing kisses to students.

What does it mean when the teachers unashamedly point to their crotches, shake their booties, and blow kisses to the excited students?

Were they appealing to students' base instincts? Were they following their former Superintendent's goal of *"loving 'em and lifting 'em up"?*

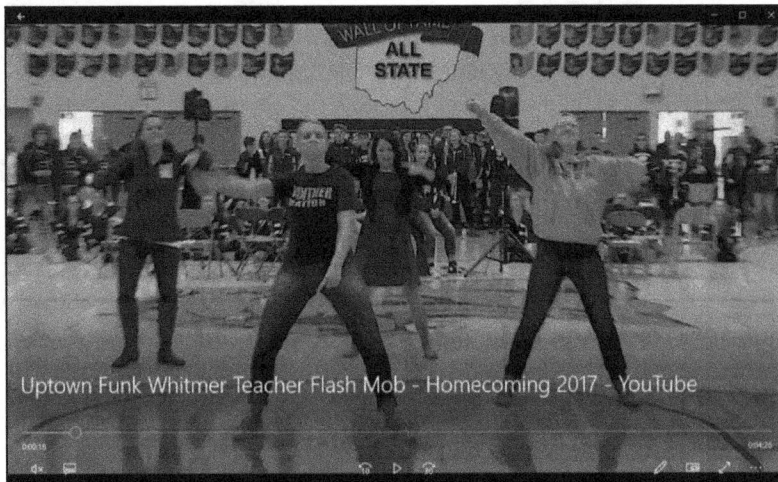

Teachers point to their gyrating crotches.

More and more teachers join in as the music climaxes.

The WLS "Uptown Funk" pep rally video is approaching *five million views* on YouTube.

Teachers resign after drinking while chaperoning 6th-grade overnight camp

Some WLS teachers viewed their off-campus chaperoning assignment as a time to party. They even left behind children in their charge to go to a restaurant to dine and drink. *The Toledo Blade* posted this in May 2017:

Five teachers and two tutors placed on paid leave by Washington Local Schools have nearly spotless employment records, according to a review of district documents.

Washington Local placed the employees on leave May 17 amid a now-complete investigation into allegations that they left an overnight sixth-grade camp to dine at restaurants that serve alcohol.

The district has said that leaving camp for longer than "a short errand" is a violation of school board policy and the state licensure code, as is "consuming alcohol during camp." [34]

The five teachers resigned as soon as the investigation was completed. The two tutors left at the end of the school year.

"The investigation did point out that all seven did drink," said school board president David Hunter. He said the internal investigation determined that each employee drank varying amounts of alcohol after leaving the YMCA Camp Copneconic in Fenton, Mich., during a sixth-grade trip. Employees receive a stipend in addition to their usual pay to accompany the students on the trip, and the job expectation is to be at the camp "full-time, 24 hours," Mr. Hunter said. [35]

The report does not describe the nature of the school's away camp.

Hickey had stayed overnight with boys in their cabin at a retreat in some past year, according to an elementary teacher who spoke at the September 12, 2015 School Board meeting. (See Chapter 14.)

More questionable WLS videos involving students produced by WLS teacher who resigned

A popular Whitmer High School teacher, Michael Punsalan (who later resigned during an investigation into his relationships with students), [36] produced the WLS promotional videos, including "Happy" and the "Uptown Funk" pep rally flash mob (described above). The teacher coached students on video projects, including the winning entries at the Tree City Film Festival in nearby Sylvania, Ohio. Emails on the school system confirm that he socialized with Hickey outside of school.

Several other videos made for WLS by the teacher (still publicly available on YouTube in 2020) include questionable sequences. In one, "Teachers Dancing behind Students" (2016, screengrabs below), teachers are shown hugging students after surprising them from behind. [37] (The video was apparently the WLS entry in a fad going around the country, [38] but in other schools' videos on the theme, teachers are not seen hugging their students at the end of the skit.)

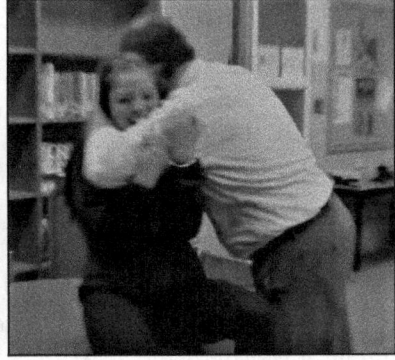

WLS video, "Teachers dancing behind students." [37]

In a parody of the movie "Breakfast Club" (2017), three girls go wild in the WLS high school library and one even does a little pole dancing. [39] Dishonest "love" is the subject of the WLS student videos awarded first and second place in the Tree City Film Festivals. "Love on Hold" (2013) [40] is about two teenage girls and their two-timing boyfriend.

"Making our Mark" (2014) tells a disturbing tale. [41] A girl follows her new boyfriend to school after hours and he shows her how to break into the building. He takes her to a secret tunnel under the school. What the viewer anticipates will be a love scene transforms into a murderous betrayal. The girl slowly realizes that many other high school girls have met their death there. The boy then turns her over to zombies. The video ends with her screams and shadow images of her being violently attacked.

"Making Our Mark" by The Whitmer Film Project - Tree City Film Festival 2014

CHAPTER 13
WLS Teachers File Complaint against Hickey
Scandalous Emails Published
– May-Sept. 2015 –

Patrick Hickey had long lived in fear that his past at Addison Schools would come back to haunt him. But could he have imagined that the relationship he had with a married high school teacher would trigger the end of his career, a Michigan State Police investigation, his guilty plea, and his imprisonment?

Teachers file "informal complaint" vs. Hickey

As the school year began in September 2015, Superintendent Hickey was nowhere to be seen around the district schools. Many events were on his calendar, but he didn't show. Why was he absent at such a crucial time?

In late August 2015, the School Board had received a complaint against Hickey by two WLS high school teachers – a married couple. In early September, the Board put Hickey on administrative leave, banning him from school properties while their attorney conducted an internal investigation.

While there had been rumors for some time about the Superintendent's behavior with women who worked for him, no one had ever come forward with an actionable complaint. But now that changed.

The married couple who filed the complaint had run smack-dab into Hickey's exploitative and manipulative personality.

In the spring of 2015, the husband had discovered communications between his wife "Anna" and her boss, Superintendent Hickey. Their relationship had been going on since "approximately the fall of 2012" (according to the "37 Charges" document; see Chapter 17).

The husband confronted Anna. The couple wanted to save their marriage; they had children to think of. The wife then told Hickey their relationship was over. The couple hoped to keep this all quiet. But Hickey wouldn't stop contacting Anna as she had requested. So on May

1, 2015, Anna filed her first "concern" (rather than a formal "complaint") with the WLS Human Resources Office about Hickey's behavior.

Then over the summer, Hickey became aggressive in tone with the husband (who had stepped in on behalf of his wife), and Anna perceived Hickey's words as a threat to embarrass her publicly if she continued with the complaint.

In late August 2015, Anna and her husband filed a summary of the escalating communications and incidents. Now it had become an "informal complaint." That is when the School Board first heard about it.

And so, Hickey's kingdom would begin to crumble. He had become reckless in his public demeanor, personal relationships, and (not-so-private) communications, so now would reap the consequences.

The angry emails between Hickey and Anna's husband were on the school email system. In these, the Superintendent comes across as impulsive, unbalanced, intimidating, and vindictive. Furthermore, the emails make clear the intimate character of his relationship with Anna.

Was this "sexual harassment" in the workplace?

But Anna still avoided calling this "sexual harassment." Certainly, she wanted to keep things quiet for personal reasons, but perhaps she was also accepting responsibility for her own role in the inappropriate relationship. Was she receiving guidance on avoiding the scandal that would follow if she charged "sexual harassment" by the Superintendent?

Furthermore, Anna was a good friend of another WLS high school teacher, "Becca," who had also received frisky communications from Hickey in 2014 and had then filed a complaint over his "aggressive flirtation" with the Human Resources Director. Perhaps Becca counseled Anna on how to protect herself while not stirring up too much trouble for the school system – or their shared love interest. (Becca's emails and dalliance with Hickey are the subject of Chapter 15.)

"There are two sides to every story," Hickey wrote to Anna's cuckolded husband in one email. The husband responded, "I have the whole story. I have seen the emails and texts." (This confirms Hickey and Anna had texted each other as well as emailing.) Hickey left taunting messages on the husband's phone in addition to the nasty emails below.

An inside source learned that Anna's and Hickey's encounters took place at local fitness centers. The professional development trips (e.g., to the private school in Atlanta) perhaps offered other opportunities for some private time. It was also apparent to this source that Anna had in fact sent sexual videos to her boss (as Hickey told the Board investigator).

Hickey asserted that those "embarrassing" nude-content videos from Anna proved that the fault was *hers* and that *she* was the sexual aggressor. *He* was the victim of sexual harassment, if anyone was, because the teacher had pursued him.

Here are the three items related to Anna's case as drawn up by the School Board's attorney in December 2015. (The full "37 Charges" document is in Chapter 17.) Note that Hickey was not formally charged with these infractions.

> 10. During your employment as Superintendent, you engaged in an inappropriate emotional and/or sexual relationship with one or more subordinate teachers of the district.
>
> 11. From approximately the fall of 2012 through the spring of 2015, you engaged in a personal relationship with a subordinate teacher of the district, exchanging emails, test [text] messages, private Twitter messages, and conversations of a personal nature.
>
> 12. Sometime during the last two years, you received inappropriate videos from a subordinate teacher of the district involving nudity.
>
> a. You were a party to the misconduct by requesting and/or encouraging that the videos be sent by the teacher, or
>
> b. You failed to take action to initiate discipline, corrective directives to the teacher for her misconduct, or any investigation of the misconduct, or
>
> c. Both a. and b.

The Toledo Blade publishes the emails

The Toledo Blade had been following Patrick Hickey for some time. A *Blade* reporter had filed a public records request to Addison Schools for Hickey's personnel file in 2012 (but no story appeared). In 2013, *The Blade* reported on the WLS administration's failure to properly inform another school system of a WLS teacher's dismissal being due to inappropriate relations with students. [1] The newspaper had also contacted former Addison student Kris Hassenzahl in 2013 (she said) about Hickey's time at Addison (but she was not ready to speak then). In early 2015, the newspaper reported the curious story of Hickey's handpicked security officer resigning in disgrace.

Teachers File Complaint vs. Hickey; Scandalous Emails

The Blade knew something was amiss with Hickey in September 2015 when social media and public Board meetings exploded over Hickey's mysterious absence and rumors he was going to be fired. Shortly after the Board's formal but light-handed reprimand of Hickey on September 16 following the investigation of Anna's complaint (see Chapter 14), *The Blade* filed a public records request for the text of the complaint.

The School Board's attorney responded to *The Blade's* request. Note that the attorney states that "the staff member had not been subject to harassment by Mr. Hickey." The investigative report (with interviews of those involved) was not shared with the newspaper due to "attorney-client privilege." So, there's no way to assess the accuracy of the conclusion that there was *no workplace sexual harassment*.

Even if Anna didn't personally believe *she* was legally harassed, what about the harassment felt by the district employees when the Superintendent was seen to be playing favorites with his paramour? (See Chapter 11 for that definition of "hostile work environment.")

The Board attorney interviewed Hickey, Anna, her husband, Becca, and possibly others. Hickey said (in a later email on the school system) that Becca was a "key witness" in the investigation. She testified *against* her formerly close friend, Anna, and in defense of Hickey's behavior. (For more on Becca's and Hickey's dalliance, see Chapter 15.)

From the Board's attorney to *The Blade*:

> Attached are the public records responsive to your request.
>
> The Board of Education's attorney conducted the investigation the Board requested. The attorney prepared an investigation report and distributed copies of that report to the Board of Education during an executive session of a Board meeting [on Sept. 15, 2015]. The Board members were informed that the report was confidential and could not be shown or disclosed to any third party. All copies of the report were returned to the Board's attorney during that executive session. The investigation report is excepted from disclosure based on the attorney-client privilege. State ex rel. Toledo Blade Co. v. Toledo-Lucas County Port Authority, 121 Ohio St.3d 537 (2009).
>
> As to records related to the investigation, the investigation concerned information (attached) provided by a staff member to the District's Human Resources Director. Because the investigation was on the advice of legal counsel rather than at the staff member's request, the personally identifiable information related to the staff member has been redacted from the enclosed records, in

accordance with *State ex rel. Dispatch Printing Co. v. Johnson*, 106 Ohio St. 3d 160 (2005). The District wishes to respect the staff member's privacy and trusts that the requester will as well.

Please be alerted that some of the information in the enclosed records is based on the writers' perceptions and was not validated.

Upon consideration of all relevant facts and witness interviews, the investigation concluded that, while the staff member had not been subject to harassment by Mr. Hickey as defined in **Board Policy 3362** [2] (also attached) or in violation of state or federal law, his subsequent communications and actions were inconsistent with good professional judgment and his office. [Emphasis added.]

The Toledo Blade published their report on the complaint in the Sept. 22 p.m. online edition and on page one of the Sept. 23 print edition. The headline: *"Staff member claims unwanted contact by Hickey; Complaint, emails reveal concerns."* [3]

People in the emails

- **Anna** – teacher at Whitmer High School in the WLS district. She had a romantic relationship with Hickey going back to about 2012.
- **Husband** – Anna's husband, also a teacher at Whitmer High School.
- **Becca** – teacher at Whitmer High School and sometime friend of Anna. She had her own inappropriate relationship with Hickey. (See Chapter 15.)
- **Coworker of Anna** – another female teacher at WLS and supporter of Hickey.
- **Patrick Hickey** – WLS Superintendent and supervisor of all the people above.

Anna's compilation of emails between Hickey, herself, and her husband from April through August 2015 are here presented in chronological order. [4]

Anna's original "concern" filed May 1, 2015

Sometime in early 2015, WLS Anna's husband discovered evidence of Anna's sexual relationship with Superintendent Hickey, supervisor of both of them. Anna then told Hickey their relationship was over and not to contact her.

Anna turned to the WLS Human Resources Office after Hickey continued to contact her. She filed a form on May 1 documenting her attempts to halt communications from Hickey. She crossed out the heading "Harassment/Discrimination Complaint Form" and wrote in "Concern." She noted that on April 10, she blocked his personal cell phone number, his Twitter, and his WLS cell phone number, and sent him an email to contact her only on school-related business.

May 18, 2015 letter to Human Resources Director

Here is the May 18 letter Anna gave to the WLS Human Resources Office Director:

> I obtained a new cell phone number and phone on April 14, 2015.
>
> At some point, after I blocked all correspondence (both personal and work phone, twitter and e-mail asking for only work related correspondence) and obtained a new cell phone number (between April 12 and May 10), he tried to persuade one of my coworkers [not Becca] to give him my phone number. He gave her a hard time about it, but she refused to.
>
> On April 14, he was sitting at Max and Erma's [restaurant] in Perrysburg at the bar. This was several days after I blocked his phone calls. He was aware that I attend trivia at Max and Erma's on Tuesday nights with one of my coworkers. He was not aware that [husband] goes with me. When [husband] and I saw him at the bar, we immediately left.
>
> On May 7, a coworker of mine [not Becca] was involved in a car accident. l went to the accident site to pick her up. While we were sitting at the corner of Alexis and Burdette waiting for the tow truck to arrive, he stopped. He spoke with her for a few minutes about the accident and prior to leaving said to me, "I know this wasn't work related, but I saw the accident and stopped." His tone was aggressive and rude.
>
> On May 10, he contacted the same coworker of mine via telephone. He asked what I wanted from him, if it was money. He said that if I "went public" with any information, he was going to pay to have messages recovered from his phone, of our correspondence, in order to make me look bad. He said that it would cost $20,000, but he has insurance so his cost would only be $4,000. He said that he had already spoke to a lawyer about it. He also indicated that I am running around telling everyone because he had a conversation with a different coworker [Becca] about it a few weeks prior. When I spoke with this other coworker, she indicated she had told him to leave me alone in a conversation which stemmed from a series of

inappropriate messages she received from him (she would like to remain out of any involvement with him and this situation and does not at any point want her name revealed or the nature of that conversation relating to her revealed).

During the course of his May 10th conversation, he indicated that he would leave me 110% alone, but he wanted all the information from the conversation relayed to me, including the threat to personally slander me with the messages.

1st Timeline submitted by Anna

Below is the timeline through late May 2015 that Anna provided to WLS Human Resources. This covers the period before the emails started coming from Hickey in June.

April 10 – Blocked personal cell phone number

April 11 – He began sending me private messages on twitter. I told him I did not want to have contact with him anymore. He kept sending and I deleted my twitter account.

April 12 – He sent me a message on his work phone. I did not respond and blocked his work number.

April 14 – I obtained a new cell phone.

April 14 – I frequently attend trivia on Tuesday nights at the Max and Erma's [restaurant] in Perrysburg. He was/is aware of this and when [husband] and I arrived that night, he was sitting at the bar. When we saw him, we immediately left.

*Sometime after April 14 and before May 10 (I don't know an exact date), he repeatedly asked one of my coworkers [not Becca] for my new cell phone number. She refused to give it to him.

April 22 – He left me a voicemail at school asking why I would not speak to him. I did not respond.

April 23 – He sent me a non-work related email. I replied and asked him to only contact me with work related correspondence. He replied that he would.

========================

On April 23, Hickey forwarded to Anna the *"Always Promoting Co. April Newsletter"* with his comment:

Hickey: "Check out 7/19/15....who knew??" [7/19/15 is listed as National Ice Cream Day.]

Anna: "Please don't send me things that are not work related."

Hickey: "I apologize and it will never happen again."

===============================

April 24 – He came into my classroom and asked me what was going on and why I was doing this (I had a class at the time). I told him I was doing what I needed to do.

April 28 – He called me on my work phone to tell me about a [redacted] project happening near a local elementary school.

April 30 – He sent me a non-work related e-mail (attached). I did not respond.

May 1 – I met with the human resources director and filed with her an unofficial complaint. I made her aware that I have asked him to stop contacting me and the dates in which I blocked numbers and attached the e-mails also. She indicated she would do nothing with the information until I told her I wanted her to and that she would keep the file at her house if I wanted her to so that it wasn't at Central Office.

May 7 – A coworker of mine [not Becca] (the same one he asked for my phone number from), was involved in a car accident. I went to the accident site to pick her up. While we were sitting at the corner of Alexis and Burdette waiting for the tow truck to arrive, he stopped. He spoke with her for a few minutes about the accident and prior to leaving said to me, "I know this wasn't work related, but I saw the accident and stopped." His tone was aggressive and rude.

May 9 – In an effort to get him to leave me alone without attacking him professionally, after meeting with and consulting with our pastor, we asked him to speak with Patrick's pastor and see if we could get him to leave us alone from that angle.

May 10 – After speaking with his pastor he immediately contacted my coworker (same as above) via telephone. He asked what I wanted from him, if it was money. He said that if I "went public" with any information, he was going to pay to have messages recovered from his phone, of our correspondence, in order to make me look bad. He was referring to messages, pictures and videos that were sent to him over the course of the relationship. He indicated that it would cost $20,000, but he has insurance so his cost would only be $4,000. He said that he had already spoken to a lawyer about it. He also indicated that I am running around telling everyone because he had a conversation with a different coworker [Becca] about it a few weeks prior. I telephoned this coworker (who knew about our relationship) and she indicated that she had in fact told him to leave me alone. This stemmed from a conversation that took place after her family discovered a series of inappropriate sexual messages that he sent to her.

Also, during the course of the May 10th conversation, he indicated that he would leave me 110% alone, but he wanted all the information from the conversation relayed to me, including the threat to personally slander me with the retrieved messages.

May 26 – [Husband] received a box of things in his work mailbox. The box contained a letter (attached) indicating he [Hickey] was returning all of the things I gave to him since I have asked him not to contact me about anything not work related. The box contained 6 books (2 of which I did not give him), a movie, a coin and a vial with his DNA in it. The vial of DNA was extracted during an experiment at the Junior High with a group of 8th grade girls (that included his daughter). I am unsure why he sent it to me.

Note the May 9 entry (above): Anna says she wants "to get him [Hickey] to leave [her] alone without attacking him professionally."

Her May 10 entry confirms that Hickey had also sent "inappropriate sexual messages" to her friend Becca.

Whatever had gone on between them, Hickey thought it serious enough that Anna might want to blackmail him. So, he shut down that possibility by threatening to release her embarrassing phone communications with him. The "messages from his phone … in order to make [her] look bad" included messages, photos, and videos, she admitted. They wouldn't be "embarrassing" unless they contained sexual content. (The full School Board never viewed these videos.)

The reference to Becca telling Hickey to leave Anna alone indicates that the two women were still friendly at this point. But they would later have a very public fight over Hickey in front of students in the high school cafeteria come November. (See Chapter 12.)

Anna's August 27, 2015 "informal complaint"

On August 27, 2015, Anna told the HR Director that she and her husband did *not* want to go forward with a *formal* complaint. They just wanted their complete chronology of communications with Hickey "on file." Clearly, they feared there might be further trouble with him.

The HR Director informed the School Board of the problem after receiving the August chronology. The Board had their attorney immediately proceed with a two-week investigation, while Hickey was put on administrative leave for two weeks at the beginning of the school year.

Here is Anna's August 27 letter:

> Dear Rachael [Human Resources Director],
>
> Per your conversation with my husband on August 26, 2015, at this time we would NOT like you to go forward with any conversation with Patrick Hickey about what we have shared with you. We at this time would not like to go through with any formal complaint and would simply like the information we have given to you to remain on file. I have included with this letter an updated timeline and additional email correspondence.
>
> If you have any questions, please contact me at…
>
> Sincerely,
> [Anna]

Her letter was accompanied by the emails from June through August.

Emails between Anna's husband and Hickey June-August 2015

On June 9, Anna's husband was out of town and concerned about her being harassed by Hickey, so he sent this email to Hickey after Anna was safely away from school. He reminds Hickey of his vaunted "core values." (See Chapter 12.)

===========================

[Anna's notes:] June 9 – [Husband] had left for [redacted] on the 7th and was worried about me being alone when he was gone. After he knew that I had left school for the day on the teacher work day, he sent the attached email telling him [Hickey] to leave me and our family alone. [Husband] sent his email at 2:52 p.m.

===========================

6/9/2015 2:52PM
To: Patrick Hickey
Dear Pat,

Do not continue attempting to contact Anna. This includes calling her friends or contacting me in any way, school related or not. This also extends to responding to this email. I hope you can find a way to live the faith and core values that you speak of, to love your family, and stop your destructive behaviors.

[Husband]
Sent from my iPhone

==============================

Hickey responds within the hour and copies Anna in the email (below), though the husband had just asked him not to contact her. Hickey is "concerned" at the abruptness of Anna's cessation of communications with him.

Hickey says to the husband, "I know you are justifiably upset and would gladly discuss this situation with you. We all make mistakes and I will own mine... There are two sides to every story." And he says he wants to help the couple "mend their relationship."

==============================

[Anna's notes:] June 9 – At 3:40 the attached response was received in which he [Hickey] lies about the following:

• That he had not attempted to-contact-me-after April 23 as outlined above.

• Not knowing I didn't want him to contact me prior to April 23, the blocking of phone numbers, discussion and blocking on twitter and voicemail all occurred prior to April 23.

• Not knowing who my friends are. He knew I was friends with [coworker; not Becca] because he too had a relationship with her.

==============================

From: Patrick Hickey
Tue 6/9/2015 3:40 PM
To: [Husband]
Cc: [Anna]

RE: Core Values

Dear [Husband],

I have not attempted to contact Anna in any way, shape, form, or regard, since she sent me an email on April 23rd responding to an email about National Ice Cream Day and informing me to not contact her unless business related. Prior to that day I did not know that she did not want contact as up until April she contacted me frequently and it abruptly stopped on April 23rd. In fact she contacted me on the Friday before Spring break (April 3rd) and was telling me about the food she planned to consume over break and how happy she was to be on break. After Spring Break and prior to April 23rd I did try to contact her as I was concerned about her and the abruptness of the request. She texted me and emailed me on a very consistent basis for a long time so abruptly stopping was very out of the ordinary. I cannot promise to not contact her friends as I do not know who her friends are but I will not discuss you or Anna with anyone with whom I speak. I also cannot promise to not contact you about school related issues as I must do so as part of my job duties on occasion.

I know you are justifiably upset and would gladly discuss this situation with you. We all make mistakes and I will own mine. If any information I can give you can help you to mend your relationship with Anna then I am available to talk to you. Your [redacted] deserve your best effort and I applaud you for putting them first There are two sides to every story [redacted] and I will give you facts if you desire them. I truly hope [you and Anna] remain employees in our district for as long as [redacted] desire. I think you are both outstanding [redacted] who make the lives of [redacted] infinitely better. I am copying this email to Anna as I think it would be deceptive to not do so.

If I do not receive an email (and you can also contact me at 419-xxx-xxxx) reply then I will know that you do not desire any non-work related contact from me regarding this issue but the offer remains. I will absolutely leave both of you completely alone and I trust you will do the same for me and my family.

[Passage redacted.]

Sincerely,
Patrick

===========================

On July 13 after he had returned from his trip, Anna's husband sent the next email to Hickey, castigating him for his "immoral and unprofessional actions." The husband notes that once Anna halted her relationship with Hickey, he "immediately started sending explicit messages to another [WLS] colleague" (Becca). He believes Hickey has "already hindered Anna's professional ambitions." He notes Hickey's claim that he is being persecuted by Board member Langenderfer who [Hickey says] is doing "evil," but turns this on Hickey and tells him,

"You are that evil that has been put in front of me, not the one being persecuted... I encourage you to get some professional help."

========================

[Anna's notes:] July 13 – [Husband] sent a response to him [Hickey] after he returned from [redacted] and spent some time deciding what we should do next (see attached). [Husband] sent his email at 3:22 pm.

========================

From: [Husband]
Sent: Monday, July 13, 2015 3:22 PM
To: Patrick Hickey
Subject: Fw: Core values

Pat:

Let me clarify a few things for you. I have the whole story. I have seen the emails and texts. I do not need to hear what you have to say on the matter. I have seen the truth.

For your information, I arranged the meeting with your pastor in hopes that appealing to your beliefs would get you to face your actions and address your immoral and unprofessional actions. I felt contacting your pastor would be the least confrontational way to approach you. Instead, you responded by threatening Anna through a mutual friend/co-worker.

The facts are that Anna asked you to leave her alone, she blocked your cell, so you tried to send her messages on twitter. Then you tried to contact her on your work phone, so she blocked that. You showed up at Max and Erma's [restaurant] knowing she would be there. You harassed her friend and co-worker for her new phone number. You left a voicemail on her school phone. You sent her non-work related emails. Messages about my dog are not school related. Having the guile to send me a box of books to give Anna is not school related. You came to her classroom. I have dates and times for all these instances. You then threatened Anna through this mutual friend "if she goes public with information".

Do not threaten my family. I am not threatening you with any public embarrassment, I am simply trying to protect my family and my professional career. I have not looked to punish you; living with yourself is probably punishment enough.

Yet amazingly, you then immediately started sending explicit messages to another [redacted] colleague [Becca], how did that work out for you? Have you explained that to [redacted] yet?

Do not talk about how much you appreciate [redacted] and that you hope [redacted] in the district along time. I believe you have already hindered [Anna's] professional ambitions. May I remind you are also nothing more than an employee of this district yourself. Professionally, there are a number of people that can contact us if need be about school related matters, figure it out.

Furthermore, I asked you to leave my family alone and I asked you to not respond to my previous email. Copying Anna was unnecessary and another form of intimidation from you. I am sure you would think I was trying to intimidate you if I copied your wife. Again, Please just leave my family alone and find a way to focus on your own.

I recall an email you sent about Mr. Langendorfer [sic], where you said "I was listening to a preacher last night who was saying that God will put enemies directly in our path, into our faces, into our lives who do evil. He will place them in order for them to find Christ in the person being persecuted and for the person being persecuted to witness to them." You are that evil that has been put in front of me, not the one being persecuted.

Before you impusivily [sic] respond to this email and feel the need to have the last word, consider if the legal representation you have admitted to contacting about this matter already, would advise you to.

I encourage you to get some professional help.

Let that be the last word on this matter.

[Husband]

===========================

Hickey responded on July 13 about an hour later:

===========================

[Anna's notes:] At 4:38, we received the attached response with lies about the following:

[That] I never asked him to leave me alone before April 23 – I did in fact on April 11 and April 12.

[That] He did not ask [a coworker; not Becca] for my new phone number and he did not threaten me to her. She indicated to me that during the week of April 14, he asked her numerous times for my new number. Also, she recapped the May 10 conversation in writing indicating that he would retrieve messages to make me look bad.

==========================

From: Patrick Hickey
Mon 7/13/2015 4:38 PM
To: [Husband]
Cc: [Anna]
RE: Core values

[Husband:]

If you want this communication to stop then you must stop emailing me about it. In my email (again responding to you) I said "If I do not receive an email (and you can also contact me at 419-xxx-xxxx) reply then I will know that you do not desire any non-work related contact from me regarding this issue but the offer remains." You replied and thus I shall reply. I copied your wife because it is imperative that she knows what I say to you and I will do so again. It is not a form of intimidation but rather communication.

Your wife never told me to leave her along [sic]. Never. The first time she said anything after she contacted me April 3rd about Spring Break and her eating plans was April 23rd when she responded to the non work related email about National Ice Cream Day. All of the contact you mentioned did, indeed, occur but it was all between April 3rd and 23rd when I was concerned that something must have happened to her over Spring Break because she consistently communicated with me and it stopped during Spring Break. I would have stopped if she ever told me to stop (just as I have since April 23rd). I did not ask [redacted] for her new phone number, I did not threaten [redacted] to [redacted]. I called [redacted] after my Pastor called me in order to find out what in the heck was going on. I don't know about the Max and Erma [restaurant] situation but [redacted] has informed me many times that she plays trivia and on one occasion I got carry out food and wanted to see what the trivia night was all about. I had no idea you intended to be there. I returned the gifts to you, and have actually found more, to let you know that your wife sent me books, dvds, videos, a gold pendant, dna, nutella spread, cookie butter, etc. so you would know that she was just as responsible as I was for the friendship we had. I would think you would understand especially given the fact that I never gave her a present. There is blame to go with Anna and there is blame to go with me. You seem to think Anna is an innocent in this situation and was somehow manipulated. If I sent her 15 presents I would understand your point. Your reference to [redacted] was also a two way street and I did give [redacted] my phone number to give to [redacted].

In terms of my pastor and living with myself please don't feel you need to save the world or that you encourage me to get professional help. I am very much at peace with who I am and how I conduct myself. I fall far short of perfect as does [redacted] as does [redacted] as do all humans.

I have not threatened your family and made it clear in my email that I will leave you alone and trust you will leave me and my family alone. I said I would support [redacted] work in this district and I have in no way, shape, form, or regard hindered [redacted] professional ambitions nor would I. On the contrary I would support them.

I would prefer that this situation ends here but if you respond (and remember it is you who has reached out to me twice, not the other way around) then it is probable that I will respond.

Sincerely,
Patrick

===========================

Hickey sends another email later that night with what Anna perceived as a threat.

===========================

[Anna's notes:] In addition on July 13 at 9:51pm, he sent the attached email, where he does in fact confirm that his lawyers are working to recover the "embarrassing, unsolicited videos that Anna sent me." That is the threat he gave to [coworker] and then placed in writing.

===========================

143

From: Patrick Hickey
Mon 7/13/2015 9:51 PM
To: [Husband]
Cc: [Anna]
[Re:] Your email

[Husband:]

Last words......I hope you are as aggressive with all men who have been evil to you and your family as you are to me. I am sure I am not the only one as evil as you present me to be.

In terms of your assertion about my attorneys, they only seek the truth and are confident in my testimony and the embarrassing videos Anna sent to me unsolicited. Truth is truth. I wish you the best.

Pat

====================================

From: [Husband]
Date: 07/14/2015 6:08 AM
To: Patrick Hickey
Subject Re: Your email

[IMAGE redacted]

http://www.wls4kids.org

"The aim of art is to represent not the outward appearance of things, but their inward significance"

====================================

Hickey apologized for his email of July 13 the next day:

====================================

[Anna's notes:] July 14 – At 6:52am, he sent the attached apology email regarding the threat of message recovery and stated that he would leave us alone if we left him alone.

====================================

Teachers File Complaint vs. Hickey; Scandalous Emails

From: Patrick Hickey
Tue 7/14/2015 6:52 AM
To: [Husband]
Cc: [Anna]
RE: Your email

I apologize for the last email. I was wrong to send it I only want you guys to leave me alone just as you want me to leave you alone.

I regret sending it and don't intend to do anything further except leave you and your family alone.

Patrick

===========================

But it didn't end with that. On August 23, Anna and her husband saw Hickey jogging past their house (very far from his own house), yelled at him, and photographed him running by, which they perceived as harassment. Hickey then sent an email to them both.

===========================

[Anna's notes:] August 23 – [Husband] was out mowing the lawn and he [Hickey] ran up to the corner at our house and started yelling things at [Husband]. [Husband] got upset, tried to speak with him and also took pictures of him running by our house. He went up to [Husband's] car and banged on the window. Later in the day, we received the attached email from him. He states that he has left us alone and [Husband] needs to stop emailing him. That email was the 4th consecutive unanswered email that he has sent [Husband] and copied me on.

===========================

From: Patrick Hickey
Sun 8/23/2015 1:18 PM
To: [Husband]
Cc: [Anna]
[Re:] Today

[Husband:]

As I said repeatedly, if you want to talk I am available. I ran 17 miles today from my house down alexis and through [redacted] and back. I have run the same course before. You videotaping me running on public sidewalks is harassment and I would ask that you not do it again. I am leaving you alone but what you did today is certainly not leaving me alone. Your incessant blocking me and

145

others and unblocking me to read my social media and blocking me again is also odd. I did not want to send an email but you have me blocked on social media and the phone number in the directory is disconnected. If you want to be left alone stop sending me emails and certainly leave me alone when I am running on a sidewalk on a public street. The f.u. was also uncalled for and I would not do that to you.

Patrick

===============================

[Anna's notes:] August 26, 2015 – 1 spoke with a coworker [not Becca] (the same coworker that he called threatening me to [sic] on May 7 and one that he admits to friendship with in his email dated July 13) and she indicated that last week for personal reasons, [Husband] blocked her on facebook. When she discovered that [Husband] blocked her, she sent Patrick an email telling me and also telling him that "shit was about to hit the fan." 1 don't know what the motivation behind sending this email to him was other than to protect/warn him. I believe this is what triggered him to run by our house on August 23, but that is just my opinion.

===============================

This jogging incident, and Hickey's response, apparently led the couple to file their collected evidence in an "informal complaint" against Hickey with WLS Human Resources on August 27, 2015.

The day after Hickey ran past the couple's house on August 23, Anna sent this email to her old friend Becca: "I don't know if you got my text, but know that I'm sorry. And sad." Becca forwarded that email to Hickey the next day, commenting, "It never ends." Becca would shortly testify *against* her old friend Anna and in defense of Hickey in the School Board's investigation.

Yes, Anna's other coworker was right:

"The shit was about to hit the fan."

CHAPTER 14
The Big Blow-Up
Community Anger & Hickey's Reprimand
– September 2015 –

An educator serves as a positive role model to both students and adults and is responsible for preserving the dignity and integrity of the teaching profession and for practicing the profession according to the highest ethical standards.

– Licensure Code of Professional Conduct for Ohio Educators [1]

The Superintendent is missing!

It's the beginning of the school year, early September 2015. But Superintendent Patrick Hickey was nowhere to be seen. The man who was *everywhere*. How very odd for the start of the school year! What was going on?

The Board was dealing with the "informal complaint" against Hickey filed by two WLS high school teachers, Anna and her husband, at the end of August 2015. (That complaint makes up Chapter 13.)

But the Board President told the community that Hickey was on a planned vacation. No one was buying that.

Rumor was that the Board was about to fire the Superintendent. Hickey's worshipful fans were enraged. Not knowing what was behind Hickey's absence, his angry supporters swarmed the September 2015 School Board meetings, praising their leader and demanding answers.

Sidebar: Hickey's blogger-defender and the three-way relationship

It was someone on the margins of WLS – blogger, former local radio producer, tabloid newspaper columnist, and WLS graduate Jeremy Baumhower – who dived in and stirred things up on social media when Supt. Hickey was mysteriously missing from the schools in early September 2015.

Baumhower led the pro-Hickey campaign on social media and at Board meetings. He had just ended work at the failing *Toledo Free Press* weekly and may simply have been looking for notoriety for his Toledo gossip blog, *IHeartGlassCity*. [2]

He would call the School Board's heightened scrutiny of Hickey a "coup" [3] – supposedly led by Board members Jim Langenderfer and Patricia Carmean – that endangered the future of 7,200 children! He helped organize protests complete with slogans, T-shirts, and signs defending Hickey and attacking Langenderfer and Carmean.

Baumhower claimed he didn't know Hickey before the scandal exploded in September 2015. There is only one email exchange between Baumhower and Hickey found on the WLS email system, dated October 29, 2015. Baumhower asks Hickey for an interview, and Hickey agrees. But Hickey's response reveals a familiarity that seems odd if he had never had contact with Baumhower before. The two men were later spotted together in a restaurant.

Somehow, Baumhower knew what was going on in the background at WLS before anyone else. Perhaps he *was* in direct communication with Hickey. (The Board's later "37 Charges" document indicates that Hickey was blind copying "persons on emails, sharing district business with persons not employed by the district" – though it did not name Baumhower.) Baumhower denied he ever received blind copies from Hickey on the school email system, and our public records request seemed to confirm that. Of course, they could have been communicating by other means.

But there was also this very strange coincidence: Baumhower confessed in his iBook, *Socked*, that he was having an affair (earlier in 2015 and possibly before) with the same teacher, Anna, who filed the complaints against Hickey in May-August 2015. [4] If this was true, Baumhower and Hickey may have met before over their shared paramour.

Pro-Hickey blogger Jeremy Baumhower, from his blog IHeartGlassCity. [5]

At about the same time that Anna was telling Hickey their relationship was over (April 2015), Baumhower's wife apparently discovered that her husband and Anna were having an affair. When Mrs. Baumhower confronted Jeremy, an altercation ensued and he injured her throat badly enough that she filed a charge against her husband. He was later convicted of domestic violence.

This was also the time Anna's husband got wind of her relationship with Hickey. Was he also aware of her liaison with Baumhower?

All of these players had a connection with the local arts scene in Sylvania (neighbor to the WLS district). Public media shows that Baumhower, Anna, and her husband were involved with the Sylvania, Ohio Community Arts Commission (SCAC). Baumhower taught a film course for 4th-8th graders there. Also frequenting SCAC was WLS teacher Michael Punsalan, Hickey favorite and producer of WLS promotional videos. WLS students won awards for their entries in the SCAC Tree City Film Festival. It is possible Hickey attended the SCAC events to see his students' entries in competition. And perhaps Baumhower met Hickey and Anna at those events.

The intertwining relationships are certainly curious.

Whatever Baumhower's motivations, he became Hickey's online champion and community rabble-rouser. He stirred up speculation that Hickey might be fired over his negotiations with Brondes Ford. He got people to engage online and at School Board meetings.

Baumhower continued with his angry posts after Hickey resigned (in December 2015). He published an iBook rant (*Socked*) on the WLS scandal (in 2017). But he went silent once Hickey was charged and convicted of his sexual crime (March-June 2018). We cannot now ask questions about his motivations since he passed away in 2019.

Aug. 5, 2015 School Board meeting

Most of Hickey's fans believed the early September controversy – with the Superintendent mysteriously on leave – centered on his advertising and sponsorship negotiations with the local Brondes Ford dealership. So people turned to the online records of the August 5 School Board meeting which included an acrimonious discussion of Hickey's negotiations with the local business. [6]

For some years Hickey had been working a contract with the dealership: WLS would receive $270,000 over ten years in exchange for field house and stadium advertising. School Board members accused

Hickey of failing to keep them properly informed, as well as prematurely having the Brondes logo painted on the field house floor without their approval.

The Board considered his Brondes negotiations a violation of proper procedure. The list of "37 Charges" later drafted against Hickey (see Chapter 17) includes this:

> #8. During 2015, you moved forward with a proposed contract between the Board and a local business [Brondes Ford] without some or all of the following: appropriate information to the Boar for its review, legal review, and/or buy-in of the Board. The proposed contract permitted the business to terminate the contract if you left the District, which was an inappropriate and self-serving item for you to include in the proposed contract.

Rumor was metastasizing on social media. [7] "OldTimer" wrote:

> Apparently Brondes name is now painted on the basketball court and Hickey was negotiating renaming the stadium in return from a donation from Brondes. These are all functions that have to go thru the board of Education First! He has pissed off the board on a number of occasions by doing things he should not be doing without their OK. A regular meeting was held this morning and it was packed.

"TrilbyGuy" posted:

> I watched the video yesterday. Not a big fan of [Board VP] Dave Hunter but I didn't see it has him throwing the (12 emails!) papers at Hickey. I don't really know what else Hickey has done to piss the board off. He may rub some people the wrong way and he is a bit of an attention whore. Having said that, he means well and has nothing but the best interests of the students, staff, families and district in mind. WLS has thrived under him and I think it would be a bad move to get rid of him.

"Reggie" wrote:

> Man, I've heard of a lot of shady things that Hickey and [Athletic Director] Snook have done over the years, some of which cost the WLS taxpayers lots of money such as this. [Links to USA Today report on WLS's $50,000 fine by Ohio HS Athletic Association.] [8] They get caught and just play dumb. Hickey and Snook are both arrogant when they are not in front of the public. Hickey means well as long as he gets his way. He spends WLS money like a drunken sailor. His "he did it for the kids" is getting old. He gets

his people on the school board then tells the board what he is going to do. There is more to this story about Hickey that the school board must not want to get out for them to turn on him all of sudden. Maybe it was all the thousands of dollars he spent on vacations for staff and students to visit Ron Clark multiple times. Maybe the board found it how he had some his administrators go in front of the board at a meeting crying like babies when they were considering cutting their pay. Hard to say. I'm surprised Hunter is attacking him so much especially after he got his whole family hired in to the district. Pretty much a good old boys network. They need to clean house and start over.

Hickey, too, may have wondered whether he was about to be fired over this after the August 5 meeting. As the month wore on – and Hickey was apparently aware that Anna and her husband were about to file a complaint – he called Board member Langenderfer to float the possibility that the Board might buy out his contract. (At that time, Langenderfer was unaware that a teacher and her husband were about to file their complaint against Hickey.)

Sept. 3 – School Board places Supt. Hickey on two-week "vacation"

As detailed in the previous chapter, since August 27 the School Board's attorney had been investigating Anna's "informal complaint" against Hickey. Clearly, though the teacher had told the Human Resources Director she just wanted the complaint kept on file, school officials realized it needed to be taken more seriously.

2015 BOARD OF EDUCATION

| THOMAS ILSTRUP President | DAVID HUNTER Vice President | PATRICIA PEDRO CARMEAN | ERIC KISER | JAMES LANGENDERFER |

At their afternoon meeting on Sept. 3 [9], the School Board adjourned the public session to go into executive session to "consider the investigation of charges or complaints against public employee or official, licensee, or student." [10] After the attorney's presentation, all five Board members voted to put Hickey on "vacation mode" (paid absence) and ban him from school property for two weeks while the investigation proceeded.

That night, Board President Thomas Ilstrup had this communication with Hickey. Note Ilstrup's aim to keep everything as "discrete" as possible. [11]

> Sent: Thursday, September 3, 2015 8:41 PM
> To: Patrick Hickey
> Subject: Board Directives Pending Investigation
>
> Patrick:
>
> Per my commitment to you to communicate following tonight's board meeting, please be advised of the following parameters regarding your employment situation pending the Board's investigation of harassment allegations. Though you may perceive some of these directives as punitive, your position in the organization necessitates unique (although Board Policy-consistent) handling of the matter.
>
> Again, it is the intention of the Board to handle this matter as discretely as possible so that all of the facts may be properly considered before conclusions are drawn, and that, as facts inevitably emerge, the community can draw on those facts, and not allegation or innuendo.
>
> At your specific request, I inquired of the Board regarding classifying your absence as "home assignment," and whether you were able to drop your daughter to school and attend football games, given your son's work as a ball boy.
>
> The consensus of a majority of the Board was that, given their desire that you have NO contact with district personnel, that your vacation NOT be "converted" to home assignment.
>
> In the interests of clarity, if you are unwilling to continue in a "vacation mode," the only alternative would be formal board action such as leave or suspension.
>
> Moreover, it is the further consensus of a majority of the Board that you have NO contact, whatsoever, with ANY district personnel – the SOLE EXCEPTIONS are: contact with myself or Assistant Superintendent Cherie Mourlam, IF SHE CALLS YOU. This PROHIBITION also applies to conducting ANY district business, or use of social media, including e-mails and tweets, for district

purposes. If you have any district issue, it must come through me to the Board.

In the further interests of clarity, please understand that if the Board learns of a violation of these directives, that that conduct will be considered insubordination, with appropriate consequences.

The Board is OK with your dropping your daughter to school, provided, however, that you have no contact in ANY form, with district personnel.

As for football, however, the Board is completely against your attendance. In fact, given the above-stated prohibitions, the Board is directing that you NOT attend any district activity or event.

Furthermore, I spoke with [attorneys] Kimball Carey this afternoon, as well as Cherie Wolff. The Board considers Ms. Wolff to be the Board's investigative arm; Spengler Nathanson is NOT our counsel in this matter. The Board considers Bricker & Eckler to be our counsel. Mr. Carey indicated to me that, while he may have recused himself from direct representation in this matter, his firm is NOT so recused. I am confirming this fact through B & E's house counsel.

Lastly, I'm not sure how you heard about interviews next Wednesday [the investigation by the Board's attorney], but I know of no specifics, except for Ms. Wolff's commitment to move forward with all deliberate speed.

Please be assured that we are moving to investigate this matter just as expeditiously as possible, to arrive at a prompt, fair resolution.

Thomas
cc: David Hunter, Board Vice-President

Ilstrup wondered how Hickey knew witness interviews were coming up. Hickey could have heard of this from his then paramour, Becca, who was called as a witness and would speak against her former friend, Anna.

Hickey responded to Ilstrup:

Subject: Re: Board Directives Pending Investigation
Date: Friday, September 4, 2015 11:21:02 AM

Tom, I did not see your email until 1046am today so I was unaware of the boards position until now. I will forward it to my attorney for his information. I am not checking work email per your directive to not work.

Following our phone call I have permission to take my sons to the football game but not attend. You will be contacting Sharon [Hickey's administrative secretary] to tell her to not contact me as she contacted me this morning about work issues and the email that you sent, otherwise I would gone to the football game so we dodged a bullet there. I did point out to you that I will inevitably run into employees in the coming days and I will keep the conversations as brief as possible.

I am copying Mr. Hunter on this email as he was copied on the original.

Patrick

Early Sept. 2015 – Rumors Hickey is about to be fired inflame community

The reaction from the community as they noted Hickey's absence demonstrates his cult-leader status.

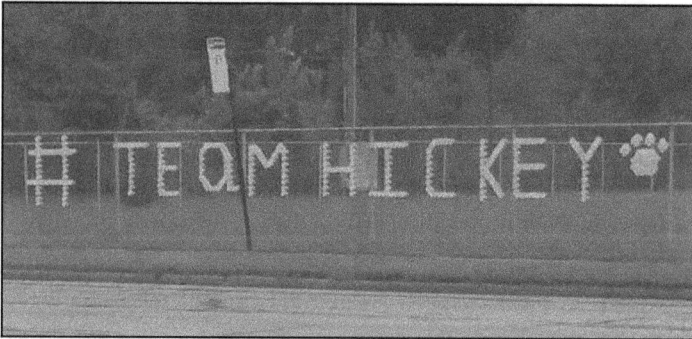

A fence in the WLS district

Pro-Hickey blogger Baumhower did a good job stirring up the community prior to the next meeting. He claimed to have learned on September 9 that a "coup" was in the works against Hickey, and the #IStandWithMrHickey campaign was born. [12] Baumhower continued to post inflammatory statements on his Facebook in the following days, including this:

I don't care about the inner workings of a school board. The only reason this has caught my attention is because of the way the Brondes Ford deal was handled, publicly, by 4 of you... The three names that vote to fire Patrick Hickey, will be ruined. I will make them famous. Don't be one of them.

The Big Blow-Up: Community Anger & Reprimand

Baumhower's efforts to turn the community against the Board were successful. He focused the community anger on three members behind the supposed "coup": Jim Langenderfer, Patricia Carmean, and Eric Kiser.

Several Twitter pages were set up prior to the next Board meeting praising Hickey, including #IStandWithMrHickey. [13] The first post is from Hickey's son: "Family over everything! I will stand with my dad no matter what." *This drew in a lot of students* who would remain focused on what would become a sex-laden scandal within just days. Sample posts over the next week include:

- Without him the WLS District would never be the same! He made this district so great!!
- [Lisa Canales, former/future Board member:] Whatever does or doesn't happen today we should be proud that the #WLS community supports students
- I don't think you could've asked for a better superintendent
- Your personal vendetta against someone doesn't mean you can vote them out of their job
- Mr. Hickey is one of my biggest role models. Such an awesome, forgiving, and inspiring man.
- loosing [sic] Mr. Hickey will bring ours [sic] school way down, not to mention, our children will suffer from this!
- ["rick fucking dalton" wrote] @SuptHickey is one of the greatest people I've ever met. Replacing him would be like replacing Batman with Shazam
- In tears that WLS4Kids would even consider replacing such an amazing man! *#Istandwithmrhickey* forever - once a panther always a panther!
- Our school district would not be as great as it is without Mr. Hickey.
- Mr. Hickey, you inspire me.
- He's always supported us. Now we return that support. This community is one big family! We stand behind @SuptHickey!
- wouldn't want anyone else as a superintendent
- Anyone who thinks Mr. Hickey could be successfully replaced under these circumstances is out of their mind.
- he's been my superintendent since kindergarten and I don't want my sisters to grow up w/out him as theirs
- I loved seeing everyone outside with signs for Mr. Hickey. [at School Board meeting]
- A 5 minute applause when Hickey showed up!!! [at Sept. 16, 2015 School Board meeting]
- forever standing by Mr. Hickey... he's a great man, motivator, educator, and friend to everyone and anyone.

- what ever happens tonight [Sept. 16] *remember we all love you*
- "Mediocrity Attacks Excellence" a wise Superintendent once said. Patrick Hickey is Excellence!!

Sept. 12 Board meeting - "Want Hickey, Need Hickey, Love Hickey"

WLS community members were confused and angry. Was Hickey about to be fired over his failed deal with Brondes?

At the next School Board meeting on Saturday, September 12, scores of people showed up to support Superintendent Hickey even though the meeting began at 8:00 a.m. on a Saturday and was billed as a Board "work session." [14]

Board President Ilstrup noted that the Brondes negotiation was slated to be the only item on the agenda, but that the deal had been withdrawn by the auto dealer.

Ilstrup flatly stated that Hickey was *not* going to be fired, and he cautioned the community about the rumor-mongering. In fact, the Board attorney's investigation of Hickey had not been completed, so the Board had not yet voted on whether or not the Superintendent's behavior warranted firing.

Hickey was not present and the attendees were told, "he's on vacation today." That only inflamed community suspicions since everyone knew the Superintendent would not take time off at the start of the school year.

Board VP David Hunter said,

> All the other speculation, about Mr. Hickey, I think he's on vacation right now. There are issues that are being discussed right now. And please trust that this Board is going to do, as we have for many years, what's best for our staff and our community. These are very difficult times for us also. OK? We're not here to hurt anybody, but we are here because this district is bigger than one person. This district is bigger than any group. This district is a community, it is a family. And if you're hearing rumors, please understand: They are rumors. The Board is not allowed to discuss many of the issues that are being talked about for legal reasons. It's not because we're trying to hide them. We are protecting people's reputations on both sides… things that are happening are not the rumors that are out there… For 22 years I've dedicated myself to this district… and this is very hard for me too… But the rumors that you're hearing are not true. All these things about Mr. Hickey's off because of Brondes has nothing to do with it. This Board did not come here this morning to vote to get rid of Mr. Hickey. There are issues that are being dealt with right now that are very sensitive to everyone. [15]

Sept. 15, 2015 meeting: "If you fire PH We WILL fire YOU!" – the same signs that were at the Sept. 12 meeting. (WLS video)

Many in the audience held signs: **"If you fire PH We WILL fire YOU!"** Social media engagement on Twitter included #Team Hickey, #IStandWithMrHickey, and #IStandWithHickey. [16]

His worried supporters mimicked his hyperbolic style in their public comments at the podium, praising Hickey and warning the Board against firing him. Their anger boils over in the video. [17] But their stories unwittingly helped document his inappropriate crossing of boundaries between educator and student, educator and community.

The quotes below are taken from the video of the Sept. 12 meeting.

Lindsay Webb, a very angry Toledo City Council member and mother of a young student in the district, is fuming. She disparages the "political double-speak" from the Board. She says that despite the 60% WLS household poverty level, the district still maintains excellent schools. She believes that Hickey should be credited since he had gotten five levies passed and is a "great leader." "You may think you are getting rid of somebody who has slighted you in one way, shape, or form, or has caused some slight problems... but you don't know what you're gonna get in his place." The Board's decision will go down in history, she says. She threatens them: "... up until this point, I haven't come anywhere near the WLS Board races, but that will change starting today. I love politics, and I know how to play politics." (She was active in the later School Board election, helping two Hickey supporters get elected.)

Hickey supporters pack the Sept. 12, 2015 School Board meeting. Toledo City Councilor Lindsay Webb walks from the podium after blasting the Board.

A fifth-grade grade teacher in the district says: "Patrick Hickey is the backbone of our school district. I would walk on water for Patrick Hickey. He encourages me, he uplifts me. I am so proud of our school district." Her college daughter's "main goal is to teach for Patrick Hickey."

An elementary teacher gives this snippet as an example of Hickey's dedication: Hickey has gone with the teacher's sixth-grade class to away camp three times as cabin leader and he "has spent the night in a cabin with sixth graders." The audience laughs. "I challenge you to find another Superintendent who would do that and love it."

A father tells of his son who treasures a photo of Mr. Hickey praying with him in the school cafeteria.

A pastor in the district says Hickey demonstrates all the qualities on the banners in the gym: *courage, dedication, dignity, excellence, gratitude, honesty, loyalty, respect, responsibility, service, teamwork, trust.* He tells the Board to "leave politics out" of their oversight. "Patrick Hickey is the best of the best."

Hickey is "a father figure to the community, students, and staff," says another.

A Whitmer High School graduate, daughter of Whitmer alumni and now a parent of WLS students, praises Hickey:

> Never before has there been a leader [here] like Patrick Hickey There are obvious victories like passing levies and reminding our community of why this district is so deserving of their tax dollars. But it's his unwavering support of our students that tells me the most about his character. He's at an astonishing number of athletic games, exchange student farewell potlucks, and countless other district events at all hours of the day or night. And every time I see him, he's cheering the loudest and smiling the biggest.
>
> He believes that each and every student matters. He relates to them in a way that nobody before him has even come close to. He's the heart of this district. And if you remove him, you will lose the love and enthusiasm that he brings with him when he walks through the door every day. It's contagious.

A bubbly, young high school teacher dressed in athletic shorts and T-shirt gives credit to Hickey for her own "awesomeness."

> I want to speak as a teacher... I want to speak with the classroom perspective about what this issue is that may or may not be going on. I am an awesome teacher. I'm really good at what I do. I'm very proud of what I do... I didn't know what I was doing as a teacher when I came to Washington Local. I had worked one year as a long-term sub in another district. I was so lost. I came to Washington Local and I can't imagine myself anywhere else. And I

don't think I could be the awesome teacher that I am if I were anywhere else.

And without Patrick Hickey as our leader, I think that I won't be as awesome because he brings so much of the enthusiasm and he encourages so many of us to be awesome teachers for our students. If Patrick Hickey is not our leader, good teachers will leave. If they don't walk physically, they will just lose their passion, and become normal, average teachers. I know some of the Board members speak often about how great the teachers are in WLS. But that's because of our leadership. We will leave, either with our feet, or everything will fizzle in the classroom.

A 23-year-old man and WLS employee tells how he learned loyalty from Mr. Hickey. As a senior at Whitmer High School, he got to shadow Hickey for a day when Hickey was handing out awards in various district schools. He looks up to Hickey and says,

I love this guy... I wish I could be half the man [he is]. Everyone that we came into contact with [that day] he hugged and thanked for their dedication and service, and they hugged and thanked him for his dedication and service to this district... He's always on his phone; people know this. He answers all his emails in a timely fashion...

At the end of the day, and we talked for hours and hours and hours, and he spent time with me, a student. He didn't have to; he's a busy man... At the end of the day, he wouldn't let me thank him. He thanked me. He let a student show him why he was here... And he said he loved me, and I believe him. Ever since then he said he loves me, and I love him back. Thank you, Patrick! I love you.

A high school student says:

Hundreds and hundreds of people are flooding to social media to show their support... We stand with Mr. Hickey. He is a man that is the face of a great and powerful district, that which the Board is shunning him. [sic] I ask that you do not look at his mistakes as negatives, but as positives, that he will get better than he ever was which is damned near impossible because a man is willing to give his all for a school district which he considers home. He is the heart and soul of the Washington Local district. Even when we fall, we make sure we get up and we brush off and stand tall. Mr. Hickey ... is a necessity to this school district. The positivity that he is able to create just by walking down the hallways of Whitmer with his huge smile, or how every time you give him a microphone, he'll make sure you won't regret it. Whether it's through his war chants or his serious down-to-heart [sic] talks, or when he lets the voiceless be heard, or even when he's doing wacky videos. He is a great man with great integrity...

Hickey with a student fan in the HS cafeteria, Fall 2015
(#IStandWithMrHickey)

A teacher in district for 17 years thanks Hickey for everything. "You're a fantastic cheerleader." She says Hickey takes popsicles to classes, attends many events, and shows how much he cares. "It's about educating the whole child." His emails to staff are important. He attends funerals and knows all the teachers by name. He hugged her when he saw her in a parking lot downtown.

A middle-aged man says, "He's a good man... What has he got? He's got something I want. What he has, he has faith in God... I'd rather follow a man that believes in God. I know when he goes to bed at night, he prays for the school district."

A woman who teaches in the district speaks through her tears:

> Patrick ... inspires me ... to be a better teacher every year. He missed his calling to be a motivational speaker. He is a very motivating person. Maybe some people say it's lip service, and maybe it is. But I don't care because I like it! He makes me happy!

He makes me want to come to school! ... If he made some kind of mistake – we all do. We all make mistakes. [Applause] I love working for this district and I would be very sad if Patrick Hickey were not a part of it.

Another woman – crying uncontrollably – says Hickey's leadership makes her proud to live in the WLS district. She believes he turned the district around, from basement test scores to top in the state.

A business owner in the community loses control and starts screaming at the Board. He wondered if Hickey was being disciplined over his negotiations with the local Brondes Ford dealership. Or was there something else? He has to be escorted away from the podium by a police officer when he refuses to halt his harangue.

A teacher says:

> We're not privy to all the information that you guys [School Board] are, and I know that there is maybe some sensitive information that we're unaware of. But I do know that this man is greatly loved by many, for many reasons. And he's loved for his character. All of these character traits on the walls that we see, he exudes. And his actions speak volumes to his person, as do yours. Personal vendettas, hidden agendas don't belong here. [Audience applauds.] We all fall, none of us are perfect... I don't know if Patrick has done something that we're unaware of, but forgiveness is a beautiful thing.

A district parent says,

> We care about our school and we love who's leading it... We love having Patrick... It's upsetting to know that we are unclear on your intentions... When we don't know what you're thinking, this is the response you get. [A huge, angry crowd.] I hope the next meeting, you are prepared for even more people... We may have elected you, but we trusted you. We thought you were here for the kids, and here for the people who were here for them. And it's upsetting that this is now what it's come to.

A WLS staff member claims that Hickey is *the greatest* Superintendent. "Short-sighted, small-minded decisions that challenge Patrick are gonna make this district less special... Any motion to challenge Patrick is gonna ... hurt the kids."

A woman chides the Board:

> Some of you are looking exasperated and are looking at the walls, or have blank stares looking at all these people. I know it may be

repetitive to hear all these great comments about Patrick Hickey, but you as a School Board are supposed to listen to what we have to say... and we've been looking at you too, and we will remember that come election time.

A man says he is "disappointed with juvenile behavior" and "lack of transparency" of the Board. "We know nothing... Sorry if I'm boring you, Sir" (addressing Board member Langenderfer). He says he is "tired of the bullshit, hidden agendas, being treated like child."

WLS high school girls for Hickey (#IStandWithHickey, Sept. 2015; still posted in 2020). One sign reads: **"Want Hickey - Need Hickey - Love Hickey"**

A very emotional woman scolds Board member Patricia Carmean and charges that her deceased husband, former Supt. Michael Carmean, "never attended school events when he was Superintendent."

Board member Jim Langenderfer told *The Blade* after the meeting that "he considered [Toledo City Councilor] Ms. Webb's latter remarks inappropriate meddling in the board's affairs. 'She has no business coming in and threatening us,' he said." [18]

Channel 13abc reported after the Sept. 12 meeting:

Some people think this is a witch hunt to get rid of Superintendent Hickey, but one school board member tells 13abc, there is an inquiry into other issues, but they are not able to comment at this time.

Lawrence [the man escorted from the podium by a police officer] feels like the Brondes fight is just a smoke screen. "As human beings we have all made mistakes. Regardless of this big bomb the board intends to drop is, [sic] Patrick's been great for our community." [19]

WTOL quoted the angry Mr. Lawrence further:

We're in the dark right now. We hear rumors, like we alluded to in the room, nobody knows. But what I do know, and what I hope to come out of today is, number one, I think it's apparent, the testimony we heard, he's a great man, great for our community, everybody's entitled to a mistake, and who knows, again, it's all speculation, and rumor. From the information that we're receiving, as a public community, and at Washington Local District, you know, it seems like there's a target on Mr. Hickey's back, and nobody really knows why. I'm hearing a lot of "that's not what this meeting is about today," but I'm worried about meetings in the future. [20]

The next day, September 13, blogger Baumhower posted on Facebook:

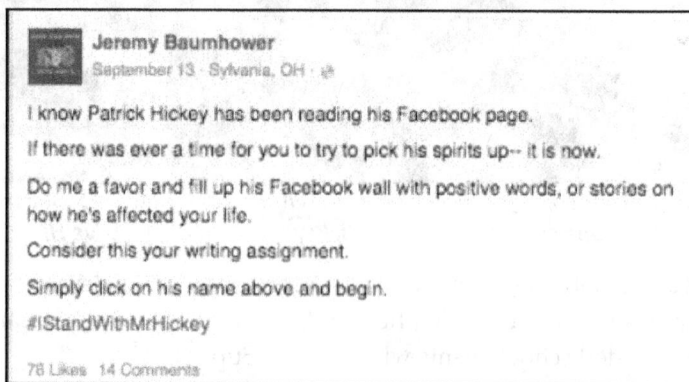

Jeremy Baumhower
September 13 · Sylvania, OH ·

I know Patrick Hickey has been reading his Facebook page.

If there was ever a time for you to try to pick his spirits up-- it is now.

Do me a favor and fill up his Facebook wall with positive words, or stories on how he's affected your life.

Consider this your writing assignment.

Simply click on his name above and begin.

#IStandWithMrHickey

76 Likes 14 Comments

Sept. 15, 2015 – Board receives investigation report

The Board met briefly in public on September 15 before entering into executive session. The announced purpose of the meeting was to "consider the employment of a public employee or official," and to "consider the investigation of charges or complaints against a public employee official, licensee, or student." In other words, they would be voting on Supt. Hickey's status.

Citizens flooded the room to advocate for Hickey and to find out what was going on. And again, many held signs: "**If you fire PH we WILL fire YOU!**" His supporters knew the session would decide Hickey's fate.

The WLS video [21] yields the following.

Board President Ilstrup tells the community to trust the Board.

Vice President David Hunter says it's been a terrible week for himself and his family (his daughter being a teacher at Whitmer High School). The atmosphere is tense for everyone, he says, and Board members themselves still don't know exactly what is going on. (They are awaiting the report from their attorney's investigation.) "I promise you, what is right will be done." He talks about his oath to "faithfully and impartially do his duties" as a School Board member.

> I sat here for the last meeting and I listened to all the accolades and things that were said about Patrick Hickey, and I agree with 99.9% of them. Patrick is a wonderful Superintendent. He has done wonderful things for this district. [Audience applauds.] He has brought us a long way and done great things, built upon other wonderful Superintendents and wonderful staff. But if issues come before this Board, I'm thinking you don't want us to rubber stamp or to go ahead without addressing those issues. And this Board is doing just that. I thank you all for the prayers you've given us to make us strong and to make the right decision. But I promise you, I will vote and do whatever it is that is right for Washington Local, what is right for our kids. And that's what this Board is going to do tonight. Trust me. We are here for Washington Local.

Board member Patricia Carmean addresses the slander of her deceased husband (the former Superintendent) at the previous meeting (referring to the woman who said she'd never seen former Supt. Michael Carmean at school events). She asks that people respect past Superintendents and not tell untruths, and she gives out her phone number for people to call her if they are displeased with *her*.

Board member Jim Langenderfer says:

> I know this is a terrible time for all of us and … we have to make some tough decisions. I just ask – I've received eight threats. I've had people stone my house. My neighbors are afraid. You know, and I've gone through [troubles] when I was a school administrator. But I've never seen this. You know, I'm going to try

to do – what I can for Washington Local. I am. But I can't believe why people want to threaten – [He is interrupted by audience members; Ilstrup says "Please hold your comments in the audience."] ... We're going to disagree, I understand that. I've threatened nobody. And my poor children, they don't even live in this city. My daughter: She's getting stuff 1,500 miles away. So please... This is going to be tough. I'm sick to my stomach half the time... That's all.

In addition to the phoned threats during this period, Langenderfer's tires were slit in his driveway, his mail was stolen, and there was frequent drive-by harassment at his home.

President Ilstrup concludes before the Board moves to executive session:

Again, members of the community, please recognize the nature of confidential information that these five individuals on this panel have that you do not. Do not let social media guide your thinking and your emotions. Please let the Board do its job that we've been elected to do.

Hickey supporters crowd the room and chant loudly during the School Board's executive session, Sept. 15, 2015. (Toledo Blade video)

Raucous chanting – **"We stand with Hickey!"** – continued during the entire executive session, which the Board members heard in their adjacent room. [22]

From *The Toledo Blade*:

A chant of "We stand with Hickey!" broke out when the board went into its closed-door executive session. Among the crowd were many teachers, there to support their boss.

Christopher Hodnicki, president of the Teachers' Association of Washington Local Schools, said that teachers enthusiastically support Mr. Hickey. Union leaders plan to meet Wednesday to discuss how the union should react, depending on board action. [23]

WTOL filed this on the Sept. 15 meeting, noting that some Board members were feeling threatened by the public:

Some board members say they felt threatened by the public as this whole situation plays out. Meanwhile, parents say they feel like the board is not listening to them.

"It didn't seem like they were too receptive. What I want them to know is that we're supporting Patrick Hickey. We don't know these board members, they don't get out and get in the community as much as he does. So, if they're not going to support the school system, the parents, the students, then they're going to be replaced," said parent David Caro. [24]

In their closed session, the Board received details of their attorney's investigation into Hickey's relationship and communications with Anna, plus testimony from her husband, high school teacher Becca, Hickey, and possibly others. The Board would meet the next day, September 16, to decide Hickey's fate.

The Toledo Blade had this the next morning: "Even though board members said Mr. Hickey is on vacation, his schedule shows numerous meetings and events he had planned to attend Sept. 3. His personnel file showed no reference to any investigations by the board or directive that he be placed on leave." [25]

Sept. 16 – Board reprimands Hickey but he keeps his job

At the September 16, 2015 special meeting (after hearing the results of their attorney's investigation the day before), the Board adjourned to executive session to decide the Superintendent's fate. They voted 4-0 to formally reprimand Hickey. [26] (Board member Langenderfer was absent due to a long-scheduled commitment. His opinion was known to the Board and his vote would not have changed the outcome.)

Hickey then entered the public meeting room and sat with the Board members when they returned from executive session. Channel 13abc reported, "As soon as Hickey walked into Wednesday's school board meeting, his crowd of supporters erupted into cheers and chants." [27]

The Board announced their letter of reprimand to Hickey *but did not share the contents*. Instead, Board President Ilstrup read this statement to the public:

> Legal counsel for Washington Local Schools Board of Education conducted an investigation of concerns raised about Patrick Hickey's interactions with staff members. We believed that the concerns which were brought to the attention of the Board were thoroughly investigated by legal counsel. The Board has appropriately addressed those concerns and has brought this matter to its proper conclusion fulfilling the Board's legal and ethical obligations to act in the best interest of the Washington Local Schools.
>
> The Board's legal counsel completed the investigation which is confidential according to law. The Board has provided Supt. Patrick Hickey with a written letter of reprimand and further directives for his conduct. Contrary to the views of many members of this community, the Board has not been considering action on Mr. Hickey's contract with respect to any school donation agreement [Brondes Ford], which proposal was withdrawn by that donor. The Board issued a written letter of reprimand and directives for future conduct for his unprofessional judgment and conduct and directed him to avoid even the appearance of impropriety and [sic] his interactions of [sic] both female and male staff members of the district. [28]

Hickey kept his job.

Why the soft reprimand by the School Board?

Below is the full letter of reprimand issued to Supt. Hickey. It had been hand delivered to Hickey earlier on Sept. 16 so that he would be able to respond at the Board meeting that night.

The Board formally scolded him for inappropriate behavior with school employees and his too-familiar, "overly personal" style. The document noted his *"repeated display of lack of judgment and inappropriate interpersonal interactions over a significant period of time."*

The Board admits the emails between Hickey and Anna's husband are "overly personal ... inappropriate and intentionally intimidating." The wording holds back on the closeness of Hickey's personal (and likely sexual) relationship with Anna. But she apparently did not *state* it was a sexual affair during the Board's investigation.

Neither Anna nor the Board wanted to take the complaint to the level of legal sexual harassment.

Anna had told the HR Director that she did not want to harm Hickey professionally. And it makes sense she would not want to hurt the school district that employed both her and her husband.

But what about the "embarrassing videos" including nudity sent by Anna to Hickey? The Board confirmed their existence in the later "37 Charges" document (drawn up in Dec. 2015). Wasn't the admitted existence of those videos enough to terminate the Superintendent? Hickey tried and apparently succeeded in shifting blame to Anna for being the aggressor, judging by the weasel words in the "37 Charges" document. Item 12 reads:

> Sometime during the last two years, you received inappropriate videos from a subordinate teacher of the district involving nudity.
>
> a. You were a party to the misconduct by requesting and/or encouraging that the videos be sent by the teacher, or
>
> b. You failed to take action to initiate discipline, corrective directives to the teacher for her misconduct, or any investigation of the misconduct, or
>
> c. Both a. and b.

Hickey stood by his version – that he was the innocent party – two years later in a statement to *The Blade*: "There was a teacher who sent me inappropriate videos. I think that's the teacher's problem." [29] But how likely is it that Anna would have been the initiator and sent the videos to her superior had they not been involved in some intimacy already? Would she have jeopardized her job by such a rash action? (The public knew nothing about these videos until two years after the reprimand.)

Had Anna or Hickey admitted the *sexual* nature of their relationship – even if consensual – the workplace for other employees could have met the description of a *hostile work environment*. That can emanate from the favoritism shown by a supervisor towards employees with whom he has consensual sexual relations:

> In the context of employees, consensual sexual relationships where such relationship leads to favoritism of a subordinate employee with whom the superior is sexually involved and where such favoritism adversely affects other employees or otherwise creates a

> hostile work environment. – Washington Local Schools policies, po3362 [30]

Surely, the Board would be happy if this condition was *not* met.

The reprimand makes no clear reference to the familiarity and sexual innuendoes in the email exchanges Hickey had with the *other* teacher, Becca (which were alluded to by Anna and her husband in the emails and complaint). The Board attorney apparently did not look at that second relationship (ongoing at the time), for which there was plenty of evidence in the school email system. (See Chapter 15.)

In light of all this, Hickey's reprimand seems a soft reaction. It refers generally to "conduct unbecoming a Superintendent." It warns Hickey "jeopardized" his leadership of the district by his irresponsible actions which went on "over a significant period of time." He didn't make just one little slip.

The reprimand letter then walks him through what constitutes proper behavior. Hickey was told not to interact or communicate with the complainants, and to avoid even the appearance of impropriety or retaliation. "You must avoid any communication or action which might be perceived, in any way, as too personal, inappropriate, forward, or flirtatious; you must exercise even more caution if you must communicate with a staff member in a private setting or manner."

That a School Board would have to give such instruction to a Superintendent makes no sense. That he should require it seems to disqualify him for the position. Nevertheless, Patrick Hickey kept his job. The question is, why? Was the Board simply afraid of a larger scandal? Of course, *that larger scandal was yet to come their way.*

According to Jim Langenderfer, he and Patricia Carmean *did* believe Hickey met the threshold for termination at this time. But they were overruled.

Here is the full text of the reprimand Hickey received prior to the public Board meeting. (The public did not hear it or see it the night of the meeting.)

Washington Local Schools
Board of Education
3505 W. Lincolnshire Blvd
Toledo OH 43606

September 16, 2015

VIA HAND DELIVERY

Patrick Hickey
Superintendent
Washington Local Schools
3505 W Lincolnshire Blvd
Toledo OH 43606

Re: Reprimand for Conduct Unbecoming a Superintendent

Dear Patrick:

This correspondence is to address concerns which came to the attention of the Board of Education of the Washington Local Schools (the Board), to provide you with our formal reprimand for your past conduct, and to set forth directives for your conduct in the future.

The Board has found that your behavior toward district staff members, including the extent and volume of your communications, were perceived as overly personal, as well as inappropriate and intentionally intimidating. Your repeated display of lack of judgment and inappropriate interpersonal interactions over a significant period of time has jeopardized your leadership of the District, and for which you are hereby reprimanded.

In the future, you must make every effort to avoid *even the appearance* of impropriety in your interactions with all staff members. Your past conduct also compels the Board to provide you with specific directives for the future, which follow.

Under no circumstances are you to have any further interaction or communication with anyone you believe has lodged any concern about you, including staff members and board members, unless that communication is confined to school business.

You are to avoid *even the appearance* of retaliation.

You must use better judgment in your interactions with, and comments to, staff members. You must avoid any communication or action which might be perceived, in any way, as too personal, inappropriate, forward, or flirtatious; you must exercise even more caution if you must communicate with a staff member in a private setting or manner.

Do not use private means of communication with staff members.

You must never make comments or take actions which might be perceived as intimidating or threatening.

September 16, 2015
Patrick Hickey
Page Two

Re: Reprimand for Conduct Unbecoming a Superintendent

Overall, you must exercise better judgment in your interactions with staff members – both female and male.

Always conduct yourself in a manner which is consistent with conduct expected of a superintendent of the Washington Local Schools. Stay well within the parameters of the Licensure Code of Professional Conduct for Ohio Educators, Board policies, administrative guidelines, and the directives of this letter.

The Board trusts that you will abide by these directives, and further cautions that your future conduct and interactions must avoid *even the appearance* of impropriety. If you fail to do so, you will be further disciplined, which may include consideration of the nonrenewal of your contract or termination.

Finally, it is the expectation of the Board that you will accept this letter and its directives in a professional manner. There is to be no retaliation against any persons who raised concerns, any staff members, or this Board or any of its members, for this letter of reprimand. Your conduct following receipt of this letter, including any social media posts – professional or personal – or discussions with community members or others, must demonstrate your highest character. Correspondingly, you will be accorded with respect and you will be charged with continuing to lead and move the District forward.

Yours truly,

Thomas G. Ilstrup
President
Board of Education
Washington Local Schools

cc: Patrick Hickey's personnel file

Hickey read his response to the reprimand while the audience listened attentively. [31] His guarded expression and quivering voice revealed his very high anxiety.

The Big Blow-Up: Community Anger & Reprimand

WLS Board Meeting
2015 September 16

More from Washington Local Schools
Autoplay next video

Hickey reads his statement after being reprimanded by the School Board.

You are the greatest community in the country. You have lifted me up in ways I cannot even express to you. I want to thank all the prayers that were said for me. And if anyone thinks this isn't a Godly district, they have something else to consider because you literally have lifted up my arms. [applause] ... I want to make it perfectly and crystally clear that this reprimand has *absolutely* nothing to do with matters or issues related to the students I love, the students I care for, and the students I am blessed to serve. [applause] I love these students as you love them, and that's what makes us so special.

I want to make it crystally clear that this reprimand has nothing to do with any romantic or sexual situation with *any* staff member or *any* person.

I want to make it crystal clear – [wild applause] I want to make it crystal clear that this reprimand has absolutely nothing to do with dishonesty, or anything that is unlawful, or anything that is fiscally irresponsible to the moneys that you give this district and you give so willingly, and that we use to raise and lift up kids. [applause]

My vacation ends today and I am blessed beyond all belief in our God. I am blessed that tomorrow I get to return to my desk and I get to serve you [wild applause & screaming] – and I will serve you with even more gusto and more love and more passion and more belief than I ever have. I will lift your kids up. I will love them as you love them. I will love this amazing staff and this amazing community. [applause]

He was not truthful about the extent of his relationship with Anna, denying even that there was *"anything romantic"* behind his reprimand. That he was prevaricating is verified by Item #19 in the later list of "37 Charges" drawn up by the Board attorney in December 2015. (Chapter 17.)

He knew he was getting off easy.

After the meeting, the WLS website (which he controlled) posted a slightly different version of his statement, including an older photo of Hickey (with a very different facial expression). [32]

Superintendent's Report & Communications
Patrick Hickey, Superintendent

WORDS to the COMMUNITY

I want to thank our community for their support over the past two weeks and the last 14 years. You are the greatest community in the country. I'm also grateful for a God who is ever faithful and provides grace that surpasses all understanding. I will never be able to fully express my thanks to the thousands of prayer warriors, but I physically felt the prayers and you have lifted me up.

The Board did the job they are elected and tasked to do. They researched a concern and came to a conclusion. I have made errors and I apologize for the distractions they have caused. They will not occur again.

I want to make it perfectly clear that this reprimand has absolutely nothing to do with matters or issues relating to the students I love, the students I care for, and the students I am blessed to serve. I love these students as you love them, and that's what makes this community so special.

I want to make it crystally clear that this reprimand has nothing to do with any romantic or sexual situation with any staff member or any person. I did not have an affair or break my marriage vows to my wife of 27 years who is the greatest wife to me and the greatest mom in the world to our four beautiful kids.

I want to make it crystally clear that this reprimand has absolutely nothing to do with dishonesty or anything that is unlawful or anything that is fiscally irresponsible to the moneys that you give this district, that you give so willingly and that we use to raise and lift up kids.

My vacation ends today, and I am blessed that tomorrow I get to return to my desk and serve you. I will serve you with even more gusto, more love, more passion, and more belief than I ever have. I will lift your kids up; I will love them as you love them. I will love this amazing staff and community.

WORDS of THANKS

I want to thank my two closest direct reports -- **Cherie Mourlam** (Assistant Superintendent) and **Sharon Giles** (Executive Secretary to the Superintendent). I work with two incredibly strong, smart, virtuous, and hardworking women. They do their jobs at the highest level while being amazing wives and amazing moms.

PERISCOPE

Periscope is the newest thing in social media and allows you to broadcast any event live. I plan to use Periscope technology to show the world the incredible things happening across our district.

Note the sentence, "I did not have an affair or break my marriage vows to my wife of 27 years," in his "Across the Board" statement (above). That was not included in the statement he read at the September 16 Board meeting.

In the list of "37 Charges" from December 2015, it was noted that Hickey was "dishonest" in that posted statement:

#19. Following the issuance of the September Reprimand and Directives, you were dishonest with the Board, students, staff, and the community when you wrote in a district publication called "Across the Board" on or about September 16, 2015, "This reprimand has nothing to do with any romantic or sexual situation with any staff member or person. I did not have an affair or break my marriage vows to my wife of 27 years…"

The Board attorney was here admitting the sexual nature of the relationship with Anna, it seems.

Public comments: Praise for Hickey & accusations of a "hidden agenda"

Following Hickey's statement at the Board meeting and before community comments began, Board member Eric Kiser praised the "love in the community." Patricia Carmean thanked the community for their involvement. Vice President David Hunter said, "This is by far the most difficult thing I've dealt with. I've been on for 22 years… We were prepared to do whatever it was that was right." President Ilstrup said he was "pleased that Patrick Hickey will be back in his office tomorrow and perhaps out in the building loving up children." (He was echoing Hickey's favorite phrase, *"We'll love 'em and lift 'em up!"*)

Hickey's supporters were relieved he had not been fired. Many rose to praise him. Some still had to vent their anger. [33]

Young children and teens were allowed in this adult forum. Parents who brought their children to this meeting – many by now suspecting that at issue was Hickey's inappropriate relationship with a teacher – apparently had no problem involving their children.

A mother in the district, Melanie Garcia, viciously speaks against Board members Langenderfer (who was not present that night) and Carmean. She tells a slanderous story that Langenderfer had run into her wheelchair-bound daughter and didn't have the courtesy to apologize. (Langenderfer explains that this is totally false and there was video confirming it did not happen.) The woman also unfairly portrays Carmean's reasonable response to the slander of her husband, former Superintendent Michael Carmean (at the previous day's meeting). The woman then calls on Langenderfer and Carmean to resign from the Board.

> If you have that much anger, and that much – just spewing from your mouth. So our people that pay taxes want answers, and some

of them aren't always as respectful as they should be. [Addressing Carmean:] You sit on our Board. You are held at a little bit of a higher standard. And we do forgive. Forgiveness is very powerful. You don't talk to people the way that you talked to us last night, or the way that Mr. Langenderfer talked to us last night. And we have no confidence. None. We ask that you step down.

(Garcia would be elected to the School Board in 2019.)

Others make digs at Langenderfer's absence that night.

Former Board member Steve Zuber takes the podium to say there was "no hidden agenda" among Board members, that Mr. Carmean (former Superintendent) was a great man, and that Supt. Hickey's style is just totally different. Later, Zuber would tell 13abc the opposite:

> … former Washington Local School board member [Zuber] is still upset about the reprimand. Steve Zuber says, "I'm glad it's over, I believe it was a witch hunt and the good prevailed." … He says much of the district's success is because of Hickey's leadership. He says he hopes the community will remember this, when it's time to vote new board members in. He says, "There are people who have a personal agenda; personal agendas don't belong on a school board. What's lacking is common sense, you don't go after someone who puts his heart and soul, 80-100 hours a week doing his job and making people happy and serving the kids." [34]

A mother of two children in the district says through her tears, "Mr. Hickey, I love you." Hickey responds, "I love you too." She tells how Hickey asks about her children by name every time he sees her. And when her elementary school daughter was having issues, Hickey looked the girl in her face and told her how beautiful she was. This meant a lot to the girl, she says. Hickey responds to the mother and calls out to the girl in audience: "Hi [girl's name]! Good to see you! You're looking beautiful as ever!" The audience applauds.

A father whose son is in a wheelchair says that disabled students get proper attention in the district due to Hickey, "one of the greatest guys I know." Hickey responds: "I know your son. He lights me up every time I see him. He is exactly as God made him and he's a beautiful, beautiful young man."

A little girl goes to the microphone and says, "Today is my birthday and I would like the best birthday present, to have Patrick, er, Mr. Hickey, back up here" (sitting with the Board). Hickey responds by leading the audience in singing "Happy Birthday," then steps away from the Board table, walks across the room, hugs the girl, and speaks softly in her ear.

WLS Board Meeting 2015
September 16

More from Washington Local Schools
Autoplay next video

*Hickey hugs a little girl the night he was reprimanded
by the Board for his "overly personal" style.*

A young woman, a recent Whitmer High School grad, is holding back tears. She's dressed in in a sports T-shirt and athletic shorts. (See photo above.) She tells how Hickey comes into the diner where she works at least monthly:

> And Mr. Hickey comes in, and he knows me by name, he gives me a hug, and he says "Hello, beautiful. How've you been? How's college?" And then he sits and he updates me on *everything* going on... It's a pleasure to see him as often as I do anywhere that I go in this community... I am not *WLS* proud, I am proud of Superintendent Hickey and he is the reason that I love this community.

A teen girl, Madison, gets ready to speak. Hickey interrupts before she begins: "I want to caution before Madison speaks that she has spent the night at my house many times and anything that happens in that house is not for public consumption here. Now go!" (meaning *speak!*) The audience laughs.

Notably, Hickey is already violating the Board's reprimand including their warning to avoid "even the appearance of impropriety." While the girl may be a friend of his daughter, the joking allusion to the Las Vegas slogan is clearly out of bounds.

A boy appearing to be high-school age speaks, his voice quivering with emotion. He says while in elementary school he wanted to be at a special luncheon just so he could talk to Mr. Hickey. He still remembers that when he was in fourth grade, Hickey had the entire classroom chant the boy's last name over and over (as a cheer). Hickey is a "great guy." He is then so emotionally overcome that he has trouble continuing, and Hickey says: "Love you, man." Boy: "Love you, yeah." The boy's shirt reads: "I stand with Mr. Hickey."

Boy's shirt reads "I stand with Mr. Hickey." Hickey tells him, "Love you, man." The boy responds to Hickey: "Love you, yeah."

When the audience finished praising Hickey, they give him a standing ovation.

Right after the meeting, Hickey engaged in what could be considered "overly personal" greetings with his supporters in the audience. One photo on #TeamHickey shows him close against a teen girl with his arm around her shoulders. Both NBC 24 and 13abc and posted images of Hickey hugging his supporters after the meeting ended. [35]

From 13abc:

> In what looked like a receiving line after a wedding, Hickey thanked his supporters with hugs.
>
> "There's nothing sexual, there's nothing romantic, there is no finance problems, there is nothing to do with a student," says Hickey of the investigation. "I can assure the district of that. Their faith is well placed in me."

Hickey says he is restricted in what he is allowed to say about what did happen.

"My leadership style is familiar. They caution me that it may be too familiar for some people," says Hickey. "You saw me hug 300 people. If there's one in there that doesn't want a hug, they need to let me know and I won't hug them." ...

Board member David Hunter told the crowd that it's time for the district to heal and move forward... [36]

Lots of Hickey hugs after the School Board let him keep his job.

Also in that 13abc report is the WLS teachers' union President's declaration of support for Hickey. Mr. Hodnicki would later regret this statement:

Christopher Hodnicki, the President of the Teachers' Association of Washington Local Schools, released this statement Wednesday night:

"Superintendent Patrick Hickey is a phenomenal leader for Washington Local Schools and our community. His leadership, vision, dedication, and passion for Washington Local is deep, enormous, and unquestionable. The Teachers' Association of Washington Local Schools commend the school board for their meticulous review of the issue prior to rendering a decision. We trust the judgement of the school board, which based its decision on facts, and not on rumor or social media, that fueled speculation on his tenure. Guaranteeing due process while protecting the integrity of those involved speaks highly of the boards conduct on this issue. As we move forward, the teachers' association will continue the successful working relationship with Patrick Hickey and the school board. In addition, our teachers will maintain the same commitment to lifting up and making a difference in the lives of our kids each day." [36]

The Toledo Blade noted:

The letter of reprimand given to Washington Local Schools Superintendent Patrick Hickey this week has plenty to say about what he shouldn't do, but little to say about the accusations made against him...

Board President Thomas Ilstrup said Wednesday that the allegations against Mr. Hickey were serious and that his job had been on the line if the investigation had supported the allegations. Mr. Ilstrup said at the meeting that the investigation, which was conducted by legal counsel hired by the board, would remain confidential because of attorney-client privilege.

The Blade has filed a public-records request for that investigation, and is awaiting a formal response from the district. [37]

So, Ilstrup told the newspaper that the investigation did *not* support the allegations without noting what the allegations were.

The Toledo Blade sensed something was off and so filed a public records request for the investigation findings. The public would soon be able to read the emails between Hickey and the husband which gave a pretty good hint what the allegations were about. (See Chapter 13.)

Sept. 21, 2015 – Hickey rewords the reprimand, nixes further comment

After his formal reprimand, Hickey published a pre-emptive response on September 21 (on WLS letterhead), anticipating *The Toledo Blade*'s public records dump on the School Board's investigation of Anna's complaint.

Note that Hickey twists the reprimand's emphasis to imply his failing was simply being "confrontational" with WLS staff – nothing about having an "affair," or being "overly personal" or "intimidating." He declares he will have no further comment. He hides behind the "thorough investigation" by the Board's attorney.

PATRICK C. HICKEY, Ed.S.
Superintendent

Ph: 419.473.8220
Fax: 419.473.8247

washington local schools

September 21, 2015

It is my understanding that the news media has requested and received the public records regarding a "concern" raised by a staff member, and as indicated in an August 27, 2015 e-mail to the human resources director, the staff member did not wish to submit a formal complaint. On September 16, 2015, Board President Thomas Ilstrup addressed this matter in a press release in which he stated, in part: "We believe that the concerns which were brought to the attention of the Board were thoroughly investigated by legal counsel." I believe that the issues have been fully resolved to the satisfaction of everyone involved. As a result of the letter of reprimand I received, I will now be more conscious of the comments I make to male and female staff members to avoid the appearance of being confrontational.

The students in the Washington Local School District are off to a great start, and I want to see that continue. Therefore, I will not be responding to or debating any issues that may arise as a result of the records that are produced as the Board of Education, the administration, the certified and noncertified staff, the parents, the students, and the community have a right to expect my entire focus to be on the successful operation of the Washington Local School District.

Patrick Hickey

individual attention. infinite opportunities.

3505 W. Lincolnshire Blvd. Toledo, OH 43606-1299 • www.washloc.k12.oh.us

---

The *Blade*'s report, revealing Anna's complaint and the back-and-forth emails with Hickey, would be published the next day.

Sept. 23, 2015 – Anna's complaint makes front-page news

The School Board's reprimand of Hickey was announced before the public knew anything about the teacher couple's complaint against him.

On September 23 (two days after Hickey posted his "no comment" letter above), *The Toledo Blade* published Anna's complaint records [38] on page one with the headline, "*Staff member claims unwanted contact by*

Hickey." (It made the late online edition September 22.) The newspaper also published the Board's reprimand [39] and Hickey's September 21 statement. [40]

> The complaint filed by the district employee, as well as copies of emails Mr. Hickey sent to her and her husband, were provided to *The Blade* following a public records request to Washington Local Schools for a copy of the investigation report and all supporting documents. Cheryl Wolff of the law firm Spengler Nathanson responded to the request, denying the request for the investigation report because it was prepared by attorneys and was covered by attorney-client privilege.

So, the public would not see everything *some* on the Board saw, perhaps including interview transcripts with the people involved, phone texts, etc. They would see just some of Hickey's "inappropriate" communications with Anna and her husband.

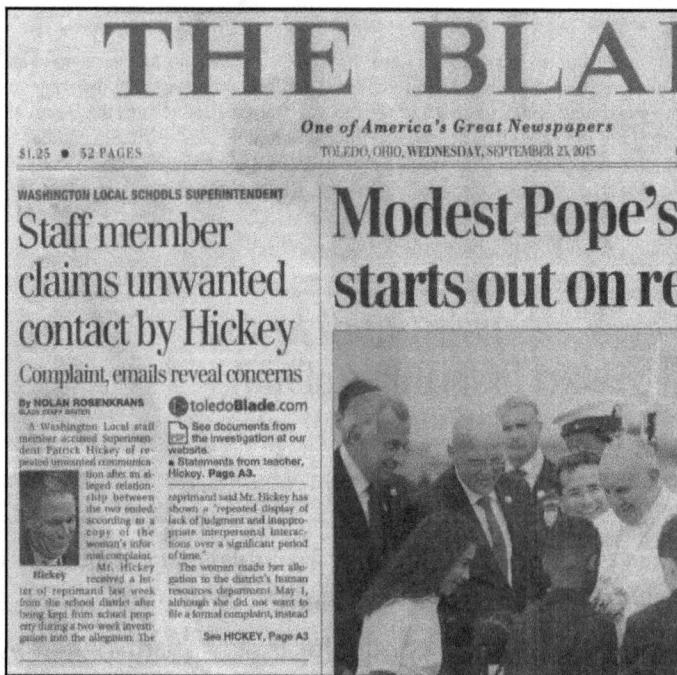

The Hickey investigation makes page 1 in the Toledo Blade, Sept. 23, 2015.

WTOL-TV 11 also published the records obtained by *The Blade* (on September 23): *"Full report of WLS superintendent's unprofessional behavior released."* [41]

WTOL was the station where investigative reporter Jonathan Walsh worked in 2007 when he spoke with victim Dawn and others in Addison regarding Hickey. Walsh's story was spiked then for lack of adequate substantiation. And in 2010, the station had tried to access Hickey's Addison personnel file. (See Chapter 9.) So WTOL was well aware of the old rumors and smelled something in the air at WLS worth following.

Social media was going crazy over the report. On September 24, blogger Chris Myers posted at *ToledoTalk.com*:

> I am sure that a lot of people feel misled now that the truth is starting to come out and Patrick Hickey's response to this whole thing is a bit shocking. Current status: Patrick Hickey's leadership is mortally wounded, the board is very weak, the district is in a bad place all because of Hickey's actions. The only way the district could move forward is for Hickey to step aside and if Hickey truly loved the district he would do this knowing he put himself, the board, and the district in a very bad spot... I doubt he will do this because he seems very arrogant. But this makes people like myself wonder what else is there, because a situation like this means there is usually more going on and an arrogant leader thinks that he can get away with other things too... The supporters are trying to justify this as two consenting adults. Baumhower is fairly quiet, stating that the documents do not say "affair" ... read between the lines. [42]

A reader responded: *"Two consenting adults* – both of whom hold public positions with one being the other's superior. Both parties should have known better but the superior needs to go ASAP."

Another wrote: "How embarrassing for both of their families that this is playing out in public. I feel sorry for those innocent bystanders of this train wreck."

Board member Patrician Carmean said that several weeks after Hickey was reprimanded by the Board and *The Blade* report was published, she apologized to Anna. "I'm sorry I did not protect you." [43] Anna later thanked Carmean for her concern and wrote to the other Board members:

> Mrs. Carmean asked a coworker for my phone number on Saturday, October 24. I called her at 11 that morning and we had a 6 minute conversation. During the course of the conversation, she apologized for not calling me sooner, asked if I was being treated fairly by my coworkers at the high school, told me I had her support and told me if I ever needed anything to call her. ... I

greatly appreciated and welcomed Mrs. Carmean reaching out to me, just as [Husband] and I have appreciated the other board members who have done the same. [44]

As we will see, the real investigation into Hickey was just beginning.

Publication of emails triggers Dawn's brother

Jim Langenderfer was just returning from a long-planned overseas vacation when *The Toledo Blade* report hit on September 23. As he was catching up with the latest developments, he received a call from "Mark," the brother of Addison victim Dawn. Mark had just read *The Blade*'s coverage of the Hickey email scandal and wanted the WLS Board to hear what Hickey had done to his sister in the late 1980s. He somehow found Langenderfer's number and hoped he would hear him out.

Mark told Langenderfer that he had tried to communicate this history to the WLS Board in 2007, but they wouldn't listen to him. Langenderfer and fellow Board member Carmean then went to meet with Mark that same day. They sensed his story was credible. He had no motive to fabricate such a story. They got Mark to put his statement in writing.

Langenderfer then hired private investigator Chris Gill to look into Mark's story and the rest of Hickey's early record. Gill got to work in October 2015.

CHAPTER 15
The 2nd Teacher & Supt. Hickey
Emails & Sightings
– 2014-2016 –

"You and I must find a venture where our amazing personality and energy will enhance people and create dollars and enrich our lives. It is out there babe."

– Hickey's email to Becca just after his resignation in Dec. 2015

Anna and her husband referred to "inappropriate" communications that Hickey sent to Anna's friend, Becca. While some of these may have been via (inaccessible) text messages or social media, some personal communications between Hickey and Becca (from 2014 through early 2016) have been retrieved.

These provide an up-close look at the techniques of an expert seducer and reveal Hickey's disingenuous nature. (Keep in mind that Becca is a young married teacher just beginning her career.)

Curiously, the School Board's investigation in September 2015 apparently failed to look into Supt. Hickey's school system emails. But Anna's complaint had referenced inappropriate communications between Becca and Hickey. Didn't the Board attorney notice that? Shouldn't the Board have been informed if anything was amiss in Hickey's communications with this second teacher?

It was Becca who had the "cat fight" with Anna in the high school cafeteria in November 2015, witnessed by hundreds of students. (See Chapter 12.) They were fighting over this man with whom they both had an inappropriate relationship.

This chapter includes private communications from two different periods.

The first group is from 2014 when Becca complained to Human Resources about Hickey's "aggressive flirtation." (The emails were acquired from a School Board member privy to the complaint.) Also around this time, Hickey reportedly told Becca that she looked "hot" dancing in the 2014 WLS promotional video "Happy." (See Chapter 12.)

The second group of emails, from 2015-2016, was on the WLS email system (acquired via public records request). The fact that Hickey had the audacity to exchange such emails on the school's system shows how arrogant and reckless he had become. After his decades of successful deception, he apparently believed he could get away with anything and no one would ever find him out (or challenge him if they did).

The later emails reveal unethical behavior between two married educators. They contain sexual content and an apparent code system for the couple's meet-ups. Hickey sometimes sends Becca his travel plans, complete with hotel reservations. He forwards her phony "weather reports" or links to his pastor's church videos (to which she doesn't respond), possibly as signals they can meet later that day. He shares information with her about Board members and school staff that she had no business seeing.

The items below from the School Board attorney's "37 Charges" document (drawn up Dec. 2015; see Chapter 17) confirm Hickey's reckless, very *public* special relationship with Becca:

> 10. During your employment as Superintendent, you engaged in an inappropriate emotional and/or sexual relationship with one or more subordinate teachers of the district.

> 25. In the fall of 2015, in violation of the September Reprimand and Directives, you worked out on more than one occasion with a certain female subordinate teacher.

> 26. In the fall of 2015, in violation of the September Reprimand and Directives, you were seen in public on more than one occasion with a certain female subordinate teacher.

> 27. In the fall of 2015, in violation of the September Reprimand and Directives, you were seen in public on more than one occasion with a certain female subordinate teacher engaging in behavior that was too personal, inappropriate, forward, and/or flirtatious.

> 28. In the fall of 2015, in violation of the September Reprimand and Directives, you continued to visit the classroom of a certain female subordinate teacher on more than once occasion.

> 29. In the fall of 2015, meetings of a district committee held at Whitmer High School were interrupted when you left to visit with the certain female subordinate teacher on more than one occasion. The committee meetings were moved to the Central Office of the district to avoid this disruption.

2014 emails

In Hickey's emails with Becca in 2014, he tells her, "you freaking rock!" He finds her "cute, blond, smart, athletic, interesting." He emails her that he is taking "pictures of his junk" for his *amour* (love) during a flight. He lets her know, "Talking smack again increases my admiration for you. Is there nothing that can reverse that trend!!" He informs her she is "UNIQUE & SPECIAL." He tells her, "I love the oddball in you...absolutely love it." They trade colonoscopy jokes.

Becca lodged a complaint with WLS Human Resources Director Nancy Brenton in the spring of 2014, concerned that Hickey's emails were "aggressively flirtatious." She "just wanted someone to know" what Hickey was up to, according to a source who spoke with Brenton. No action was taken against Hickey at the time. (The Jan. 31, 2018 Michigan State Police report confirms that a teacher filed a complaint against Hickey in 2014, but does not name the teacher.)

Becca's friend Anna was involved in a relationship with Hickey at this time, so that may have been one reason she had a problem with his flirtation. Becca became more receptive to his advances as time went on.

Below are some of the messages between Hickey and Becca from 2014.

==========================

From: Becca
To: Patrick Hickey
Date: 3/20/2014 12:04 PM
You know, before I sent the first email I contemplated instead a nice, modest response of something more like, "YOU also rock!" I figured you already knew that!

From: Patrick Hickey
To: Becca
Subject: Re: CALAMITY MAKE UP [after a school closure day]
Date: Thursday, March 20, 2014 12:06 PM
I can always benefit from hearing it.....especially from someone I admire and respect :-) Who doesn't love a compliment.
PH
PS -- I think you are amazing....so there.

PASSING the TRASH

From: Becca
To: Patrick Hickey
Date: 3/20/2014 12:34 PM
Thank you x4+3! You are quite the complimenter! Also,
a master wordist! That's like a punctuationalist -- spell check
puts squiggles under both.
I've managed to multi-task throughout this exchange. Have
you?

From: Patrick Hickey
To: Becca
Date: Thursday, March 20, 2014 12:35 PM
I multi task every minute every day.
I even sent an email to my doctor thanking her for sticking a
camera up my butt on Monday.
PH

From: Patrick Hickey
To: Becca
Date: Thursday, March 20, 2014 12:36 PM
PS thank you for the compliments and for not sticking a
camera up my butt as you are not trained in that area of
expertise.

From: Becca
To: Patrick Hickey
Date: 3/20/2014 12:37 PM
Yeah, wow, she definitely deserves some gratitude for the job
she does!
There is going to be a lot of multi-tasking through next week.
I don't know if you've heard, but I think there are some
basketball games on *right now*. And there is an app on the
iPad to let them play off to the side while I do my teacher and
[redacted] duties!

From: Patrick Hickey
To: Becca
Date: Thursday, March 20, 2014 12:41 PM
Sadly, my multi tasking is work, with work on the side, with
work on my devices, with work on my brain.
Did I tell you that you freaking rock?
PH

==============================

The next exchange about a week later begins with talk about the WLS "professional development" trips to Ron Clark Academy in Atlanta, GA, which was then a subject of debate at School Board meetings. Here we see flirtation posing as an exchange of substance, while including inappropriate personal details.

===========================

From: Becca
To: Patrick Hickey
Date: 3/26/2014 12:18 PM
All received and understood. I don't advocate for homeschooling, charter schools or private education, but I understand why Ron Paul does. There is no reason Americans cannot take back control over education in order to restore public education to what it once was. Of course, I mean without the antiquated methods and strategies. Every child can learn *something* regardless of ability level. Ron Paul and those like him support alternatives to public education because it's in such a sad state. I want to change that. This is why I love RCA [Ron Clark Academy]. Although it's a charter [it's a private school], there is no reason we can't implement their ... [cuts off]

From: Patrick Hickey
To: Becca
Date: Wednesday, March 26, 2014 12:23 PM
I understand your points fully. I like your brain.
Less government would be ideal but the horses are so very far out of the barn.
Obviously I am a believer that much of what is happening at RCA can be replicated here. It is all about Rigor, Climate, Culture, and Engagement. However, without LOVE, none of it can occur anywhere. Feel free to keep calling me a liar until you realize that I dig truth and honesty…. ALOT. I am flawed but truthful. I would be quite a fibber if I manufactured that I listen to the music he listens to.
Patrick

(Interim email from Becca to Hickey is missing.)

From: Patrick Hickey
To: Becca
Date: Wednesday, March 26, 2014 12:40 PM
You just happened into someone I admire and who young

people (including me) read and devour his words. A YA [young adult] website of his is very cool and it lists what he is reading, listening to, and watching. Somewhat narcissistic but very cool. I am an English major remember.
http://jamespattersonya.com/about
In terms of headphones, I ran from the age of 13 through 23 as a full time job. 365 days a year. It paid for my college education. It defined me. In all those years I never wore anything as I concentrated on improving and bettering myself and monitored breathing and pace and gait. Today, I run for the pure joy and rarely compete. I run in every city I visit. I become depressed when I cannot run due to injury or illness. I don't pay attention to anything regarding the actual running. I learned to love to listen to things when I run as it broke the habit of the 10 year job of monitoring. I then moved to noise canceling bose headphones so you hear absolutely nothing but the beauty of the sound. I don't find it cumbersome but I know I look goofy as fuck.
PH

From: Becca
To: Patrick Hickey
Date: 3/26/2014 12:45 PM
Gotcha. When I started running (in July 2011!) I did the ear buds thing. I got kinda tired of them so I started running with music without the ear buds. Then I got a Garmin and realized how much I enjoy not carrying anything, be it in my hand, ears, or elsewhere. I do listen to music while I'm on a treadmill usually but not with headphones. I'm the annoying person who plays music directly out of my phone until someone tells me that it's annoying.

From: Patrick Hickey
To: Becca
Date: Wednesday, March 26, 2014 12:50 PM
Who is the idiot who has a cute, blond, smart, athletic, interesting female running next to them and points out anything annoying? What an idiot.
PH

From: Patrick Hickey
To: Becca
Date: 03/26/14 3:21 PM
I use google maps as there is a reason they are taking over the world and a reason they trade at $1,131.94 a share...Ford

motor company trades at 15.25 and sirius radio at 3.00 if you
need a comparison.
Talking smack again increases my admiration for you. Is
there nothing that can reverse that trend!!
PH

From: Becca
To: Patrick Hickey
Date: 3/26/2014 4:18 PM
Is Waze the app that guides you based on road conditions? I
used to use that. I got into trouble talking smack to another
driver on Waze in a traffic jam once. Shhhhhh!

From: Becca
To: Patrick Hickey
Date: Wednesday, March 26, 2014 5:33 PM
I'm embarassed. [sic] I typed "your" in my last e-mail instead
of "you're." Ugh. I deserve punishment. Seriously, that's
horrible.

===========================

In the next exchange, Hickey tells Becca he is taking photos of his
"junk" (while on board a flight) for his *amour*:

===========================

From: Becca
To: Patrick Hickey
Subject: Re: 36000 feet
Date: Tuesday, April 8, 2014 12:44 PM
The only non work email I will be sending will be to you [her
initials here]......U R UNIQUE....SPECIAL....

From: Becca
To: Patrick Hickey
Subject: Re: 36000 feet
Date: 4/8/2014 12:46 PM
Wow! What an honor! I am definitely unique. In fact, my
superiors today told me that I'm an "oddball." They meant it
as a compliment! You've put me at ease. Mmmmm, 7:37
miles...

From: Patrick Hickey
To: Becca
Subject: Re: 36000 feet
Date: 4//8/2014 12:50 PM

Easy, I am sitting next to two French speaking dudes....bad
time!! (if there is such a thing)!!
I love the oddball in you....absolutely love it.
Passion!!
Patrick

From: Becca
To: Patrick Hickey
Subject: Re: 36000 feet
Date: 4/8/2014 2:03 PM
The Frenchmen probably like you.

From: Patrick Hickey
To: Becca
Subject: Re: 36000 feet
Date: Wednesday, April 9, 2014 1:17 PM
They did like me and were talking about me ..... no doubt?!!
Something about the fucked up American taking a picture of
his junk to send to his amour.

2015-2016 emails

By 2015, Becca was apparently engaged in a close relationship with
Hickey.

Most of the exchanges below from 2015-2016 between Hickey and
Becca were sent during the school workday. They indicate an intimate
relationship and include explicit sexual jokes (referencing oral sex,
erections, dicks, pussies, big breasts, pooping, etc.).

They exchange instructions on how to get certain emoticons to show.
Some seem to reference oral sex.

Various emails seem to be coded communications (e.g., long, phony
weather reports), and are possibly signals to meet up. Hickey sometimes
shares his travel plans (flights and hotels) with Becca.

He blind copies or forwards Becca emails involving other administrators (and even his wife). They share criticisms about district staff or
Board members. Hickey says Langenderfer has a "scattered mind and
intellect." They joke that Carmean might actually be "human" after she
sends Hickey a friendly email.

Hickey shares his dislike of particular teachers with Becca. He says of
one: "Makes me want to spew..." On another: "Absolutely ridiculous ...
unacceptable." They criticize a union leader's survey on teacher morale:
"It was poorly done and poorly written."

Becca emails Hickey about her daily issues as a teacher, sometimes expressing her frustration, for example, as "Blech."

In the fall of 2015 (after Hickey had been reprimanded by the School Board following the cursory investigation of Anna's complaint), Hickey and Becca were seen together on various occasions interacting inappropriately. Of special note was School Board member Carmean's sighting of the two at a local fitness center in late October 2015. (See Chapter 16.) That sighting and others are documented in the "37 Charges" the School Board attorney drew up in December 2015, as the Board was considering firing Hickey.

Anna admitted to a source that she and Hickey would have encounters at fitness centers, so it is likely he continued this same pattern with Becca. In April 2015, when the two women teachers were still friends, Hickey sent them both this email referencing "hot ladies" at his local gym:

> From: Patrick Hickey
> To: Anna & Becca
> Subject: FW: Ladies Locker Room, Massage Service, and Pool Closed
> Date: Tuesday, April 7, 2015 9:49:44 AM
> Those old ladies are so hot that they started the sauna on fire!!!!!!
> *"Last night Wildwood Athletic Club had a fire that was started and contained in the ladies sauna. There is water damage in the ladies locker room, massage rooms, and back hall leading to the pool. The club is open as usual with the exception of the ladies locker room, massage service, and the pool. These areas will be closed until further notice. Ladies will have access to some small lockers and the restrooms on the second floor."*

The Wildwood Athletic Club (not far from the WLS high school) is where Board member Carmean saw Hickey and Becca together in late October 2015.

Below is a sampling of emails between Hickey and Becca from early 2015 through early 2016. To start, here is their exchange on emoticons, including what looks like references to oral sex:

> RE: Restaurant Invitation to …
> **Hickey:** I am told when you put a smiley face into outlook it comes out as J? Hence I better learn to live without the smiley.
> **Becca:** It worked that time. :)
> **Hickey:** I had to override the smiley J :-)

Becca: This is a wildly inappropriate string of e-mails.
Hickey: [response is colon followed by P yielding "sticking my tongue out" emoticon, implying oral sex]
Becca: [replies with same emoticon]
Hickey: Don't do the symbols you showed me via text:-)
Becca: You mean the one that starts with an 8 and ends with ~? [sexual connotation]
Hickey: That would be the most critical one fo sho – Doesn't it end with a whole lot of ~~~~?
Becca: Only between me and you.
Hickey: Not necessarily between but sometimes between.

In one apparent meet-up code, Hickey sends Becca a video link which goes to his Cedar Creek Church pastor speaking about church business – but there's nothing of note at the 59 second mark he tells her to check. He sends this same video link on different days. In one instance, the subject heading is "Pause." Becca responds: "We're on pause?" Hickey: "I thought it was funny that my pastor used the same lingo." Becca: "So did I. Except I think he used it in a more proper context. :)"

In early January 2015, Hickey emails area Superintendents inviting them to join him in his office for morning prayers. Becca is blind copied on the email and responds, "Are you going to pray for me?"

There are silly exchanges like the next – perhaps just to stay in touch during the school day – about his bonus miles on an airline:

RE: PATRICK, Your FREE SPIRIT [airline] Statement
Hickey: I love your word pictures but as an English Teacher [Hickey referring to himself] you referred to the plane as the plan twice. I do not Spirit, I do not like them Sam I am, I do not like them as a firm, I do not like them on any term, I do not like them when they fly, I do not like them when they dry. I do not like them Sam I am. Thank you for sharing your adventure.....I like how you use words. Patrick
Becca: It's a long a. Duh.
Hickey:
ooooooooooooooooooooohhhhhhhhhhhhhhhhhhhhhhhh

Hickey and Becca share their orders for running shoes. One exchange includes this:
Becca: Does the "TRACK YOUR PACKAGE" button make only me laugh every time I look at it?
Hickey: :-) Especially with the words above it!! [which read: "Get ready to show the world your creation."]

Becca: It has so much more meaning for a man.
Hickey: ;-)

Hickey forwards emails from his buddies who go sailing together. One of the men in this group is a psychotherapist and marriage counselor. (Recall this is all *on the school email system*.) The therapist sends this to Hickey, which Hickey then forwards to Becca:

> W, YOU NEVER WERE THE FREAKIN COOK ! But I really was the captain--right--right--am I right about that -- right---after all I was able to avoid a mutiny form a group of nasty, pussy obsessed rascals for 30 years. I will now share a deep captain's secret form the Captain Survival Manual actual title is "How to survive as a Captain of a small sailboat designed to hold two persons with a motley crew of 4 very uncouth and stinky freakin passengers who thought they were a crew". From the Great Book - three rules on how to prevent mutiny...
>
> Rule 1 – Distraction. Intently focus on a rather large chested female wench on the dock and loudly whisper-wow, look at the rack on her.
>
> Rule 2 – Oral Stimulation. Interrupt the mutinous whispers by saying loudly— "The Blue Bird has a great buffet today"
>
> Rule 3 – Work Avoiding. In your best command voice shout--- "OK crew let's put up the Conestoga cover" ...at that moment all the discussion of mutiny stops as the crew quickly disperses. C finds a picnic table to lie on and reads the same book he has taken on the trip for 10 years--but each chapter is different ... Patrick very quickly put on his sneakers and jogs all the way to the next town and back while W suddenly decides to take a shower despite the fact that he took one only 2 hours ago. It seems that touching yourself approximately is more important than any mutiny. Captain, if you happen to find the cook lying in his bunk and he says he is watching the cooking channel, you might ask him why his pants are down.

Here is another joke from the buddy group that Hickey shares with Becca:

> My Female Urologist. As men age, we start seeing more of the medical world, which nowadays seems to include an increasing number of women as our physicians and therapists. And in my case, a new urologist. My family doctor recently referred me to a just-out-of-medical-school female urologist. I saw her yesterday, and she's absolutely drop-dead gorgeous as well as unbelievably

sexy. She told me that I must stop masturbating. I asked her why. She said, "Because I'm trying to examine you."

In another of the group's emails shared with Becca, the psychotherapist says to one of the buddies, "I found you a little pussy for your Big Birthday!!!" (signed "Cappy" for Captain). The fellow answers, "Well that's a switch ...... a pussy that could eat me!" Becca responds,

> **Becca:** Inappropriate.
> **Hickey:** If somebody ever requests these emails....they will think you are serious!!
> **Becca:** See my picture? THAT IS MY SERIOUS FACE! Pussy.
> **Hickey:** You, again, made me laugh. Out loud. Pussy.
> **Becca:** Inappropriate. I love cats.
> **Hickey:** As do I.
> **Becca:** You love a cat. She is white and grey.
> **Hickey:** I like all cats.....3 in particular.

Becca asks Hickey if she can come to his birthday party at a restaurant, Stella's in Perrysburg. He answers, *"Yep"* and *"Wowzers."*

Becca says a runner in a news story "can't be much younger than you." Hickey answers: "Lets find out....my mind was damaged while at Siena [college] with booze....women....and.....other stuff. PH"

Hickey forwards Becca a notice (originally sent to a group of men) of a sports awards event for his son at an away location, where "it is so fun and far enough away where we can act like kids... Road trip!" She says she'll bring the ventis (coffees). He gives her the date and time of the game. She responds: "PS, I'm all about that bass." Hickey: "Bass is a yummy fish." Becca: "No, bAss. No treble."

They arrange to run together. Hickey says, "If the golf course is deserted I can show you my high school course... Ps.....I could also show you my training regimen of sprinting tee to green and recovering green to tee." Becca answers: "Swoon."

Hickey responds to Becca about photos she has sent him: "the ... pic of you is adorbs [adorable].....how is it possible to be cute in such a stark location...but you pulled it off. I also love you in the group shot."

In late August 2015, when Hickey was on a two-week "vacation" just as the School Board was about to deal with Anna's complaint, he emails Becca about a monthly luncheon with his extended family:

> **Hickey:** I would invite [you and your husband] but i would have lots of splaining to do
> **Becca:** What about just [me]?

Hickey: Even more splaining!!!!
Becca: You are thinking about us [Becca and her husband],
right? How about [Anna and her husband]?
Hickey: Yes. And No to the latter. In my previous situation
with which we have spoken ..... we were couple friends.
Eeeekkkkkkk. PH

Note that Hickey says "we were couple friends" (apparently meaning with Anna and her husband). Does the "we" include his wife? Is he still "couple friends" with Becca and her husband?

In late September 2015, there were reports of a nearby shooting, so a lockdown of district schools was declared. Then there's this exchange on pooping:

Becca: WOW! That [Hickey's email to staff] is positive and
powerful. Keeping after it I am!
Hickey: My lovely daughter was pooping at WHS when her
father called for the lockdown!! Poor girl!! PH [Seconds later:]
Thank you PH
Becca: Wow. That's impressive. It took me a couple of
decades before I was comfortable enough to poop in public
places. Good job, dad!
Hickey: On the other hand never pooped at WHS in 4 years. I
can poop anywhere .... Anytime ..... Fyi Patrick
Becca: I think it's either a runner thing or a shame/dignity
thing.

Hickey forwards Becca his exchange with a Board member, asking him if he would be going on the "professional development" trip to Ron Clark Academy in Atlanta.

Becca: I thought you were asking me! I'll go again.
Hickey: Change your name. This will be my fourth trip ....
Whooooooofuckinghoooooo
Becca: To what?
Hickey: Anything ..... we check names against a data base.
Go as one of the dumb bunnies who hasn't gone. [He names
Teacher "LU"] PH

In another exchange, Hickey admits his "man crush" on Ron Clark, headmaster of Ron Clark Academy. He asks Becca what she thinks of Atlanta, after her "professional development" trip there. He tells her, "I like Atlanta but I have had multiple great experiences with my man crush there."

PASSING the TRASH

A nastiness is on display in this exchange that makes light of a situation where a local widow hopes to bury her veteran husband in Arlington National Cemetery but can't cover the expense. Hickey forwards this to Becca and they carry on in a cynical vein. This is from the Superintendent who has made a big deal about recognizing veterans. (From March 2015.)

> **Teacher email to Hickey:** I am watching a story on 13 ABC tonight about [Conni U-B] and wanting to go to Washington DC to bury her husband in Arlington National Cemetery but that she cannot afford to get herself there. I find it appalling that we did not know about this and that one of our own was crying on the news asking the public for money so she can get to Washington DC to have her husbands ashes put at Arlington Cemetery. After the story she had over the $1500 needed in donations but it is still sad to me. I guess I am letting you guys know, hoping that if something like this ever happens in the future that the Social Studies Department would be more than happy to make sure that a Veteran and their spouse gets to where ever it is they want to be buried without having to worry about the cost.

> **Hickey** to teacher: I had no idea.

> **Teacher:** I just learned about it from watching the news this morning. I spoke with her this morning and she just came up with the fund raising idea. I'm not sure she wanted this shared across the district.

> **Hickey to different teacher and others:** I am appalled that someone is appalled without doing their homework. Appalling. :-)

> **Becca:** I am appalled that you are appalled by the fact that someone is appalled by something so appalling. Yours in appalledness, Becca

> **Hickey:** The fact is that the situation is not appalling because it was based on incorrect assumption and now I am appalled that you are appalled that I was appalled. I am also appalled that you thought the original situation was appalling. Sincerely, Patrick

> **Becca:** You are appalling.

Just ten days before Anna and her husband would file their complaint (in late August 2015), Hickey sends a highly complimentary email to the new Human Resources Director and forwards it to Becca. (He may have known from Becca that Anna was about to file the complaint.)

> **Hickey to HR Director:** ... You know that one of my favorite quotes is "Great spirits will ALWAYS encounter violent opposition from mediocre minds". Albert Einstein said it and he was routinely attacked by mediocre minds. Know that the attacks will come. Know that I have walked this path and welcome the attacks as jealousy and evil are not in short supply in our world. Embrace the attacks......they are a clear indicator of courage and ground breaking work.

In late August, just days after Anna and her husband filed their complaint with Human Resource Director, there's this:

> **Hickey:** Sometimes your door is thankfully closed :-) You are a very good leader!!
> **Becca:** What do you mean "thankfully"? [smiley face]
> **Hickey:** Didn't we have this discussion? Trust me I am thankful. PH
> **Becca:** I was being playful, boss.
> **Hickey:** :-)
> **Becca:** [1 min later] I am doing something really fun right now.
> **Hickey:** [6 mins later] Do tell. PH
> **Becca:** I pressed "9" fifty times to delete that many voice mails. I didn't listen to any of them.
> **Hickey:** I just left you one
> **Becca:** Priority!!!!
> **Hickey:** You and I are so diff ..... I would have had to listen and follow up that I was unable to respond. You need to re-record your name.....
> **Becca:** absolutely. Oh. My. Goodness. NOT DELETING THAT ONE!!!

Hickey is forced to resign as Superintendent on December 11, 2015.

Becca continues to forward him emails from the WLS network. (His WLS email address was still functional in early 2016.) In January 2016, following an email Becca forwarded to him from the Interim Superintendent:

Hickey: [It was] My idea to get rid of kia [Kids in Action program]. Superficial bullshit. The 20 new traditions we started organically were truly kids in action. Thanks for sending.

Becca: KIA, to me, was a waste of effort and time. There were never clear expectations for teachers and student groups. I cannot tell you what exactly my students and I were supposed to be doing or why.

Hickey: Exactly!!! Hence don't do it. You and I must find a venture where our amazing personality and energy will enhance people and create dollars and enrich our lives. It is out there babe.

Hickey even forwards to Becca a very personal exchange he had with his sister in March 2016, months after his resignation, where he speaks of his suffering.

His financial aid application difficulties with his son's prospective college are also shared with this young teacher, Becca.

The emails retrieved from the WLS system end at about this time.

CHAPTER 16
Investigations Begin
Hickey Placed on Administrative Leave
– Oct.-Nov. 2015 –

School Board members Jim Langenderfer and Patricia Carmean had lingering concerns after Superintendent Hickey's formal reprimand on September 16, 2015. They believed he got off too easy in light what they had learned from the investigation of Anna's complaint. Those findings provided an adequate case for his termination, they thought. They were concerned that the district would continue to experience turmoil due to his arrogant and inappropriate style. But they were outvoted. Other Board members may have worried that terminating the litigious Hickey would prove too costly for the district.

But how embarrassing and disruptive to the district to have a Superintendent with a wandering eye and a touchy-feely style! The Board could hardly be confident that Hickey would follow the behavior guidelines laid out in their Sept. 16 reprimand. Would he really be able to change?

And there were other concerns: his mysterious absences and missed meetings during the school day; his rogue negotiations with local businesses; his favoritism among the staff; his disrespectful treatment of support staff; the questionable "professional development" trips to the private school in Atlanta; his dubious expenses submitted for reimbursement; etc.

The events of October-November 2015 would confirm Langenderfer's and Carmean's fears of more disruption by Hickey.

Langenderfer initiates investigation of Addison rumors

Sometime after seeing Anna's complaint and emails in *The Blade* (in late September), Dawn's brother Mark contacted Jim Langenderfer. He was fuming that Hickey was still in education given what had happened to his sister at Addison High School. (Mark had attempted to warn WLS about Hickey in 2007 but was brushed aside.)

Langenderfer and Patricia Carmean then met with Mark and found him credible. With his own funds, Langenderfer hired private investigator Chris Gill to look into the Addison stories. If it turned out there was nothing to them, fine. Then the air would be cleared and the rumors would stop.

Langenderfer did not view this as a rogue action, rather as an insurance policy for the WLS district. This was his community, too. He'd lived there for 40 years and both his children had gone through the Washington Local schools. He was doing this for the good of his community. If he had an "agenda," that was it.

Beginning in October, Gill spoke with many Addison residents (former students and staff) contemporary with Hickey's time at the high school. He contacted former WTOL investigative reporter, Jonathan Walsh, whose report on Hickey was spiked in 2007. He talked to Dawn's brother, Mark. And in December 2015, Dawn agreed to speak with Gill.

Langenderfer and Gill told the other School Board members what they had learned. The Board attorney would follow up starting in late November.

Media for and against Hickey

Meanwhile, Hickey got back to his public relations work as Superintendent in October, highlighting his participation in the "Panther Prowl" school fundraiser. [1] The WLS online newsletter noted that he helped a disabled girl participate in the walk, "not knowing if she would be able to maneuver the terrain in her motorized wheelchair." When Hickey featured disabled children in his posts, he garnered accolades.

In early October, criticism of Hickey heated up on social media. The community had read *The Toledo Blade* report and emails from the teachers' complaint, and they wondered about the soft discipline from the School Board. Several nasty and crude websites appeared that attacked Hickey and published raw gossip. Their titles, "Making a Predator" and "Hickey Leaks," indicate their tone. These sites were, in fact, harmful to the legitimate investigations going on and eventually ceased publication.

Hickey complains to Board about Carmean and Langenderfer

In October, Hickey complained in an email to the other three Board members that Carmean and Langenderfer were "harassing" him. [2] He said he had earlier explained to everyone "the gap in [his] work history."

He was upset that Carmean wanted to see emails between him and a female administrator.

From: Patrick Hickey
To: Tom Ilstrup; David Hunter; Eric Kiser
Subject: Harassment
Date: Saturday, October 24, 2015 4:47:13 PM

Gentlemen,
I have tried to take the high road with Mrs. Carmean and Mr. Langenderfer. I have been kind and polite. In the last two years Patty [Carmean] has requested my contract multiple times and has requested my expenses. A board member can certainly request those items. However, her behavior has become increasingly hostile. She called my previous employers and identified herself as a board member and requested information on my work history. Our attorney warned her against using her title to do things the full board has not authorized. She has repeatedly brought up the gap in my work history 25 years ago which is detailed in my application, was explained to Mr. Carmean, was explained to my last board, and was explained to her and Mr. Langenderfer.

She demanded all 35000 emails between [an administrator] and myself. When I inquired she said it was because people have been talking about an inappropriate relationship for years between [administrator] and myself. She asked about the executive physical in my contract and asked me questions about my health in violation of HIPAA. The board justifiably asked questions about my 7 year practice of buying each board member a nominal gift on their birthday. The board did their due diligence and felt the purchases were not in the public interest. I incorrectly felt that they were proper and each purchase was processed through the Treasurers office. I was not hiding anything and thought they were proper. I went so far as to pay over $2000 for the skyjump documentary for opening day despite our attorneys saying it was a proper public expense and purpose. I thought it was an olive branch in terms of expenses. Despite the board handling this situation and correcting it, Patty and Jim wrote our auditors and spoke to our auditors about the practice.

When Patty said she had no choice but to do the "right thing", I bit my tongue because her multiple recommendations for employment by her husband (and recommendations for his son's employment) violated statute but I never "did the right thing" as it would have embarrassed him, her, her family, and the district. Patty is "liking" defamatory posts about me on facebook. Our board policy and

AUP [acceptable use policy] both state that such behavior violates our policy. She has repeatedly questioned the General Truck donation despite it being explained several times. A two week investigation into [Anna's] concern resulted in a two hour executive session where I assume the situation was thoroughly explained. The culmination of the instigation resulted in a finding I did not violate our harassment policy. A letter of reprimand was delivered and accepted.

Despite this culmination Mrs. Carmean requested emails between [Anna] and myself. Today she called [Becca] and asked her for [Anna's] phone number. [Becca] was a key witness in the investigation and felt this call was extremely improper. The investigation has been high profile and is concluded. Can you imagine if I did all of these things to an employee? I am an employee. If one of my direct reports treated an employee this way there would be discipline imposed. Mr. Langenderfer has violated executive session with Mr. Peters, Mr. Bell, Mr. Johnson, and Mr Hughes. He divulged investigation information to each of them. The detail I provided is just what I can confirm. I have been given many heresay [sic] examples that are not detailed. I have concerns that Patty has provided my contract, a payroll spreadsheet and other items to a blogger who is under investigation for violating her counseling license by calling me a sociopath, narcissist, asshole, and accuses me of having sex with students and harassing staff members at WLS and my previous employers. I have been given the impression that the board "can't do anything." I need direction. My wife and I believe I am being harassed. Our HR Director reports to me. I think my next step, as an employee, is to file a complaint of harassment. I think that I would need to file it through our WLS attorney rather than our HR Department. I do not think the district needs anymore negative publicity but my health, well being, livelihood, and family are suffering due to this incessant harassment. It is my desire for this behavior to stop and for us to handle it in house but it must be addressed. I intend to bring this up at the November board meeting. Please let me know your thoughts.

Sincerely, Patrick

Hickey references Langenderfer supposedly divulging information from a School Board executive session. [3] Langenderfer – knowing what he did about Hickey's history – had in fact discussed with a community resident the possibility of that man running for School Board to oppose Hickey.

Within an hour, Hickey added a PS to his note:

From: Patrick Hickey
To: Tom Ilstrup; David Hunter; Eric Kiser
Subject: RE: Harassment
Date: Saturday, October 24, 2015 5:21:35 PM

PS While still being improper, Mrs Carmean could have asked HR for an employee number, could have asked CTC Director, or could have asked HS Principal. Patty [Carmean] called someone who confidentially testified in a very difficult circumstance [i.e., Becca against Anna]. How do you think it made [Becca] feel when a board member calls a witness [Becca] and asks for the phone number of the person she testified against [Anna]? This testimony led [Becca] to lose a friendship and take a risk to testify only to be called on a Saturday morning by a board member. She [Becca] thought her testimony was confidential.

Patrick

Hickey tangles with Board member Carmean

Tensions were high. A week after Hickey's note to the three Board members, another blow-up occurred the afternoon of October 30. [4]

Hickey's version is that Patricia Carmean followed him to a local fitness center. But she said that she was going to see about joining the fitness center herself. What makes the encounter significant is that Carmean saw Hickey and Becca exit the building at about the same time.

Carmean said she arrived at the Wildwood Athletic Club around 4:30 to inquire about a membership. When she arrived, she saw Becca leaving the gym. Carmean later stated in court that Hickey exited the gym about five minutes later. Carmean watched from her car as Hickey leaned in through Becca's open window and spoke with her for some time. Then Hickey got in his car and drove away. [5]

Hickey turned the encounter against Carmean. He claimed she was stalking him and that *he feared for his safety*.

Hickey wrote [6] to three members of the School Board at 6:16 that night (leaving Carmean and Langenderfer off the recipient list):

I left my gym this evening at 545. I was talking to someone [Becca] in the parking lot and I noticed Patty Carmeans car. I pointed out to the person [Becca] that I thought it was Patty Carmean. She [Carmean] then moved her car four spots over and hastily entered the building. I am now fearing for my safety. We must meet on this very soon. I look forward to speaking to each of you. I am fearful for the safety of my family.

Patrick

Here is the text Hickey sent to Carmean on her cell phone at 6:37 p.m. that night:

> Mrs. Carmean - following me to my gym has crossed the line as has calling employees about me. I would like this to stop immediately. I fear for my safety and that of my family. [7]

That Hickey should have feared for his safety at the hands of a petite, female senior citizen is hard to believe. He was a fit male, much younger, and about twice her weight.

Beyond a doubt, Carmean's sighting of Hickey with Becca would have put him over the edge. He must have realized others were noting that inappropriate relationship, especially after the Board's reprimand of September 16, warning him not to have "overly personal" or inappropriate interactions with staff. The list of "37 Charges" against Hickey (prepared by the School Board's attorney in Dec. 2015) verifies that in the fall of 2015:

> 25. ... in violation of the September Reprimand and Directives, you [Hickey] worked out on more than one occasion with a certain female subordinate teacher.

> 26 ... you were seen in public on more than one occasion with a certain female subordinate teacher.

The document states that others observed Hickey together with Becca multiple times. The emails between the couple (Chapter 15) hint at a sexual relationship.

Hickey criticizes Carmean in letter to entire WLS staff

Following the encounter at the fitness center, in the wee hours of Saturday, October 31, Hickey sent an email from his phone to *all 850* on the WLS staff, criticizing Carmean. [8]

> From: Patrick Hickey
> Date: 10/31/2015 12:07 AM
> To: WLS-Everyone
> Subject: Mrs. Carmean
>
> Dear Washington Local Family,

Investigations Begin; Hickey Put on Leave

I have tried to protect you from the politics of our current situation but, sadly, I can no longer do so.

Mrs. Carmean has taken it upon herself to contact some of you to discuss my leadership and relationships with each of you. Let me be emphatic and clear. Mrs. Carmean is acting alone and not with direction from the board. You have no obligation whatsoever to respond to her individual and destructive questions into my leadership. I am intensely proud of what we have accomplished together. Her email, and that of the board, are attached to this email. Please let your voice be heard about your feelings and our current path.

Mrs. Carmean, today, told our administrators and TAWLS/OAPSE [teachers' and support staff unions] leadership that morale is the lowest she has seen and she is embarassed [sic]. I might suggest that morale is awesome as evidenced by our Top Workplace designation [from two years earlier], levy victories, and excitement in our buildings. Morale may have taken a hit when administrator salaries were voted to be slashed despite an agreement to not do so in exchange for a health care percentage. To go back on our deal would be reprehensible. Morale may have been damaged when 200 teachers advocated for the finest PD [professional development trips to Ron Clark Academy in Atlanta] they have ever received. Mrs. Carmean voted no despite never visiting the school workshops.

Patrick Hickey
Superintendent - Washington Local Schools [etc]
Sent from Samsung Mobile

Later that morning, he sent the same critical email from his phone to all five Board members, including Carmean.

From: Patrick Hickey
Sent: Saturday, October 31, 2015 7:13 AM
To: WLS-Everyone
Cc: Tom Ilstrup; Sharon Giles; Jim Langenderfer; Pat Carmean; Eric Kiser; David Hunter; Jeff Fouke; Cherie Mourlam
Subject: RE: Mrs. Carmean

I did not attach the board email addresses, they are now attached. Thank you for always putting kids first despite any distractions. You are the most amazing staff in the world. Keep after it!!

Patrick

Hickey kept going and dug his hole deeper. He sent the next email a little over an hour later that Saturday morning (leaving off Carmean and Langenderfer). Note that he includes a hit on Board President Ilstrup.

> From: Patrick Hickey
> To: David Hunter; Tom Ilstrup; Eric Kiser
> Cc: Yount, Sue [Board attorney]; Dennis Pergram [Hickey's attorney]
> Subject: Mrs Carmean
> Date: Saturday, October 31, 2015 8:36:02 AM
>
> I spoke to [Board VP] Mr. Hunter last evening and once again was told there is nothing the board can do regarding Mrs. Carmeans stalking and "investigation" (which includes calling staffers during their work day and on weekends). I am confused by this response. When Mr. Ilstrup spoke to basketball families during the Bruce Smith bias case he was immediately brought into executive session and each board member made it very clear that he was being rogue and asked for the behavior to be stopped immediately. I also believe the board did not promote him from VP to President during the next cycle due to that incident. Mrs. Carmean's behavior is far more egregious (calling previous employers, repeatedly asking for my contract, violating HIPPA by asking me about my health and heart condition, insinuating an inappropriate relationship with my assistant and asking for emails, asking for emails after the investigation into me was concluded and calling the key witness to intimidate her and ask for the complaintants [sic] phone number, calling staffers at work and on weekends to ascertain if I have ever disrespected them or anyone they know and other questions in order to set up a meeting surrounding these issues, and stalking me at 6pm on a weekend at my gym). I am at a loss as to why the board is not reacting as the previous board did to Mr. Ilstrup's far less egregious behavior. It is far past time that her destructive behavior is confronted.
>
> Patrick

On November 2, Board President Ilstrup wrote to Hickey, [9] making it clear that the Board viewed his October 31 email to all WLS staff as seriously out of bounds:

Investigations Begin; Hickey Put on Leave

From: Thomas Ilstrup
To: Patrick Hickey
Cc: [Hunter, Carmean, Kiser, Langenderfer, Mourlam, Fouke,
Atty Yount]
Subject: e-Mails over the Weekend, Including at Midnight
Friday, October 30
Date: Monday, November 2, 2015 4:10:19 PM

Mr. Hickey:

I was under the distinct impression that Mr. Hunter had asked you
to call me, not that you would text me asking if "I wanted to talk,
that I should call you." Under the circumstances, frankly, I don't
believe that a one-on-one telephone conversation would be
effective in addressing, with you, the issues raised in your
weekend e-mails. I simply cannot begin to convey to you how
disappointed I am by those e-mails.

The e-mail which you sent to the staff at midnight Friday, October
30, 2015, was an attempt to silence members of the Washington
Local community, by chilling any dialog which may have
occurred/may occur with Board members. By virtue of that e-mail,
you are in violation of your letter of reprimand of September 16,
2015, insofar as your e-mail was designed to intimidate those who
HAVE expressed concerns to the Board or who MAY otherwise
express concerns in the future. You also inappropriately brought
your dispute with a Board member to the attention of all staff
members, and to the community. You used your position of
authority to attempt to influence others in with your personal
employment situation.

Though you have requested an immediate board meeting, I do not
believe that a special meeting would be good for this District –
which is my only focus and concern. We will address these issues
as adults, and speak to them specifically at the next scheduled
meeting.

In the interim, and as Board President, I specifically direct that you
disseminate no "all-WLS" e-mails, no voicemails, no tweets, and no
other communications, which discuss the Board, its members, or
any of these issues. Our staff is also especially concerned that they
are intentionally being inserted in the middle of these issues for no
good reason. I agree. That is not healthy for the District.

Moreover, your reference to my treatment in an executive session
of a previous Board was clearly designed to embarrass and
intimidate me into a course of action which I did not believe was

warranted – nor, frankly, did/does legal counsel, with whom I have been in regular contact. Furthermore, you incorrectly presumed that I thought that previous Board action was anything but intimidation; moreover, even though you opined that Mrs. Carmean's behavior was far worse than mine, you still, incorrectly, presumed that I felt that formal action was warranted – I do not.

While Mrs. Carmean's comments of last week may have been unprofessional, they were not illegal, nor unethical, especially so as to warrant formal Board action. Be that as it may, I have counseled Mrs. Carmean to be more professional in Board dealings with you, particularly in public – which is the extent that I believe is even remotely appropriate for "Board action" at this juncture.

Furthermore, whether you like it or not, as a public figure, your public presence – including your physical presence in public places, as well as e-mails, texts and tweets at all hours of the day and night – includes the legal ability of others to observe your activities and behavior. Legal counsel concurs.

In order to address your midnight e-mail, and to send a clear message to the Washington Local community that conversation with Board members is absolutely appropriate, I will be proposing the following Board resolution at the next meeting of the Board…

[He includes proposed text of a resolution to be agreed to at the Nov. 18 Board meeting, "encouraging free and open dialogue between the Board of Education and community including students and staff."]

Yours truly,
Thomas Ilstrup
President, Washington Local Schools Board of Education

Hickey then realized he'd made a mistake sending the two emails to all WLS staff and Board members, and his later email on Oct. 31. He then sent this to the Board on Nov. 2, apologizing and proposing a "third-party intervention" for Carmean and himself:

From: Patrick Hickey
To: [Board members Ilstrup, Hunter, Carmean, Kiser,
Langenderfer; Asst. Supt. Mourlam, Treasurer Fouke, Atty.
Yount]
Subject: RE: e-Mails over the Weekend, Including at Midnight
Friday, October 30 Date: Monday, Nov. 2, 2015 6:24:59 PM

Thank you Tom [Ilstrup]. Mr. Hunter told me Friday night [Oct. 30] that Mrs. Carmean is acting alone and there was nothing the board could do about it. I was confused because I had seen the board intervene previously. In that the board would not convey that she was acting alone I felt compelled because multiple staff members felt intimidated, did not want to be contacted, and asked that something be done. My email was meant to educate, not intimidate. I apologize if it was taken that way and it won't happen again. I was upset after the situation that occurred earlier that evening outside Wildwood Athletic Club. I also apologize to you because I was not trying to intimidate nor embarrass you, I was just confused about past precedent. I am sickened that you took it that way and I, again, apologize. I will comply with your directive and I firmly believe that your resolution is spot on. I also think a board retreat in the new year and/or 3rd party intervention for Mrs. Carmean and myself would be beneficial.

Respectfully,
Patrick

That same day, WLS teacher "L" wrote to the Board [10] defending Carmean and explaining that Hickey's email to all WLS staff got it wrong:

> After receiving Mr. Hickey's email this weekend I felt compelled to let my voice be heard. First, I do not feel that I need [to be] protected from our "current situation."
>
> We need strong board members and leaders who will get answers to our questions and concerns, and quite frankly will continue to ask questions. I felt Mr. Hickey's email was directed at me, as Mrs. Carmean did speak directly with me a few weeks ago ... [but] not to discuss his leadership as his email suggests... It was me, however, who had questions for her regarding our leadership in this district. I openly shared with her my concerns...
>
> The one glaring concern I have regarding the latest email from Mr. Hickey, besides the fact that I find it intimidating in nature, is that he has lied to our WLS family. Carmean is NOT acting alone in her quest for the truth. There are other board members who have reached out to our staff and are having conversations regarding our "current situation."...
>
> I would hope that the board would discuss these lies, as it seems to violate his letter of reprimand. Specifically the lines in which he is to "avoid even the appearance of retaliation" and he "must never

make comments or take actions which might be perceived as intimidating or threatening."

Anna also reacted to Hickey's email to all WLS staff. On November 3, she emailed the Board [11] disputing Hickey's portrayal of the situation and defending Carmean's actions, both in acquiring her phone number from Becca, and Carmean's "checking in" with her to see how she was doing.

> From: Anna
> To: Tom Ilstrup; Jim Langenderfer; Pat Carmean; Eric Kiser;
> David Hunter
> Subject: email
> Date: Tuesday, November 3, 2015 1:08 PM
>
> I have thought a lot about the email we [all WLS staff] received in the early morning hours Saturday [from Hickey] and I feel compelled to respond to all of you. I believe that I am at least one of the intended recipients. I wanted to let you each know, on record, about the conversation I had with Mrs. Carmean.
>
> Mrs. Carmean asked a coworker [Becca] for my phone number on Saturday, October 24. I called her [Carmean] at 11 that morning and we had a 6 minute conversation. During the course of the conversation, she apologized for not calling me sooner, asked if I was being treated fairly by my coworkers at the high school, told me I had her support and told me if I ever needed anything to call her.
>
> Contrary to the email we received, she never once asked me about the district leadership or my relationship with anyone. I greatly appreciated and welcomed Mrs. Carmean reaching out to me, just as [husband] and I have appreciated the other board members who have done the same.

The Hickey-Carmean confrontation was not over. On November 2, Carmean filed a complaint against Patrick Hickey with the Toledo Police. She cited Hickey's text message telling her she had "crossed the line" by "following" him to the gym and implying she was a threat to his personal and family's safety. And she cited his email demeaning her to the entire WLS staff. She saw all this as intimidation.

Here is the report she filed:

Investigations Begin; Hickey Put on Leave

Suspect
Name   HICKEY,PATRICK C   SSN ████████
Race   White   Sex M   Age 52   DOB 4/25/1963
Height   600   Weight 200 Hair BRO   Eye Blue
Address
   BUSINESS   3605 W LINCOLNSHIRE BLVD TOLEDO OH 43606
   HOME ADDRESS   1952 BRIM DR TOLEDO OH 43613
Phone
   CELL   (419) 261-0832
   BUSINESS   (419) 407-4070
Person Notes   SUPERINTENDENT OF WASHINGTON LOCAL SCHOOLS   RB# 054208-15

Reporting Information
Supplemental Date/Time 11/02/2015 12:49
Officer 1   8034 - BROWN,CHRISTINE
Narrative
         VICTIM STATES THAT SUSPECT, WHO IS THE SUPERINTENDENT,WASHINGTON
         LOCAL SCHOOLS SEND THE VICTIM A TEXT ON HER CELL PHONE QUOTE"MRS
         CARMEAN FOLLOWING ME TO MY GYM HAS CROSSED THE LINE AS HAS CALLING
         EMPLOYEES ABOUT ME. I WOULD LIKE THIS TO STOP IMMEDIATELY. I FEAR FOR
         MY SAFETY AND THAT OF MY FAMILY(10/30/15 1837HRS)". THIS IS JUST ONE (1) OF
         THE TEXT MESSAGE, THE SUSPECT SEND THE VICTIM PLUS 850 EMPLOYEES, A
         ORIGINAL MESSAGE ON 10/31/15 0831 AM, THIS MESSAGE TALKING ABOUT THE
         VICTIM. THE VICTIM HAS A SCREEN PRINT OF THE SCHOOL E-MAIL AND THE
         PERSONAL E-MAIL SEND TO THE VICTIM'S CELL PHONE, ON 09/16/2015 A LETTER
         WAS SEND TO THE SUSPECT, RE: REPRIMAND FOR CONDUCT UNBECOMING A
         SUPERINTENDENT, THE VICTIM HAS A COPY OF THAT LETTER. THE VICTIM WOULD
         LIKE TO FILE HARASSMENT CHARGES ON THE SUSPECT BECAUSE SHE ALSO
         FEAR FOR HER SAFETY TOO. THE VICTIM WAS ADVISED TO FOLLOW UP THIS
         INCIDENT AT THE PROSECUTOR'S OFFICE.
```

*The Toledo Blade* laid out the dispute between Hickey and Carmean:

... Mr. Hickey claims that Ms. Carmean has called staff, asking them probing questions about him, a charge Ms. Carmean says is untrue...

"He sent that email out to 850 employees. That's slander. Harassment," Ms. Carmean said. "To send that to people that I taught with? It's unfathomable that he would do something like that."

Mr. Hickey said staffers had complained to him that Ms. Carmean was investigating him and that her questions made them uncomfortable.

He framed his email as one in defense of staff. He said Ms. Carmean has made repeated allegations against him in the past and called his past employers. The pair both say they are fearful for their own safety.

Board President Thomas Ilstrup said that the school board will discuss Mr. Hickey's email at its next meeting, which is Nov. 18.

"In my opinion it may have, and that will be the basis of our discussion," he said when asked if the email had violated Mr. Hickey's letter of reprimand.
```

Ms. Carmean said she received about a dozen emails from staff following Mr. Hickey's email. She said she believes the board should discipline him, and claimed he has violated the terms of his letter of reprimand. [12]

The later list of "37 Charges" against Hickey (from Dec. 2015) agreed with Carmean: Hickey had "engaged in intimidation and/or retaliation of Mrs. Carmean."

Langenderfer's investigation reaches Board's attorney

In the first week of November an attorney for the Board, Sue Yount, called Jim Langenderfer and asked him what he knew about Hickey's time at Addison. But she did not then believe what he told her.

Around this same time, another of the Board's attorneys, Cheryl Wolff, spoke with Langenderfer and investigator Gill. They told her to call former Addison teacher Jim Driskill (who witnessed Hickey's time in Addison and was a School Board member there in 2015). They also directed her to former Addison student Brooke Brooks Kelly and others in Gill's preliminary investigative report. Wolff believed the reports about Addison after speaking with the people there.

On Nov. 18. the Board voted to have their attorney to initiate an investigation into Hickey's time at Addison.

The importance of Hickey's sudden departure from the Addison Schools in November 1990 was eventually recognized and included as the first two points in the "37 Charges" drawn up against Hickey. However, that issue was never discussed by the full Board prior to Hickey's resignation, according to Langenderfer.

According to Gill, Board members Ilstrup and Kiser did not read his preliminary report until after Hickey's resignation on December 11, 2015. Gill also suspects Hunter never read it, though he did speak with Gill about his findings.

Pro-Hickey blogger Baumhower has his own drama

In early November, pro-Hickey blogger Jeremy Baumhower (who started the campaign #IStandWithMrHickey) posted a call to defeat former OAPSE union President, Cindy Perry, in the upcoming School Board election. He said the attempted "coup" she was part of against Hickey had to be halted. [13]

The very next day, Baumhower was charged with domestic violence after having assaulted his wife in the spring of 2015. The incident apparently happened after his wife discovered evidence that he was involved in a relationship with Anna. (Baumhower stated in his iBook *Socked* that he and Anna *were* having an affair.) He was later found guilty and was sentenced in 2016.

Hickey sends incriminating email to Dawn

In early November, investigator Gill first spoke with Dawn's brother Mark. Mark had earlier given his written statement to Jim Langenderfer.

Somehow, Hickey found out that a private investigator was looking into his past at Addison High School. Who tipped him off – a friendly School Board member? This is possible, given that the Board knew that Langenderfer had hired Gill to investigate.

Hickey was also feeling the pressure of imminent Board action on his apparent violation of his September reprimand (namely, his public criticism and intimidation of Carmean).

So, it's not surprising that Hickey would take yet another erratic action around this time.

He now made a fatal mistake: He contacted Dawn and *asked her to keep quiet* about his sexual abuse of her decades earlier. Here is the message he sent her on Facebook on November 11, 2015:

Patrick Hickey   11/11 5:30pm
[Dawn,]

This is Patrick Hickey and I am sorry that I have to bother you 25 years later I have a crazy lady down here trying to dig up all kinds of dirt from Addison. I am still married to Sue and have 4 kids (a college Junior, twin Seniors in HS—one who is cognitively disabled, and a Freshman daughter. I see from Facebook that you have a wonderful family as well. This person has hired a private investigator. I would bet that he will try to contact you. If you would like to discuss this my number is 419-xxx-xxxx. I don't want your family disrupted, nor mine. The last 25 years I have pieced my work and my family back together. If you are going to talk to him, can you let me know so that I may prepare for the heartache, publicity, and destruction. If you aren't going to talk to him can you let me know that too. You can also text me at that number if you don't want to call. I hope your life is amazing.

Patrick

Hickey's Facebook message to Dawn, Nov. 11, 2015

Dawn shared the message with Gill and it was later verified by the Michigan State Police. [14] It proved to be key evidence of Hickey's guilt.

(The "crazy lady" Hickey mentions could refer to School Board member Patricia Carmean or the woman he suspected of running the gossip websites targeting him, Terri Kern.)

The message shows that he was running scared. It was not a smart move for a supposedly intelligent man.

Might Hickey also have contacted his other rumored victim at Addison High School, "Julie," with a similar request? She would not speak against Hickey, either in 1990 or in the recent investigations by Gill and the Michigan State Police. But the MSP state *there is evidence* of that relationship, without specifying what it is.

"Cat fight" in the high school cafeteria

On November 17, former friends Anna and Becca had a loud argument over Hickey in front of students in the packed high school cafeteria. Anna's husband also got involved.

The Toledo Blade had reported a week earlier that the next Board meeting would look at Hickey's possible violation of the terms of his September reprimand. [15] Later, the newspaper confirmed, "At about noon on Nov. 17, Mr. Ilstrup announced further discipline against Mr. Hickey could be forthcoming" at the next day's meeting. [16] This may have sparked the argument between the teachers.

All three teachers were suspended for the next three days. But no notice of formal disciplinary action was placed in their personnel files. [17]

This squabble naturally fueled student and staff gossip. Teachers reported that after the incident, students were talking about the women teachers' affairs with the Superintendent. It was a huge distraction for the entire school community.

This incident impacted the School Board's decision to further discipline Hickey at their meeting the next day.

Hickey seen outside Anna's classroom in locked school building

That same night (November 17), security cameras at the high school captured Hickey taking photos outside Anna's classroom after the school building was locked. Hickey said he was at the school to watch his son play basketball and that he often wandered the halls after hours to keep an eye on things.

He was photographing Board member Carmean's business card which was stuck on Anna's classroom door. According to *The Toledo Blade*, [18] Hickey "walks by the door of the teacher who claimed Mr. Hickey harassed her, stops, notes something on her door, and stays around it for a few minutes before leaving." He left, then returned to the door three more times, and took photos of the business card.

> [Board President] Mr. Ilstrup returned to the school that night, saw the surveillance video [of Hickey returning several times to the classroom] and met with concerned staff members.

> "I could see the fear in the employees' faces," he said.

> Mr. Ilstrup said Mr. Hickey was suspended [on November 18, 2015] because it could appear his returning to the door and taking pictures could be a form of harassment or intimidation, and that it also initially appeared that Mr. Hickey was trying to "frame-up" Ms. Carmean...

> "It was kind of creepy or weird that he was coming in a locked building, going in front of the classroom of the teacher who had alleged victimization," Mr. Ilstrup said. The first and second times Mr. Hickey comes to the door can be justified, he said. "But when he came in a third time, and he immediately turned and left when staff saw him, that caused me concern."

A month after the event, Interim Superintendent Cherie Mourlam tried to clear Hickey of any wrongdoing that night, explaining she had asked him to retrieve Carmean's business card (when he contacted her after seeing it on the door). "It was much to-do about nothing," she said. [19] But it is unclear why Mourlam would want the card – and why Hickey was wandering the halls and stopped by Anna's classroom to begin with.

Ilstrup later stated that this incident was not a cause for Hickey's resignation in December 2015, though it was a factor considered at the time of his suspension in November. [20]

Nov. 18 Board meeting: Hickey is "confrontational" with Board, placed on paid administrative leave

Hickey's intimidation of Mrs. Carmean, his strange behavior in the locked school building, sightings of him with Becca, and the "cat fight" between the two female teachers (with whom he had relationships) would all be discussed at the Nov. 18 Board meeting. Prior to the meeting, Board President Ilstrup told *The Toledo Blade* that the Board would:

> ... announce a "plan to move the school district forward" that could include discipline for Superintendent Patrick Hickey and "additional steps" regarding board member Patricia Carmean...

> Mr. Ilstrup said that Mr. Hickey's recent behavior may have violated the terms of the [September 16] letter of reprimand. In a statement Tuesday, Mr. Ilstrup and board Vice President David Hunter said the board will discuss at Wednesday's board meeting whether Mr. Hickey violated the letter of reprimand, and if further discipline is warranted.

> The board also plans to discuss Ms. Carmean's interactions with Mr. Hickey, and whether "additional steps may need to be taken." Mr. Ilstrup also said he will try to arrange mediation between Mr. Hickey and Ms. Carmean.

> ... In an email, Mr. Hickey said his sole focus was "teaching and learning."

> "I stand hand in hand with the board to do all we can to move this great district forward," he said. [21]

Unknown to the public, also on the Board members' minds were the stories they were hearing from Addison.

It was clearly going to be a meeting of consequence. There were policemen standing behind the Board members. Hickey was not present at the public session. [22]

Two policemen guard School Board members at the Nov. 18, 2015 meeting.

The meeting began with community comment. An angry mother, Melanie Garcia, called for "sanction" of Carmean and asked community members to sign a petition against her. Another woman called for Carmean's resignation.

Then, in a two-hour 40-minute executive session, the Board took up Hickey's latest offenses. Hickey was questioned by the Board and an angry exchange ensued.

The list of "37 Charges" later drawn up by the Board attorney confirmed: Hickey *"raised [his] voice with individual Board members and with the Board as a whole in an insubordinate, intimidating, and/or retaliatory manner."*

After Hickey left the room, the Board voted to put Hickey on paid administrative leave.

When the Board members returned to the open session, they announced only these two resolutions:

> **Resolution** that the Asst. Supt. and Human Resources Director shall report directly to the President & Board of Education on complaints/concerns about Superintendent or Board Member.

> **Resolution** encouraging free and open dialogue between Board of Education and community including students and staff. [23]

Among other things, the latter resolution underscored that Carmean had done no wrong speaking with staff about their concerns with Hickey, no matter who initiated the conversation.

In the public session, Board VP Hunter apologized to Asst. Superintendent Mourlam who, he said, was "put through the wringer," and thanked Human Resources Director Rachael Novak who was "put through fire." President Ilstrup added that they are "both true professionals."

Hunter said it was embarrassing that $35,000 was already spent on legal fees related to the scandal, but a new investigation was beginning. (What exactly would be investigated was left unspecified.) He said the WLS community was "asking for an investigation. We will find the truth and bring it to the community." He admits that teachers have been distracted by the scandal. The public must "trust us," he said.

Then at the end of the public session, Ilstrup told the audience that during the executive session, Hickey was put on paid administrative leave while the new investigation would take place. "He is not being punished," he emphasized. Ilstrup said he could make no further comment.

The Toledo Blade featured this on page one in the second section:

> Washington Local Schools has placed Superintendent Patrick Hickey on paid leave while the board investigates new, unspecified allegations against the embattled school leader.

> After a nearly three-hour, closed-door meeting Wednesday, the board took no immediate action against Mr. Hickey, but Vice President David Hunter said the board will be investigating unspecified charges.

> "We are once again going to have an investigation into all these charges," he said. "We are hearing charges from right and left."

> Mr. Hickey left the building after the closed-door portion of the session and did not participate in the open meeting. He did not return calls seeking comment Wednesday night.

> Board President Thomas Ilstrup said that the paid leave was not punishment, but will continue while Mr. Hickey is under investigation…

> While school board audiences earlier in the year were larger and seemed nearly universally in support of Mr. Hickey, Wednesday night's meeting drew a smaller crowd that was apparently divided in its support. [24]

The group of Hickey fans at the meeting may have been smaller than in September, but they were irate. The *Blade* report featured a photo of a woman calling on Langenderfer and Carmean to resign. Angry women in the audience front row held signs reading "RESIGN NOW!!"

The audio exists somewhere

Days after the Board placed Hickey on paid administrative leave (and he knew they were starting their own investigation of his time at Addison), a school employee overheard him speaking to someone on his phone while in the field house lobby. This was on or about November 20. The employee hit *record*.

The recording gave a glimpse of what went on in the Nov. 18 Board executive session, when Hickey was apparently confronted on his history at Addison. Had he violated a student there?

Joey Horan in *Belt Magazine* (March 2018) calls this one of "Hickey's 'Access Hollywood' tapes":

> One such tape, a clip of audio recorded by a WLS staff member who wished to remain anonymous for fear of retaliation, showed

Hickey privately displaying a prove-it attitude concerning the Addison allegations. The recording, later posted to an anti-Hickey Facebook page, WLS Predator Watchdog, which has since been taken down, captured a 2015 phone conversation in which Hickey said to someone on the other line, "You could bring 20 witnesses that say that I fucked students. Go ahead! Unless you have someone who says, 'I was fucked,' you have nothing." [25]

Hickey had to eat his own words in 2018. Dawn *did* come forward then and said exactly that – and she provided quite a lot of detail.

WLS Board Attorney launches new investigation

And so, the Board voted to look into in the Addison rumors. They'd also had enough of the Hickey drama tearing the district apart. The rumors had to be dealt with.

Board attorney Cheryl Wolff sent a public records request to Addison Schools for Patrick Hickey's personnel records on November 25, 2015. [26] She requested:

- Any notice of resignation
- Any agreement related to that separation from employment
- Any communications related to that separation from employment
- Any investigation report or any other records or notes dealing with allegations related to that separation from employment

The Addison Schools Superintendent responded on November 30, supplying some documents but said there are none described as "any investigation report or any other records or notes dealing with allegations related to that separation from employment." [27] (It's unclear what the unavailable last bullet point refers to. Was Addison saying there was no *police* report in the file?)

Addison Supt. Kersh's 1990 memo (see Chapter 3) addressed the reasons Hickey was convinced to leave in November 1990. The WLS attorney apparently had the Kersh memo when she drew up the list of "37 Charges" of employment violations by Hickey. That document shows that WLS knew that Hickey lied about the date and reason for his departure from Addison High School:

1. On your application for employment with the Board as Superintendent, you indicated that you left Addison Community Schools in August of 1990, which was not accurate.

2. The reasons that you provided the Board for your departure from Addison Community Schools were not accurate. You left Addison Community Schools as a result of allegations that you had a relationship with one or two students of that school district, and your relationship(s) became too close and too personal.

CHAPTER 17
Hickey Resigns as Superintendent
The 37 Charges
– December 2015 –

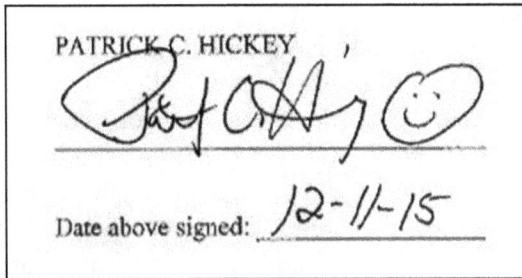

Hickey's signature on his termination agreement.

Dec. 2, 2015 School Board meeting

Patrick Hickey knew he was in big trouble with the new investigation underway by the School Board's attorney. He had been dreading this moment of truth for decades.

On December 2, 2015 the WLS Board met in executive session for only 17 minutes. [1] They reviewed their attorney's findings from her investigation of Hickey. By then, they had proof from Addison Schools that Hickey had lied on his WLS applications about the date and reason for his departure from Addison.

Board President Tom Ilstrup and the Board attorney were then quietly refining a list of 37 employment violations by Hickey ("Notice of Pre-Disciplinary Hearing and Allegations-Charges"), as well as a severance proposal. The letter containing the charges appears later in this chapter. Apparently, Ilstrup's mind was now made up on Hickey's future.

This list of "37 Charges" was compiled without input from some of the other Board members. Langenderfer, Carmean (and possibly other members of the Board) were not even aware of the list of charges at the time.

The full Board agreed at the December 2 meeting to push Hickey to resign.

Dec. 11, 2015: Supt. Hickey resigns at School Board meeting

The Toledo Blade's coverage of the Dec. 11 Board meeting began:

> The soap opera-like saga over the fate of the Washington Local Schools superintendent took another sweeping turn today when the board of education voted 5-0 to accept Patrick Hickey's resignation. [2]

Patrick Hickey was never presented with the "Notice of Pre-Disciplinary Hearing and Allegations/Charges" – the list of "37 Charges." If he had been, a hearing on those charges would have followed at the executive session of the Board meeting that night.

Hickey said he never saw the charges until they were published in *The Toledo Blade* almost two years later in October 2017, when he was running for School Board. Nor had Langenderfer and Carmean seen the document before then.

The Board attorney and President apparently determined that it was too problematic to attempt to *terminate* Hickey at this time. So, the list of charges was not made a part of his resignation agreement. [3] But the document shows where the Board President was coming from during the negotiations.

Hickey's administrative secretary, Sharon Giles, later wrote that Board VP "David Hunter directed [her] to meet Patrick off Lincolnshire [administrative office] grounds to retrieve his resignation in December, 2015" which she described as "a cowardly act." [4] (Hickey was on administrative leave at this time, so was not in the administrative offices.)

Discussions between Ilstrup, Hunter, and Hickey had led the Superintendent to agree (prior to the evening's meeting) to resign that night without any dispute. Hunter would later tell the public (in Feb. 2016) that the Board "allowed Mr. Hickey to resign in lieu of an inevitable termination of his employment, which would have resulted in his separation from Washington Local and his receiving less than one-quarter of the separation package he received." [5]

The four-minute video of the public session shows a policeman behind the Board members. Another shows a policeman at the rear of hall. Hickey was not present in the public session. About 90 members of the community were there awaiting the Board's action. [6] Several audience members still held signs reading "I Stand with Hickey," including a woman with a young child. [7]

In executive session, the Board voted 5-0 for Superintendent Hickey's resignation: "Motion to approve the resignation of Patrick Hickey effective July 31, 2016, to approve the agreement with Mr. Hickey as presented, to authorize the Board's President and Treasurer to execute the agreement." Hickey signed the separation agreement with a smiley face.

Hickey told WTOL that night that he would file a complaint with the Ohio Ethics Commission against Board members Langenderfer and Carmean for their "numerous ethics violations." A parent in the district planned to do the same, claiming Langenderfer released confidential information and asked someone to run for School Board be the "third vote" against Hickey. [8]

Hickey's termination agreement

Board President Ilstrup did not share the final terms of Hickey's severance package with the entire Board prior to obtaining Hickey's signature. In particular, Langenderfer and Carmean were not fully informed. Langenderfer believes the severance agreement was far too generous in light of what was known then about Hickey's past and recent behavior.

The agreement [9] states Hickey would be considered to be on paid administrative leave through January 2016, then on sabbatical through the end of July 2016. He would continue to receive his salary and insurance benefits through that period. His total payout was $217,000. "No evaluations, directives, or disciplinary material of any kind shall be added to Mr. Hickey's personnel file ... except as required by law."

Item 12 – which banned Hickey from school properties (unless his children were involved in an event) – would prove problematic after Hickey was elected to the WLS School Board for the term beginning January 2018.

> 12. Mr. Hickey agrees that ... he will not enter upon the grounds of any properties of the Washington Local School District, except for the purposes of attending parent-teacher conferences, athletic events, performances, or other school functions in which one of his children is a participant, or unless prior written permission is provided by the Superintendent or Board President.

(Even the exception for his children's events would be upended by the School Board within a few months.)

Hickey's public statement

Hickey did not enter the public session after the vote. The Board handed out copies of his statement to the audience:

December 11, 2015

The last 14 years serving the Washington Local community have been the most satisfying, rewarding, and successful of my 29 years in education.

To the students of Washington Local -- I will miss you. Each one of you is sunshine and hope and love in my life. You are amazing people from beautiful families. Love does not die, and my love for you will be in my heart forever. You have made me love life in powerful and eternal ways.

To my team and the teachers and support staff of Washington Local -- I love you! You are what make us "not normal." It is your love, your care, empathy, and compassion for our kids that is the wind beneath our wings. You know that the kid in front of you may just be a kid in the world, but to mom and dad and grandma and grandpa, they ARE the world. I will miss each of you in varied and different ways. ALL of you have made a profound impact on me.

To the parents in the Washington Local community -- You are the most supportive, enthusiastic, loving, and compassionate school community in the country. I was humbled to walk with you, laugh with you, cry with you, and love you. Your children were my sole purpose, my focus, and my passion. We encourage our students to find their passion and to fuel it. Your kids were my passion, and together we loved them, lifted them up, and assisted them to their destiny.

To those of you who are disappointed in my decision -- Know that I can never repay your love, support, dedication, courage, and loyalty. The last two years have been difficult, painful, and taxing. I spent inordinate hours defending myself and our work. My family suffered from horrific rumors and innuendo about their dad and husband. The dad and husband they know was not the person being vilified, mocked, and ridiculed. I apologize to you that I could no longer subject the people I love to the evil and viciousness that seemed to never end.

To my family -- Thank you for being a superintendent's wife and a superintendent's kid. I would not wish that on anyone. My love for you fills my heart to overflowing, it brings me to my knees, and it literally sustains me. You are my reason for breathing, and I will redouble my efforts to love you powerfully, unconditionally, and passionately.

I wish nothing but the best for Washington Local Schools. Together we accomplished unprecedented success. The success we had seemed complex but it was really very simple -- love kids unconditionally, lift them up, fuel their passion, embrace their beautiful diversity, and celebrate their families.

My hope is that with my departure kindness -- simple kindness -- can fill my gap.

Sincerely,
Patrick Hickey

School Board statement

The School Board issued a brief statement following the meeting entitled, "Washington Local School Board Moves Forward – Patrick Hickey Resigns."

> The Washington Local School District Board met at 5:00 on December 11 to approve the resignation of Superintendent Patrick Hickey. Mr. Hickey will remain on paid administrative leave through January, and then he has requested and the Board approved a sabbatical leave through July 31, 2016, when his resignation is effective. Mr. Hickey will not return to perform any work duties for the Washington Local Schools. Board President Thomas Ilstrup stated, "We believe that it was in the best interest of the district to approve the resignation of Mr. Hickey and the agreement with him. Cherie Mourlam was previously appointed Interim Superintendent, and she will continue in that role."

News coverage after the Dec. 11 meeting

After the meeting, WTOL found Hickey outside the room:

> [Patrick Hickey] spoke exclusively with WTOL about the decision [to resign].

> Hickey says he wishes this was a bad dream, but it's not and he doesn't want to put his family through any more.

> "I want to say to my supporters that I'm sorry I disappointed them, because they wanted me to fight and I couldn't keep fighting," he said. "I probably could have kept fighting, but it wasn't worth it to, you know, a 14-year-old girl, two 18-year-old boys. I have a kid in college. It just wasn't worth it anymore to me."

> Hickey calls the allegations against him horrific rumors and innuendo, citing problems with school board members.

> "The kids deserve my leadership, the staff deserve my leadership, but the current board of education doesn't at this point," he said.

> Some people at the school board meeting Friday agreed. They were angry at board members for Hickey's resignation. [10]

Board VP Hunter still sided with Hickey to some extent and told WTOL that he was unhappy with the Board's action. He still believed Hickey was a "great leader." But he said it's time to get back to focusing on the students. WTOL's report continued:

Hickey says that's his hope for the district, too.

"I love WLS, probably more than myself," Hickey said. "It's time for them to heal. It's time for the focus to be off me. It's time for the focus to be back on the kids. I hope they make decisions to bring in a leader who's going to love and lift up kids, because that's what we've been doing for 14 years."

The Toledo Blade gave front-page coverage to the news of Hickey's resignation. [11] Note that Hickey said he had been considering resigning for the six months prior. (He had approached Langenderfer in August, floating the idea of a buyout.)

In a telephone interview after the meeting, Mr. Hickey said the school board had agreed to pay him $217,000 in severance. He said he had contemplated his future with the district for about six months, and decided hours before the meeting he didn't want to put his family or the district through more turmoil.

"$217,000 is a lot of money. I think it's better spent on students and the district, but it allows me a couple years to move on to somewhere else where I will be appreciated and loved by a board or by a boss," he said.

Board President Thomas Ilstrup refused to comment. Immediately after the meeting, he hugged several in the audience, but walked away as a reporter asked him questions, saying he couldn't discuss details at this point…

Mr. Hickey's backers continued to express support. One described the ongoing drama as "a circus."

Another faulted board members Patricia Carmean and James Langenderfer, against whom Mr. Hickey said he plans to file complaints with the Ohio Ethics Commission.

"I feel like he was going to go anyway, one way or another. Once all this ended, who wants to stay in a district where you have specific individuals that are constantly trying to dig through your garbage and find things against you to discredit your name?" said Carly Sifuentes, a district parent…

The Blade's coverage confirms that Hunter still saw Hickey in a positive light:

Board member David Hunter called the occasion of the board's vote to accept the resignation a "terrible day." The district "lost a very good superintendent" who is a great motivator and energetic leader, he said.

"Everybody makes mistakes, and you know Patrick probably made a few that got him into these issues where you had to investigate," Mr. Hunter said. "I think with all the frustration and everything, it got [to be] too much for all of us."

A smiling Patrick Hickey, looking disheveled in T-shirt and sweatshirt, spoke with NBC 24 News after the School Board meeting on Dec. 11, 2015. He is saying, "No, it's not entirely true" that he resigned of his own accord.

Hickey told NBC 24 News his opponents are "vicious" and "evil." He said he still hoped to "love and lift up kids" – signaling his intention to somehow stay involved in education.

"We all make mistakes – Patrick might have made a few," [Board VP] Hunter said. Hunter said Hickey resigned on his own accord.

"No, it's not entirely true," Hickey told NBC 24 Friday night. "I wouldn't leave this district if it was on my own accord."

Hickey has twins who are seniors at Whitmer High School and a daughter who is a freshman.

"I wasn't going to put her through six more months of fighting and viciousness and evil."

After more than eight years as WLS superintendent, Hickey said things started to turn in the last two years – with constant battles between he [sic] and the Board of Education.

"They just made it so difficult to work and today I was thinking do I want to go through six more months of hurt and vitriol and anger? Or do I want to accept the $217,000 – which would have been much better spent on students, much better on our activities, on our athletics than on me, but I had to look out for my family. So with that offer on the table, I acquiesced to the Board's wishes and I'll be moving on to ... hopefully love and lift up kids in some way or some form." [12]

SwampBubbles blogger Chris Myers reacted:

The Washington Local School board voted 5-0 to accept Patrick Hickey's resignation this evening closing his almost 8 year stint as superintendent of Washington Local Schools.

It is an interesting development since his resignation would mean he decides to exit the system. His resignation is probably the best thing for everyone including Hickey. He can move forward quickly and not look like he has an axe to grind with the board and members of it. It is in his best interest to move forward because too much baggage would come with looking backward, but only time will tell if this is the case.

With a polarizing figure now out of the picture, things will hopefully begin to get back on an even keel and the community can come back together. [13]

But that was not to be. A commenter added:

Good. However, there are three remaining problems:

1. It still takes an enormous effort to get rid of a ruinous alpha male from a system.

2. The system is still presided over by a WL Board of Education that are obviously filled with "weak sisters". They permitted Hickey to run rampant. They all need to go.

3. Ultimately, such a Board of Education exists because the moron voters emplaced [sic] them.

It all boils down to the mental retards who purport to be the middle class, who live in the Washington Local school system, who vote like total idiots. There are just too many idiots there.

A WLS parent mourned her fallen hero the day after he resigned. She had drawn her young daughter into the salacious events surrounding his reprimand and resignation. She posted on Hickey's Facebook page:

Today I had to tell my 10 yr old 6th grader that you resigned. She cried and cried. We've been telling her as much as we could, and she sat with us to support you at the Board meetings. I'm Pissed as Hell at those crazy, hateful people! I had to explain to my daughter that there are people out there that will do ANYTHING, say ANYTHING just to HURT someone they dislike. I had to watch her eyes fill with tears as she lost some of her innocence. I had to tell her that the ADULTS, that are in charge of our school system, chased out a man of great faith and integrity – they HARASSED him and his family until he had to leave to protect his family. I am a woman of faith, and I will continue to pray for our Board Members, but I will have a vile taste in my mouth as I do...

The day after his resignation, Hickey went on Toledo talk radio (Q105.5) with host Denny Schaffer and complained about Board members Carmean and Langenderfer. He said he'd taken a polygraph test on the day of his resignation regarding his time at Addison Schools and "passed." (But he would later decline to take a polygraph test – in March 2018 at his interview with the Michigan State Police. His attorney then said he did not trust them. See Chapter 23.)

Hickey just couldn't contain his ambition. *He announced on the show that he would run for a seat on the School Board in the fall of 2017.*

37 Charges against Hickey drawn up by Board attorney

The 37 specific charges against Hickey for employment violations were compiled by the Board's attorney but were *not* delivered to Patrick Hickey (nor all Board members) in December 2015. They were not made public until *The Toledo Blade* published them in late 2017. We include the document here as evidence of what most Board members – certainly the President – knew then and believed were adequate reasons to call for Hickey's resignation.

Why wasn't the draft of the "37 Charges" shared with the whole Board in December 2015? Why didn't the Board leadership pursue terminating Hickey, instead of negotiating his resignation? Were the 37 Charges tabled in order to cover up Hickey's malfeasance? Why wasn't the entire Board included in the resignation negotiations that did take place with Hickey?

The 37-point document [14] only came to light when an anonymous source leaked it to *The Toledo Blade* in October 2017, during Hickey's campaign for a seat on the School Board. [15] (Langenderfer was not the leaker.)

The Blade explained, "Those charges were detailed in a document provided to *The Blade* that was the official notice and charges prepared to comply with state law for the termination of a teacher or superintendent." [16] *The Blade's* Oct. 2017 report clarified what happened in December 2015:

> District officials say since Mr. Hickey resigned before he could be presented with the charges, the document was not signed nor provided to him. And since he resigned, Mr. Hickey was never given a hearing to contest the charges.
>
> But the document is authentic, district Treasurer Jeff Fouke and former board chairman and current board candidate Tom Ilstrup both told *The Blade* last week.
>
> Mr. Hickey said he has never seen the document outlining the allegations against him and contends it is being used as a "political ploy" to prevent his election to the board in next month's election. [He was, however, elected in November 2017.]
>
> "The board said there was no document," he told *The Blade* last week about conversations he said he had with Washington Local officials after he resigned. "They told myself and my attorney."
>
> He denied many of the board's assertions and said if they were true he should have been fired rather than allowed to leave with a severance package of $300,000.
>
> "If these were true, I would fire me," Mr. Hickey said. "I would not give me $300,000."
>
> Mr. Ilstrup said the document was not given to Mr. Hickey because conversations between the board and Mr. Hickey turned to negotiating a severance package in exchange for his resignation, instead of termination.
>
> "As I recall, I was still in the process of discussing that with our attorney when everything sort of took a different direction," Mr. Ilstrup said.
>
> When asked why the district never made the findings of the investigation public, Mr. Ilstrup said he didn't have a good answer for that. He said he personally felt his hands were tied, as he was about to leave the board, and worried about plunging the district into a lengthy and contentious legal process while he was on his way out.

Board members said little at the time about why they paid Mr. Hickey to leave, but framed it as a way for the district to quickly move on from the months of contentious drama surrounding the former superintendent. [17]

The following pages lay out the "37 Charges" against Patrick Hickey that were never formally presented.

===============================

PASSING the TRASH

Washington Local Schools
Board of Education
3505 W. Lincolnshire Blvd
Toledo OH 43606

December 11, 2015

Via Hand Delivery
Patrick Hickey
Washington Local Schools
3505 W. Lincolnshire Blvd
Toledo OH 43606

     Re: Notice of Pre-Disciplinary Hearing and Allegations/Charges

Dear Mr. Hickey:

    This letter is to provide you with the allegations/charges against you for which the Washington Local School District Board of Education (the "Board") will consider on December 11, 2015, a resolution to suspend your contract without pay and initiate termination of your contract of employment.

    The allegations/charges against you include:

1.   On your application for employment with the Board as Superintendent, you indicated that you left Addison Community Schools in August of 1990, which was not accurate.

2.   The reasons that you provided the Board for your departure from Addison Community Schools were not accurate. You left Addison Community Schools as a result of allegations that you had a relationship with one or two students of that school district, and your relationship(s) became too close and too personal.

3.   During your employment as Superintendent, you submitted requests for reimbursements that were not for public purposes or were not authorized to be reimbursed to you. Examples include paraffin wax for services rendered to you by the cosmetology program, raffle tickets, pancake breakfast, license renewal, and BCI check.

4.   For several years, you purchased birthday gifts and get-well gifts for Board members. You gave no indication to Board members that the gifts were paid for with Board funds.

5.   During your employment as Superintendent, after you were advised that birthday gifts or get-well gifts for Board members would not be an expense for which you

5683485v1

234

would be reimbursed, you used Board credit cards to continue to make purchases for Board members from Board funds.

6. During your employment as Superintendent, you purchased clothing for yourself after the Treasurer indicated that such expenditures would not be a valid public expenditure.

7. During your employment as Superintendent, you spent Board funds to skydive with a special needs student who had already graduated from the district. Following this, the Board communicated to you that skydiving was expensive and Board funds were not to be used for you to skydive. Thereafter, you went skydiving with a WWII summer class, using Board funds to do so.

8. During 2015, you moved forward with a proposed contract between the Board and a local business without some or all of the following: appropriate information to the Board for its review, legal review, and/or buy-in of the Board. The proposed contract permitted the business to terminate the contract if you left the District, which was an inappropriate and self-serving item for you to include in the proposed contract.

9. During your employment as Superintendent, you failed to report use of sick leave or any other leave when you were absent from your work duties. Examples include:

   a. Absence due to visiting hours and funeral of your mother-in-law;
   b. Doctor's appointment for your colonoscopy;
   c. Illness that caused you to cancel a cabinet meeting, when your executive secretary indicated you were "sick as a dog";
   d. Emergency room visits for your illness.

10. During your employment as Superintendent, you engaged in an inappropriate emotional and/or sexual relationship with one or more subordinate teachers of the district.

11. From approximately the fall of 2012 through the spring of 2015, you engaged in a personal relationship with a subordinate teacher of the district, exchanging emails, test messages, private Twitter messages, and conversations of a personal nature.

12. Sometime during the last two years, you received inappropriate videos from a subordinate teacher of the district involving nudity.

   a. You were a party to the misconduct by requesting and/or encouraging that the videos be sent by the teacher, or
   b. You failed to take action to initiate discipline, corrective directives to the teacher for her misconduct, or any investigation of the misconduct, or
   c. Both a. and b.

9746196

2

235

13. You engaged in unwelcome contact and/or intimidation of a female teacher in April 2015 after your relationship with her ended. Examples included:

   a. You called her work phone several times;
   b. you left her a voice mail on her work phone;
   c. you emailed her after she asked you in writing not to send her things that were not work related (or words to that effect);
   d. you showed up at a restaurant where she and her husband were socializing;
   e. you went to her classroom to see her;
   f. you were running near the teacher's home;
   g. you drove by a park near the teacher's home.

14. You engaged in unwelcome contact, unprofessional conduct, and/or intimidation of a male teacher of the district (the husband of the female teacher with whom you had a relationship), beginning in April/May 2015. Examples included:

   a. You showed up at a restaurant where the teachers were socializing;
   b. You were running near the teacher's home;
   c. You drove by a park near the teacher's home;
   d. You emailed the teacher;
   e. You continued to email the teacher after he asked you not to email him or not to respond;
   f. Your emails to the teacher were inappropriate and unprofessional;
   g. Your emails to the teacher were intimidating;
   h. You delivered a box of items to the male teacher's school mailbox with a note indicating, among other things, that the items were given to you by his wife.

15. You were dishonest with the Board's investigator in August/September 2015. Specifically, you failed to admit the extent of the emotional and/or sexual relationship you had with a subordinate teacher.

16. In August/September 2015, you blamed a subordinate teacher for the inappropriate relationship you had with her.

17. You were issued a reprimand and directives on September 16, 2015, ("September Reprimand and Directives") for the following misconduct:

   a. Behavior toward district staff members, including the extent and volume of your communications, were perceived as overly personal, as well as inappropriate and intentionally intimidating.
   b. Your repeated display of lack of judgment and inappropriate interpersonal interactions over a significant period of time has jeopardized your leadership of the District.

18. You were directed by the September Reprimand and Directives, in part, as follows:

    "Under no circumstances are you to have any further interaction or communication with anyone you believe has lodged any concern about you, including staff members and board members, unless that communication is confined to school business.

    You are to avoid *even the appearance* of retaliation.

    You must use better judgement in your interactions with, and comments to, staff members. You must avoid any communication or action which might be perceived, in any way, as too personal, inappropriate, forward, or flirtatious; you must exercise even more caution if you must communicate with a staff member in a private setting or matter.

    Do not use private means of communication with staff members.

    You must never make comments or take actions that might be perceived as intimidating or threatening.

    ... The Board trusts that you will abide by these directives, and further cautions that your future conduct and interactions must avoid *any appearance* of impropriety. If you fail to do so, you will be further disciplined, which may include consideration of your contract for nonrenewal or termination.

    ...There is to be no retaliation against any persons who raised concerns, any staff members, or this Board or any of its members, for this letter of reprimand."

19. Following the issuance of the September Reprimand and Directives, you were dishonest with the Board, students, staff, and the community when you wrote in a district publication called "Across the Board" on or about September 16, 2015, "This reprimand has nothing to do with any romantic or sexual situation with any staff member or person. I did not have an affair or break my marriage vows to my wife of 27 years ..."

20. You further stated in the "Across the Board" article, "I have made errors and I apologize for the distractions they caused. They will not occur again." But, your behavior *has continued to cause distractions* for the district, the Board, and the staff.

21. At the September 16, 2015 Board meeting, you made remarks about how you would be using "periscoping" and you indicated you would periscope certain classes, including the courses taught the female teacher who had submitted the

informal complaint against you. Your action was in violation of the *just issued* September Reprimand and Directives.

22.   On October 31, at approximately 12:07 a.m., you sent an email to all staff members of the district, which violated the September Reprimand and Directives. Specifically, the email was intimidating, threatening, and/or stifled communications, and/or caused some staff members to feel threatened or the subject of retaliation by you.

23.   On October 31, at approximately 8:13 a.m., you sent another email to all staff of the district, which again violated the September Reprimand and Directives. Specifically, the email was intimidating, threatening, and/or stifled communications, and/or caused some staff members to feel threatened or the subject of retaliation by you.

24.   On October 31, at approximately 8:36 a.m., you sent an email to several board members in which you referenced a prior meeting involving Mr. Ilstrup, in an effort to justify your earlier all-staff emails. This email to Board members was an attempt to intimidate Board members, including Mr. Ilstrup, which again violated the September Reprimand and Directives.

25.   In the fall of 2015, in violation of the September Reprimand and Directives, you worked out on more than one occasion with a certain female subordinate teacher.

26.   In the fall of 2015, in violation of the September Reprimand and Directives, you were seen in public on more than one occasion with a certain female subordinate teacher.

27.   In the fall of 2015, in violation of the September Reprimand and Directives, you were seen with a certain female subordinate teacher engaging in behavior that was too personal, inappropriate, forward, and/or flirtatious.

28.   In the fall of 2015, in violation of the September Reprimand and Directives, you continued to visit the classroom of a certain female subordinate teacher on more than one occasion.

29.   In the fall of 2015, meetings of a district committee held at Whitmer High School were interrupted when you left to visit with the certain female subordinate teacher on more than one occasion. The committee meetings were moved to the Central Office of the district to avoid this disruption.

30.   In November of 2015, you were dishonest with a Board member about your interaction with a teacher, Matt Kizaur. Specifically, you denied to Mr. Hunter that you had spoken with Mr. Kizaur and told him to return to his classroom (or words to that effect) while he was speaking to a certain female teacher of the district.

31. Following an incident among three teachers of the district in November 2015, you requested by the Assistant Superintendent not to be in the central office when two of the teachers would be there, at 7:30 a.m. the next day. You appeared at the central office at that time anyway.

32. You engaged in intimidation and/or retaliation of Mrs. Carmean. Examples include:

    a. Your interactions with Mrs. Carmean in one or more district committee meetings at which she attended as the Board's representative was inappropriate, unprofessional, and/or retaliatory.
    b. Sending the October 31, 2015, emails to all staff referencing Mrs. Carmean.
    c. Your personal interactions with Mrs. Carmean in a public place, the parking lot at a gym.
    d. Your personal interactions with Mrs. Carmean following the encounter at the gym parking lot and your communications about that encounter in the days following it.

33. In the fall of 2015, you raised your voice with individual Board members and with the Board as a whole in an insubordinate, intimidating, and/or retaliatory manner.

34. Over the course of your employment as Superintendent, you have blind copied persons on emails, sharing district business with persons not employed by the district. This behavior has deteriorated relationships with your subordinates and Board members.

35. You have exhibited a pattern of intimidation against staff, Board members, and others.

36. Your conduct and pattern of dishonesty has resulted in a lack of trust by the Board.

37. Your conduct has resulted in a lack of trust by staff members, such that you can no longer lead the District effectively.

The above charges, each separately and independently, constitute violations of the Licensure Code of Professional Conduct for Ohio Educators and good and just cause for considering discipline, including termination of your contract of employment. Evidence to support the charges includes district records, first-hand observations, witness reports, written statements, public records, social media posts, and other evidence.

You will be provided with an opportunity to respond to the charges against you in a hearing in executive session at the meeting of the Washington Local School District Board of Education at its office on December 11, 2015, at 5:00 p.m.

Sincerely,

Jeff Fouke,
Treasurer

Cc: Dennis L. Pergram, Attorney for Patrick Hickey, via email

Note: All persons not specifically identified by name in these charges have been identified and all such names have been shared with Attorney Dennis L. Pergram by Sue W. Yount, Attorney for the Washington Local School District Board of Education on December 10, 2015, and before that date also, in prior conversations.

===============================

The 2015 drama wasn't over yet

At the December 16, 2015 Board meeting, Asst. Superintendent Cherie Mourlam was confirmed as Interim Superintendent (a title she had held since Hickey was placed on paid administrative leave on November 18).

Community members made vicious speeches calling for Langenderfer and Carmean to resign from the Board. [18] Some examples:

A parent says she is "disgusted with the blatant lack of transparency and unethical behavior of the Board." She says the taxpayers were stuck with a $30K bill for the investigation of Hickey. The only information released was the concern by the teacher whose name was leaked by Board members. The Board should release the entire official investigation, "not the one paid for by Mr. Langenderfer. I don't consider that investigation to be credible, objective, or valid," she says. The Board is aligning itself "with persons who seek to terrorize the parents and taxpayers of this district through threats and harassment." She calls on Langenderfer and Carmean to resign. (Note, however, that the Board sought Hickey's resignation *without* reference to "Langenderfer's investigation" findings.)

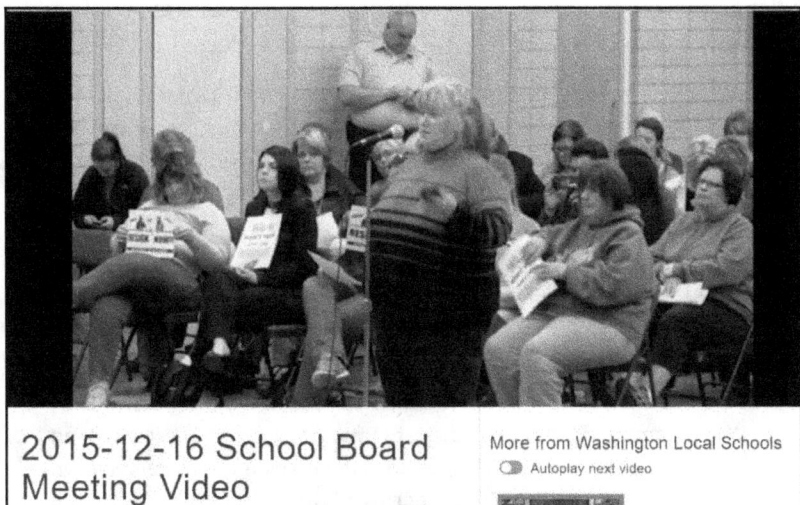

2015-12-16 School Board
Meeting Video

More from Washington Local Schools
Autoplay next video

*Angry women hold signs calling for Carmean and Langenderfer
to "RESIGN NOW!!"*

Another Hickey supporter claims that her 12-year-old granddaughter saw a Board member smiling and laughing after the last meeting (on December 11 when Hickey resigned), "when most were in tears." She cites "behind-the-scenes activity such as police reports, getting on the Board to fire Mr. Hickey, friendships you have with people who spew hate and attack citizens, threatening their jobs on social media ... or other friends who get in community members' faces..."

A woman wants Hickey to be allowed on school properties. She says that when Hickey attends events it shows someone actually cares about students and encourages them. She goes on:

> I'm appalled at the childish and petulant behavior of the district, of the Board members over the last several years, and more so over the last several months. Yet the behavior ... is nothing less than a bunch of toddlers having some temper tantrums all directed at one person. The move [to ban Hickey from school properties] was clearly spiteful and vindictive, designed to deliberately hurt someone who's done nothing more than lift the kids to succeed... If he's not allowed to attend the events, we don't want you to attend them either... We can accept nothing less than the resignations of Patricia Carmean and Jim Langenderfer from this Board.

Melanie Garcia says she is starting a petition to force the resignation of Langenderfer and Carmean. (In the fall of 2017, Garcia would run for a seat on the School Board but lose. She was later elected in 2019.)

> We have one [Langenderfer] that sits on our Board that has nothing to do [with our district] – and by the body language, you can tell that he doesn't really care to be here – doesn't listen to what people say, doesn't have the common courtesy to show up at any events or to do anything. Then we have another one on the Board [Carmean] who says the most hateful things to people, has her people come from out of district that have nothing to do here and say nothing but the most hateful things and spew nothing but venom. And you think that's OK.

> This is a district where we lift each other up. We love each other. We're family. You don't play by those rules.... There was an investigation which went on, besides the investigation we know of. And we all want to see that other half [Hickey's side of the story]. We get to see one half from a teacher; we need to see the whole thing. It's been so put out there that it's all one-sided. Nobody can see what actually went on, and I think you guys like it that way. [She demands resignations of Carmean and Langenderfer.] We have no confidence in you. You are not trustworthy; you are not truthful. You don't tell us or show us that you want to be a part of this community. You're interjecting yourself into all the events now because you think it's gonna do some kind of rally for you. It's not; it's more of a distraction. People don't want you there, and you still interject yourself. [She again calls for their resignations.]

Blogger Jeremy Baumhower posted a Change.org petition slamming Patricia Carmean:

Jeremy Baumhower
4 mins · Change.org · ✔

Although I am not a resident of Washington Local; I feel that Ms. Carmean is doing everything in her power to bring down the district.

Washington Local Board of Education: Remove Patricia Pedro Carmean from WLS Board of Education - Sign the Petition!

43 signatures are still needed!

JEREMY BAUMHOWER JUST SIGNED THIS PETITION O...

Hickey celebrates his new life

Baumhower posed with Hickey at a celebration a few days after the resignation:

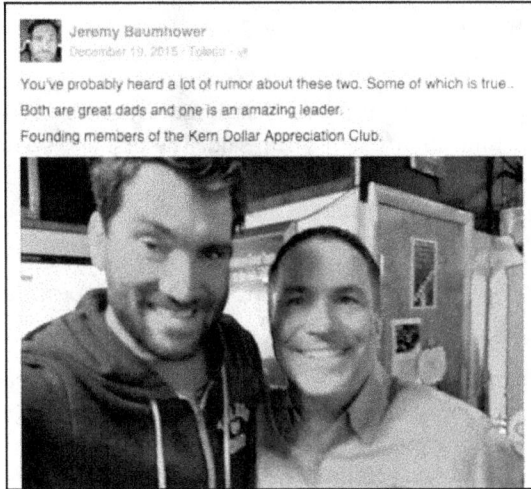

> **Jeremy Baumhower**
> December 19, 2015 · Toledo ·
>
> You've probably heard a lot of rumor about these two. Some of which is true.
> Both are great dads and one is an amazing leader.
> Founding members of the Kern Dollar Appreciation Club.

Baumhower takes a swipe at community resident Terri Kern who he believes is posting the "gossip" about Hickey from Addison sources.

As for the gossip, here's a comment at *SwampBubbles* on December 21, 2015:

> Anyone here attend the big party that some of the loyal Kool-aid drinkers gave for their messiah Patrick "too familiar" Hickey last night at Pat and Dandy's [pub]? It was a gala event. Bumhower [Baumhower] was there as well as assistant super Cherie Mourlam [now Interim Supt.]. The was a lot of hugging going on in between the tears of joy by his followers. They must of [sic] been congratulating him for beating the rap and making fools out of the BOE [Board of Education] and the taxpayers. [Interim Supt.] Mourlam, a Hick disciple will carry on his work, with his direction of course. The Hick will have a lot of time now, while he is sitting home collecting his 200K+, to keep causing dissension and animosity towards some of the BOE [Board] members and staff. Still trying to find out if [Board VP] Hunter was there paying homage to his master. This just keeps getting better! [19]

Hickey traveled to Florida the next week, accompanying his daughter and the Whitmer High School girls' basketball team.

And to end 2015, *The Toledo Blade* ran a report on December 30 (front page, second section) [20] that reviewed one of the concerns the Board had about their Superintendent. The report referred to the Nov. 17 incident when security cameras picked up Hickey outside teacher Anna's classroom door at night after the school was locked. The odd behavior was one consideration for the Board when they placed Hickey on paid administrative leave on Nov. 18.

> "It was kind of creepy or weird that he was coming in a locked building, going in front of the classroom of the teacher who had alleged victimization," Mr. Ilstrup said. The first and second times Mr. Hickey comes to the door can be justified, he said. "But when he came in a third time, and he immediately turned and left when staff saw him, that caused me concern."

But it was all innocent, according to Asst. Superintendent Cherie Mourlam:

> He said he was at the high school to watch his son play basketball, and that he occasionally walked the district's halls at night, sometimes taking pictures of student art or achievements posted on the wall... "It was much to-do about nothing," Ms. Mourlam said.

CHAPTER 18
More Investigations, More Hickey Drama
– 2016 –

The year 2016 began with two billboards popping up in the district, thanking Patrick Hickey for his "14 years of service" to Washington Local Schools. Hickey's critics believed he paid for the billboards himself. But Hickey said he didn't "know who was so kind to purchase" the billboard. From his Facebook (January 6, 2016):

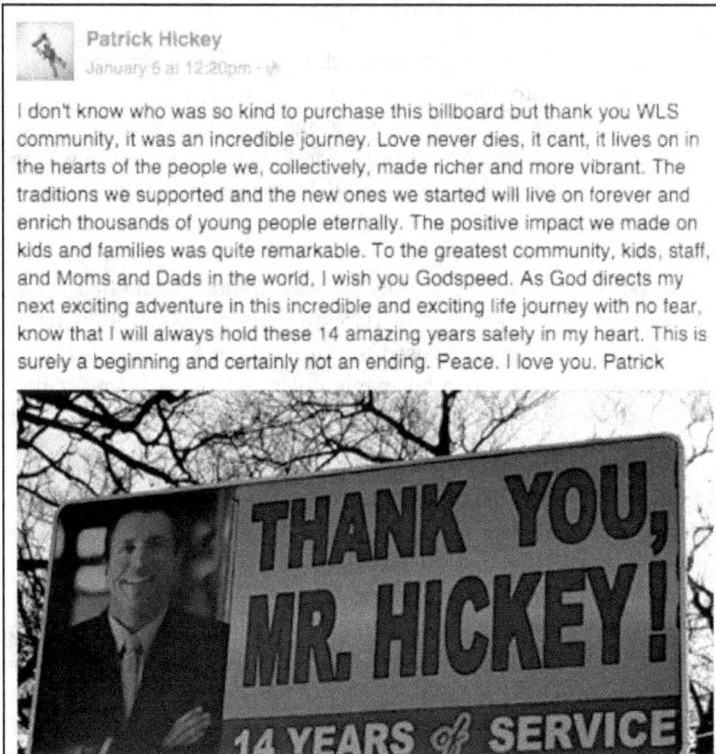

Patrick Hickey
January 6 at 12:20pm ·

I don't know who was so kind to purchase this billboard but thank you WLS community, it was an incredible journey. Love never dies, it cant, it lives on in the hearts of the people we, collectively, made richer and more vibrant. The traditions we supported and the new ones we started will live on forever and enrich thousands of young people eternally. The positive impact we made on kids and families was quite remarkable. To the greatest community, kids, staff, and Moms and Dads in the world, I wish you Godspeed. As God directs my next exciting adventure in this incredible and exciting life journey with no fear, know that I will always hold these 14 amazing years safely in my heart. This is surely a beginning and certainly not an ending. Peace. I love you. Patrick

Perhaps this was the first campaign ad for his School Board candidacy in the fall of 2017. He had announced his plan to run the day after he resigned as Superintendent.

January 2016: Dawn talks to private investigator

When first contacted by private investigator Chris Gill, Hickey's Addison victim Dawn did not want to speak with him. But then, things changed.

In late 2015, Patrick Hickey had gotten wind that an investigator was hot on his trail. He then blundered and took the incriminating step of contacting Dawn on Facebook on Nov. 11, 2015, asking her to keep quiet about what happened at Addison. (See his message to her in Chapter 16.)

Dawn did not respond to Hickey. But she preserved his Facebook message. And this unwanted contact from Hickey made her receptive to investigator Gill's request for an interview.

So, in early 2016, Dawn spoke with Gill via phone. Below are his notes from that taped conversation (dated Jan. 12, 2016) which became a part of the Michigan State Police investigation. [1]

> On listed date I was able to conduct an interview with "Dawn" to gain insight into her inappropriate sexual relationship that occurred between her, starting at the age of 14 and continuing until her graduation from High School, and Patrick Hickey who was in his mid-20's at the time. Patrick Hickey was Dawn's high school basketball coach at Addison High School in Addison, Michigan at the time. I started out by telling her that I was going to use the Jonathan Walsh [former WTOL reporter] interview she had a few years ago [2007] when he was trying to bring this out, but the news director he worked for refused to put it on the air. I assured her I was going to try to keep her name quiet as long as I can for her. Dawn states that she just wants this behind her and to get on with her life.
>
> I asked her what happened and she stated that Patrick Hickey started grooming her when she was 14 years old at the time. She states that it started as a basketball coach and an athlete just being friends and working on her basketball moves and her game in general. She states that their first time of intercourse was when Patrick Hickey took her to a basketball game in Pittsford, Michigan. She states that she waited in the car while Patrick ran into the school. She states that he was in the school for about 5 minutes and then returned to the car and stated that he had forgot his checkbook. Patrick and Dawn then returned to Patrick's home in Addison and they both went into the residence and that was the first time that they had sexual intercourse. Dawn did not allude to how many times they had sexual intercourse during this interview.

Dawn states that after her graduation from Addison High School she went on to college and Hickey sought her out after she graduated. At this time Hickey had become involved with another student by the name of "Julie"... Julie refused to speak with this investigator at the time, but [he] has recently been told she may have had a change of heart and might talk to Law Enforcement Officers.

Hickey started right out of college in 1987 [sic; 1986] at Addison H.S. He was JV coach and would stay after practice to help Dawn. She states that they would have dinner at his house with his fiancée and Hickey and Dawn would know they were having sex with each other, but Sue, his wife now, had no idea. Dawn would meet Patrick at the North Adams Cemetery and he would pick her up because she could not drive yet. He did the same exact thing with Julie. When the sexual relationship started with her [Julie], Tom Britsch, her former coach, confronted Dawn and asked if she had a sexual relationship with Hickey and at first she said no, but then called him back and came clean about the sexual relationship.

Dawn states that Hickey is very charismatic and is a good talker. He really knows how to pull you in to him.

Dawn is scared for her children ... Dawn states she is scared because you never know what someone is going to do when they are pushed into a corner, sometimes they just snap.

Dawn states that on November 11, 2015, she received an email from Hickey stating that it has taken him 25 years to rebuild his life and family and wants her to contact him in the event that she is going to talk to the Private Investigator or the media. It's all about him as it always has been [she said].

I told Dawn I'm going to use the interview she gave Jonathan Walsh and I forwarded it to her to highlight if anything he put in the interview was not her words.

She stated that she was invited and went to Patrick Hickey's wedding. She states that it never bothered Patrick that she was only 14-15-16 years old when they were having sexual intercourse. She states that she does not believe there was ever a Law Enforcement investigation into either her or Julie's sexual relationship with Hickey. Dawn forwarded the email [from Hickey on Nov. 11, 2015] for our records. Dawn was left with our phone numbers and she stated we can contact her if we have any other questions in regard to this case.

Feb. 12, 2016 – Michigan State Police open investigation

Shortly after this, Gill turned over his findings to the Michigan State Police. MSP Detective Larry Rothman then filed his initial report on the Addison findings on February 12, 2016. [2]

Rothman contacted Dawn on two occasions by phone. He confirmed the basic facts of her attendance at Addison Schools. Rothman reported:

> I then read over some of the statements she made to Chris Gill as well as the recorded statement she made to former Channel 11 News Reporter Jonathan Walsh in regards to Patrick Hickey. I was advised by Dawn that the allegations of her having a sexual relationship with Patrick Hickey were true. She stated they started having sexual intercourse when she was 14 years old and on the Junior Varsity Girls Basketball Team. She stated that her relationship with Patrick Hickey continued until she graduated from Addison High School in 1989.
>
> I advised Dawn that the relationship she had with Patrick Hickey was in fact against the law and Patrick Hickey could still be charged with a crime. I asked if she wanted to pursue charges against Mr. Hickey and she hesitated and then said, "no". Dawn stated that she is currently happily married and has children. She stated one of her children is currently going to college ... and she has some concerns about their safety. She stated what happened between her and Patrick Hickey was a long time ago and that even though she knows the relationship was wrong she has suffered no ill effect from it. She stated that as long as Mr. Hickey is no longer having those sorts of relationships with young girls then she does not want to disrupt her life for something that happened so long ago. She did say however if there we [were] other victims then she would gladly come forward and pursue the issue.
>
> I asked Dawn if Patrick Hickey made contact with her via her Facebook account and she stated he did. She stated he had sent her a Facebook Private Message on 11-11-2015.

2nd Addison student denies relationship with Hickey

Might Hickey have sent a message to "Julie" – his alleged second Addison victim – similar to what he sent Dawn in November 2015? Did he ask Julie not to speak with investigators?

Julie was the girl whom Mrs. Brooks and her daughter Brooke saw in the bouncing car with Patrick Hickey at a local cemetery one night. When Mrs. Brooks reported that sighting, it triggered the Addison administration's brief internal investigation of Hickey in the fall of 1990 and resulted in his abrupt resignation.

Julie had earlier refused to talk to investigator Gill in late 2015, slamming her door in his face. In early 2016, MSP Detective Rothman traveled to Julie's home but there was no answer at the door. He left his business card and later that day received a phone call from her. After Rothman explained the reason for his contact, Julie...

> ... sounded as if she were upset and frustrated over the phone. She stated at no time did she and Patrick Hickey have sex or have a relationship of any kind. She stated all of the allegations involving her and Patrick Hickey were untrue and she is frustrated with people calling her and disrupting her family. Julie stated she had nothing else to say and then we ended the phone call.

> NOTE: I found "Julie" very agitated and frustrated with my phone call. She stated she has been contacted by private investigators and others who continue to try to dig things up that are not true and she stated she has no interest in a "witch hunt" against Mr. Hickey.

Hickey not charged, case put on hold; Dawn did not want to proceed

Detective Rothman wrote in his March 23, 2016 wrap-up: "Based on the fact that no victims want to come forward and pursue the complaint I felt no need to contact Patrick Hickey at this time."

On April 21, 2016, the Lenawee Country Prosecutor's office declined to authorize criminal charges against Patrick Hickey. The May 13, 2016 MSP document states:

> Victim [Dawn] has requested "no authorization," is uncooperative or cannot prove adequate facts. Furthermore, this appears to have been reported well outside the statute of limitations for the alleged crime. If further information becomes available please resubmit.

The Detective's report noted that the information surrounding Hickey's resignation from Washington Local Schools showed "a continued pattern of behavior on his part" (with women subordinate employees) that might lend credence to earlier stories of malfeasance.

Dawn would later change her mind in November 2017 and ask the MSP to proceed with an investigation (which was then reopened in January 2018).

On the question of the statute of limitations, the Prosecutors later determined that Michigan law would allow prosecution of this sort of crime even decades later, since Hickey was not a state resident in the years after the incident, the victim was underage at the time, and it was a teacher/student relationship.

2016 School Board

The School Board President at Hickey's resignation , Tom Ilstrup, had ended his term. The new 2016 School Board President was David Hunter, who had repeatedly praised Hickey during the scandal-filled year 2015. New Board member Lisa Canales was a long-time Hickey supporter and had been Board President when Hickey was promoted to Superintendent in 2007. Canales was now the new Board VP. Jim Langenderfer and Patricia Carmean were still on the Board (through 2017). [3]

Elected Officers: **President Hunter, VP Canales**

SEATED: Superintendent **Cherie Mourlam**, Board President **David Hunter**, Board Vice President **Lisa Canales**, Treasurer **Jeff Fouke**.

STANDING: Board members **James Langenderfer**, **Patricia Pedro Carmean**, and **Eric Kiser**.

Hickey flips out at Feb. 12 basketball game

Patrick Hickey was no longer Superintendent. The terms of his resignation included his ban from Washington Local Schools properties, unless attending one of his children's school activities.

On the night of February 12 – the same day the initial Michigan State Police investigation report was filed – Hickey attended the Whitmer High School boys' basketball game. Because his son was playing, Hickey was allowed on school property.

During the game, Hickey totally lost control in an altercation with the referees and Athletic Director. He yelled at them and refused the authorities' requests to leave the court baseline.

It was first reported that the Athletic Director removed Hickey "from the gym three separate times, and each time he removed him, Mr. Hickey would appear from another door. On the last occasion, while in the corridor, Mr. Hickey was yelling and became verbally abusive" to the Athletic Director. If it had been any parent other than Hickey, the Athletic Director said, "he would have had him arrested and law enforcement may have done more."

To top it off, Hickey assaulted Interim Supt. Cherie Mourlam with unwanted embraces. For some time, she struggled to free herself as the entire gymnasium full of people watched in amazement.

According to Hunter's later statement (on behalf of the Board): "His arms were wrapped around her in a hug; she had her arms down at her sides." Twice Hickey loudly said to her, "Are you afraid you'll get in trouble?" And as she continued to try to break free, he said, "Are you trying to get away from me?" Then he released her. "The whole scene last night was extremely embarrassing for the district, most uncomfortable, and unwanted by Mrs. Mourlam." The High School Principal and Athletic Director "were trying to deal with a man that at one time they had utter respect for and who was their boss... both were shaken up very badly by these incidents."

NBC 24 News quoted Board President Hunter:

> What I saw [at the game] just wasn't the Mr. Hickey that we all know. It was very strange, it was embarrassing, it put our athletic director and our school principal in a really strange situation. They were very, very upset as was I. I felt myself in a position to have to apologize for behaviors. It was almost surreal watching this unfold... [4]

The station also noted:

> Hickey's son, who plays on the Whitmer basketball team, tweeted a photo with the following on Saturday: "Didn't know being passionate and getting upset at a bball game was a crime. WLS board needs to worry about doing their jobs rather than bothering a man trying to support his family." [5]

Could Hickey's erratic behavior have been triggered by knowledge of the first filing by Michigan State Police investigators? Someone might have tipped him off. The date coincidence is certainly odd.

Blogger Jeremy Baumhower explained (in his iBook *Socked*) that Hickey's behavior followed a sleepless night before the day of the basketball game:

> On Thursday, February 11, the night before Patrick Hickey's public meltdown, an audio clip was released by "David Morgan" on Facebook. It was 9 seconds of muffled audio that had proclaimed Hickey's admission of guilt. It was anything but.
>
> The audio link was uploaded as a Facebook video. The video portion displayed the "Thank You Mr. Hickey" billboard and then scrolled the words. This link was repeatedly sent to Hickey and he was not bothered by what he had allegedly said, but how he was recorded. Hickey was convinced the brief audio was a recording from a board member during executive session… It was not. It was part of a seven-minute recording by someone standing next to him, as he talked on the phone. The conversation had taken place months before [Nov. 2015 in the field house lobby].
>
> That Thursday night, after receiving the video, Hickey did not sleep… Hickey was obsessed with trying to remember when he said those words… The lack of sleep stemming from the "leaked audio" combined with the ruthless attacks on him and his family, and a close basketball game with rising tension, caused him to snap.
>
> Hours after the basketball incident, the emergency WLS board meeting [Feb. 13] and another website was launched. [The anti-Hickey website] featured the entire seven-minute phone call of which [sic] the audio clip was lifted. It shared details of when it was recorded as well [as] the transcript. The full audio proved nothing new but gave insight into what Hickey had been saying the months previous: "Prove it." [6]

Baumhower failed to quote some of the telling lines from the audio. Hickey said, "You could bring 20 witnesses that say that I fucked students. Go ahead! Unless you have someone who says, '*I was fucked*,' you have *nothing*." (See Chapter 16.)

Feb. 13 – School Board calls emergency meeting

The day after the fiasco at the basketball game, February 13, the School Board called an emergency meeting. Board President Hunter read a statement to the audience describing Hickey's disturbance. He noted that the Board "allowed Mr. Hickey to resign in lieu of an inevitable termination of his employment, which would have resulted in his separation from Washington Local and his receiving less than one-quarter of the separation package he received." [7]

February 13, 2016

The Washington Local Board of Education met in emergency session pursuant to the rules in the Administration Building, 3505 West Lincolnshire Boulevard on February 13, 2016 at 11:00 a.m. The following members were present:

Mrs. Patricia Carmean	Also, Mrs. Cherie Mourlam, Superintendent,
Mr. Eric Kiser	and Mr. Jeffery Fouke, Treasurer.
Mr. David Hunter	
Ms. Lisa Canales	
Mr. James Langenderfer	

Mr. Hunter asks for a moment of silence in honor of Mr. Frank Erne. | **Moment of Silence:**

It was moved by Mr. Langenderfer and seconded by Mr. Kiser to accept the Superintendent's recommendation to enter into Executive Session to: | **Executive Session: 142-2/16**

    4. Consider the discipline of a public employee or official.

Yes: Mr. Kiser, Mrs. Carmean, Mr. Hunter, Ms. Canales, Mr. Langenderfer (5)

The Board entered into Executive Session at 11:03 a.m. The meeting was reconvened at 11:50 a.m. and did, in fact:

    4. Consider the discipline of a public employee or official.

All five board members are still in attendance.

Board President, Mr. Hunter, addressed the audience regarding an issue that occurred at the Whitmer boys' basketball game involving Mr. Patrick Hickey. | **Board Comment:**

"One of the promises that this 2016 Board of Education made to the community was that we were going to move forward and put the past behind us. We promised to place the students of our district first. We also promised to be as forthcoming, honest, and transparent as allowed by law.
It's for this reason we call this special emergency meeting of the Board.
Last year there were lots of questions concerning the investigations, allegations, and resignation of Mr. Hickey that we, as a board, were not allowed to discuss publicly, due to attorney/client privilege and Executive Session mandates.

Last night, at our boys' varsity basketball game against Lima Senior, several incidents occurred that were disturbing, disruptive, embarrassing, and inappropriate. I know that the rumors are flying and that the social media is a "buzz" again. It's for this reason that we're going to set the record straight and make sure the facts about the board actions resulting from these incidents are understood and not exaggerated.

Last year, the board allowed Mr. Hickey to resign in lieu of an inevitable termination of his employment, which would have resulted in his separation from Washington Local and his receiving less than one-quarter of the separation package he received. Part of that separation resignation

---

Board Comment- Continued: package included a stipulation that Patrick will not be allowed on Washington Local property. This was done, in fact, that several of the allegations made against him included charges that he was harassing members of our staff. I urged my fellow board members to allow Patrick to attend activities and sporting events that his children were involved in and I felt, as a father of three, who plays sports myself, that this was a nice thing to do. Last night, during the course of the boys' basketball game, Mr. Hickey, became very verbally aggressive and began to shout out at the referees. He moved from his seat in the stands to the far corner of the gym, located down the out-of-bounds lines were Whitmer basketball players would enter the hallway to go to the locker.

From this point, Mr. Hickey, made a comment to the referees to the point where the referees had to ask the Athletic Director to remove him from the gym. Mr. Snook was forced to remove him from the gym three separate times, and each time he removed him, Mr. Hickey would appear from another door. On the last occasion, while in the corridor, Mr. Hickey was yelling and became verbally abusive to Mr. Snook.

I also learned that earlier in the game, Mr. Hickey, approached our Superintendent, Mrs. Mourlam. His arms were wrapped around her in a hug; she had her arms down at her sides. When she did not reciprocate the hug he became agitated and began saying, "Are you afraid you'll get in trouble?" "Are you afraid you'll get in trouble?" Mrs. Mourlam tried to move away from Patrick and he would not let her go. He said "Are you trying to get away from me?" "Are you trying to get away from me?" and at that point he released her.

This whole scene last night was extremely embarrassing for the district, most uncomfortable, and unwanted by Mrs. Mourlam. When I asked Mr. Snook what would he have done had we been any other parent other than Mr. Hickey? He responded that he would have had him arrested and law enforcement may have done more.

I would like to make it very clear that this board does not fault Mr. Snook or Mrs. Martin, our high school principal, who are also present and extremely upset and embarrassed by Mr. Hickey's behavior. Rather, under circumstances considering they were trying to deal with a man that at one time they had utter respect for and who was their boss, they did as great a job as they could to control the situation. When spoken to after the game and Mr. Hickey had left the building, both were shaken up very badly by these incidents. They were at this time promised that action would be taken by this board to make sure neither of them would be put in this type of situation again as was Mrs. Mourlam.

It is for this reason that after speaking with our board attorney who has been in contact with Mr. Hickey's council, that I am requesting a board motion, from this board, to prohibit Mr. Hickey from coming to school functions on board property. I have a resolution that each board member has that was prepared by our attorney."

> It was moved by Mr. Langenderfer and seconded by Mrs. Carmean to accept Board President, Mr. Hunter's recommendation to prohibit Mr. Hickey from coming to school functions on Board property as presented:
>
> *Resolution Re:Patrick Hickey-143-2/16*
>
> ### Resolution
>
> Whereas, on February 12, 2016, Patrick Hickey reportedly engaged in inappropriate conduct at a Whitmer High School boys' basketball game, and specifically, Mr. Hickey:
>
> 1. engaged in inappropriate and/or abusive conduct toward one of the officials of the game;
> 2. was directed by a game official to leave the game;
> 3. was escorted out of the Whitmer High School gymnasium two or three times;
> 4. returned into the gymnasium after being escorted out of the gymnasium two or three times;
> 5. was verbally confrontational with the district's Athletic Director during the game; and
> 6. embraced another district administrator and continued to embrace the administrator despite her attempts to push Mr. Hickey away, while he was at the game.
>
> Now therefore, be it resolved that:
>
> 1. As a result of the safety concerns for its employees and the need to maintain decorum and order at its school functions, Mr. Patrick Hickey shall not be allowed to come onto Board premises, and he shall not be permitted to attend any function of the Washington Local Schools on property owned or controlled by the Board, effective following the hearing with the Board in item 2. below and until further action of this Board;
> 2. Mr. Patrick Hickey shall be provided with notice of this action, and an opportunity in executive session of this Board at 5 p.m., on Monday, February 15, 2016, to respond to the charges contained in this resolution and to otherwise explain his actions.
>
> Yes: Mrs. Carmean, Mr. Hunter, Ms. Canales, Mr. Langenderfer, Mr. Kiser (5)

The entire Board then approved a resolution to temporarily ban Hickey from *all* WLS properties and events until the Board could take further action.

Feb. 15 School Board action: Hickey banned from school properties - even his children's events

Hickey was then given a chance to respond to the charges before the Board in a meeting on February 15. [8] He was present at the executive session, and his attorney participated via conference call. His statement (below) was then considered by the Board. (Board President Hunter initially refused to release Hickey's statement to the public.)

Hickey's statement tells a different story about his interactions with the referees. And he sees nothing wrong with his over-the-top physicality with women. His excuse for giving Interim Supt. Mourlam a bear hug is that they "have been colleagues and friends for many years." He said they have "publicly hugged each other a countless number of times," and he did not realize "that she was trying to break away" from him.

February 15, 2016

Board of Education of the Washington Local School District

**RESPONSE TO CHARGES SET FORTH IN
BOARD OF EDUCATION RESOLUTION**

As you know, Cherie Mourlam and I have been colleagues and friends for many years. We have publicly hugged each other a countless number of times. I am sorry for embarrassing her and did not perceive that she was trying to break away from my hug.

I received via e-mail a document titled Resolution pertaining the evening of February 12, 2016 at the Whitmer High School boys basketball game. I was sitting at the game with my wife, and as a fan, I made remarks to one of the officials. Being an official myself, I noticed the official making eye contact with me and sensed his displeasure with my remarks. Therefore, I left my seat and stood with Athletic Director Snook at the end of the gymnasium and continued to observe the basketball game with Mr. Snook.

I did not perceive any of the officials directing me to leave the gymnasium, but apparently Mr. Snook heard or perceived something and advised me to go upstairs. On my way toward the upstairs, I saw Brian Meyer and stopped to watch the game with him rather than going upstairs. Mr. Snook saw that I had not gone upstairs and was visibly upset and yelled at me to get out and go home. I did exchange words as I left, telling him that I have supported him and that I was upset and embarrassed that he had ordered me to leave the gym. Nonetheless, I left.

I have sent an e-mail to the official apologizing to him for my remarks.

I have shared your resolution with Brian Meyer, the director of security, and he has first-hand knowledge as to what happened and does not agree with all of the facts set forth in the resolution.

My presence at Friday night's basketball game was to support the basketball team and my son and I apologize for any attention that was drawn to me and for embarrassment to the Board, the district, and my family. As you know, social media has ran rampant with defamatory statements about me and I have taken down my Twitter account and Facebook page that had close to 6,000 followers. I am not seeking media attention. Quite to the contrary, although I was contacted by the media today, I informed the media that I would not speak to them. Nonetheless, it was reported by the Board's attorney to my attorney that I was contacting radio stations to plead with them to allow me to speak on the radio and that, in fact, one of the radio stations called the Board president to ask me to stop. After my attorney made further inquiry, he was informed that the facts relayed to him were not accurate and that I had, in fact, refused to speak to the news media. Quite frankly, I do not know how my refusal to speak with the news media gets translated to the false assertion that I have been pleading with the news media to put me on the radio and that someone from the radio station had to call the Board president to ask that I quit contacting them.

I trust that I have adequately responded to the Resolution as I have been asked to do.

Patrick Hickey

The Board found Hickey's excuses inadequate and voted unanimously for a longer resolution (below) which *completely* banned him from school properties, not even allowing him to attend his children's events. The Board's attorney later wrote to Hickey's attorney,

"Mr. Hickey certainly was provided with due process of law before the ban was adopted by the Board."

Resolution

Whereas, on February 12, 2016, Patrick Hickey reportedly engaged in inappropriate conduct at a Whitmer High School boys' basketball game, and specifically, Mr. Hickey:

1. engaged in inappropriate and/or abusive conduct toward one of the officials of the game;
2. was directed by a game official to leave the game;
3. was escorted out of Whitmer High School gymnasium two or three times;
4. returned into the gymnasium after being escorted out of the gymnasium two or three times;
5. was verbally confrontational with the district's Athletic Director during the game; and
6. embraced another district administrator and continued to embrace the administrator despite her attempts to push Mr. Hickey away, while he was at the game.

Whereas, Mr. Hickey was provided with notice of the charges against him and notice of an opportunity at 5:00 p.m. on February 15, 2016, to appear before this Board in executive session to respond to the charges and to otherwise explain his actions.

Whereas, Mr. Hickey was provided with an opportunity to present a response to the charges and to otherwise explain his actions on February 15, 2016, and the Board has considered all of Mr. Hickey's responses to the charges.

Now therefore, be it resolved that:

1. The Board hereby finds that during the Whitmer High School Boys' Basketball game on February 12, 2016, Mr. Patrick Hickey was not asked to leave the facility by an official of the game, but rather the official asked that Mr. Hickey be removed from standing on the baseline, and Mr. Hickey did not comply.

2. The Board further finds that Mr. Patrick Hickey engaged in inappropriate conduct at the Whitmer High School Boys' Basketball game on February 12, 2016, and that Mr. Hickey's interaction with district administrators at that basketball game was unacceptable;

3. As a result of the safety concerns for its employees and the need to maintain decorum and order at its school functions, Mr. Patrick Hickey shall not be permitted to come onto Board premises, and he shall not be permitted to attend any function of the Washington Local Schools on property owned or controlled by the Board, effective immediately and until further action of this Board; and

4. Mr. Patrick Hickey shall be provided with notice of this action.

Channel 13abc quoted Hunter, whose reflex continued to be to support Hickey: "I thought Mr. Hickey was very genuine in his statements," Hunter said. "I believe from his tone of voice and the way he acted today, that he also wants to put this behind him." [9]

The Blade had this:

The board's resolution on Monday clarified that a game official did not ask Mr. Hickey to leave the facility, but instead the official asked that he be removed from standing at the court's baseline...

Mr. Hunter said the board will "see how things go and talk about" whether or not Mr. Hickey will be permitted to attend his son's graduation, which is not held on district property. Mr. Hunter said attorneys have said that the district could deny him access since the district has "control" of the venue during that time.

Mr. Hunter said the board did not discuss changing Mr. Hickey's roughly $217,000 resignation package.

He said he was pleased Mr. Hickey had discontinued using Facebook and Twitter. The former superintendent's social media accounts had been a "real source of consternation" because it led to rumors, Mr. Hunter said.

"It seems like we are spending way too much time on this type of issue," Mr. Hunter said, after the meeting. "I pray that this is the end of it." [10]

As will be seen, Hickey's disruptions would *not* cease after this latest reprimand.

Also at the Feb. 15 meeting, Hunter addressed the latest rumors about the pirated recording. (This is the same recording discussed in Chapter 16 and referenced above in this chapter by blogger Baumhower.)

There's been a lot of rumors and innuendoes once again in our district. This Board does not take any pleasure in what just happened. We are hoping that we can get on with everything. I promised you that this Board has complete honesty and transparency. We've been as honest with you about the details about what happened. There have been rumors about items from executive sessions and Board comments being leaked out to the public, I understand. I have not seen them or heard them myself. However, I understand that people are in the belief that words mentioned in an executive session with this Board were taped or are being played on the Internet. I can tell you with 100% certainty, 100% honesty, that those words that are being transmitted on the web are not from an executive session... when the rumors first came out, that it was something that came from an executive session, I asked for the resignation of any Board member who was responsible for said action. I allowed each Board member some time to think about it, and they did not make that recording...

We're all extremely sad that this is happening. I believe we are going to be able to go forward from this time. I know Mr. Hickey has done several things in the last day [taking down his social media accounts] that have been very positive toward solving some of the issues that are going on. I believe that silence in most of these cases is what's going to be needed...

This has been very difficult. I'm hoping this is the last time we have to deal with this issue. And looking back, this is not easy for many of us. Please trust that this Board will offer you 100% honesty and transparency. The facts will always be in front of you. Anything discussed in executive session, if it involves an attorney, we cannot discuss it. However, all the facts, I just told you, concerning this recording will be aired publicly. They will not be hidden. [11]

Though Hunter promised more facts concerning the recording, none were later revealed to the public.

Feb. 17 School Board meeting – Union leaders support Board

During community comment at the Feb. 17 Board meeting, the Presidents of the WLS teachers' union (TAWLS), Christopher Hodnicki, and support staff union (OAPSE), Karen Gilliam, spoke in support of the entire Board of Education, the Treasurer, and Interim Supt. Mourlam. [12] Their disillusion with Patrick Hickey was now public.

Hodnicki read his statement:

This school year has been trying and challenging for this district community. The time has come for this district to move on... To say that one man or person is the district is insulting. It gives me and my fellow colleagues great pain to hear these remarks time and time again. It is the community, it is the parents, it is the kids, and the staff that make Washington Local...

The time has come for the district to move forward. The events that culminated in the resignation of Patrick Hickey are in the past. As President of the [Teachers'] Association, I have enjoyed the professional relationship [with former Supt. Hickey] to advance the district...

As I learned about the events that would eventually culminate in his [Hickey's] resignation, I went from being surprised to being angry. All that had been accomplished now lay in question. Clearly, these are not the acts of a vengeful School Board, but of a man whose choices were being acted upon that led to a ripple effect throughout the district. In the end, let it be clear: He has taken responsibility for his actions, made a choice to resign, and he shall not be coming back.

History has taught us that idolizing or following any *one* without question can have serious consequences. As we move forward, we need to come together to advance this district by putting away the hostility, by setting a better example for our children. What example does it set for our kids when an individual attacks School Board members, by stealing their mail, or slashing their tires, or holding signs at Board meetings, or turning their backs when certain individuals speak? [Referencing actions directed at Langenderfer and Carmean.] I ask that this community put their energies into making real and beneficial change in this district by getting involved in parent clubs, booster organizations, or helping to close the achievement gap, petitioning the state to restore funding for public schools, or advocate for less reliance on test scores to determine students' achievements, or for other methods to positively improve our schools. The time has come. Let us come together and stand together.

Gilliam seconded Hodnicki's sentiments.

Hodnicki later explained the delicacy of the late 2015 circumstances:

Teachers were divided. Plus, the union was kept in the dark. We did not know any details or the extent of the situation. All we saw was a Board going after a popular and beloved leader, who we believed (at the time) was good for the district. So, the best course – as we afford all our teachers during an investigation – is for due process to occur and not to leap to judgment. My and others' perception (at the time) was that Patricia Carmean and Jim Langenderfer – who we called a carpetbagger from Michigan because no one knew anything about him other than he had worked and lived in Michigan – were enemies.

We later learned more about Jim's personal life. Then I met with Jim, the private investigator Chris Gill, and Patricia Carmean. Once I later saw all the evidence and multiple statements [from the Addison people], I was convinced we had been duped by Hickey. Of course, Jim became a major figure in this entire drama and his house was under constant surveillance. I was discrete about later meeting at his house. However, the day after one meeting a teacher came up to me and said, "I saw you at Jim Langenderfer's last night." [13]

Hunter said, "it speaks volumes that presidents of both unions have come forward" with their support. The other Board members thanked both unions, and Interim Supt. Mourlam thanked them for their courage in coming forward. [14]

June 11 School Board meeting

A high school student addressed the Board during the public comment period: "I'm kind of here today to wonder why you guys ain't gonna let Hickey sit with..." (referencing the upcoming high school graduation). Hunter cuts the boy off and says,

> I'm sorry, we're not discussing that topic. It is a discussion which has been had with legal attorneys. It's been handled with executive session. We're not allowed to speak to that issue. I can tell you that the concern right now of this Board is that everything's handled at our graduation with decorum and gracefulness for all students. And that issue right now has been discussed by attorneys and we can't discuss that publicly.

A woman in audience mumbles, "So much for compassion." [15]

A student set up an online petition to "let Mr. Patrick Hickey Speak at the Class of 2016 Graduation." [16] It got 626 signatures and regurgitated this photo:

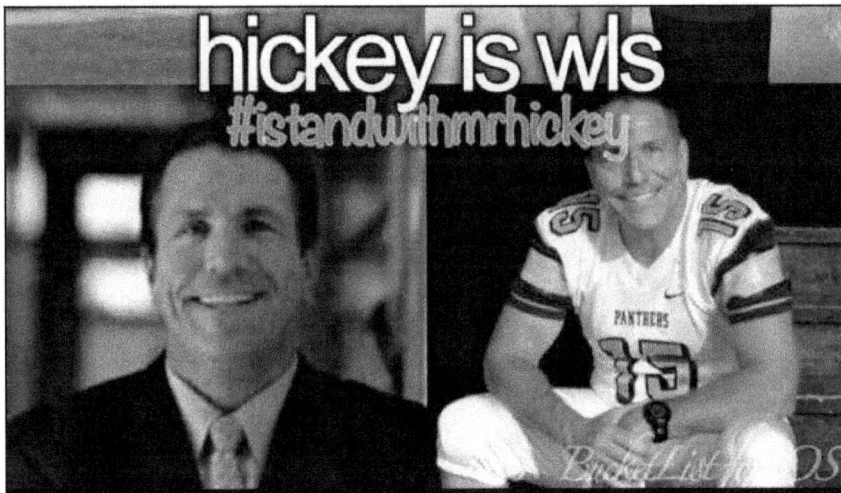

Excerpts from the petition page:

> **Kim** started this petition to Washington Local Board of Education. Mr. Patrick Hickey has always been a leader to the Washington Local Community and the Class of 2016. I, along with those who have signed the petition, ask that at the Class of 2016 graduation

ceremony, Mr. Hickey give a speech as he always did when he was the Superintendent of Washington Local.

Patrick Hickey [posting under his wife's name since he had agreed with the Board to stay off social media]: *If the majority of seniors want me to do so then I would be honored!!*

Laura: For any child in the WL school system Mr. Hickey's speech at graduation is a right [sic] of passage. Seniors look forward to Mr. Hickey speaking and motivating them as they begin the next part of their lives. I, as a parent, was looking forward to hearing the speech that he was going to give to my child and the rest of the class of 2016. The ban on Mr. Hickey from WLS events should be dropped and let him continue to support the kids of WLS even if in an unofficial capacity.

Nathan: Mr. Hickey is a great man. I've been looking forward to his speech for our class for years. Either way, with all of the rumors around, I still look up to him and respect him.

Grace: I'm signing because Mr. Hickey was more involved than any other superintendent and made it extremely clear that his heart beat for the students of Washington local.

Daniel: … First off this guy is great, awesome, and out going for our community. He has done so much for our schools in Washington local and I am much appreciative for him doing what he has done. I'm currently in the United States Air Force and till this day I can honestly say that the one speech he does for everyone every year right around prom is still played through my head every weekend or weekday that one of my family members or even I drink. That one speech he gave us I'll never forget. It was about drinking and driving and what had happen [sic] to him was a real life situation that happens daily, and he was just looking out for us but at the same time not trying to scare us. It was an emotional story but he got the point across to me at least that drinking and driving is not ok to do. And I would like to say thank you to him.

A Toledo talk radio host at WSPD (who would interview people from Addison) posted, too. He obviously knew something was up:

Fred LeFebvre: Not signing. Until Michigan State Police speak with him, I'll withhold any endorsement for him to speak.

More taunts from Hickey

According to the gossip at the *SwampBubbles* blog, Hickey violated his ban from school grounds and "ran past the WLS Administration Building" on August 23. A neighbor to the Administration Building witnessed this. "It was about noon. He was shirtless and wearing a skimpy pair of blue running shorts... He trotted on WLS property towards West Lincolnshire [administration building] and directly in front of the window of his old office/the new superintendent's office."

On August 29, Hickey emailed the School Board, administration, and some teachers requesting permission to be on school property for a fundraising event, his daughter's parent-teacher conferences, and her athletic/extracurricular events. Permission was denied. He also mentioned his plan to run for School Board in the fall of 2017 and that he would need to access school grounds if elected.

In October, blogger Jeremy Baumhower continued to target Carmean, taunting her for her defense of her deceased husband, the former WLS Superintendent. Hickey had at that time submitted a public records request on Mr. Carmean's tenure, apparently attempting to find dirt to use against Mrs. Carmean (as he prepared to oppose her in the 2017 School Board election).

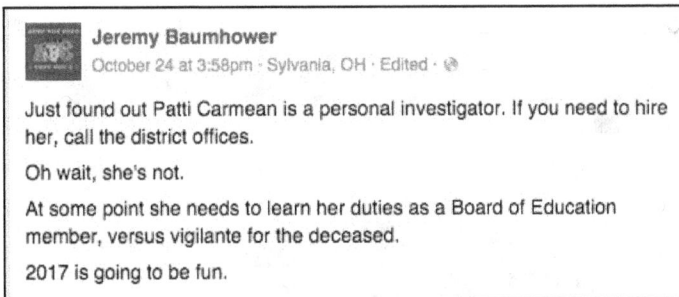

> **Jeremy Baumhower**
> October 24 at 3:58pm · Sylvania, OH · Edited · 🌎
>
> Just found out Patti Carmean is a personal investigator. If you need to hire her, call the district offices.
>
> Oh wait, she's not.
>
> At some point she needs to learn her duties as a Board of Education member, versus vigilante for the deceased.
>
> 2017 is going to be fun.

Ohio Dept. of Education begins investigation of Hickey

In August 2016, Board member Patricia Carmean got a call from the Ohio Department of Education (ODE), Office of Professional Conduct. They asked her to turn over any information she had on Patrick Hickey's malfeasance. [17]

In late August, TAWLS (WLS teachers' union) VP, Fritz Schermbeck, was interviewed for an hour by an ODE staffer. *He gave them names of WLS teachers who'd had sex with students.* He told the staffer whom they needed to contact to root out this evil. [18]

On August 31, the ODE subpoenaed Addison Community Schools for Patrick Hickey's personnel, disciplinary, or investigative file. [19]

In October, Board member Jim Langenderfer received a subpoena from the ODE for all information he had on Hickey. [20]

In November, TAWLS President Christopher Hodnicki received a subpoena from the ODE for the same. [21]

There was no timely follow-through from the ODE on any of this information, as far as the WLS sources knew. Possibly the bureaucracy was just moving at a snail's pace. [22]

But the ODE took no public action concerning Hickey until May 2018 – *after Hickey had pleaded guilty in Michigan court* to his crime against Dawn. It was only then that the Ohio DOE revoked his educator licenses through administrative action.

2016 ends poorly for WLS

In September, the School Board revealed the State Report Card for 2015-16 with grades of mostly Ds and one F. [23] For all of Hickey's big talk, scores had not been great in previous years either. The new Superintendent said the district had "struggled from 2012 on" in some areas. Even making allowances for the state's new grading system, things did not look good.

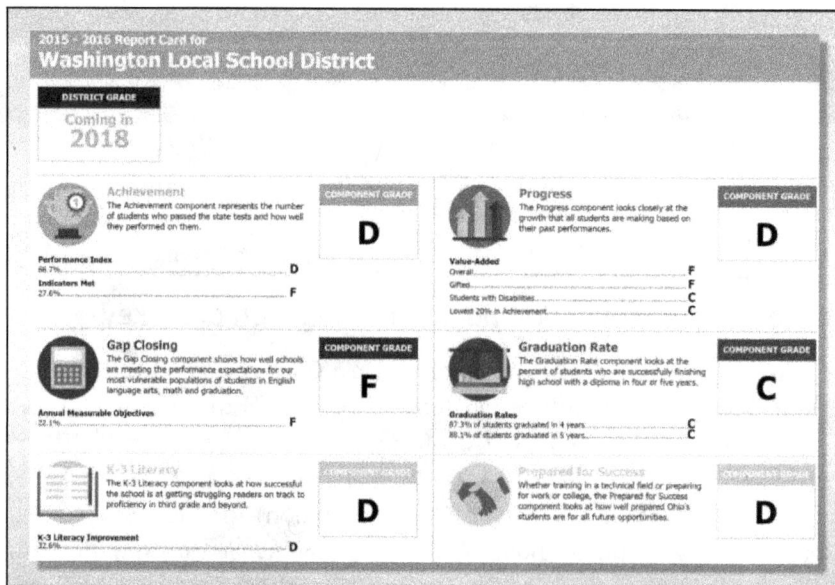

2015 - 2016 Report Card for
Washington Local School District

DISTRICT GRADE

Coming in
2018

Achievement — COMPONENT GRADE **D**
The Achievement component represents the number of students who passed the state tests and how well they performed on them.

Performance Index — 66.7% — D
Indicators Met — 27.6% — F

Progress — COMPONENT GRADE **D**
The Progress component looks closely at the growth that all students are making based on their past performances.

Value-Added
Overall — F
Gifted — F
Students with Disabilities — C
Lowest 20% in Achievement — C

Gap Closing — COMPONENT GRADE **F**
The Gap Closing component shows how well schools are meeting the performance expectations for our most vulnerable populations of students in English language arts, math and graduation.

Annual Measurable Objectives — 32.1% — F

Graduation Rate — COMPONENT GRADE **C**
The Graduation Rate component looks at the percent of students who are successfully finishing high school with a diploma in four or five years.

Graduation Rates
87.3% of students graduated in 4 years — C
88.1% of students graduated in 5 years — C

K-3 Literacy — COMPONENT GRADE **D**
The K-3 Literacy component looks at how successful the school is at getting struggling readers on track to proficiency in third grade and beyond.

K-3 Literacy Improvement — 32.6% — D

Prepared for Success — COMPONENT GRADE **D**
Whether training in a technical field or preparing for work or college, the Prepared for Success component looks at how well prepared Ohio's students are for all future opportunities.

Dec. 2016 – Hickey complains about rumors

Towards the end of the year, Hickey complained to the Board about his ongoing ban from school properties. He emailed the Board and Superintendent on December 6:

Dear Board,

Your latest refusal to allow a Dad and taxpayer to see his daughter participate in her school activities is disappointing. I have never missed any of my kids activities and it is a shame that you are taking out whatever ill will you feel towards me onto her.

Even more gruesome is the email sent out from [teachers' union President] Chris Hodnicki and discussed at a staff meeting warning teachers and staff to report if I am on campus. [Hickey's daughter] heard of this email within 30 minutes of it being sent. I received notice from staff and the email in question, and my wife heard from a parent (all within an hour).

I have not been on school property since you made your edict despite rumors of banging on the Superintendent's window and this incident of "waving at teachers" recently. It is as simple as checking your surveillance footage coverage to discover these claims have no merit. My family files such claims with the ones that my wife left me, that I was in rehab, that I am a pedophile, that I leaked emails to Jeremy Baumhower, that I had work issues with the Findlay City Schools, that I ignore summonses, that I am about to be arrested, that Sharon Giles [his former secretary] leaked emails to me, that I was escorted out of WHS and snuck back in three times the night of the Lima Senior game [February 2016], and the multiple conclusions from the private investigator hired by board members to re-investigate a situation I told the Board about and that was fully investigated 26 years ago with a conclusion that the charges were unsubstantiated.

I will no longer ask you to allow me to attend my daughter's activities. I will not seek an injunction, at this time, to do so because of the embarrassment it would cause the district and my daughter. I highly encourage you to challenge strongly those who bring you information about me, my activities, my exercise, my lifestyle, my hour to hour living, to prove their accusations rather than allowing more emails and innuendo to spread like wildfire. I have avoided such wildfires by continually turning down the electronic and print media for interview requests and by not publishing anything on social media. I would request that you all do the same.

I cannot be hurt anymore, but the damage you have done to my family and specifically to a 15 year old girl in your care is shameful. I will continue to go to all of her away events at our sister schools. I have attended hundreds of events since your edict for [sons and daughter]. I have interacted with your staff who approach me, and all without incident. Allowing one night in February to define me and all my future activities is sad and lacks compassion, mercy, and empathy.

– Patrick Hickey

PS I drop my daughter off at Whitmer High School on Clegg Drive every morning and have done so every morning since your edict. If you hear that I do so, it is correct. As you are well aware Clegg and Whitmer Drive and the sidewalks on both of those streets are not WLS property. [24]

He also emailed the Board attorney on December 21, wondering why his latest public records request had not yet been fulfilled, saying he is "confused by [the Superintendent's] flaunting [sic] of the law." He was trying to retrieve the email sent by teachers' union President Hodnicki regarding Hickey's "presence on school property," his former secretary's "settlement-resignation" documents, and "dirt" on the former Superintendent, Michael Carmean.

Meanwhile, Hickey was dreaming about his business plan to open several fitness centers. He posted a graphic on his social media [25] of young women holding bottles of liquor and laughing it up in a locker room. His caption read: *Cyclebar in Toledo SOON!! Stoked!!*

CHAPTER 19
Hickey Roils the District;
Elected to School Board
– 2017 –

Hickey again tangles with Board member Carmean

The Superintendent of Washington Local Schools through the summer of 2007 (just prior to Hickey's tenure) was Michael Carmean, who passed away in 2009 after a difficult struggle with scleroderma. [1] His widow Patricia Carmean had retired as a Washington Local teacher in 2013, then began a four-year term on the School Board starting in 2014.

Mrs. Carmean said her husband did *not* recommend Patrick Hickey to be his replacement as Superintendent in 2007. [2] Mr. Carmean was not involved in that selection process; it was entirely run by the School Board.

Mrs. Carmean was well aware of Hickey's uneven performance as Asst. Superintendent (2002-2007). She therefore had a ready skepticism about Hickey's truthfulness. It is not surprising that the relationship between the two was filled with animosity.

In early 2017, Hickey and Carmean had yet another run-in, after Hickey formally announced he was running for a seat on the School Board. The election was coming up in November. (He had first floated the plan in a radio interview the day after his resignation as Superintendent in December 2015.)

He just wouldn't go away.

Some believed Hickey was plotting his return as Superintendent. If he could get a majority on the Board – two allies plus himself – he could be hired back to run the district. Or he could be satisfied with ruling the Board and hiring a Superintendent he could control. He already had his long-time ally, Lisa Canales, on the Board.

But Patricia Carmean was planning to run for re-election. Hickey clearly wanted her to fail.

Sometime before April 16, Carmean responded to a Facebook post on a Hickey supporter's page regarding his campaign announcement:

Carmean: This person [Hickey] resigned as the Superintendent of WLS. He resigned to heal the district. He has requested my husband's public records. My husband Superintendent Michael W. Carmean died 8 years ago. Why would the resigned Superintendent make this request? He is very disrespectful and needs to leave WLS alone. Kids and community members are being hurt by his blatant disregard for their lives!

Hickey supporter: The district has not healed. And will not heal until you and James Langenderfer are no longer on the board. Your policies have done nothing but burden the school district. Mr. Hickey resigned as the Superintendent of WLS because of the unfair pressure that was put on him. And if you don't think the school district is behind him. Go look at the support he is getting.

Carmean: As I stated this man resigned. You are saying he resigned because of unfair pressure. Bottom line he resigned!

Hickey then messaged Carmean directly on April 16:

Patrick Hickey:

[9:13 pm] A positive person? Really. Positive? SMH. [shaking my head]

[9:36 pm] I look forward to November. Please run on your record and what you have done for this district. Please avoid you were hired illegally by Mike. [her husband, former Supt.] Let the district know what you have done as a "positive person." Please avoid the police report that you filed after stalking me, [Nov. 2, 2015] that won't play well my friend.

[9:44 pm] I saw you mentioned my public records request about Mikes spending. His spending was outrageous Patty, please don't make me make it public. I made the request due toy [sic] my knowledge of what he did at taxpayer expense in Columbus and NSBA [National School Boards Assoc.], please don't make me make it public. There are records that are very embarrassing for your family. Your call Patty.

[9:54 pm] *The Blade* and TV and Radio have requested his records. Let me know what you want me to do. I am sure you have sent all of these to Terri Kern [anti-Hickey community resident]. Patty, she has failed at every turn, every accusation, don't hitch your future to someone who has been proven wrong at every turn. Summons, fail. Email leaks, fail. Addison, fail. My license, fail. Leaked emails, fail. I see you are active, let's talk. Ok ..... the media begins Tuesday.

Hickey Roils the District — Elected to School Board

Let me know of [sic] you want to talk. Peace. If not of [sic] Still active? Let's talk.

[10:08 pm] I give up.

[10:38 pm] I tried Patty. Know that I tried despite your evil.

Then on April 17:

Carmean:
[5:30 pm] Please do not contact me. Thank you

Hickey:
[6:17 pm] Patty, you can block me. Otherwise, you allow people to contact you. It is a social media contract. When one posts they are a positive person, and when they make assertions about my resignation, and when they assert my reasons for [getting records on] Mikes spending then you can expect contact. I have a deal Patty. I won't contact you if you stop stalking me, talking about me, and having me be the focus of your life. Deal?

Carmean:
[9:07 pm] Please do not contact me. Thank you

Hickey:
Ok, I won't contact you.

Carmean had also suspected Hickey of removing a magnet with sentimental value (related to her husband's terminal illness) from her car earlier in 2017. She thought this had occurred at an away girls' basketball game on February 16 which Hickey also had attended. At that same event, he took a photo of her in the stands and tweeted it out, asking his followers why she was sitting on the side of the gym with the opposing team. (She later explained she sat there in order to avoid having a run-in with him.)

Adding that to the messages above, she filed for a civil protective order against Hickey for stalking on April 20.

> NARRATIVE
>
> THE VICTIM PATRICIA STATED THAT A SCLERODERMA MAGNET WAS TAKEN FROM THE RIGHT REAR HATCH DOOR. THE VEHICLE WAS PARKED IN WELL LIGHTED AREA NEAR THE FLAG POST. PATRICIA STATED THAT HAS REASON TO BELIEVE THAT THIS NAMED PERSON PATRICK TOOK THE MAGNET AS HE WAS AT THE BASKETBALL GAME. SHE STATED THAT PATRICK KNOWS THE MAKE OF HER VEHICLE AND HE KNOWS HER HUSBAND DIED OF COMPLICATIONS OF SCLERODREMA. PATRICIA STATED THAT PATRICK LEFT THE BASKETBALL ARENA BEFORE THE END OF THE VARSITY GAME. AND HE LEFT BEFORE HER. PATRICIA STATED THAT SHE ALSO BELIEVES PATRICK TOOK PICTURES OF HER AND POSTED IT ON TWITTER ACCOUNT WITHOUT HER PERMISSION. SHE STATED THAT SHE HAS HAD THIS MAGNET FOR MANY YEARS AND THE ONLY TIME IT WAS REMOVED WAS WHEN SHE WASHED HER VEHICLE.
>
> PATRICIA HAD PATRICK DOWN AS SUSPECT BUT HE WASN'T SEEN DOING IT AND SHE STATED THAT VIDEO TAPE WASN'T CLEAR.

In the video of her preliminary hearing, Carmean states Hickey made no physical threats, but she doesn't know what he's capable of. She is worried by his past harassing behaviors (jogging past his victim teacher Anna's home, sending an email to all WLS employees criticizing her, etc.). She says, "I don't know what to do. I'm pleading with someone to stop this man." She conveys her strong feeling that she's dealing with an unbalanced person, so she was afraid for her physical safety. [3]

The Toledo Blade called this squabble part of a "seemingly never-ending saga." It made top spot in the second section of the paper. [4]

Carmean was granted a temporary order of protection. From *The Blade* on May 4:

> Ms. Carmean testified that Mr. Hickey has not threatened physical harm.
>
> Mr. Hickey, meanwhile, told the magistrate he felt Ms. Carmean and board member James Langenderfer "made my life heck for years." When asked by his lawyer if it was fair to say he did not like Ms. Carmean, he briefly struggled to answer.
>
> "As a Christian," he said before verbally stumbling for a moment, "I have no feelings toward her one way or another." [5]

At that hearing, *The Blade* asked Hickey how he would serve on the WLS School Board if elected, since he is banned from all WLS properties. He had no comment.

Shortly after the May 3 hearing, Carmean's petition for a protective order was denied on the grounds that Hickey had not made any threat of physical harm.

Hickey challenged on Toledo talk radio

Hickey's candidacy for the School Board and his ongoing run-ins with Patricia Carmean caught the attention of Toledo talk radio. On his April 18 show, host Denny Schaffer (Q105.5) did his best to boost Hickey. [6] But an unexpected challenge came from Brooke Brooks Kelly who called into the show.

Hickey was live in the studio with Schaffer. They addressed his plan to run for School Board. Hickey says that his tenure at WLS ...

> ... ended poorly, and the Internet had a whole lot to do with that and the pressure that comes from a bunch of people making up a bunch of things... but it's the best thing that ever happened to me 'cause of what my family and I have accomplished since then, the

plans that my business partners and I have for the coming months...

He said that as head of the Jeanne Hickey Memorial Fund, he and his siblings had given over $1 million for inner city kids' education. [7] The WLS severance package allowed him freedom to plan his new business, and he would soon be opening "three boutique fitness studios" in northwest Ohio. On his run for the School Board, he said he is uniquely qualified to help manage the $75 million WLS district budget. When asked if he would be a distraction if elected to the Board, Hickey answered:

Hickey: I don't think so. Thousands of people have asked me to run. I'm an expert in education. Two members of that Board ran to get rid of me. That's not the right reason to be on the School Board... It's insane that [his ban from school property] is still going on. If I win, the school district has spoken [and] they can't keep me from doing the job that the community has hired me to do... My wife is prompting me constantly to sue the district... For them to do this is petty. I'm not going to streak across the basketball floor. Come on!...

Schaffer: If you don't think the cloud is still around you, then you're fooling yourself. You are gonna be a huge distraction... And there's all these other unanswered questions. [Earlier] you said you were gonna sue these people and clear your name, and you never did it. Why?

Hickey: I was advised by both Toledo Police and my attorney you can't sue people for saying whatever they want on the Internet unless they direct it directly to you...

Here is our transcript of what followed:

Unidentified caller: When you worked at Addison Schools, why you were asked to leave their property?

Hickey: In November 1990, there was an investigation that completely cleared me of any wrongdoing in 1990, and then this [WLS] Board spent $10,000 more to investigate the same situation with the same conclusion: rumors, innuendoes at Addison. I decided to leave, my wife encouraged me to leave – both times, unsubstantiated. [*His voice quivers.*]

Schaffer: Then what we have here, inappropriate stuff at WLS? ... controversy ... Is there a pattern?

Hickey: Two instances in 30 years? A pattern? And I was cleared of both.

Asst. Host: Why put this guy on the School Board if this is in his past? It's serious – there are children. What do you have that supersedes all this? It's serious stuff. Controversy should be overlooked? Being around kids?

Hickey: I have a lot to offer. This is the beauty of the USA. Voters will decide. I lifted up kids. We were the exemplar of how to educate kids in poverty.

Schaffer then took a call from Brooke Brooks Kelly. Schaffer challenges her, but not Hickey:

Brooke: I was a student there. He was my basketball coach. I actually saw you in the cemetery with a student in a bouncing car (etc.)...

Hickey: You said that in 1990 and it was debunked.

Brooke: No, it wasn't. Your victims were scared to come forward... [Schaffer challenges her.] I was a military criminal investigator for several years. Don't tell me what is criminally needed.

Hickey: In 1990 it was debunked, that you made it up. OK, then I should be in jail!

Schaffer: Brooke, why is he not in jail? Why didn't you come forward?

Brooke: I was a child! [Her mother *did* go to the Addison School officials, and that is what led to Hickey's departure.] Why is he contacting another victim, begging her not to come forward?

Schaffer: You aren't answering the question.

Brooke: I am. *He's* not answering the question. He's just *deny, deny, deny.* Can he please speak for himself, and not you for him, Mr. Schaffer?

Schaffer: It's my show!

Hickey: It was re-investigated and debunked again. You are making this up, you've been doing it for 30 years!

Brooke: Why would I? I have no dog in this fight.

Hickey: You *love* this attention!

Schaffer: Why'd you call?

Asst. Host: Can you testify as a witness? Why haven't you done it?

Brooke: Because someone needs to come forward. The victim.

Asst. Host: Oh, I see.

Hickey: [to Brooke] What do you want me to do?

Brooke: Quit lying.

Hickey: You have been debunked twice.

Asst. Host: So, what is he getting out of this, Brooke? What is his motivation?

Brooke: In every school he went to, he's left under mysterious circumstances.

Hickey: That's not true of St. Anthony Villa, or Findlay.

Brooke: There was not one person in Addison that didn't know what was going on.

(Schaffer cuts her off.)

Schaffer went on to promote Hickey's upcoming "friend-raiser" (event to gather volunteers) for his School Board campaign. He continued to stick up for Hickey in the next segment. [8]

Toledo media criticize Hickey for running for School Board

All of Toledo was watching the spectacle of Hickey's continuing disruption of the WLS district, especially his plan to run for School Board.

On May 13, 2017 *The Toledo Blade* editorialized on Hickey's "office-seeking as grudge sport." [9] The editors were astonished that he would run for School Board after his forced resignation, his ban from school properties, and his ongoing run-ins with Patricia Carmean.

> ... Mr. Hickey is running for school board despite being barred from district grounds and despite a restraining order requiring him to stay away from a current board member...
>
> Local politics is not an appropriate forum for personal grudges.
>
> School districts need board members who show that they respect rules and the bounds of civility, as well as fellow human beings.
>
> Mr. Hickey is clearly not a person with the temperament for public office, and even less so *this* office in *this* community.

The best thing Mr. Hickey could do to help the district and the schoolchildren he professes to love would be to drop his bid for school board. But if he doesn't, voters in the district should recall the acrimony and chaos of 2015 and 2016 and render a final verdict at the polls.

Hickey's candidacy for the School Board brought this ridicule by Johnny Hildo at the *Toledo City Paper*, an entertainment guide (June 1, 2017):

Keeping Score in City Politics

It's a topsy, turvy world out there.

We never would have believed that, as we enter the official start of the local political season, we'd be writing about the Washington Local school board race. Toledo Public Schools? As a former Miss Idaho might say, "You betcha!" But not sleepy little Washington Local. Yet there it is…

Hallelujah and pass the peanut butter! The accused superintendent, Patrick Hickey, was investigated by the WLS Board and resigned so he wouldn't be dumped. Seems ol' Patty H has decided not to leave well enough alone. He is now a candidate for WLS school board, which brings him directly into our laser beam sights.

Love bites

Here's our best shot. Hickey allegedly harassed a WLS teacher after an affair with her ended. He denied it all, but then a video of him lurking around her classroom at night surfaced. At the time these allegations were ruminating around in the WLS school board, Hickey had several run-ins with WLS board member Patrician Carmean. That led to more allegations of Hickey stalking and harassing.

Not one to fade into the woodwork, Hickey subsequently got banned from WLS property after belligerent shenanigans at a Whitmer HS basketball game. In that incident there was questionable physical contact between Hickey and the female WLS interim superintendent who had replaced him. Teacher, board member, interim superintendent. Three professional WLS women, three strikes for Hickey.

Three strikes should mean he's out, right? We already revealed the punch line, and it isn't Hickey's last name. He's now running for a spot on the board, the same board that investigated him, suspended him, accepted his resignation, and banned him from WLS property.

Like the old infomercials used to say, wait, there's more. He is running in the same election with Carmean, who has new allegations of intimidation and harassment against Hickey. You say you want more? Both Hickey and Carmean have sought the endorsement of the Lucas County Democratic Party.

Let that all marinate a bit. Hickey wants a seat on the board in a district that has banned him from its property. He wants to run on the same ticket with a woman who has twice accused him of harassment and intimidation. He wants to regain the ultimate employment authority over a female teacher who has accused him of harassment after an affair.

We lied about the punch line. Here it is. And his last name is Hickey.

You can't make this stuff up, folks. [10]

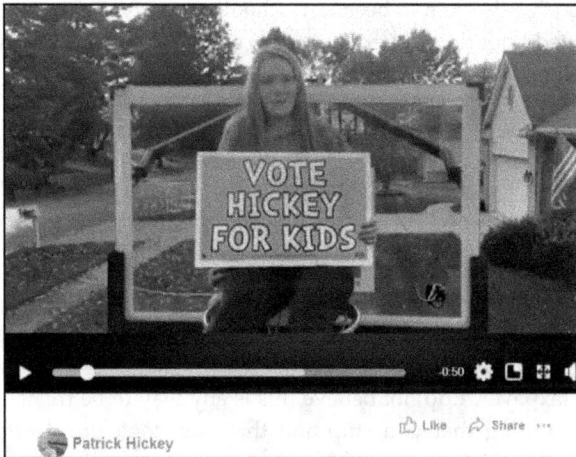

Hickey featured young girls in his Facebook campaign videos. (His daughter was in the high school at the time.) The narrator says: "As for me and my family, we know Mr. Hickey and we're voting Hickey for Kids!"

Hickey's angry email to teachers' union president

On July 13, 2017, Hickey sent a threatening letter to the teachers' union President, Christopher Hodnicki, unhappy that many in the district were still concerned about his behavior and felt the need to monitor him. [15] Hickey had been seen on school properties (from which he was banned), and Hodnicki had heard reports from various

WLS staff. At the same time, Hickey still had many supporters in the district. Hickey wrote:

> Chris,
>
> It has been brought to my attention by those in attendance at your latest TAWLS union meeting that I was the subject of some discussion. I was informed that you discussed publicly stating prior to the November [2017] School Board election that I am harassing/stalking [teachers Anna and her husband].
>
> This pattern of behavior on your part includes two emails in my possession, and sent to me by your members, indicating by you that I was on school property and soliciting staff to inform you if they see me on school property. There are also emails you sent to two staff members, forwarded to me, asking them to meet with you about me being on school property. These follow your assertion to staff that I hacked your twitter account.
>
> Be clear Chris, I have not harassed or stalked [Anna and her husband], I have not been on school property since the board requested I not do so over a year and a half ago, and I did not hack your email account.
>
> You need to cease and desist this pattern of defamation and slander. Know that I will take all legal remedies against you personally if you continue this behavior. I have copied my attorney (Jerome Phillips) on this correspondence and I suggest you consult an attorney before you continue this assault on my character.
>
> I faithfully served the district for 14 years. My wife and I are parents of a current student and three graduates, I am a school board candidate and a WLS property and business owner. I am also a taxpayer. I do not believe this is any way to be treated and I am requesting that you stop and that you don't direct others to make untrue claims.
>
> Sincerely,
> Patrick Hickey

The campaign proceeds

All of Toledo was watching the School Board election in the Washington Local district.

In September, Hickey asked the Board for permission to be on WLS grounds to join in prayer at the Whitmer High School flagpole, but was denied. Then through his social media (which he recently had restarted), he asked people to contact the Superintendent to reverse that decision.

The Toledo Blade reported:

> He wrote that he was "stunned" [that his request was denied]. The post has been shared more than 100 times. The district responded with its own post on its Facebook page, reiterating that the 2016 board action prohibiting the former superintendent from school grounds still stands. [12]

Hickey told the newspaper he was running for School Board because "hundreds of community members, students, and parents" asked him to. If he was elected, "The board would be absolutely foolish not to lift the ban, because the community is speaking." According to the Ohio School Boards Association, a Board vote would be needed to lift the ban on Hickey.

Thomas Ilstrup was also a candidate for the Board in this same election. He had been Board President when Hickey resigned in December 2015. Ilstrup said he was running in 2017 to "help bring some calm back to the district. His chief concern is that if Mr. Hickey is elected there will essentially be two superintendents trying to run the district" and that Hickey would be constantly second-guessing the Superintendent. [13] Later Ilstrup said, "he didn't think Mr. Hickey should be involved with a school now or in the future. 'I think there's too much of a cloud over his past that I don't think he has a place in public education'." [14]

In October, WSPD radio talk show host, Fred LeFebvre, questioned why Hickey was "friending" girls on his Facebook:

> There's a controversy brewing in the Washington Local School district. Former Superintendent Patrick Hickey who had to leave the district is now running for school board. As part of his campaign he apparently is reaching out to underage girls on Facebook despite the fact that they are not eligible to vote.
>
> Parents are upset that their daughters are being approached this way and that begs the question, should an adult man friend underage girls on social media like Facebook? [15]

Furthermore, the School Board had asked Hickey to take down his social media prior to this run for School Board.

Oct. 2017: Truth comes out on Hickey's malfeasance as Superintendent

As the WLS School Board election heated up in October with a surprising amount of support for Hickey, *The Toledo Blade* published a stunning flashback.

A list of "37 Charges" of employment violations – prepared by the School Board's attorney in anticipation of possibly terminating Hickey in December 2015 – was leaked to *The Blade*. Apparently, someone hoped this document would doom Hickey's campaign.

The complete letter with the "37 Charges" is in Chapter 17.

The report made the front page of *The Blade*. [16] From the lengthy article:

> **Washington Local Schools considered firing Hickey before resignation in 2015** – October 17, 2017
>
> Former Washington Local Schools Superintendent Patrick Hickey, who is now a candidate for the district's board of education, was facing charges that could have led to his firing in 2015 when he suddenly resigned during an investigation into his behavior, according to a document obtained by *The Blade*.
>
> The document, a letter dated Dec. 11, 2015, from the district's treasurer to Mr. Hickey, stated in the first paragraph that the board intended to meet that night and consider "a resolution to suspend your contract without pay and initiate termination of your contract of employment."
>
> What follows in the letter are findings of an investigation by Columbus-based law firm Bricker and Eckler, hired by Washington Local to look into numerous allegations of misconduct by Mr. Hickey as superintendent.
>
> That investigation, and its findings, have now surfaced within weeks of the Nov. 7 election with a copy of the "Allegations–Charges" letter prepared for the board of education given to *The Blade* by a person who had a copy of it and offered it to the newspaper on the condition that its source remain anonymous...

Hickey told the newspaper that he never saw the document at the time of his resignation. A hearing on the specific charges did *not* take place. Rather, Hickey agreed to resign with a generous severance package. That was apparently after private discussions with the President and VP of the School Board.

Hickey said that the "37 Charges" document was full of falsehoods, and its release was a "political ploy" to hurt his chances in the School Board election.

More from *The Blade*:

> "The board said there was no document," he told *The Blade* last week about conversations he said he had with Washington Local officials after he resigned. "They told myself and my attorney."

> He denied many of the board's assertions and said if they were true he should have been fired rather than allowed to leave with a severance package of $300,000. "If these were true, I would fire me," Mr. Hickey said. "I would not give me $300,000." ...

> It [the document] stated that he lied about why he left the Addison district, and that he left Addison "as a result of allegations that you had a relationship with one or two students of that school district, and your relationship(s) became too close and too personal."

> Mr. Hickey told *The Blade* that he denied the board's charge that he left Addison Schools because he was accused of having personal relations with students.

> "There were rumors that I had inappropriate relations with students," he said. "That was investigated by Michigan State Police in 1990 and unsubstantiated."

But the Addison situation was never investigated by the Michigan State Police or any other police department, and there is no record that any child protective agency investigated at the time, according to the recent Michigan State Police investigation.

Hickey went on to deny to *The Blade* that he had engaged in any inappropriate sexual relationships with personnel in the Washington Local Schools leading to his resignation. He even blamed Anna for anything inappropriate that happened, claiming he was the innocent party:

> Mr. Hickey told *The Blade* last week he objected to most of the allegations in the document: "I did nothing sexual, romantic, financial, nothing involving a student, nothing unlawful, and I violated no policies."

> Mr. Hickey was placed on administrative leave twice in 2015 before he resigned. The first leave stemmed from a district investigation into an informal complaint by a husband and wife – both teachers

in the district – who claimed Mr. Hickey harassed them after an alleged affair between the wife and Mr. Hickey ended.

The document received by *The Blade* last week stated that Mr. Hickey received videos from a teacher that included nudity.

"You were a party to the misconduct by requesting and/or encouraging that videos be sent by the teacher, or you failed to take action to initiate discipline, corrective directives to the teacher for her misconduct, or any investigation of the misconduct, or both," the document stated.

Mr. Hickey denies that he engaged in behavior that was "too personal" or "inappropriate" with teachers. He did admit that a Washington Local teacher sent him videos involving nudity, but denied he solicited any inappropriate communication from the teacher.

"There was a teacher who sent me inappropriate videos," he told *The Blade* on Thursday. "I think that's the teacher's problem."

The night *The Blade's* report came out, there happened to be an election forum for the nine School Board candidates, including Hickey.

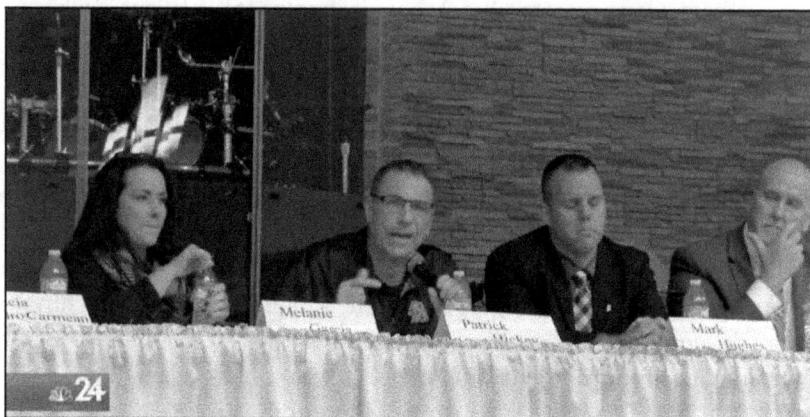

Hickey at the Oct. 17, 2017 School Board candidate forum. He is flanked by two allies, Melanie Garcia, who was not elected, and Mark Hughes, who was.

At the forum, Hickey objected to an opponent's campaign website that grouped him with Harvey Weinstein, Bill Cosby, and Anthony Weiner.

NBC 24 News covered the event:

> A polarizing candidate, Hickey undeniably has a lot of experience... But in 2015 he resigned amidst controversy...

"Washington Local community is a very smart community," explained Hickey. "So if there are people who think that that divide can't be lessened, then they won't vote for me. But I believe strongly that we can help the district resurrect itself. Be back to the best school district in the state of Ohio, and I will work tirelessly to do that."

But it still has some voters concerned. One woman did not want to go on camera, but said she wasn't sure how he was allowed to run when he's not even allowed on school property. However, other voters say the charges were over-hyped in the first place for political reasons, and that Hickey is the best qualified candidate for Washington Local's future.

"This whole thing's garbage," shared Ronald Williams II, a Washington Local School District resident for 11 years. "I just think he was dragged through the mud. I think that even today, they brought up stuff from way back, that why [sic] didn't they bring up when he was superintendent." [17]

Hickey's statement that WLS was once "the best school district in the state of Ohio" was typical hyperbole.

Hickey's campaign appeal on Facebook

Hickey was very active on his Facebook page leading up to the election. He posted the photo below in the fall of 2017:

Hugging little girls at a school Halloween party. This appears to be in a school building, though he was banned from WLS properties. Possibly the photo was taken before his ban.

On October 25, he mused that love would overcome evil:

> If elected, I just want to return to loving and lifting up kids. Nothing more, nothing less. I truly, truly believe the drama will end when love overcomes evil. I love our school district so much.

> End the hate, end the outside influences, vote on my 14 years in the district and what was accomplished. Allow me to assist Dr. Hayward [Supt.], Mr. Hunter [Board President], and Mrs. Canales [VP]. Allow me to help the teachers and support staff. Your support of me will be rewarded, of that I absolutely guarantee.

On October 26, Hickey posted his campaign appeal and promised "the drama will end November 8th." He included his family photo in this post.

Patrick Hickey
26 October 2017

We send a Christmas pic each year, the out takes (especially with pets) can be more fun than the final pic....

On November 7th, please vote for the Patrick Hickey that you have known for 14 years, that took care of your kids, that inspired an amazing staff to embrace our mission and core values, and who assisted the district to unprecedented success academically, financially, extra curricularly, and with facility improvements.

Please take your district back from two years of hate, negativity, lies, agendas, and fake/vile websites.

My campaign has remained positive, loving, uplifting, and strong. It will remain so. My only goal is to assist Dr. Hayward, Mr. Hunter, Ms. Canales, and the people who are voted to this board. The drama will end November 8th. To be clear the following statements are true. You see truth is truth.

1. I have been married for 30 years and have 4 amazing kids who have had a great experience in the Washington Local Schools.

2. I have never, ever been charged with a crime.

3. I currently hold valid licenses from the state of Ohio to be a Superintendent, Principal, and English Teacher. [18]

4. In 30 years in education I received exactly one reprimand. [19] It was from a board that included 2 members who have admitted to wanting me gone from day one of their service to the district. The one reprimand [by WLS Board, Sept. 2015] followed a two week independent investigation by a law firm which concluded (by them, not me) that I did "nothing romantic, sexual, [20] financial, did not involve students, and was not unlawful." They further concluded that I did not violate board policy. I was given a letter of reprimand after the board put me on a two week "vacation", interviewed multiple witnesses, and made a conclusion that I did not discipline a teacher who sent me unsolicited gifts and videos. I did not discipline the teacher because I did not want her family embarrassed. [21] I made a mistake and it clearly has cost me dearly.

5. I left Addison Schools in 1990 with the written assurance from the Superintendent that I left in good standing with the school district. [22] There was an investigation of rumors by Children Services and the police in 1990. The results were unsubstantiated. [23] Board Member Jim Langenderfer paid thousands in 2016 to have the same rumors investigated with the same results. My wife and I made a mutual decision to leave that district.

6. After Addison I was extremely successful at St. Anthony Villa and was promoted to their director, [24] was very successful at the Findlay City Schools where Mr. Carmean came to talk to all my supervisors and who promoted me from an Assistant Principal to Assistant Super-intendent, [25] and 14 years of extremely successful leadership in Washington Local. All of my experience has been listed on all of my applications. [26]

7. In the state of Ohio every expenditure by a Superintendent must be approved as a legitimate public expense by the Treasurer. It is a good system. Every single expenditure was approved by our Treasurer and auditors. [27] I paid for skydiving with staff and a special needs student for our opening day video and for a WW2 class despite the Treasurer receiving a legal opinion that it would have been a proper public expense.

8. The board placed me on leave because 2 teachers had an exchange in the cafeteria [28] and I was seen taking pictures in the CTC [high school Career & Technology Center]. That leave resulted in the board discovering that the exchange had nothing to do with me and that the photo I took was of a board members card on a complaintants [sic] door 2 weeks after an investigation concluded. They also know the Assistant Superintendent Mrs. Mourlam, and

my secretary, Mrs. Giles texted me to take the picture. I gave those texts to the board. [29]

9. The board paid me $300,000 to leave the district. They did this because I violated no policies. Had I done so they would have fired me with cause. [30] They later paid my secretary 6 figures to leave and she, also, violated no policies.

Vote Hickey on November 7th, let's take back our district from special interests. It is the only way this ridiculous drama will end.

I have much to offer our school leaders, you will not be disappointed.

More bombshells dropped on Hickey's campaign

NBC 24 News highlighted billboards that popped up against Hickey and his two allied candidates running for School Board. [31]

Many feared Hickey's plan was to regain personal control of Washington Local Schools by dominating the Board. It would only take three votes (including his own) to hire him as Superintendent again. Since the Ohio Board of Education had not yet confiscated his educator's license, what could stop him?

On November 1, a week before election day, Hickey posted on his Facebook:

IT IS THE EXCITING CRUNCH TIME TO TAKE BACK OUR AMAZING DISTRICT FROM SPECIAL INTERESTS AND AGENDAS. DO NOT LET ANONYMOUS BLOGGERS AND ANONYMOUS BILLBOARD BUYERS CONTINUE TO DAMAGE OUR DISTRICT.

On November 2, WSPD talk radio host Fred LeFebvre interviewed Brooke Brooks Kelly, who was a key witness with her mother to

Hickey's inappropriate behavior with one of her high school classmates. (LeFebvre would cover Hickey again in early 2018.)

Brooke Brooks Kelly in the WSPD studio

In their Nov. 4 print edition – just three days before the election – *The Toledo Blade* revealed the 2016 Michigan State Police investigation: *"Woman claims sex with Hickey as a teen; School board candidate was her teacher then."* [33] Hickey was front-page news once again. The article linked to a PDF of the investigation reports filed through May 13, 2016. [34]

> A woman ["Dawn"] told a Michigan State Police investigator that she had sex with former Washington Local Schools superintendent and current school board candidate Patrick Hickey when she was 14 and he was her coach and teacher at Addison High School more than two decades ago, according to a 2016 state police report.

> The Lenawee County Prosecutor's Office declined to press charges because the woman requested that they not, and because it was reported outside the statute of limitations, according to both the police report and Scott Baker, chief assistant prosecuting attorney for the county.

> "If there is additional information, we will review," Mr. Baker told *The Blade.*

> Mr. Hickey refused to respond to most questions on Friday by a *Blade* reporter, saying only that he "vehemently denies all accusations." He first said the allegations were investigated in 1990 and that he was exonerated – adding the 2016 investigation was prompted by a private investigator hired by Washington Local board member Jim Langenderfer and that he was again exonerated.

When told that the case was closed because of statute of limitation and witness cooperation problems, he then repeated "I vehemently deny all accusations" in response to every question posed by a *Blade* reporter...

The report states she told the detective the "allegations of her having a sexual relationship with Patrick Hickey were true," and that they started having sex when she was 14.

"She stated that her relationship with Patrick Hickey continued until she graduated from Addison High School..." according to the report.

The investigator told her that was a crime, and asked if she wanted Mr. Hickey charged. She hesitated, the report shows, then said no, because she is married with children, was worried for their safety, and that it happened a long time ago.

"... Even though she knows the relationship was wrong she has suffered no ill effect from it," the investigator wrote. "She stated that as long as Mr. Hickey is no longer having those sorts of relationship with young girls then she does not want to disrupt her life for something that happened so long ago."

If investigators could find other victims, she said, she would come forward to press charges.

The Blade also quoted from Hickey's Nov. 11, 2015 Facebook message to Dawn from the police report. Its high significance came through.

"I don't want your family disrupted, nor mine. The last 25 years I have pieced my work and my family back together," he wrote in the Facebook message, which was included in the police report. "If you are going to talk to him [the investigator], can you let me know so that I can prepare for the heartache, publicity, and destruction?"

Mr. Hickey refused to comment Friday to *The Blade* about why he sent the woman that message.

Hickey responded on his Facebook page:

The Blade will be doing their 4th front page story about me in the last month. Ask yourself why the information they will share has been public record for years. Ask why on the weekend before the election do they attack. Judge me on what I have done for your kids and our community. Judge me on 30 years in education. 30 years.

Of course, Dawn's statements and the "smoking gun" message Hickey sent her had *not* been in the "public record for years." They were only on record since early 2016 (in the MSP report) but had not been reported publicly. *The Blade's* news story was the first time the general public was seeing this.

A supporter responded on Hickey's Facebook: "Smart voters will recognize a smear campaign. Curious voters will wonder why they are so afraid of you. Most voters will line their puppy crates with *The Blade*. Any publicity is good publicity."

The next day, Hickey tried to switch the focus to his campaign platform (which he had first posted in September). His Facebook post from November 5 tells voters, "Give the boot to cowards, anonymous sources, and agendas."

Two days after *The Blade* summarized the Michigan State Police investigation (not exactly an "anonymous source"), Hickey rolled out praise of his wife and family on Facebook. He included a photo of himself wearing a T-shirt, posing with his wife in front of their house.

He wrote on Facebook:

6 November 2017 - This amazing woman has been married to me for 30 years. With WLS our son Luke earned a baseball scholarship and now teaches special needs kids in Lima, our special needs son, Noah, works at Kroger and is proudly in the union, our son Sam is on a basketball scholarship at Ohio Dominican, and Abby is a Junior at WHS with Div 1 basketball offers. WLS has served our family well. Please let me continue to love, lift up, and cherish your

kids. Please vote Hickey tomorrow. Our amazing district and future truly depends on a return to our shared values. We must, must, must vote!! Let's roll friends!! Please share.

This is an enormous election for the future of our kids. The last four years you can see first hand what agendas do to a school district. From the mountaintop of the top workplace, top leader, excellent ratings, incredible honors and initiatives to police reports, lies, innuendo, anonymous bloggers, leaks from executive session of the board to blogger and newspapers and radio and potential board members (all against the law).

I would love your vote but if not me, please vote for the other 5 candidates who are not on the board or served on the board. This board has failed to be courageous and did not stand up to special interests. My daughter and all our kids deserve better.

No matter what, you must VOTE!!

In his outdoor election-day Facebook livestream on Nov. 7, Hickey said, "I was scared coming here. I'll be honest with you, with the negative publicity, and the agendas, and the lies, and the vitriol."

Early Nov. 2017: Dawn asks Mich. State Police to go forward with investigation

Patrick Hickey just couldn't let go of his power in Washington Local Schools. He craved that seat on the School Board. *If he hadn't decided to stay in the spotlight, perhaps his Addison victim, Dawn, would not have changed her mind about coming forward with her accusations.*

In early November – just days before the School Board election – Dawn again contacted Detective Rothman at the Michigan State Police. On November 6, 2017 she submitted a written statement detailing her sexual relationship with Hickey. Her statement is in the Jan. 3, 2018 MSP report. (See Chapter 22.) It concludes:

> I know the question everyone has is, why come forward formally now? My answer is simple – I'm tired. I'm tired of the constant phone calls / voicemails / texts / letters from Attorney's [sic] – the disruption in my life and my family's life. I was nervous and scared for my family, but at this point, with other's [sic] coming forward, I just want this to be over! Having to tell my children was heartbreaking and humiliating. They shouldn't have to deal with this – MY past. How can I ever talk to them about making good

decisions when here I've been sitting silent hoping this just goes away? I finally have to do the right thing.

I also never wanted to be labeled a "victim". I didn't (still don't actually) want this part of my life to be public knowledge open to have people judge me or my family for one reason or another. I realize that it's inevitable whether I formally admit it or not, but at least the truth will be out there instead of assumptions being made. The final straw was the Jeremy [Baumhower] blogger! Reading his comments and [his] laughing about it has pushed me to finally come forward …

Could Jeremy Baumhower ever have imagined that his over-the-top pro-Hickey activism would be a factor in bringing Hickey down?

The Michigan State Police would formally reopen the investigation in early January 2018.

Hickey wins seat on School Board

Despite the revelations of the "37 Charges" (Dec. 2015) and the 2016 MSP investigation, Hickey won his seat on the School Board. He came in second out of nine candidates. Former Board President Thomas Ilstrup was the top vote-getter. Patricia Carmean was not re-elected.

Either the voters didn't want to believe anything bad about their beloved leader, or they simply didn't think the revelations were disqualifying. After all, *everyone makes mistakes.*

Significantly, Hickey ally Mark Hughes was elected. Should Hickey take his seat in January 2018 (despite his ban from school properties), he would control the majority on the Board along with allies Lisa Canales and Hughes.

Hickey and his fans were ecstatic. But some on Facebook showed concern about his suitability for the Board:

Patrick Hickey - 8 November 2017
Thank you so much to the community and the hundreds who have reached out to me. I promise to respond to each of you but it will take time. You humble and amaze me. Thank you for your love, support, and trust. Today is the first day of the next 50 months where the board will not have agendas or special interests. We will focus solely on kids, family, and community. The healing begins today!!

Allison
Rapist

Jim
great day for the lawyers!! Patrick do the right thing and step
down. The district is better off without you around. If you
really cared about the district, our children and the teaching
staff you wouldn't have behaved as you have in the past.
They say the past repeats itself. Shame on the voters for not
doing their homework!!

The day after the election, Nov. 8, he was interviewed in his home by
13abc Action News. Dressed in brief running shorts, he "man spread" on
his sofa next to the female reporter. [35]

He told her:

> I just believe this is a day of healing for the district, and a day to
> move forward where we can return to the kids being the sole
> focus... I deny *emphatically* the accusations that have been made
> against me.

Hickey said if the charges were true, he would have been fired rather
than given a $300,000 severance package by the district. And he would
be in jail.

> If all of those things were true, one, I would have been fired or two,
> I would be in jail. I've never been charged with a crime in my life...
> There was never given the opportunity to respond to any of it [the
> "37 Charges" the Board drew up]. I deny... It's complete
> falsehoods. The 37 things that are listed on that document are
> complete falsehoods...
>
> The Superintendent [Dr. Susan Hayward] has never spoken to me.
> I think that [allowing him on WLS properties] is under the

direction of her Board. So I look forward to working with Dr. Hayward.

In fact, the Superintendent works for the Board. The Board is not "hers." She cannot tell them what policies to set.

There was a School Board meeting that night. How would they address seating Hickey on the Board in January, given that he was banned from WLS grounds? Hickey had in fact emailed the Board and Superintendent earlier that day, requesting the issue of his ban be placed on the agenda and voted on that night. [36] But that didn't happen.

The WLS administration did register Hickey for the upcoming Ohio School Boards Association (OSBA) conference, as he requested.

Board President David Hunter said that many community members had called about lifting Hickey's ban from school properties, but the question would be left to the Board's attorneys. No public comments were allowed at that evening's meeting on the issue. Hunter said,

> We hope that over the next few weeks many of the concerns can be addressed and settled. We must remember that our primary concerns and obligations involve [sic] around our students... I have reached out to all three of our newly elected members ... inviting them to contact our Treasurer... We must heal and work as a team... I am sure that the rumor mill will continue to grind out nontruths, innuendoes, and inaccuracies as it has over the past few years... I have asked everyone here today and those who truly care about Washington Local to step back, take a deep breath, and allow our Superintendent, Treasurer, and our staff to do the job that they were hired to do: educate and care for our students. It's time for the ugliness, the hatred, and the viciousness to stop. We do not all have to agree, but we must learn to disagree in a manner that is civil and can serve as an example to the students and community we serve. [37]

WTOL covered the meeting:

> While there was no public comment at the Washington Local School Board meeting Wednesday, several in the audience had the election on their minds.
>
> Some liking the outcome of Patrick Hickey on the board while others disagree.
>
> "I am a strong believer in fact and I think there's been a lot of rumor a lot of innuendo and no proven fact of anything," said

Jackie Semelka, a supporter of Hickey. "I've got 15 kids who have gone through this district and he's done great things."

"I was ashamed for the first time in my life to even say, this was last night, to say that I was a panther. Today I am back to being proud to be a panther, we just had a little hiccup," said Chris Weills who was disappointed Hickey was elected. "You had two candidates that the teachers backed, they didn't even make it. They weren't even in it."

Weills said she will watch Mr. Hickey closely and the election has ultimately made her become more involved. She plans to attend every board and council meeting to be more active in the future...

The board president hopes the current board can come up with a decision on the ban, but if not the new board will address the issue come January.

"I think it is important that we wrap our arms around the community's decision," said Hunter. "The community made a decision to put these three people on the board, they will be on for four years and I think we need to make sure that their focus and our focus is for the kids."

Hunter hopes they can move on from all this and get back to what matters most their students. That's something Patrick Hickey agrees needs to happen.

He said he's ready to get to work and will be dedicated to keeping voters [sic] trust.

"I'll be good to our kids and I'll be good to our staff and our community and when you do that the district can soar and the district has soared before and it will soar again," said Hickey. [38]

Over the next days, Hickey stuck with the "time to heal" message and promised the district would "soar" because he was going to be on the Board.

Patrick Hickey - 9 November 2017
It is time to heal. It is time to focus on kids. Thank you so
much for your support.

David
Congrats Mr Hickey I have to tip my hat off to you for
keeping your composure and up beat Spirit throughout your
campaign there's a lot of negative powers that be that wanted
to see you fail especially the Toledo Blade and 1370 [WSPD

talk radio]. Now that the election is over and the parents of Washington local have spoken hopefully they will back off now and let you do your job to the best of your ability to serve our children.

Patrick Hickey - 11 November 2017
The next 50 months I will keep the trust of my amazing supporters and earn the trust of my detractors. In partnership with Dr. Hayward, the board, the parents, and the community we will soar as never before, let's get to work!! Hunter, Canales, Hughes, Ilstrup, Hickey. A true team for kids!!

The Toledo Blade's cartoonist disagreed:

Kirk Walters for The Toledo Blade, Nov. 12, 2017.

Citizens want Hickey's ban from school properties to continue

Meanwhile, five days after the election, people in the district ("Citizens for a Safe WLS") posted an online petition to the Board, *"Keep Patrick Hickey's Ban from WLS Property in Place."* [39] It summarized the "37 Charges," threw in Hickey's wild behavior at the Feb. 2016 basketball game, and mentioned the Addison rumors. It drew 2,146 signatures. The petition explained:

The vote total on November 7th did not show the whole picture of the Washington Local community. The community isn't only the voters who live in WLS. The community is the teachers, staff, alumni, and family members of students, many of whom live across the country, not along Alexis Road. Everyone connected with WLS should have a say in how their district is managed, especially when the mismanagement lends itself to embarrassing articles in the *Washington Post* [sic; *Washington Times*, endnote 40], and a potential danger to the students and staff of the district. Alumni across the country are answering difficult questions as to what is going on back home in Toledo.

The numerous allegations against Hickey prove that he is a risk to the safety of staff and students; therefore, he should not be allowed to interact with them on school grounds. As a board member, he should receive access to only the Lincolnshire Administration Building. This should be sufficient to fulfill his elected duties to attend board meetings.

Patrick Hickey's behavior has garnered negative attention for the district, which has taken the spotlight away from students, staff, and residents who do so much good for the school community. Please do what is right for Washington Local, and work to keep Hickey away from school grounds.

Here are three of the comments that were posted at the petition:

CSM (Ret) S B: Mr. Hickey ran and won. Allowing him to unfettered access to the students and staff at WLS will perpetuate his ability to coerce his victims and send a message he is untouchable. Given his reprehensible behavior with female staff and past history of criminal sexual behavior with minors, it is the job of this board to protect the employees and students of WLS.

H M: While I do sympathize with Patrick Hickey's children that they are not able to have their father at their school event, I feel it is in the best interest of the children, staff and WLS district to err on the side of caution and keep the ban in place for Patrick Hickey. This is mainly due to the allegations of him having inappropriate relations with a 14 year old at his previous employer (Addison School) along with the 37 charges the WLS board members documented prior to Patrick Hickey resigning in 2015. With the WLS board members having knowledge of the past allegations and charges against Patrick Hickey, it could be a tremendous liability to Washington Local Schools if any new allegations were to be made in the future. I feel it would also send a message to the community and others that the actions behind the allegations and charges are not acceptable and will not be tolerated for any WLS staff or board member.

Woman: I have signed because this kind of behavior is not okay and by allowing him to come back it will send such a negative message to these young future adults. Regardless, he knew what he was doing was wrong and yet he did it anyway!!!

Hickey demands his rights as Board member

Hickey just couldn't lie low but continued to make contentious demands. As a victor in the recent election, he asserted his rights to contact WLS staff. He also wanted passes to WLS athletic events. The Superintendent denied his requests. *The Toledo Blade* had this:

Emails provided to *The Blade* through a public records request show Mr. Hickey began pressuring the school board and Superintendent Susan Hayward to lift his ban the morning after he was elected Nov. 7...

In his post-election emails, he linked support for him with support for future district tax levies, told Ms. Hayward to remove his separation agreement from the district's website, asked her to unblock him from social media and, asked her to instruct other administrators to unblock him as well.

"I will use every legal recourse at my dispisal [sic] if you attempt to suppress my ability to do the work I have been duly elected to do," he wrote in a Nov. 10 email. "Lift the ban, take the slings and arrows and move on. Furthering this ban is unacceptable."

The Board's attorney explained in a Nov. 11 email to Hickey that he is not yet a Board member and won't be until he is sworn in. "Until and unless there is further action from the Washington Local School District Board of Education, he is not to contact any employee of the district." Hickey's attorney then "asked what authority the district had to stop him from contacting staff. 'Last I heard Toledo was still in America,' he wrote."

Mr. Hickey claimed in an email to his attorney that district employees are contacting him "in droves" since the election.

"Contact by employees is certainly not unwanted when they are reaching out to me in astonishing numbers. I will absolutely respond to them as their elected representative as it is my duty," he wrote. "This harassment and these threats need to end immediately."

But the WLS teachers' union was having none of it.

> Union President Christopher Hodnicki said in an email to members last week he intended to address the "divisive" aspects of the election and the union would "remain vigilant to keep our kids and staff safe by taking all necessary actions to do so."

> Before the election, Mr. Hodnicki and union Vice President Fritz Schermbeck spoke to *The Blade*. Union leadership once supported Mr. Hickey. Now, while some teachers continue to support Mr. Hickey, others are "terrified of retaliation" if they speak against him, Mr. Schermbeck said, and worry that his election to the board is divisive for the district.

> "It's hard to put into words the fear you hear from your own members," Mr. Schermbeck said.

> Mr. Hodnicki said Mr. Hickey has twice threatened him with defamation lawsuits. Union leaders say they are concerned about their members' safety.

Hickey ordered to reimburse WLS for inappropriate expenses

Shortly after the disagreement over contacting WLS staff, the Board's attorneys ordered Hickey to pay back certain expenses totaling over $1,123 that he had claimed while Superintendent. This included clothing, gifts to Board members, beverages, donations, a license renewal, and even skydiving.

Hickey claimed that the WLS Treasurer had earlier approved those expenses, but the Treasurer took issue with that. From *The Blade*:

> Disputes about Mr. Hickey's use of public funds while he was superintendent are long-running, but often overshadowed by other allegations of misbehavior... The list of questioned expenses included gifts for board members and others, as well as reimbursements for donations Mr. Hickey made to district programs...

> Mr. Hickey's use of public funds to pay for skydiving sessions with a special needs student and district staff was also questioned. He later said publicly during the campaign that he felt the expenditure was proper, but paid the district back when questioned.

> A $2,231.50 check dated Aug. 26, 2014, to the district did not come from Mr. Hickey himself, but from the Jeanne Hickey Memorial

Fund, which was created in memory of one of Mr. Hickey's sisters, who was killed by a drunken driver ... when she was 15. Mr. Hickey is listed as the sole trustee for the foundation in tax records. [42]

Hickey would often cite that memorial fund set up for his sister (killed by a drunk driver). [43] It was his big charitable work. Perhaps he later paid the fund back.

Hickey had to pay back the WLS district for his skydiving.
This was one of his signature photos on his social media.

School Board votes to keep Hickey banned from school properties

At the final School Board meeting of the 2017 on December 20, the audience was primed for more Hickey drama. [44]

Board President Hunter commented that the primary focus of the WLS Board is the safety, welfare, and education of children, and it should not be centered around any one Board member. But Hunter went on to make a motion to *waive* the ban on Hickey from school properties temporarily, for just the organizational meeting of the Board on January 3, 2018 where newly elected members would be sworn in and Board officers elected. But if Hickey were to be allowed at that meeting, he and his two allies could to take control of the Board, electing themselves as officers. (The innocuous argument for letting Hickey participate at the

Jan. 3 meeting was that the *new* Board would decide then how to handle his ban in the longer term.)

While Hunter continued to favor Hickey, the three outgoing Board members held the line. Eric Kiser joined Langenderfer and Carmean to keep the ban, voting Hunter's motion down.

Treasurer **Jeff Fouke** administered the Oath of Office to the 2017 officers -- President **David Hunter** and Vice President **Eric Kiser**.

SEATED: *Superintendent **Susan Hayward**, Board President **David Hunter**, Board Vice President **Eric Kiser**, Treasurer **Jeff Fouke**.*

STANDING: *Assistant Superintendent **Brian Davis**; Board members **Lisa Canales**, **Patricia Pedro Carmean**, and **James Langenderfer**.*

Outgoing 2017 School Board members Carmean, Kiser, and Langenderfer held the line and voted to keep Hickey banned from WLS properties in 2018.

The Toledo Blade covered the meeting:

> Washington Local Schools' board of education refused Wednesday night to allow Patrick Hickey, the district's former superintendent, to enter district property to be seated early next month as a newly elected board member, at least initially.
>
> At the outgoing board's final meeting Wednesday, members upheld their previous decision to ban Mr. Hickey from district property. Outgoing board members Patricia Carmean, Eric Kiser, and James Langenderfer voted against temporarily removing the ban, while David Hunter and Lisa Canales voted in favor.

The 3-2 decision was met with cheers from the standing-room-only crowd, many of whom wore yellow shirts in a silent show of solidarity in their effort to see the ban upheld.

"I'm extremely happy. I'm proud of this school board," parent and WLS graduate Tina Wagner said. [45]

The Board also defeated (3-1) Hunter's motion to move the Jan. 3 meeting off-site, which would have allowed Hickey to attend. (Hickey ally Canales abstained.)

More from *The Blade*:

"Nobody should be afraid to send their child to school or go to work," Mr. Kiser said. The comment was met with applause.

Ms. Wagner said she helped organize the movement of citizens concerned about allowing Mr. Hickey on school property. The group sent roughly 400 postcards to current board members urging they maintain the ban.

"We want students and teachers to be safe in the district. There are some predatory behaviors that I don't feel comfortable with," she said.

It was a rancorous meeting. [46] The crowd appeared to be evenly divided pro- and con-Hickey. [47]

As Hunter makes his opening statement, a woman in the audience interrupts and yells, "How many postcards did you get?" (to keep Hickey banned from school properties). Hunter warns her to be courteous or leave the room.

He says, "This is one of our problems. *We have to heal.* Please, hold your comments." He repeats his statements from the November meeting: "The ugliness, hatred, and viciousness must stop." He says no discussion of the ban issue would be allowed from the public as it is an ongoing legal issue.

In the public comments, [48] Kathy Mayfield (WLS resident and alumna, and teacher in a nearby district) says:

When it comes to safety in the workplace – and stop me if I go too far – our nation is experiencing a time of reckoning. Men in power have seen their careers come to a sudden end when it's learned that their actions have made others feel uncomfortable...

She is stopped there by Hunter.

A woman yells out: "The voters want to know why you're silencing people." Hunter continues,

These decisions that are being decided concerning this Board and the next Board and [Hickey] are very legally involved. To allow that microphone to be open allows liability to this Board and we have to be protected to protect the moneys of this school system.

More interruptions come from women in audience.

Mayfield then says she speaks for "... students and staff... their safety and their protection should be put before the popularity of one man." She had a petition from small group of alumni. She gives it to the Board, accompanied by applause.

She later tells NBC 24 that night that she knows "teachers who have had personal experiences with Patrick Hickey that have been negative and they've been fearful to speak out." [49]

Another woman speaks: "Silence is consent. I refuse to remain silent when safety of the district is at risk." She reads a quote from Elie Wiesel:

We must take sides. Neutrality helps the oppressor, never the victim. Silence encourages the tormentor, never the tormented. Sometimes we must interfere when human lives are endangered, when human dignity is in jeopardy. That place, at that moment, must become the center of the universe." We must protect this community, we must protect these students, and you must protect the staff. I ask you not to modify the ban.

She is applauded when stopped by Hunter.

The various speakers who referred to "protecting the staff" were apparently thinking of the female staffers Hickey took advantage of from his position of power.

Karen Gilliam, OAPSE (support staff union) President spoke, with Teachers' Union President Christopher Hodnicki standing at the podium with her signaling his union's agreement.

Social media is killing Washington Local... it doesn't do any of us any justice, no matter what your position is. [It] has made it impossible for a lot of our teachers and staff to do our jobs... As a human being, I stand with victims. I don't victim shame.

Hickey responded on Twitter after the meeting: "Tonight 3 members of the WLS board voted against the will of 3,300 voters. The will of the people is a cornerstone of our democracy. Shame!!" [50]

The Blade ran this after the meeting:

[Hickey] has insisted his ban from school property be lifted because of his election to the board.

"This board, as they've done the last two years, they've thwarted the will of the people," he said Wednesday. He added he is confident the new board will lift the ban in January, "and then we'll move forward. The president told me last night that the ban will be lifted," Mr. Hickey said. [51]

Hunter was roundly criticized two weeks later for stifling comments on Hickey's ban at this meeting. From *The Blade's* lead editorial on Jan. 1, 2018:

No shushing Hickey critics

Muzzling public comment at school board meetings does not help Washington Local with its Hickey woes… However the board decides to handle the ban question, one thing is certain – it botched the debate…

School boards are required to do the public's business in public. And when they allow public comment, they are not allowed to limit the topics. Yes, a public debate over the lightning rod that is Mr. Hickey is bound to get disruptive.

But because he was elected, Washington Local school board meetings are bound to be disruptive for the foreseeable future. The district IS disrupted. Voters put a disgraced, ousted superintendent with a history of drama and legal issues in office. [52]

The issue of how Hickey could serve on the Board – or even be sworn in – when he was not allowed on school properties would become the first order of business for the Board in January 2018.

Students drawn into the scandal

Students were closely watching this drama. In the videos of the Board meetings, there are often quite a few children present. Which details of the Hickey scandals did they know and talk about?

Joey Horan in *Belt Magazine* (March 2018) confirms the high school students' involvement. They even sat according to which "team" they were on.

… more than two years later [after his December 2015 resignation as Superintendent], Hickey continued to enjoy support from a large contingent of students. At the final board meeting of 2017 … a large group of students expressed their support for Hickey. "We started out with Hickey," two students told me, sitting among more than a dozen of their peers in the pro-Hickey section.

In a mock school board election [in November 2017] held at Whitmer High School – the only high school in the district – they said Hickey won by a landslide. Many would want him to speak at their graduation, too. [53]

Did teachers or administrators instigate or approve this mock election?

Hickey closes out 2017

Hickey wasn't done yet. He closed out 2017 with a demand that $2,231.50 – the amount he had reimbursed the school in 2014 for his skydiving adventure – be returned to him. *The Toledo Blade* reported:

> "In that the board has asked me to pay 6 year old expenses [the $1,123 noted above] that they deem to be not legitimate expenses, I am asking that the $2,231.50 be reimbursed to me as it was a proper public expense," he wrote.

> In his letter, he also defended the credit card purchases.

> "He paid the money because he was told it wasn't appropriate, and as far as I'm concerned, it's over," Board President David Hunter said Friday in response to Mr. Hickey's letter.

> He [Hickey] also asked for "records provided to the Ohio Department of Education concerning Patrick Hickey." That appears to be a request for documents in relation to an educator misconduct report sent to the state in January, 2016 by Mr. Hunter regarding Mr. Hickey.

> The report states Mr. Hickey resigned under threat of termination, while in the course of an investigation into conduct unbecoming the profession, and that he "has engaged or may have engaged in conduct unbecoming to the teaching profession."

> The state can remove an educator's license as discipline for conduct unbecoming the profession. State law prohibits the education department from even acknowledging investigations unless an educator is disciplined. [54]

Note that the Ohio Department of Education had begun an investigation of Hickey in early 2016. Later that year, they subpoenaed Addison Schools for his personnel records, and contacted WLS Board members and teachers for any concerning information on him. An educator's license can be revoked for "conduct unbecoming to the teaching profession." But two years later, Hickey still had his educator's license.

On December 31, Patrick Hickey once again won a top spot in *The Blade*'s front-page story on the city's "tumultuous year" 2017.

> Often when a prominent public official is pushed out during an internal investigation into misconduct, they either fight it in court or quietly recede into the background.
>
> Patrick Hickey did neither. Instead he ran for – and won – a seat on the school board…
>
> But, Mr. Hickey ended up throwing himself back into the WLS ring in 2017, running for the Board of Education, arguing that if he won that the ban would be effectively lifted through the will of the people. He was elected, and so far, the ban is still in place. But a new board will be seated in January, meaning the drama will likely continue. [55]

And this was just a hint of the discord to come in 2018, when the Michigan State Police would formally reopen its investigation into Hickey's time at Addison High School.

Hickey plans his future business

While all this chaos swirled, Hickey was working on his business plan to open three Cyclebar fitness centers. He also posted on Facebook that he was vacationing in Orlando with "Whitmer [High School] staff and kids."

Patrick Hickey
18 November 2017
I love the cities where we will bring Cyclebar. Toledo, Ann Arbor, and the amazing Chicagoland!! Our staff will transform lives. Sooooo exciting!!

25 December 2017
Looking forward to a week in Orlando with Whitmer staff and kids. Feels a little different as a board member than it did as Superintendent. Go Panthers!!

29 December 2017
Awesome location Cyclebar Orlando!! Patrick Hickey's Cyclebar opening in 2018 in Toledo, Ann Arbor, and Chicago.

PASSING the TRASH

Working in fitness allows me to meet the most amazing people and transform lives.
We are going to ROCK YOUR RIDE!!

Patrick Hickey gets ready to rock 2018.
(From his Facebook)

CHAPTER 20
Chaos as Hickey Is Seated on School Board; Michigan State Police Reopen Investigation
-- January 2018 --

Acrimonious start to 2018

The 2018 New Year did not start quietly for Washington Local Schools. With Patrick Hickey poised to claim his seat on the School Board – but still under a ban from school properties – chaos and division would continue.

A commenter at *ToledoTalk.com* wrote:

> If the Washington Local School district continues to be a dramatic shitstorm for months or years to come, then all the blame for the embarrassment and chaos belongs to Hickey and his fanatical supporters. He could have taken the huge buyout two years ago and drifted from public view, but he chose differently. With his new role as an elected official, Hickey desires to look only forward and ignore the past, but that's not how it works in a free society. [1]

Because of Hickey's resignation agreement (Dec. 2015) and the Board's later action banning him from school properties even for his children's events (Feb. 2016), he could not attend the January 3, 2018 organizational meeting at the School Board office.

But it was crucial for Hickey to be at this meeting so his new majority on the Board (Lisa Canales, Mark Hughes, and himself) would elect the new Board President and Vice President, and thereby control the School Board and its future hiring decisions.

Anticipating the discord over the Jan. 3 meeting, the Board's attorney, Sue Yount, had emailed Hickey on Dec. 23, 2017. [2]

> Mr. Hickey:
>
> Board President David Hunter is providing the draft board agenda for the January 3, 2018 board meeting to board members via various means. Mr. Hunter asked me to forward a copy of the draft agenda to you with this email. The draft agenda is to keep you informed, but as you know, a board resolution to permit you to

attend the board meeting has not been approved at this time. Mr. Hunter also asked me to forward the following message to you:

"Patrick, in the spirit of complete trust and honesty I want to tell you that due to events and issues that have come to light in the past few days including a letter from the OEA [Ohio Education Association], threats of litigation against the board by staff members, and our unions' concerns about their members safety, I am not willing to modify or change the ban nor the Separation Agreement. I do not know how the other members of the board will vote, and I will not ask. It is their decision. However, I want you to know that you may have been right when you told me that it may end up in the hands of a court, if that is the direction you choose go... Please understand that I do not believe in social media or media exchanges and debates, so I will now request that any and all communications between us go through the board attorneys."

Hickey responded the next day:

Sue, Let Mr. Hunter know that a federal judge may grant me unfettered access to the entire district, just as other duly elected board members enjoy. The board has an opportunity to restrict such access on Jan. 3. I also think a letter from OEA, unions, and threats of litigation against a duly elected person who has never been charged with a crime, did not violate our harassment policies, and received one piece of discipline in a 30 year educational career should be seen as threats, and we have never bowed to threats in the past. Mr. Hunter and Ms. Canales voted to lift the ban December 20th and flip flopping two weeks later also may not sit well.

I worked closely with students and staff in this district for 14 years and safety of staff or students was never called into question. Once sworn in and seated I, obviously, will communicate directly to Mr. Hunter. Going through attorneys is not cost effective to our community. I trust other board members will not vote for the Presidency, (which Mr. Hunter has campaigned for and made promises to other board members, and board member elects to retain that seat), until the entire board is seated after a TRO [temporary restraining order] and injunction is granted. (We did not allow a vote on the Ron Clark academy because a member was sick and waited until he could cast his vote. The vote for the Presidency after our community voted so loudly in November should receive the same consideration).

I, obviously, cannot pursue such court action until the board, and any members who vote to not allow me to the job I was elected to do by the will of the people, act to damage me on January 3. It might be prudent to let them know that it is my understanding that board attorneys cannot represent them if called into federal court individually and they may want to consult an attorney before overturning the will of the people. I would also ask that the agenda be modified because you are not swearing in newly elected board members. Based on this correspondence I am not permitted to attend so you are swearing in some members, but you are not swearing in newly elected board members.

He added on Dec. 27:

Sue,
Please deliver to all members of the Washington Local Board and respond no later than 1-2-18. As a duly elected board member, I request to be sworn in by one of the board members or the Treasurer prior to, or at the organizational meeting, on January 3rd, and prior to any vote to elect a President and Vice President. Please advise as soon as possible and no later than January 2, 2018, as to the date, time, and place for this to be done. Thank you.

Hickey posted on his Facebook on New Year's Day, 2018:

Patrick Hickey – 1 January 2018

READ AND SHARE: Imagine 3,300 WLS residents and voters packing Whitmer Memorial Stadium's home side. On the visitor side is a handful of people (most do not live in the district) attempting to thwart the will of the residents. On Wednesday [January 3] the 3,300 could be silenced. I am 54 years old and have never been charged with a crime, ever. In a 30 year educational career (including 14 leading WLS), I never violated a policy. In 2015 the board paid tens of thousands of dollars to investigate me. The independent law firm concluded I did nothing romantic, sexual, financial, or unlawful. Because of that decision the board gave me $300,000 to leave. Nobody's safety is in danger, the hysteria must end. Absolutely no votes should be taken until all members of the board are present. We must take back our district. Dave Hunter, Lisa Canales, Mark Hughes, Tom Ilstrup must end this madness before the district spends thousands more of your money on out of town attorneys who will be ordered by a Federal Judge to honor the will of the people. Be courageous, the 3,300 who pass levies are watching!!

Jeremy Baumhower: People need to be at the meeting to speak up for the 3,000 voters. The voters clearly spoke.

Joshua: We Love you Mr. Hickey.

On January 2, Hickey expressed his dismay to Yount that he had not heard back regarding his participation in the Jan. 3 meeting.

Meanwhile, Hickey was busy mobilizing his troops on Facebook, and even published Hunter's personal cell phone number:

> **Patrick Hickey**
> 2 January 2018
> If you are one of the thousands who voted for me, feel free to email David Hunter at [xxx] or call/text 419-[xxx-xxxx] as he has said he does not check email. It is time to get the district back on track and out of the hands of special interest and Columbus attorneys. It is beyond ridiculous.

> **Catherine:** Washington local school board meeting Wednesday at six! Patrick Hickey was elected to serve on the board now let him serve!!! No one has been banned for life!! He done a fantastic job when he was superintendent with the highest rating. Let him show other board members how to serve an elected board member. Other board members need to learn how to be for the kids! Patrick Hickey done an excellent job of keeping us at the top of all districts! Now we are at the bottom with a **F** rating!

Local media continue coverage

On January 1, *The Toledo Blade's* lead editorial [3] blasted 2017 Board President David Hunter's handling of the Dec. 20, 2017 meeting when he shut down public comments on Hickey.

> Washington Local School Board members were intent on avoiding any disruption when they recently took up discussion of whether to lift the ban forbidding former Superintendent Patrick Hickey from setting foot on school property.

> In fact, the board was dead set on restricting that discussion as much as possible.

> School Board President David Hunter announced that *public comment from the audience would be limited.* No one would be permitted to address the topic of Mr. Hickey or the ban the school board slapped on him after a 2016 incident at a Whitmer High School basketball game that included giving an unwelcome embrace to then-interim Superintendent Cherie Mourlam...

In restricting public comment on the matter Mr. Hunter mangled both logic and Ohio open meetings law:

"This is a meeting of the public, not a public meeting. These decisions that are being decided, concerning this board and the next board, are very legally involved. So to allow that microphone to be open allows liability to this board, and we have to be protected to protect the monies of the school system."

School boards are required to do the public's business in public. And when they allow public comment, they are not allowed to limit the topics. Yes, a public debate over the lightning rod that is Mr. Hickey is bound to get disruptive...

Also on Jan. 2, WSPD radio talk show host Fred LeFebvre criticized Hunter. LeFebvre said school boards do not have the right to limit *topics* of public comments; they may limit time but can't stifle debate. [4]

LeFebvre again interviewed Brooke Brooks Kelly, a prime witness from Addison against Hickey, on the movement to force the WLS Board to block Hickey from being seated. "We want this man out of education," she said. She noted his "his arrogant, snobbish, just in-your-face behavior," and his threats of lawsuits. [5] She would give her account of Hickey's time at Addison to the Board meeting the next day, Jan. 3. (See her statement below.)

Hickey swears himself in with Notary

Hickey live-streamed his personal swearing-in ceremony at the local library, with the oath administered by his former administrative secretary. [6] State law allowed her as a Notary Public to swear him in.

He did this in the afternoon prior to the Board's official organizational meeting that evening (January 3).

He says "the will of the people" is all-important. He believes his ban from WLS properties is "completely political" and the talk about "safety" is "hysteria." He denies ever violating the policies of Washington Local Schools. He states there was nothing sexual in his behavior with WLS teacher Anna (who filed the 2015 complaint). He notes that no charges were filed against him in Addison. He threatens to go to federal court for an injunction if he is not seated on the Board.

> We live in the United States of America where the will of the people is always the strongest, strongest gift we've been given by our Founding Fathers... As of today [I] cannot go to the Board meeting because in 2016 I yelled at a basketball official. I was asked to leave and I did. I apologized to the official the next day. [The ban keeping him off school properties is] completely political. [Talk about] safety is group talk, hysteria.

> I spent 30 years in education. Never did I ever violate any policy, including any policy at Washington Local. All of you know the two-week investigation that happened in 2015. And in that investigation, the law firm said I did nothing sexual, I did nothing romantic, I did nothing unlawful, I did nothing financial, and nothing involving a student. Um, nobody was at risk. No policy was violated. Those of you who have read the news of 1990 in Addison – an allegation there 30 years ago – also resulted in no charges.

> And so, I'm 54 years old and never charged with a crime, I've never violated a policy in a school district. I worked at Addison, and St. Anthony Villa, and the Findlay City Schools, and 14 years I was in every classroom in Washington Local, every day. And of course everyone was safe. I just spent a week with our kids and our staff in Florida. We need to listen to the 3,300 voters, and not hysteria, and not unfounded allegations, and we need to let the people speak. I do not want to waste any more of the taxpayers' money going to federal court and getting an injunction, and ensuring that the voters' voice is heard. On November 7, I was elected to the district. There was a Board meeting on November 8, and the simplest thing to do at that time would have been to allow me to be placed on the Board, figure out my separation agreement however that's going to look. But instead, I'm now – I'm not even allowed to talk to the Board President. I've been ordered that I can

only speak to the Columbus-based attorneys who charge $300 an hour. This madness must end. It must end today.

Um, I'm going to be sworn in, um, right now, um, taking my oath of office, uh, under the law of the State of Ohio. Um, a judge could swear me in, a Board of Education member, a Treasurer, or any notary in the State of Ohio. And I've chosen a very special notary to swear me in today. So in a little moment you'll see me take the oath of office. At that point I will be seated as a Board member.

Uh, tonight the Board will meet and on the agenda is to vote for President and Vice President. On the agenda is to vote for the calendar of events. On the agenda is to vote for committee assignments. I *implore* the four members of the Board of Education –The voters spoke very, very loudly… They want change. They want this over. The want us to move on. They want the next 48 months to return to the dignity of the school district, and to get it out of the hands of special interests, and to get it out of the hands of the people who do not live in the district, and to listen to the voice of the people… That is our duty, that is our obligation, that is the Constitution of the United States.

I have a 14-plank agenda that I would like to get introduced as soon as possible… One of the items on that agenda is to stop paying out contracts. The $300,000 taxpayer money that was given to me, because of 37 items that you've seen publicized everywhere were indefensible, uh, would have been proven wrong in court, and they gave me $300,000 to leave. Shortly thereafter, they paid my assistant to leave. If someone has done something wrong in the district, don't do that. You don't do that! Fire them! And don't waste taxpayer money. But they didn't do that. And you probably won't read that anywhere.

Sharon Giles is going to swear me in. She was my long-time assistant. She was treated unfairly, with no dignity. Those of you who didn't vote for me: I will gain your trust over 48 months, trust me. I asked for them to swear me in, um, prior to the meeting – the [Board] Treasurer or any Board member – they didn't even get back to me.

I'm looking forward to working with Superintendent Hayward; I think I offer a great deal in terms of sounding board, in terms of expertise. I'm not looking to *be* the Superintendent, I'm looking to open Cycle Bar in Ann Arbor… [He implores the Board:] Please don't waste taxpayer money and make me go to federal court… [7]

Hickey signed his oath of office document with a smiley face. After his self-swearing-in on Jan. 3, Hickey emailed the Board attorney:

> On December 27th I emailed Mr. Ross and Ms. Yount requesting that the board swear me into my duly elected position on the School Board. Your attorneys ignored my request to respond. At 1:00pm today I was sworn in and took the Oath of Office and am now a Board Member of the Washington Local School District for the next four years. I have attached the oath and the statute which allows a Notary to administer the Oath. I was honored to have an amazing exemployee of the District, Sharon Giles, administer my oath. I strongly and emphatically believe that I should be present to vote for President, Vice President, Calendar, and Committee assignments. I am obligated and honored to represent the thousands of people who voted for me and to represent the entire district community as well. Any suppression of the will of the people should not be tolerated, especially by members who solemnly swear to support the Constitution of the United States and to faithfully and impartially discharge their duty. The board can vote to have me be present this evening to vote, schedule a new meeting off campus so I can vote, and can table the votes mentioned until I can vote at the next meeting of the board of education on such vital and important topics. I reiterate that I take the will of the people extremely seriously as it is a cornerstone of our great democracy and I trust this new board will understand the gravity of the situation as well. In closing, I am pleased that [law firm] Bricker Eckler and Sue [Yount] and Richard now represent me [he is claiming their legal representation as a Board member], as it is hoped that my requests will now no longer be ignored.
>
> Sincerely,
> Patrick Hickey

Board attorney Yount replied within minutes:

> It has come to our attention that you intend to force your way into the Washington Local School District Board of Education's organizational meeting this evening, which has been noticed and scheduled for the Board office. District administrators, District security officers, and individual Board members have no authority at this time to disregard: (1) the Agreement you entered into in which you agreed not to come onto Board property [Dec. 2015], or (2) the Board's resolution banning you from entering Board property [Feb. 2016]. The Agreement and Board resolution must be followed unless amended or overturned.

Please be advised that if you choose to try to enter Board property this evening before any Board action to allow you to enter Board property, you will be asked to leave. If you choose not to leave, you will be arrested.

This evening, the Board will have the opportunity to consider your attendance at this evening's organizational meeting before the election of officers. If the Board decides to allow you to come into the Board meeting this evening, you will receive a call from Mr. Hunter – as I indicated to you in an earlier email. If you are called to come to the Board meeting and you cannot come to the meeting because you have been arrested, that will be a problem for you.

Please be advised that this firm does not represent you (or any individual board member); rather, this firm represents the Board of Education as an entity.

Five minutes later, Hickey responded:

Sue,
Don't be ridiculous. Please confront who brought this fable to your attention. This email and your work on it is a ludicrous waste of taxpayer money. This isn't the first time you have put your trust in rumor mongers. As an attorney, you should be ashamed. You ignore my legitimate requests and respond to the theatre of the absurd. Yes, you represent the board, of which I am a member.
Patrick

He posted his exchange with the Board attorney on Facebook later on Jan. 3 with the comment, "This is an example of your tax dollars at work with Columbus attorneys and my response. I hope you are as angry as I am."

Here are some responses on Hickey's Facebook to the letter from the Board's attorney, and on the Board meeting that night:

Misty – This is RIDICULOUS!!!

Erica – Ok. I have had enough!! More threats!! Who do we call? What do we need to do?

Ron – Go to the meeting tonight. This is ridiculous and unwarranted for being a little loud at a sporting event. We all get a little excited for our team but not kicked out for years at every location. It's time to take back WLS for the kids.

Deena – What exactly can be done by attending the meeting tonight?

Ron – Deena S, it shows support for positive change. Patrick can't have a voice in voting if not in attendance. That's what some of the old board wants by staying in power. I'm not sure a lot will be done but it's a start to show support and this district has higher values. Good question.

Liss – I asked that before and no, legally the board member must be physically present to vote. hence why everyone is up in arms. All board members should have the right to vote for the president of the board…

Hunter – That sucks.

Melissa – I would suggest [to Hickey] to not go to the meeting but be ready for Mr Hunter's call. Should that call not happen, I give you my blessing to move forward with legal action against the board. Forcing your way into the meeting at this time I think would go against everything you're trying to do. I know how upset you are. And it's frustrating to me too as a tax payer and voter of the district. Calmer heads always prevail!

Beverly – They should schedule the voting of officers for another meeting when Mr Hickey would be allowed to attend if this is the case. I feel they are trying to get officers elected without him there. The present board is very deceitful!

Liss – Well there are new board members that will not "drink the koolaid" so to speak. Hopefully things settle down and the focus can be out back on the kids where it belongs

Kristen – This is getting ridiculous! The board needs to do what's right. I'm ashamed to be part of Washington Local right now. The board is making a complete mockery of us. The entire area looks at like we are a joke.

Carly – So either Dave or Lisa the only current sitting board members contacted the attorney to send you this letter?!? I'm guessing Dave because he doesn't Internet very well and probably got his information second hand and acted on it without looking into it! Hmmm sounds familiar I thought with patty and jim gone this bullshit was over?!

Liss – Well, there's still at least one that will need to go asap.

Donna – The letter is an outrage, as is the fact that the new board allows this nonsense to continue. They are attempting to ban a duly elected official from performing the duties of his job....

Jeffrey – This sounds so pathetic, immature and unprofessional. Enuff said

Liss – My friends told me. Rumor and I'm going to threaten you over it [Hickey forcing his way into School Board meeting]....did we revert back to grade school behavior? I mean really? What are we paying her for? She couldn't even take time to look into the claim before taking $300 of taxpayers money and firing off this dirt?

Tara – I really feel right now that me as voter am not being heard!! And that is very frustrating. What can we do? Feeling a bit helpless with this matter because they obviously don't care what we think or want for that matter. I'm so tired of this drama ...

Jeffrey – Wow these people r a joke grow up.

Tom – What a bunch of BS. Hang in there, they cannot keep an elected representative out.

Mindy – "Yes you represent the board, of which I am a member." (BOOM!) Mic drop....

Molly – This is bullshit get over this shit and everyone on the board need to grow up

Jordan – Everyone should call their office and send as much email as you can expressing your support for Patrick Hickey to their office

John – do it legally.....the voters of Washington local have a right to be heard through you.....best wishes

Hickey's plan to control School Board foiled

Hickey's plan to control the School Board was foiled. He never received a call from the Board to join their organizational meeting the evening of January 3. He waited outside the building in vain. *Toledo Blade* reporter, Nolan Rosenkrans (who had covered Hickey since 2015), tweeted: "Hickey was outside meeting in his car. Would not talk to me on the record. Had a heated discussion off the record ..." [8]

That evening, the other two newly elected Board members, Tom Ilstrup and Mark Hughes, were sworn in. The WLS website news later congratulated the two, with no mention of Hickey. Ilstrup was elected President and Hickey ally Hughes was elected Vice President.

The Board struggled in two executive sessions that night to address Hickey's ban. Eventually, they acknowledged that since Hickey was elected, he had a right to participate in Board activities. They noted that he was sworn in by a Notary early on the afternoon of January 3. A proposal was finally approved (4-0) that January, February, and March meetings would be held off district property so Hickey could attend.

Once again, the Washington Local Schools drama made the front page of *The Toledo Blade*.

> Former Washington Local Schools' Superintendent Patrick Hickey is still banned from district property, but will be seated on the school board after other members voted Wednesday to temporarily move board meetings off campus.
>
> Wednesday's meeting was raucous at times, with shouts from the crowd, standing ovations, and strong feelings all around. Allegations of inappropriate conduct by Mr. Hickey dominated the public comment portion.
>
> A motion by Mark Hughes to hold meetings off site for several months so that Mr. Hickey could attend failed after it was not seconded, but the board at the end of the meeting re-voted and unanimously decided to move meetings so Mr. Hickey could attend. [9]

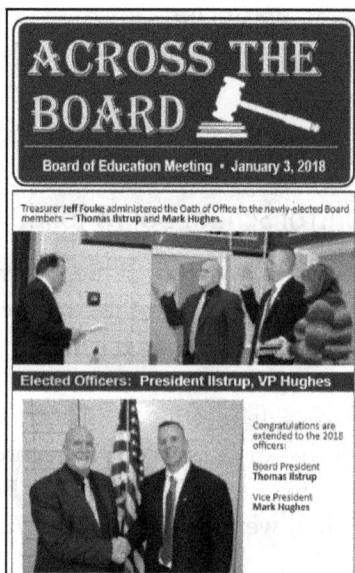

ACROSS THE BOARD

Board of Education Meeting • January 3, 2018

Treasurer Jeff Fouke administered the Oath of Office to the newly-elected Board members — Thomas Ilstrup and Mark Hughes.

Elected Officers: President Ilstrup, VP Hughes

Congratulations are extended to the 2018 officers:

Board President
Thomas Ilstrup

Vice President
Mark Hughes

The online WLS newsletter (above) featured the new Board President Thomas Ilstrup and Vice President (Hickey ally) Mark Hughes. [10] But no mention of Hickey.

After the meeting concluded without Hickey in attendance, his attorney complained about communications from the Board. He wrote to the Board's attorney:

> On January 3, 2018, you sent an e-mail to Mr. Hickey setting forth an unfounded allegation that he intended to force his way into the organizational meeting. Your e-mail contained the threat of arrest… If Mr. Hickey had been permitted to participate in the [Board officer] election in in his official capacity as a Board member, he would have voted in favor of Ms. Canales being elected as Board President… Ultimately, Mr. Ilstrup was elected Board President only because Mr. Hickey had been barred, in his official capacity, from voting.

Hickey's attorney threatened a lawsuit in federal court over denial of "a liberty interest" to Hickey for his being banned from public property. He also requested that the Jan. 3 vote for 2018 Board officers be rescinded and a new vote be taken with Hickey participating.

The Board's attorney then wrote to Hickey's attorney:

> The Board has procedures for swearing in its new members, and rather than following those procedures, Mr. Hickey asked for action to swear him in in advance of the organizational meeting – an action that was not authorized by the Board. Nevertheless, he had a notary public swear him in on January 3, 2018.

Hickey's supporters posted on Hickey's Facebook after the meeting:

Jennifer – Love your [Hickey's] response! Forgive my language, but two words….Shit Show! Totally ridiculous and absurd! I attended the meeting tonight in support of you. Oh how I wish I could have been interviewed by the local tv station… I don't have a "dog in this race". But as an American Citizen, I resent the arrogance of a system that doesn't respect the Will of The People! A slap in the face to Democracy. I guess we will have to see where this goes…best of luck moving forward!

Ernie – New board president [Ilstrup] who gave a 20 minute speech on his dislike for PH [Hickey]. This is getting worse not better. SMH [shaking my head]

Jason – Wow, unbelievable

Public comments at Jan. 3 meeting

The video of the January 3 meeting includes public comments on whether or not the Board should keep the ban on Hickey accessing school properties, or even seat Hickey.

Tina says: "It's no longer about him [Hickey], it's about you [Board]. Uphold the ban. If you don't, you will be responsible for anything bad that happens. Protect the kids!"

Kathy Mayfield, WLS alumna and district resident, says Hickey reopened wounds by running for the School Board. "We cannot stand idly by as he continues to harm the image of his district that he claims to love." Respect the will of the voters but put in place the strictest measures to protect students and staff. Hickey has openly criticized the new Superintendent Hayward's leadership. He emailed her the day after the election and demanded staff in the district unblock him from social media. He gave back misused school funds but now asks for that money back. He repeatedly threatened litigation but then blamed the district for spending too much on legal fees. This is not what healing looks like. Hickey just attacked on social media an involved and respected parent who spoke in favor of the ban. On January 2, Hickey posted the personal cell phone number of one of the Board members on Facebook and Twitter. His promises don't align with his actions. His bullying behavior should not be rewarded with lifting the ban. [Applause]

André has 22 years in law enforcement and has two children in Washington Local schools. He wants all kids protected. He points to the March 23, 2016 Michigan State Police report: An unnamed female admitted a sexual relationship with Hickey while she was underage. That's not OK for any adult male or female to be involved with a high school student. Hickey denied it. But the report states: *"There is evidence."* The former Addison student also said she was contacted on November 11, 2015 by Hickey telling her an investigator would be contacting her. He asked her to let him know if this happened so he could prepare his family for heartache. This only makes sense if Hickey had done something wrong. "I have six daughters and a son. I'm not OK with him on any property, not at all. He's shown a pattern of behavior that's destructive and brought this Board and this school district down." He mentions Hollywood figures being brought down for similar charges, three local pastors facing life in prison, a local law enforcement officer, etc. "Yet we're supposed to send our kids to a district where a gentleman

[sic] who's done the exact same thing has a say over their future, and I'm not OK with that."

Jackie, a staunch Hickey supporter: She congratulates the newly seated Board members. She knows they'll do a fine job. She wants the district to "put hysteria and drama behind us... Peace!"

Tracy, WLS teacher: "Do not modify or lift the ban." She is expecting harassment for speaking out. "Silence is consent." The safety of the district and her own safety as an employee are at risk. The *community* did not create the ban imposed on Hickey. A series of events beyond the basketball game (2016) have left the safety of students, staff, and community at risk. Hickey has flirted with the boundaries of the ban:

> Videos taped outside the stadium, menacing emails to staff, and runs past the campus of WLS despite the many places to run in Toledo. As a teacher in this district, I should not fear coming to work because of the threat someone poses with the possibility that I may be harmed in some way because actions were not taken to secure my safety. By lifting or modifying the ban, you will be imposing a ban on every uncomfortable, intimidated, or threatened teacher, student, or community member from any event or building you allow Mr. Hickey to attend. I am entitled to safe working conditions and I am entitled to support my students, past and present, without fear. And lifting the ban will jeopardize that safety... Just because no one has been convicted of a crime doesn't mean they pose any less threat. This district has been robbed of its progress, of its security, and of its focus for two years because of the common denominator of Mr. Hickey's noise. Well, I'm here to make some noise of my own, because silence is consent...

Wendy, mother of five, employee of the WLS district: She is speaking for friends who are afraid to speak out from fear of retaliation from Hickey. She shares that concern for herself. She is cringing at things seen on social media. It's hard to sit in a meeting when people laugh at others. She is very concerned and wants to keep the ban in place.

Tom Ilstrup, newly elected Board member (who will be elected the new Board President later in the meeting): He says he has mixed emotions himself about his return to the Board and that he filed only one week before the candidacy deadline. The teachers' union endorsed him. This will be his third term on the Board. He says he did not abandon the district as trouble began in late 2015, but that he had already decided not to run for the term starting in 2016 because he was tired of dealing with Hickey's "BS." He mentions Hickey's inappropriate public criticism of the new Superintendent, Dr. Susan Hayward. Ilstrup says Hayward has his total support (along with Treasurer Fouke's). On Hickey's remarks about the election results being the "voice of people," he says Hickey received about 3,000 votes (about the same as Ilstrup received).

Ilstrup reviews the history: Hickey's separation agreement was signed with a smiley face, meaning he voluntarily agreed to leave. The Board was contractually obligated to pay most of that money. Hickey has been banned from school property as part of the agreement except for his kids' events, but he couldn't even handle that well. Ilstrup says:

> Folks, you've heard the concerns of teachers, of staff, of former students. And I'm so sorry for what happened to you ladies [from Addison] so many years ago. Don't let this man destroy this district. He is not here to heal. He is here because he wants his name in the paper; he wants the attention. Do not support him.

(The audience applauds.)

Eric Kiser, former Board member: Kiser thanks Ilstrup. "You've taken the words out of my mouth." He's had his own experiences watching out for Hickey's harassment and wants it to stop. Speaking as a father, he says:

> Maintain the ban [on Hickey]. He knew what he was signing [when resigning]. It doesn't change anything that he ran and got elected. The Board is not being mean. Each time I felt, "Well, I might be getting close to letting him come back on the property for his daughter's games," he would do something that made someone feel unsafe, made them feel uncomfortable.

Patricia Carmean, former Board member: She apologizes to the audience that no comments were allowed at the December 2017 meeting about keeping Hickey's ban in place. She has lived in the district for 43 years and her children went to WLS schools. She never felt more disrespected personally – as was the entire district – than during the last 2½ years. She continues:

> I was given information about this former employee [Hickey] when I was on the Board. And yeah, I was in shock because I don't know people like this. If you look around this room, you see the core values. As a teacher, we were encouraged to memorize them, have our children memorize them. It was a game. These are not bad things; these are great things. This man brought these core values, but this man did not live these core values. He has no integrity, in my opinion.

He resigned to "heal" the district. When is it going to happen? He has disrespected every leader that has come before him. He has verbally attacked me, he has intimidated and defamed my character. He told people I ran for the Board to fire him. I did *not* give him any negative evaluations. I had no idea of his lack of good judgment until I sat in the meeting with the rest of my Board members and read these emails [between Hickey, teacher Anna, and her husband].

I was a reading teacher before that. I ran, and I thought that my experience being a teacher and my knowledge of education would only add to the Board.

This person has brought hurt, humiliation, and untruths to our district. This person has caused fear among some, actually many, of our staff members that I've spoken to. I worked in this district when this man was the Superintendent, so I get it. None of you have, until you're there. And someone comes to you, because I was a building Rep, and they want to give me information and they don't want it to go any further than me.

I want our staff to work in peace, tutor our kids without distractions (which I know they've done their best to do). As a member of the Washington Local community, I urge the Board to do the right thing and keep the ban in place. Our kids and staff deserve the best.

Board members Mark Hughes and Lisa Canales – Hickey's allies – declined the opportunity to comment.

Addison people speak at Jan. 3 meeting

Especially significant were the powerful testimonies by four people who were witnesses to Hickey's time at Addison High School: two of his former students, a former teacher, and a former Athletic Director. [12] These comments were allowed by newly elected Board President Ilstrup.

Jim Driskill – former Addison HS teacher, current Addison School Board member

In 2018, Jim Driskill was serving on the Addison Schools Board of Education and the Lenawee County Commission.

Hi. I'm Jim Driskill. I'm a former teacher for 31 years in the Addison Community School District. I was teaching across the hall 27 years and 59 days ago, on Monday, November 5th, when Kelly

PASSING the TRASH

Wynn was sent down to escort Mr. Hickey to Mr. Dieck, our Principal's, office.

I must admit I was fooled like everyone else at that point in time. In fact, that morning I said, "Patrick, you have my complete and full support." At the end of that hour – I was asked to watch that, because – his room – because I was right across the hall, he came back and got his keys and he left. He left, not due to the relocation of his wife as it says on his application for employment here; he left because he was told, "Either leave or you would be prosecuted for inappropriate relations."

He left with two weeks to go in his basketball season. His girls had a game the following night in a dismal 5 and 12 season. And that much superior team that next night – those girls with a new coach – beat, and they beat them the next week in the first week of the districts. Not only did he leave, his wife left. And she was the coach of my 8th-grade daughter. And my wife and I had to explain to our daughter why she did not get to present Sue Hickey with a sweater that they had made for her.

From 1978 until his retirement in 1993, Don Dieck [HS Principal] and I ran every night after school. I have a record of it, back to that day. So, I know what happened in that meeting that day. And I know why he was no longer employed at Addison Community Schools. And I know, if you look at the memo that is on Facebook dated November 5th, 1995 between Mr. Hickey and Mr. Kersh, who was a Superintendent at Addison at that time, he says his employment dates are May 12th, 1986 to November 5th, 1990. But if you look at his application for employment, it says that he was employed at Addison from August of 1986 to August of 1990, on both his applications to this district. He also used a letter of reference from Don Dieck in his employment here. That letter of reference was undated and was from 1988, because Don Dieck says, "In the past two years that I've known you." That was a generic letter of reference. What you've seen reported in *The Blade* – and I can show you those items presented there in *The Blade* –

[Board President:] Three minutes is up. Please finish in one sentence if you could.

[Driskill:] I just want to tell you that if I were in your shoes, and I am a present member of the Addison School Board, that I would – I [don't] envy your position – but I will assure each and every one of you that my daughter would have never, ever played for Patrick Hickey in high school basketball at Addison. [Applause]

Ken Mullin – former athletic director at Addison Community Schools

Hello. My name is Ken Mullin. On the day that Pat was asked to leave Addison Community Schools, I was the Athletic Director. I was at an Athletic Director's meeting. I came back from the meeting. The principal called me in and told me what had ensued: that Pat had been asked to resign or be prosecuted. I was a little worried about Pat, being – I don't know how to say it – but I don't – I was worried about his mental well health – his mental well-being.

And I asked the custodians, "When he comes in to clean out his room, come and get me." And they came and got me. And I went down and Pat was in there with his spouse and an older couple, either his parents or her parents. I asked him out in the hallway, and I said, "Pat, I just want to make sure you're all right." And Pat said, *"I want you to know it wasn't all my fault."* At that point I turned, walked away, and I haven't seen or spoken to him since. I don't envy you gentlemen, the job you have. It's tough. I was an educator for 32 years. I hope you do the right thing. Thank you. [Applause]

Brooke Brooks Kelly – former Addison HS student and basketball player

Hello. My name is Brooke Kelly. This is the second trip I've made from Georgia to come up here and talk about Patrick Hickey. I was a student and I was also a member of his basketball team.

I witnessed, along with my mother, Patrick Hickey, after one of our home games, go into a cemetery at approximately ten o'clock at night along with one of my fellow players and classmates, park in the back of the cemetery they both were in, both got into one vehicle. Very shortly thereafter the vehicle starts bouncing.

My mother and I sat and watched, had a very short discussion over, "Mom, don't do it because I have to go to school there. You don't know what hell I'll receive when I go back to school tomorrow." Thank God, my mother did not listen to me. My mother called the School Board, reported what we saw, and I believe it was five days after, Patrick Hickey was gone and no longer a threat to any more students. That student I saw him with was only the second, it was not the first student, but the second student I know that he has done inappropriate things with.

I am a former military member, a military police investigator, and also a violent crimes investigator with the Richmond County Sheriff's Office in Augusta, Georgia. I've handled many cases like this. And for Patrick Hickey to say that he has been cleared of *any* wrongdoing in police investigations is a lie. I'm looking at each and every one of you in your eyes, and I'm telling you, that is a lie. The only investigation that has *ever* taken place started in 2016 [by the Michigan State Police]. And that case is not closed. It is not closed.

The more Patrick Hickey talks, boasts, and has his head inflated because he thinks he keeps getting away with everything that he does, more people from Addison that he has hurt are going to come forward and talk about what they know and what they have seen. I will not name the victims, because I will not victimize them again. That is for them to decide, when they are ready to talk.

But I'm telling you: Please do not lift this ban. Children need to be protected. Employees need to be protected. This man has not – he keeps saying he wants to heal. "Let the wounds heal. Let's move on." The best way to have done that was to "walk away and let things die down." That man stood up for a fight because, you know what? – God bless Washington Local School District board members who actually had the nerve to call him to the carpet and answer for what he had done in your district.

I beg you, I beg you: Keep this ban. Keep this ban and protect the people that have voted for you, the children, the parents, and your employees. Thank you very much.

Kris Hassenzahl – former Addison HS student and basketball player

My name is Kristina. I go by Kris Hassenzahl. And I'm one of those former students from Addison. I live in Jackson, Michigan now. And I'm the face of the destruction, not two years ago that you guys are dealing with, but almost 30 years ago. I was a 14-year-old student. He was my coach. He was my English teacher. He was my mentor. He groomed me sexually. I watched him victimize two of my players. And for you guys to support him?

I looked around the gym, you know. [referencing the "core values" posters around the room] "Loyalty" – Does he have it? For himself. "Honesty"? – None. And I didn't say a word because I'm still that 14-year-old child after 30 years that's now speaking out. And I'm asking you. I have nothing to gain. He doesn't want to heal. He wants to continue his reign of terror. And if you want to see faces like this of your own community's children, that [School Board] seat should stay empty, or you should find a loyal person that truly cares about the kids.

I kept my mouth shut because who was gonna believe us? Who was gonna believe a 14-year-old? They wanted to keep it away from their bruised eyes, so they just lifted that rug and swept it under there. I'm done sweeping it under. I'm done! [Applause] I'm asking you for there to be no more Addisons. No more Addisons! [Applause]

The room becomes quiet, with one person commenting, "Pathetic!" – referring to Kris. Kris continues: "You want somebody with dignity. And he doesn't have it. And what he did to you guys for two years, he will continue to do."

Hickey threatens a lawsuit

Hickey's reaction? On his Facebook the next day, Hickey does not directly respond to the accusations at the meeting. Instead, he posts a photo from his daughter's basketball game.

Patrick Hickey
4 January 2018   Findlay, OH
I love watching her [his daughter] and her teammates play. Everyone is safe!!! Stop the insanity!!

Liza
Will it ever stop :-(

Patrick Hickey
Hope so. The will of the people rocks!!

Though Hickey knew that he would be able to participate in the next School Board meeting (Jan. 16), the urge to file some legal action still coursed through him. On Jan. 7, he wrote to former Board members Langenderfer, Carmean, and Kiser threatening a lawsuit for an "unlawful and egregious action." He suspected one of them had leaked to *The Toledo Blade* the list of "37 Charges" that had been drawn up at the time of his separation agreement in December 2015. But Langenderfer and Carmean had not even heard of the document until it was published in the newspaper in late 2017.

From *The Blade*:

Mr. Hickey sent an email to James Langenderfer, Patricia Carmean, and Eric Kiser, asking them who leaked a document that listed 37 charges against him when he was superintendent of Washington

Local. In his email – which was copied to district Superintendent Susan Hayward, Treasurer Jeff Fouke, and two attorneys for the board – he claims the document "severely defamed me and was key to my separation agreement."

"I chose to forego due process in exchange for stipulations in the agreement that were agreed to by my wife and myself. If you have zero knowledge of who sent it to *The Blade* let me know that as well," he wrote in his email.

Mr. Hickey's separation agreement included a stipulation that no "evaluations, directions or disciplinary materials" would be placed in his personnel file after he resigned. [13]

Carmean wasn't too worried anything would come of Hickey's threat, because "he has too much baggage." She saw it as just more of his intimidation tactics. Langenderfer was surprised to get the email and said, "He's always threatening to sue people."

Meanwhile, in order to accommodate Hickey's attendance, the Board was left scurrying to find a location (off WLS properties) for the upcoming meetings. They wanted to keep the rental cost down, yet have enough room for the expected large audience, adequate parking, and handicap access. [14]

The WLS Board soon announced the nearby American Legion Post as the site for the Jan. 16 meeting. *The Blade* pointed out, "The move could allow a board majority – likely Mr. Hickey with board members Lisa Canales and Mark Hughes – to rescind Mr. Hickey's ban from district property, and renegotiate his separation agreement." [15]

The Blade anticipated more craziness. The headline on their Jan. 11 editorial read: *"With Hickey: watch and wait."*

Uproar, outrage, and melodrama seem to rule these days in Washington Local School District. The election of disgraced former Superintendent Patrick Hickey to the school board has set off a firestorm of disruption from Mr. Hickey's critics, his supporters, and from Mr. Hickey himself...

Mr. Hickey is a master at creating contention and chaos. The *students* of Washington local are an afterthought. So, what next? Where is all this heading? It will all have to play out.

The challenge for serious educators and parents in the Washington local district is to not buy in to the psychodrama and to stay focused on the kids and their education...

Ohio law does not provide for recall elections to remove school board members. And none of Mr. Hickey's actions before he was elected can likely be used to force him from office.

School board members who commit misconduct in office, however, can be removed via the state court system. The misconduct that can lead to this process involves willfully neglecting a person's legal duties as a board member or abusing the board member's authority. Mr. Hickey *is* likely, over the course of the coming months, to neglect his duty and abuse his authority... [16]

Jan. 16 School Board meeting

The Board next met in the nearby American Legion Post on Jan. 16. Hickey was present for the meeting, which was mostly held in executive session. There was little discussion before the public. [17]

Board President Ilstrup told the audience after the executive session that Hickey's attorney had corresponded with the Board's attorney. He also stated, "There was a good exchange of ideas in the executive session among all five members. We are all going to come together."

Hickey said, "the meeting was extremely positive... Respect was shown by all. I'm very confident about the future of this district" based on the time the Board members had just spent together.

> **Patrick Hickey** – Facebook – 16 January – Awesome and productive WLS BOE meeting. Kindness, respect, and common goals for kids and community ruled the evening.

> **Darcy** – Finally

> **AnnaLiz** – #YES!!!

> **Amy** – I wish you all the best, you are such a BLESSING to WLS!! When will the people wake up and see what you are truly TRYING to do?!?

Jan. 18 School Board meeting

Patrick Hickey hoped things would remain calm for him after the "kind and respectful" meeting on January 16. He posted on Facebook about his planned new business:

> **Patrick Hickey**
> 18 January 2018
> Cyclebar Toledo will be an amazing life affirming place!!

But later that day, things would blow up in his face.

That evening at the Jan. 18 Board meeting, Hickey sat facing the audience. There were several policemen in the room. Just in case. [18]

Some fearless and powerful voices spoke directly to Hickey during the public comments. Several of the speakers were also giving their statements to the Michigan State Police at this time and they knew something was in the works.

First up was André, a police officer and father in the WLS district, who ripped Hickey with facts taken from the 2016 Michigan State Police investigation (reported by *The Blade* in November 2017). André had also spoken at the Jan. 3 meeting.

André, police officer, father in WLS district

> I want to start by addressing Mr. Hickey. I've never met you. But I've heard so much about you in the past two to three years that I feel I know enough about you and your character. After hearing from two Addison School District employees and a former student athlete at the last meeting, it strongly appears that you abused a position of trust and upon doing so, became an abomination and embarrassment to teachers, administrators, coaches, mentors, fathers, and men in general.

> You have repeatedly stated that you were found not guilty, and that's impossible. Based on my understanding, you were never tried criminally or charged. You repeatedly stated that you were cleared of any wrongdoing which again, by my understanding, is not true because the latest Michigan State Police report indicated that although the victim admitted to the investigators that she had been involved in a sexual relationship with you from the time that she was 14 until she graduated, and upon being informed by the investigating officer that this relationship was in fact a criminal act, it is my understanding that the investigator decided not to interview you at the time due to the victim's unwillingness to pursue criminal charges at the time – which thankfully means the possibility that at some point charges might still be filed.

> Since resigning from yet another school district, Washington Local, you have put on this huge distraction which you may call a fight for your life, a fight for our kids, and a fight for this district – which apparently 3,000 voters fell for and pressed a button next to your name. It is my understanding that based on witness observation that you and the 14-year-old victim [were] having sex in the cemetery. And it is again my understanding that the 14-year-old victim admitted to this to the investigators. Addison School District gave you an ultimatum: Resign or be prosecuted. I've never heard

you say during this entire process that you welcomed an investigation to clear your name, protect your integrity, your career, your livelihood, or your family. You simply packed your bag and bounced.

It is again my understanding that you contacted the victim to warn her of the possibility that an investigator would be contacting her to 'dig up dirt' on you and ask … that she inform you if she chose to talk to him so that you could prepare your family for the heartache and destruction. [I'm] thinking: What could she possibly have said that would cause any of this if nothing ever transpired between the two of you? I can only imagine that your family has been aware of these allegations for quite some time, so why would they be destroyed or heartbroken by her statements when investigated [if she] said nothing happened? It is my belief that you were concerned that she was going to tell the truth and reveal the real reason behind you leaving Addison Schools.

According to a Michigan State Police report, the victim admitted to the private investigator, the WTOL news reporter, and the Michigan State Police Sergeant Detective that she had sex with you basically her entire high school career. To think that a man in his 20's was having a sexual relationship with a 14-year-old high school student is nothing any decent human being should be able to [inaudible]. I'd like your supporters to ponder that. She could have very easily when approached with these questions by investigators said that nothing ever happened and went on about her life. But she didn't. She told the truth. [3-minute time limit signal sounds.]

And you keep blabbing about how you want Washington Local district schools to heal, but that's impossible with this one-man clown act you have dominating everything associated with this district. It appears that it eats you alive to see the district has strong leadership with Dr. Hayward and Mr. Fouke in the Treasurer's office and no one's paying attention to you…

[Ilstrup:] Sir – Your time is up.

[André:] Can I finish?

[Ilstrup:] Quickly.

[André:] You want Washington Local to heal? Sit your family and supporters down and tell them the absolute truth about what happened at Addison Schools and why you resigned. Because I'm sure the truth always comes out.

Police officer and WLS father, André, addresses Hickey directly as Hickey looks down at his papers and checks his laptop.

Jim Driskill, former Addison HS teacher

Jim Driskill, who had also spoken at the January 3 meeting, had suggestions and a warning for the Board:

> Hi, I'm Jim Driskill. I'm speaking on my own behalf. As you well know, I'm a member of the Addison School Board, but I'm here solely on my own. On Saturday the 6th, I sat at home and I was dismayed, disgusted, and distraught as I thought about what happened on the 3rd of January. And then I read the *Sunday Blade,* and found out that some people thought things were "pathetic," etc., but things were still all right. And I sat there, and I sat there, and I came upon a statement by Walter Pater, a 19th-century essayist, and in it he said, "You cannot tell the people the truth. You can only put them in the position in which they can discover it for themselves." Unless we discover the truth for ourselves, it remains a second-hand and external thing. And further, unless we discover truth for ourselves, we will almost certainly forget it quickly....
>
> I have two suggestions for the Washington Local School Board I'd like to share with you. So I'm offering to the Board, if you really want to get to the truth, ask Ken Mullin and myself to come into executive session with you. I will not speak any more about what I said, and I will stand behind what I said on the 3rd of January. But I'm on a Board like yourselves. So I would only do anything else in executive session...
>
> I have a second option if you don't like that one. Let me take a truth-detector test. In the state of Michigan where I come from, if

your house burns down and they think it might be arson, you take a truth-detector test. I'll take that, and if I fail, I'll pay. But if I pass, you pay... I won't fail it...

And I'm here to greatly encourage you to not be embarrassed. Some of you who want to hold onto the facts as you think they are, someday soon you're going to be embarrassed. I've waited 27 years and 74 days to have something happen. And something is going to happen.

Secondly, as a Board member, I would hope that all of you will do as it appears that you did after your first Board meeting. I would encourage you all to be in the same boat, row together. You have a great leader in Dr. Hayward ... Thank you for my time. [Applause]

Brooke Brooks Kelly, former Addison HS student and basketball player

I'm Brooke Kelly. This is my third visit from Georgia to Ohio to speak about Patrick Hickey in as many months. I know you've all heard my story before... As a 16-year-old, I had to talk to my mother, scared to death – because he was such a popular, charismatic, and energetic man in our district – that to speak up against him, and to tell our truth and what we witnessed that night – I knew what hell I was going to face. This was a 16-year-old. I'm an adult now. I don't care what this man thinks of me, I don't care about the district I come from, or actually any of his supporters, or the people on the other side. I know the truth. The truth always wins out. You don't have to have a great memory when you know the truth.

I beg you. I would not put the time, effort, and energy away from my family, away from my home, just to tell you that this man is not good for your district. You guys have to know that. Two years ago, you guys recognized this. And again, I thank Washington Local Schools for being the first ones to call him to the carpet. My school didn't do it. They didn't protect us. After he left, they didn't protect us. Protect your students. Protect your teachers. Protect your staff. Please. A 27-year history of destruction and pain. It's not worth it. He keeps saying, "I want to heal the district." ... Then let it heal! Back away. Have the common decency to care more about the students than you do your own ego – for once. Thank you. [Applause]

PASSING the TRASH

Kris Hassenzahl, former Addison HS student and basketball player

I'm Kris Hassenzahl, a former student from Addison. Patrick Hickey was my basketball coach from 1986 until 1990. 27 years, 5 months, and not much has changed. [To Hickey:] You were at my graduation open house, you bought me a fifth of Tia Maria and I have a picture of it.

See, predators don't always come from the shadows. But they come from where they earn trust. I found comfort in that small town that I came from. We were family, even extended families. We'd look out for one another. And this man came in, with his charm, his own personal plan, deceit, and he was able to divide a community, cause fear and doubt, shame – until November 5, 1990.

When you were asked to leave, or be prosecuted, and you walked – because you would have had to pay for the destruction you did on us. Well, 30 years is long enough. This isn't a witch hunt. Because I've let you occupy enough space that I don't rent out for free any more. See, you don't have power like you did then. I'm not 14. I don't look up to you. I don't respect you. You haven't earned any of it. You were supposed to be my coach, someone that protected us, educated us, and a mentor. Instead, you used our community as your own personal playground. And when things got tough, you ran like a coward.

Well, it's time that I give you the guilt and the shame that I carried for 30 years back to you. Do I need to remind you of the inappropriate comments, the grooming, that you used to do? The things that you could teach me that a 14-year-old boy couldn't teach me. Degrading a student in front of their graduating class, saying that I would never amount to anything? Well, for that, I tell you I have [inaudible]. I have respect.

I no longer will give you any power. I take ownership for my mistakes. I have compassion for other people. I'm a loyal person. My question to you, Patrick Carl Hickey: Do you have the same? *Do you have the same?*

I got backlash from some of your followers asking me if I thought of you and your children and what this would do to them. That's a great question, it was just asked of the wrong person. I ask you: Did you think about Sue and your children when you raised havoc and continued to do so over 30 years? It needs to stop! [Applause]

Other speakers at Jan. 18 meeting

Heather: She is a teacher elsewhere in Toledo. She was on Hickey's JV basketball team at Addison High School. Heather says she was not personally a victim of Hickey's, but a witness to his behavior. She lived in the WLS district until two years prior to her statement.

> I personally enrolled my child – who is a girl – in my school [in a different district] because I did not want her anywhere near Patrick Hickey. When we moved two years ago … I was sad because … I'd heard good things about Washington Local. I thought, how much contact is she really going to come into with him? And then these pamphlets started coming to my house with his face all over them, about him going to the honor roll luncheons or breakfasts, or whatever. And my child – she's pretty bright. I knew she would be at one of those breakfasts. So, there was no way I was enrolling my child at Greenwood Elementary... no way....
>
> As a girl myself in his class and on his basketball team, I did not feel safe. I never even told my mom half of what was going on until two years ago when this all started coming out, because I was afraid. And I watched things happen from the background. Did I see anything? No. I saw people disappear at camp – that's what I saw – and I didn't know where my coach was, and a certain member of the basketball team. I do remember that. So, there's no way I would ever allow my child to go to Washington Local Schools and that is why. When I came to Toledo, I was looking to get a job, that's how I found out he was still involved in education. And I was doing the Internet search, trying to maybe, you know, work at Washington Local, who knows... I needed a job... When I saw his face on the Washington Local webpage, I physically got sick, and I never, ever put an application or a résumé in at Washington Local. I just want you to know, I'm shaking, and this is still very real for all of us who were on that team 27 years ago. It's very real. And it's sad that I have to tell my 10-year-old daughter to never be alone with a male teacher, ever.

A young woman criticizes those in the audience at the Jan. 3 meeting who made fun of Hassenzahl's testimony (calling her "pathetic" and telling her to "get over it"). She says their ridicule was "disrespectful."

Kathy Mayfield, WLS alumna and district resident:

> Knowing that I would have a chance to finally address Mr. Hickey in person, I admit the first thought in my mind was to list all the accusations and the salacious emails that I could cite. But to the

relief of some and the disappointment of others, I'm not going to do that tonight. In fact, I'd like to go in another direction and make an allusion to the Bible. Mr. Hickey, I know how valuable your faith is to you. So, this story will perhaps sound familiar. [Tells story of King Solomon and the two mothers arguing over the baby.] ...

Mr. Hickey, by running for the School Board ... you fought to reclaim ownership of something you had lost. You proved yourself willing to split our community apart. And I can't argue that you didn't do great things for Washington Local. But since then, due to your own actions, too much damage has been done. There is no going back to the good old-Mr.-Hickey days. And your continuing fight for power is only damaging those that you love, it's tarnishing your legacy, and it's worsening the community divide. If you really do love the staff and students as you claim you do, and if you truly want for us to heal as you have said, and if you truly support Dr. Hayward and her incredible efforts to lead our district in a positive direction (since you left it in ruins), the right thing to do would be to walk away – for Washington Local, for your family, and for yourself. You would walk away and let us heal. Thank you. [Applause]

Karen is a WLS district resident and executive assistant to the Superintendent of Ottawa Hills schools nearby. Both she and former Board member **Patricia Carmean** praise Superintendent Susan Hayward.

Mrs. Carmean objects to holding the Board meeting at the American Legion Post. She points out that the ban has *not* been lifted on Hickey being at *school-related* functions. So why is he at this meeting, she wonders. She is concerned that children are still seeing and hearing negative things in the community and wishes parents wouldn't discuss this situation in front of children.

Cindy Perry, former OAPSE support staff union president, 51-year community resident, voices her concern about Hickey's continuing presence.

[Addressing him by name]: Patrick Hickey, I have worked in this district for 31 years. And I have never seen a Superintendent treat people so disrespectful, treat people as if they were the dirt beneath your feet, not only the classified staff, but also the teaching staff. If somebody didn't agree with you, they were in trouble. The intimidation was out of sight here. I hope this doesn't continue. What I need to say is I think you need to walk away. That's the only way that this is going to heal. I have grandchildren that go to this district. And if I have to get an attorney to tell you to not even speak to them or hand them a piece of paper, I will. [Applause]

Cindy Perry at the podium. Hickey (far left at table) busies himself with papers as she and other speakers chide him.

A woman yells out from the audience, "He won't even look at people when they're talking to him! It's ridiculous!"

Ilstrup calls for order. He halts the public comments segment with this: "Thank you all for the courage you had to speak tonight."

Hickey's last-ditch attempt to control the School Board

A significant vote was taken at the end of the January 18 meeting. Supt. Dr. Susan Hayward's contract extension was *not* approved at that meeting because *Hickey and his two allies on the Board (Canales and Hughes) abstained.*

Hickey was already at work undermining his replacement as Superintendent, and apparently still holding to his plot to take control of the WLS district.

After the tongue-lashing that he received at this meeting, he got a sympathetic interview with Jerry Anderson on WTOL television the next day. Anderson begins:

> Patrick Hickey from the Washington Local School Board joins me on "Leading Edge" this week. He says he loves his district which made me ask "knowing that your election would fan the flames of division already burning because of you, does one do that to a district he loves?" Here's how he handled it. I was impressed. Should I be?

Hickey's answer: Because of *his presence* on the Board, he believes that:

... in four years, we'll be right back where we were before, where kindness, and loving and lifting up kids will again rise to the surface. I believe *fully* in that. I believe fully that the district is going to be a better place in four years than it is now. [19]

Hickey shared the interview on his Facebook: "Thanks to Jerry Anderson for a great and fair interview."

WTOL later quoted Hickey at that interview, as he continued to deny any wrongdoing while he was a teacher in Addison:

> "No, it didn't happen," Hickey had said in a "Leading Edge" interview with Jerry Anderson earlier this year. "The best part is, the thing that isn't being brought out is a lot of school districts got in trouble when they would have someone leave and then not do anything. Addison Schools had that allegation investigated in 1990. It was investigated and unsubstantiated in 1990." [20]

Hickey on WTOL TV, Jan. 19, 2018.

Note that WTOL is the station that spiked Jonathan Walsh's investigative report in 2007 on Hickey's time in Addison. (See Chapter 9.)

Michigan State Police reopen investigation, interview Dawn

Did Patrick Hickey know during these early 2018 Board meetings that the Michigan State Police had reopened their investigation into his sexual relationship with Dawn?

On Jan. 4, Detective Rothman began his documentation of the restarted MSP inquiry. This followed on Dawn telling him in early November 2017 she wanted to proceed with charges against Hickey.

On Jan. 9, Rothman was granted a search warrant and traveled to Addison, Michigan to retrieve Hickey's personnel documents from the Addison Community Schools.

On the morning of Jan. 25, Detective Rothman met with Dawn at the Michigan State Police Lansing Post. (See Chapter 22.)

That same day, 13abc [21] and *The Toledo Blade* reported that the investigation was reopened. From *The Blade*:

> Michigan State Police Lt. Tony Cuevas said investigators have reopened a criminal sexual conduct case they were looking into in 2016....
>
> Lenawee County prosecutors at the time declined to press charges because the woman requested that they not, and because it was reported outside the statute of limitations, according to both the police report and Scott Baker, chief assistant prosecuting attorney for the county.
>
> "The same victim wants to move forward with criminal charges, and the statute of limitations for that particular crime is no longer an issue," Lieutenant Cuevas said Thursday...
>
> Mr. Hickey could not immediately be reached for comment. He has previously denied wrongdoing...
>
> Board President Tom Ilstrup said he was "saddened that all this is coming as it is" and that the full board will have to discuss the situation with their legal counsel.
>
> "I intend to let the Michigan State Police continue their investigation and move forward. It is out of our hands. At this point, he is a member of the board and we'll deal with it on that basis," he said... [22]

The Blade also quoted Kris Hassenzahl, who had spoken twice before the School Board in January. She stated that Hickey "made repeated sexually suggestive comments to her" when she was a student at Addison High School. She said the Addison victim and witnesses "have found our voices. We are not backing down, and he is going to have to answer."

A commenter at WLS Politics on Facebook [23] complained, "This guy is under investigation for criminal sexual conduct with underage kids, while serving as a board member of a district with over 7,000 underage kids. #wls4kids #messedup #resignnow."

The Adrian, Michigan *Daily Telegram* reported on Jan. 27:

Assistant Lenawee County Prosecutor Angie Borders said an investigation into Hickey and his relationship with the student began in 2016 after someone who is not the victim [private investigator Chris Gill] contacted the state police. The alleged victim at that time did not want to participate in the investigation.

"That has changed," Borders said.

She said the investigation is ongoing and she has not received the results of it to decide if Hickey will be charged with a crime.

The statute of limitations on filing charges is not an issue, Borders said, because of the nature of the alleged offense and a provision in state law regarding defendants who live out of state. [24]

The *Daily Telegram* also summarized the two-page investigation report in Hickey's personnel file at Addison Schools written by then Supt. Kersh. (See Chapter 3.) This meant the entire WLS community had that detail at their fingertips.

Hickey's devoted former administrative secretary, Sharon Giles, was apparently triggered by the bad news out of Michigan. Her response was to write a poison-pen letter to the School Board and new Superintendent Dr. Hayward (dated Jan. 29, 2018). She accused them of incompetence, malfeasance, hatred, and evil. [25]

And that same day, former Addison student Kris Hassenzahl was interviewed on WSPD radio. Host Fred LeFebvre noted that Hickey had turned down three invitations to come on the show. [26]

CHAPTER 21
Michigan State Police Build Their Case
Hickey Arraigned & Pleads Not Guilty
-- Feb. - March 2018 --

Michigan State Police closing in on Hickey

By late January 2018, Patrick Hickey must have sensed his days were numbered. It was now public knowledge that the Michigan State Police (MSP) had re-opened their investigation.

After Dawn had decided to press charges, things progressed quickly. Besides the many Addison people giving similar testimony about Hickey's behavior, there was that incriminating Facebook message Hickey had sent to Dawn on November 11, 2015.

As the MSP continued to collect more witness interviews, Hickey's behavior in the Washington Local community became more erratic. After fighting so hard to get on the WLS School Board – and the Board jumping through expensive hoops to find an off-campus location so he could attend – he graced the Board with his presence only a few times.

Feb. 1 School Board meeting – Resolution for Hickey to resign

On February 1, Hickey was absent from the School Board meeting. He said on Facebook that he was at his son's college basketball game. It was announced at the meeting that "he had a prior commitment."

At this meeting, the Board passed a resolution (3-0) calling for Hickey's resignation from the Board. [1] Board member Lisa Canales was absent due to illness but was reported to agree with the resolution. Even Hickey's allies (Hughes and Canales) had to face the facts now.

Board President Ilstrup explained this action was "premised upon charges by the Michigan State Police as outlined in news articles that have been contained in *The Toledo Blade* and the *Daily Telegram*" in late January. Board VP Hughes lamented the divided community.

> ... we are very divided. What we see in our neighborhoods, what we see on social media ... People who used to be friends, neighbors, community members, are enemies. We are not in a good

place. We have too much distraction in this district at this particular time. We are not moving forward with the issues regarding kids. We're not talking about our buildings. We're not talking about anything right now.

Admitting his friendship with Hickey, Hunter said the distractions had to end.

I don't want my personal feelings about one man or one issue to cloud anything... My pledge is that we march forward now, asking for a resignation, not because we hate or dislike a person, but because it's the right way to go forward, not distracted.

So, the Board had to take decisive action and call for Hickey's resignation. The Board also clarified that Hickey was still banned from all WLS properties and was only allowed to attend the meetings through March at the off-site location.

From 13abc News following the Feb. 1 meeting:

In a unanimous vote at special meeting Thursday, members of the Washington Local School Board unanimously approved a resolution calling for Patrick Hickey's resignation.

This comes after information released last week that Hickey, a current Washington Local board member and former superintendent, is under investigation by the Michigan State Police...

Cuevas says there is no statute of limitations in Michigan. He adds the age of the victim at the time, the suspect's position of authority and the nature of the alleged crime would have allowed police to reopen the investigation either way.

MSP says they expect the investigation to take some time. Investigators say they want to talk to potential witnesses so anyone with information is asked to contact them. [2]

Ilstrup emphasized that by law the Board cannot force Hickey to resign or "discipline him for something that happened outside of the board room."

The WLS drama was gaining national attention. Associated Press reports were being picked up by major newspapers around the country. [3] But Patrick Hickey still refused to step down from the Board.

Hickey remains defiant; Critics speak at Feb. 21 Board meeting

Hickey defiantly attended the next Board meeting on February 20. [4] Entirely in executive session, the meeting was focused on security issues following a serious incident at one of the junior high schools. (A student had stabbed a school security officer.)

The next night, February 21, another Board meeting was held. [5] Hickey was absent. He posted on Facebook:

> **Patrick Hickey** – 21 February 2018 – Tonight I will be attending my daughter's state tournament game as Whitmer takes on St. Ursula in Genoa. I will not be in attendance at the WLS board meeting. Family always comes first in the lives of Sue and me. I look forward to our March meetings and the vital and important work that faces our district, kids, parents, and community. Go Panthers!

Then came these reactions on Twitter:

> **@NolanRosenkrans** (Toledo Blade reporter) – Patrick Hickey says he won't be at tonight's meeting, where a crowded room is full of many who hoped/expected him to attend.

> **Kim** ...Replying to @NolanRosenkrans – At this time when safety at schools is of utmost concern and he knows it is on the agenda, he misses what is his 2nd meeting in 2 months since fighting tooth and nail to get on the board??? He could give a shit about WLS!!

> **@WLSPolitics** Feb 21 It seems like @SuptHickey would prefer not to do the job the voters hired him to do. The district went out of its way to pay extra costs associated with allowing him to serve on the board while his ban is still in place, and he chose not to show. How disrespectful of the voters.

At the February 21 Board meeting, most of the public comments were focused on Hickey. [6]

Terri Kern: "Is Mr. Hickey going to be at the next Board meeting?" (No answer from the Board.) "So, if Mr. Hickey is arrested between now and the next Board meeting, are steps going to be taken for him to be off the Board?"

Board President Ilstrup: "This is not a question and answer... I appreciate – this is simply a comment period. If you would like to call me..."

Terri Kern: "All right. Let me rephrase that. In between now and the next Board meeting, if he does get arrested, I will be very diligent with making sure that steps are taken to get him off the Board."

Kris Hassenzahl, former student at Addison High School, again speaks:

> I spoke several times... I don't want to hold your school district hostage, by any means. I had no vested interest in your district other than the fact that there's a man on your Board who held our district hostage when I was a student. And I don't want you to be – 30 years down the road – fractured more than you already are. Try to pull your district back together... The things that he's done at our district – yes, there is criminal trouble. I can't speak on it, but his days are numbered.

> I would just hope that everyone that holds a seat on the Board – because I know he has a personal agenda, he's not gonna let you heal. I've watched everything that's been on the news, held onto every word, more than I wanted to let that man occupy. But I've done it because I hope that he loves this district, as much as he claims he does. And when he was Superintendent, he [was holding] all his employees to these pillars of dignity, and integrity. Then be a man of his word, walk away, and allow the Board to do what it does for this district. And you people on the Board have to put aside any personal agendas you may have that may include him and do the job that you were elected to do which is to protect, and take care, and nurture this district...

> I know that you voted to have him resign. But he's not going to go out without a fight. We all know this. But do what is in your power and what you were elected to do on this Board and that is what is in the best interest of your students and your community.

Jim Driskill, former Addison teacher when Hickey was there, current Addison School Board member and Lenawee County Commissioner, makes his third appearance. He sent the Board an email earlier in the day which he reads:

> I write this with the utmost sincerity as a fellow Board member, albeit in a rather small Michigan district. I wish to express two observations and concerns, with the express interest of the Washington Local school district at heart... First and foremost, I

believe that – if it's not already too late – the first order of business should be to extend your excellent and outstanding Superintendent's contract... [More praise for Supt. Hayward.]

Her truthful experience and background is not the six pages of lies back from 2002 and 2007 [referencing Hickey's WLS job applications]. I further must add, and I'll bet the house on it, and the farm, that she doesn't do outlandish things on YouTube videos, or two pictures of her on each month's calendar that I received back in 2010. Nor does she post pictures of beer on her Twitter account, as some Board members do. That's amazing to me. And until I pointed it out, he [Hickey] actually didn't have anything about his daughter on there, in the 16 tweets I looked at. That's just amazing to me. And if you don't understand the rage I have from back at Addison, these ladies have portrayed it, and more. OK?

And just Tuesday night, I just happened to remember who worked at Boysville and St. Anthony's Villa, that I kept trying to think of. And I called Timmy up – and Timmy is as big as that gentleman over there in uniform – OK? And I said, 'Hey, do you remember Pat Hickey who worked at Boysville St. Anthony's Villa?' 'Yeah." "Was he Executive Director and Principal?" "Heck no! He was a Treatment Specialist just like I was. And I was there for 16 years, and the five years that he was there, and then he left." That's the kind of Board member you have.

And I think it's a sad state of affairs in this climate for the Board members here to abstain from voting on your current Superintendent... and I agree with Mr. Hunter when he said on the 18th of January or the 1st of February – whichever date it was, sir ... this Board needs to move forward. And the way to do it is to extend that lady's contract right there. [Supt. Hayward] She's overqualified.

The Hickey scandal had attracted the attention of the district's **State Representative, Teresa Fedor**, who calls for his resignation and highlights the problem of schools "passing the trash":

I taught for 18 years. Before that I was in the military. Thank you for being School Board members. I have to commend you also on your bold, courageous move, asking for the resignation of Patrick Hickey... School Boards are about oversight and accountability, setting a direction for the school community, based on the voters and what they want, and listening to them... I also commend you for listening. I've been listening online. [Not even the Ohio State House has cameras hooked up, she adds.] And you're stuck here, in a very, very tough spot. And right now, Washington Local Schools is, through no fault of its own, not able to follow through on these obligations because they are dealing with a distraction, and I mean a great distraction. As we go down this road – and our hearts are broken – but what I know, in my talking to investigators and people in the community and hearing their heartbreak – our hearts are going to break soon. This distraction takes time away from the true duties and goals of this institution.

Multiple meetings have now been dedicated to the discussion of the resignation of a School Board member, Patrick Hickey. His refusal to resign, amid allegations and his colleagues' resolution, signals that he would rather continue to be a distraction from the needs of our community than graciously step down. It's time for Washington Local Schools to heal from this. It is time for Mr. Hickey to resign...

Young people know we are not protecting them as adults... So, I implore you to continue your effort to work in a way that is ... respecting the children. And I will work with you because I am looking at peeling apart this onion. Is there a law that I can create in the State of Ohio so we don't "pass the trash"? I don't apologize for that comment. I never will. Because I've been in teaching for 18 years, I've been a legislator for 18 years. I'm a lawmaker.

There are ways that we can take this situation and we can figure out where the guardrails need to be so that this never happens again. And that's part of what I call in my work with human trafficking the "rape culture." This is real. The "MeToo." This is real. And so, we're going to have to deal with this in this generation because we're the role models for those students. So, I'd love to work with you to find out – I've already talked to the law enforcement, they have suggestions. They're writing me. They're writing a paper this weekend. And I'm going to make the law [bill] by Friday... You did the courageous thing by calling for his resignation... We're going to have to forgive each other. This is tough. But we can do this.

Fedor is now an Ohio State Senator. As of early 2020, the Ohio legislature had not enacted a law to prevent "passing the trash."

Eric Kiser, former Board member: Superintendent Hayward and Mr. Fouke (Treasurer) worked very hard last year and a half under difficult circumstances with Hickey "sniping at their every action, questioning their decisions," and making public records requests that wasted employee time.

A woman speaks:

> Thanks for asking Hickey to resign, but it was overdue. You guys [on the Board] owe everyone an apology for moving this meeting so Hickey could attend. He should never have been allowed to attend the meeting. You did the wrong thing letting him be around all his victims. They're still feeling hurt, that's why so many people are at meetings. If you want this to stop, apologize. If not, maybe have a town hall where people can come and tell what they've experienced, where you will look them in the eye instead of ignoring them. Make sure every victim of Hickey is listened to and believed.

A man asks: "Why was Hickey at the previous night's meeting? If he truly cares about the community, he'd resign." He hopes something will happen soon "to end the circus." In the business community, he is constantly questioned about what's going on in his school district, and it's totally embarrassing. The Board could have solved the problem easily two years ago.

A woman yields her three minutes to **Kris Hassenzahl**:

> "Circus"? To me it's real life. It's not a "circus." This stuff happened to us. I don't stand to gain anything other than I'm trying to protect any other child... And the question of why we didn't come forward? Well, I was 15. And he was my English teacher, he was my coach. And who was going to believe me? Because my own administration knew about it, and they turned a blind eye. [paraphrase:] Hickey is not here tonight because his personal agenda wasn't going to be met. He's a coward... The circus that's created, he was allowed to create in this community... We're doing what we need to do now because we're not 15 and we know how to handle it... There will be no more Addisons. And Patrick Hickey will no longer be a factor. Protect your district.

Teresa Fedor, State Representative, speaks again. She says that in going through the work that will have to be done, the Board really needs to consider an independent investigation and find out where the inadequate gaps are.

Ilstrup reminds audience that this Board does not have the legal authority to remove an elected member.

Patricia Carmean, former Board member, begins by referring to the attempted "mini-coup" by three of the five School Board members (Hickey, Canales, and Hughes) at the January 18 meeting. They blocked the extension of Superintendent Hayward's contract by abstaining on the vote. Hickey's motives were unclear, she says. But some suspected he somehow hoped he could regain the position of Superintendent.

> I was a teacher in the district when that person [Hickey] was Superintendent and Assistant Superintendent. I am humiliated by what happened to Dr. Hayward last month by several people [when the three Board members – Hickey, Canales, and Hughes – refused to extend Hayward's contract]. It's just unbelievable that you would do that to a person. You know what she has gone through trying to get the education and safety of our children and every day she had to deal with that person... I'm ill at ease with Board, I can't possibly understand Mark [Hughes]. I'm very disappointed that you would do that to Dr. Hayward.

> I understand the importance of going to your children's sporting events... I understand things come up, and we have to miss them as a parent. I don't understand, if you're elected ... and then you are not here. I understand he wants to see his daughter. But we moved this meeting [for Hickey] – which I'm still not happy about... I think we could move this back to central office if he's not going to be here... I know what the truth is though, and I know what the lies are. And people are going to continue to hear and see and read both. He has too much baggage, and he should not be on our Board. He should not be in any capacity with our staff and with our students. I'm only concerned with the children and the staff... We have evidence...

Jennifer says she is disappointed in this meeting and said she doesn't care about Hickey. "You're doing your job letting the law take care of it. What we need to do now is stop all the open comments about something we have no control over." She's sick of hearing his name. "Enough is enough. I don't want to hear his name again... So, Addison, please, go back!" She is loudly booed, and there is chaos and shouting in the room. Ilstrup tries to restore order.

A woman yells, "Shame on you!" Another yells: "What if it happened to you?"

Jennifer answers:

> I was respectful to every person that stood up here... All I'm asking you is to let our district do its job. These Board members cannot force his resignation. They can't. They asked for it. He didn't agree. So now it's out of their hands. And laws, as Ms. Fedor said, need to be passed. I agree with that. Protect our children. Pass laws to protect our children... What I disagree with is reliving the story every day, over and over.

Sue says: "I will say what a lot of people are thinking… We need to extend [Superintendent] Dr. Hayward's contract. We can't stop Pat [Hickey]. You can't … remove him, but we can stifle him… In Hickey World, he thinks he is going to remove Dr. Hayward and move right back in… In the real world, we need to keep Dr. Hayward."

Hickey was present at the next Board meeting on March 1 which focused on school security/emergency protocol issues. But Hickey left the executive session about 1½ hours before it ended. No explanation was given for his early departure by Board President Ilstrup. [7]

March 14: MSP Detective interviews suspect Patrick Hickey

The Michigan State Police investigation proceeded with the Prosecutors' legal determination that since Hickey had been a non-resident of Michigan after leaving Addison, he was not protected by the statute of limitations. Furthermore, the underage status of his victim and the teacher/student status would allow for prosecution.

By mid-March, the MSP had collected enough evidence to speak with suspect Patrick Hickey. On the afternoon of March 14, Detective Rothman conducted a lengthy interview with Hickey at the MSP Monroe Post. The Detective had also asked Patrick Hickey's wife Sue for an interview. She declined. (See Chapter 23.)

It's no wonder Hickey did not attend the Board meeting on March 17 (which was focused on curriculum). [8] He knew something big was about to come down.

March 19: Patrick Carl Hickey charged with felony sex crimes in Michigan

PASSING the TRASH

Patrick Hickey's mug shot (March 2018) was featured in
People Magazine's crime section. [9] The national magazine
linked to the Adrian Daily Telegram's video of his arraignment.

On March 19, 2018, Patrick Carl Hickey was charged on three counts of Third Degree Criminal Sexual Conduct (against a person age 13 through 15), with the date "on or about 01/01/87-03/31/87." The Michigan State Police issued a warrant for his arrest the same day.

Hickey's attorney Lorin Zaner "notified *The Blade* of the charges Monday afternoon [March 19], but said his client still maintains his innocence and has passed a polygraph test." [10] The polygraph test likely referred to the one he took on the day he resigned as Superintendent (Dec. 11, 2015), which Hickey mentioned in an interview the day after his resignation. Tellingly, just a few days earlier at Hickey's March 14 interview with the MSP, Zaner had said "he does not trust a polygraph" as Hickey declined to take one then.

The Blade report continued:

> "It's disappointing," Mr. Zaner said, "but let's see where the evidence goes."

> Scott Baker, chief assistant prosecuting attorney for Lenawee County, confirmed Monday that police forwarded information late last week to the prosecutor's office for consideration of possible charges against Mr. Hickey. He said prosecutors do not comment on pending charges until sworn statements are made in court...

> Mr. Hickey voluntarily agreed to be interviewed by investigators and [Zaner] said he had asked prosecutors to allow Mr. Hickey to turn himself in if he is indicted to avoid the cost of extradition to Michigan.

> "He's denied the accusations and will continue to deny them," Mr. Zaner said. "He's never changed his position."

> Jim Langenderfer, a former Washington Local school board member and frequent critic of Mr. Hickey who funded a private investigation into his conduct, said in response to the charges that "I just would like to see justice be done and the truth to come out."

> Glass City Investigations' Chris Gill, a former Lucas County sheriff's detective, was the investigator hired by Mr. Langenderfer. "I just hope the victims can get some closure during this whole process," Mr. Gill said.

Hickey resigns from School Board, maintains innocence

Hickey resigned from the Washington Local School Board the next day, March 20, saying that he didn't want to "be the focus" of the Board's business. WTOL published his letter of resignation. [11]

March 20, 2018

To whom it may concern,

The charges filed against me are false. I voluntarily spoke with investigators and voluntarily took a polygraph test with a Forensic Psychophysiologist with 30 years of experience. His conclusion was that I told the truth and have not had sexual activity with any student, ever.

I led the Washington Local School District for 14 years and we achieved unprecedented success as we cared for and lifted up students in amazing ways. Being named the Top Workplace, with the top leader, in a district that loved all kids equally will forever be in my soul.

At the advice of my attorney I will be resigning my seat on the Washington Local School Board. The kids, staff, and community deserve better than for me to be the focus over the coming months. While it breaks my heart, it is the right thing to do. I apologize to the thousands who voted for me and who knew I could make a difference in the lives of kids, teachers, and staff.

I will now fight for justice and truth. My wife, kids, parents and siblings deserve for their Dad, husband, son, and brother to fight for them.

Sincerely,

Patrick Hickey

Hickey's letter proclaimed his innocence and announced his resignation from the School Board.

Hickey states in his letter that his voluntary polygraph (apparently from December 2015) confirmed that he has "not had sexual activity with any student, ever." He vows that he will "now fight for justice and truth" and his family's honor.

Also on March 20, Brooke Brooks Kelly was again interviewed on WSPD radio. [12] Private investigator Chris Gill had told the host, Fred LeFebvre, that Brooke's story of what she and her mother saw in the cemetery (Hickey in a bouncing car with Julie) was key evidence. Brooke said, "So many people knew for so long... No one even bothered to talk to these girls to be sure they were OK ... and he was allowed to move on and affect other districts." LeFebvre noted the cost to Hickey's family as well. He saw this man as driven by hubris and ego.

13abc had this from Hickey's attorney who continued to maintain his client's innocence:

> "This was a very difficult decision for him," Lorin Zaner, Hickey's defense attorney said. "He has done wonderful things for the school system. He is not guilty of these charges. He did not molest any kids and it's a shame after 30 years that he now has to fight a case that is so old. It just makes sense to take the focus off him and let's get it back to school business." [13]

In the same report, a former supporter of Hickey spoke out.

> "It's been a really trying time for our district," Robin Ramm, a mom with a senior at Whitmer said... "I was one of his biggest supporters," Ramm said. "But over time, my eyes were opened to the allegations and with some things you can't just look the other way. Our kids, our teachers, our parents; we're a good district," Ramm said. "Let's get back to what we are."

Hickey arraigned in Lenawee County Court, pleads "not guilty"

On March 21, Hickey turned himself in and was arraigned in Lenawee County Circuit Court in Adrian, Michigan. He pleaded "not guilty" and was released on $25,000 bond.

The Michigan State Police announced that their investigation had expanded because there could be one or more other victims (in addition to Dawn). According to MLive.com on March 21, First Lt. Tony Cuevas, commander of the Michigan State Police Monroe post, explained that the alleged crime during Hickey's tenure in Addison Schools was *not* reported at the time to either the Michigan State Police or the Lenawee County Police. The statute of limitations did not apply because Hickey did not live in state in the years following the alleged crime. And attorney Zaner continued to profess his client's innocence. [16]

The Daily Telegram (Adrian, Michigan) posted a video of the March 21 arraignment. It shows Hickey looking disheveled in blue jeans and a sloppy orange hooded sweatshirt. [15]

Hickey is arraigned in Lenawee County Court on March 21, 2018 in the same orange sweatshirt he wore the night of his resignation as Superintendent. (Toledo Blade photo) [14]

Lenawee County District Court Judge Laura Schaedler set Hickey's bond at $25,000. He was ordered to remain in Lucas County (Toledo area) and Lenawee County (Michigan), but was granted permission to travel to Washtenaw County (Ann Arbor area) where he had plans to open an indoor cycling business "in 6-12 months." He was to have no contact with any child 16 or under (except his daughter), or contact the alleged victim (Dawn) and her family. He had to stay away from Washington Local Schools properties and school functions (even if off school property). The Judge said her order extended to anywhere in the counties where children under 16 are present (such as a library, ice cream shop, etc.). [17]

From 13abc:

> After the hearing, Hickey's attorney commented on the severity of the restrictions. "Everybody is disappointed on some of the procedures that happened, but that's what happening [sic] in court,

nothing goes as smoothly as you hope," Lorin Zander [Zaner] said. "He is ready to do battle and we will proceed accordingly." [18]

And from *The Toledo Blade*:

First Lt. Tony Cuevas of MSP's Monroe post said detectives investigating claims about Hickey's contact with the first woman [Dawn] received information about a second possible victim [Julie] – also a former student who would have been 14 or 15 years old at the time.

Lieutenant Cuevas said information from the victim in the ongoing case and other witnesses indicate Mr. Hickey's alleged inappropriate relationships were known to students at the school.

"It was pretty common knowledge that he was having a relationship with at least one, if not two, students," he said.

While the charges would have been first-degree criminal sexual conduct under current state law because of Mr. Hickey's position of authority, he must be charged under the code in place at the time of the alleged incident, the lieutenant added.

Mr. Hickey is to appear for hearings March 28 and April 13 before Judge Jonathan Poer. [19]

March 21 School Board: Farewell Hickey!

There was an empty seat at the March 21 School Board meeting that night. [20] School Board President Ilstrup began the meeting saying he appreciates the citizens' right to comment at Board meetings and recently gave latitude on that, but it was now time to refocus on the work of the Board. He asks the community to be judicious and restrained, particularly considering "the developments of recent days." He announced Board meetings would return to WLS property on April 11.

The Board voted to accept Hickey's resignation.

Hickey was again in focus at *The Blade*. Their March 21 editorial declared, *"No more Hickey circus at WLS."* [21]

CHAPTER 22
Dawn Speaks with Michigan State Police
-- Nov. 2017 - April 2018 --

Dawn changed her mind in early November 2017 and decided to go public with what had happened between herself and Patrick Hickey during her high school years. She gave the Michigan State Police (MSP) a written statement on November 6, 2017. That was the day before Hickey was elected to the Washington Local School Board.

This chapter refers to the 2018 MSP reports that include Dawn's statements from late 2017 and early 2018. Digital images of the reports are included in the *Kindle edition* of this book. [1]

Jan. 4, 2018 MSP report

The MSP filed their first report on the reopened investigation of Patrick Hickey on January 4, 2018.

That was the day after Hickey had sworn himself in as a newly elected member of the Washington Local School Board.

MSP Detective Larry Rothman states in the January 4 incident report:

> After "Dawn" stated she wanted to pursue possible criminal charges against Mr. Hickey, I made contact with Angie Borders who is a senior Trial Attorney for the Lenawee County Prosecutors Office. We discussed the case and possible limitations given the extended amount of time that has gone by. We discussed possible statute of limitations issues and determined that the allegations and circumstances surrounding this case did not fall under the 6-year statute of limitations in Michigan.

Dawn detailed her relationship with Hickey in her November 2017 statement for the MSP. Fleshing out her statement at Hickey's June 2018 sentencing hearing (Chapter 1) – that Hickey hurt her to the point she thought she could die – she gave Rothman this description of her experience on Hickey's wedding day in 1988.

> It was the most horrible day of my life. He invited me to the wedding, which I went [sic]. I guess I was hoping deep down that when it came to saying "I do", that he wouldn't be able to, but that obviously wasn't the case. There were just a couple other students

that attended so I wasn't by myself, but I remember it being so difficult not to cry. I excused myself often to go to the restroom to dry my eyes. When I finally left, I got to my car (I was 16 now) and cried harder than I have ever cried. I nearly hit a semi head on while driving home because I was crying so hard. I will never forget that as long as I live. One of the most painful experiences I've had from heartbreak in my life to this day.

Our day to day didn't really change after the wedding We were together when we could be and stole moments in school for a kiss or a hand squeeze when able.

Because so many people were touched by Hickey's malfeasance over the years, his violation of Dawn continued to torment her and she could not continue to just wish it away.

I know the question everyone has is, why come forward formally now? My answer is simple...I'm tired. I'm tired of the constant phone calls / voicemails / texts / letters from Attorney's [sic]...the disruption in my life and my family's life. I was nervous and scared for my family, but at this point, with other's [sic] coming forward, I just want this to be over! Having to tell my children was heartbreaking and humiliating. They shouldn't have to deal with this...MY past. How can I ever talk to them about making good decisions when here I've been sitting silent hoping this just goes away? I finally have to do the right thing. I also never wanted to be labeled a "victim". I didn't (still don't actually) want this part of my life to be public knowledge open to have people judge me or my family for one reason or another. I realize that it's inevitable whether I formally admit it or not, but at least the truth will be out there instead of assumptions being made. The final straw was this Jeremy blogger! Reading his comments and [his] laughing about it has pushed me to finally come forward and let him know the truth and that he [Jeremy] was snowed by this man [Hickey]!

Here is the rest of Dawn's statement to the MSP on Nov. 6, 2017:

Per our conversation, I am writing a statement confirming that Patrick C. Hickey and I had a sexual relationship during my sophomore year of high school (86-87) through the end of my senior year ending when I went to college (1989). Being that this was 30 years ago, some details are a little foggy, but I will explain to the best of my ability to the detail I remember. I first met Hickey at age 14 when he joined Addison Schools as high school English teacher and JV Girls Basketball coach. He was never my actual coach, but he assisted my varsity coach as most JV coaches do. So he would attend our practices and do drills with the team occasionally. I would frequently stay after practice to do additional drills or shoot free throws, etc. Hickey would also stay after to rebound for me or play one on one. Eventually during the one on one, he began touching me in areas that I knew were inappropriate and rubbing his erect penis on me (clothed). This went on throughout the basketball season. In school, I remember passing notes back and forth throughout the day to each other, some written in code (acronyms) while others were not. I remember one specific time we exchanged notes. We were talking about my boyfriend at the time. I told him that my boyfriend and I had just had sex for the first time. His response was "That's too bad. I wanted to be your first."

Then came the night of the Addison Boys Basketball game against Pittsford. I was now 15, but I still couldn't obviously drive so he offered to take me with him. During the drive to Pittsford, we discussed the rumors that were going around about us spending so much time together. It was obviously noted. When we got to Pittsford, I/we decided that we should not go into the game together as the rumor mill already had enough to talk about, so I stayed in the car. Hickey went in to make an appearance, but came back a little while later and we left. I remember sitting next to him with some hand holding and touching going on both on the rise there and back. On the way back to Addison he wanted to go to the grocery store but forgot his checkbook at his house so we stopped there so he could grab it. Instead of simply running inside to get it, he invited me in. I went in, he went back into his bedroom while I laid down (on my stomach) on his chair/ottoman. He came out a few minutes later and laid on top of me. I could feel his erection through his jeans on me. He asked me to turned [sic] over so I was on my back and I did. He was still on top of me and he kissed me. We kissed for quite a while and we continued to grind his erection into me (again clothed). He told me that he didn't have any condoms so we would wait for another time until he could buy some. He took me home a while later.

Soon thereafter we had our first sexual encounter at his house. I don't remember the logistics of how I arrived there as it's been 30 years, but regardless I was in his bed and we had sex. The relationship went on until I went to college in 1989 having many sexual encounters during that timeframe. We would meet at his house, my house, his car or on his parent's boat (I believe it belonged to his parent's [sic] but can't remember for sure).

Being that he and Sue were not yet married, he was by himself during the week mostly and Sue would come back on the weekends. We would call each other every morning around 6am (when Sue wasn't there) to start each day off with hearing the other's voice and to tell each other "I love you." Occasionally I would join him and Sue for dinner and he would also have dinner at my house now and then with me and my mom.

… [Dawn's description of the wedding day, highlighted above, is given here.]

My senior year came and went with more of the same. Still loving each other (so I thought) and being together any moment we could. Before I went to college, I told him that I would NEVER say anything about our relationship as long as he NEVER had another relationship with a student. Well – During my sophomore year of college, I was called out of class to my basketball coach's office because of an important phone call. When I arrived and answered the phone, my heart sank into my stomach. It was my High School basketball coach, Tom Britsch. I immediately knew that the conversation was not going to be a delightful one. He began to talk about Hickey and told me some of what was going on with Hickey and other students. At first I told Mr. Britsch that nothing had happened between Hickey and myself – we hung up the phone and I was a mess. You need to understand, Mr. Britsch was like a father to me. He was my mentor and I looked up to him and I loved his family. I had many emotions running through me during this time. I was scared, I was physically sick to my stomach, I was angry (that Hickey put me in a position to lie to my mentor) and I was hurt to find out he moved on to another student.

Later that day, I saw Hickey's car pull up to my apartment. I asked my roommate and a couple of other friends from my basketball team to hide me and take me to my college coach's house. I believe my roommate talked to him to tell him I wasn't there. He drove from Addison to … College in order to make sure I didn't talk to Mr. Britsch and tell the truth. Once at my coach's house, I immediately called Mr. Britsch back and told him the truth. I couldn't live with myself lying to him. I was devastated and embarrassed and humiliated. Now everyone was going to know what I had kept secret for so many years – all because Hickey couldn't behave himself.

Detective Rothman emphasizes Hickey's failed attempts to add more positive content to his Addison personnel file (that he "left in good standing" to the reference letter), and to have Supt. Kersh's two-page report from 1990 removed from his file. (See Chapter 7.)

> It is apparent that several attempts have been made by Mr. Hickey to remove the memo which lists the allegations against him and what appears to be the reason for him resigning as an employee at Addison Community Schools. Mr. Hickey not only requested the memo be removed but to add or replace the memo with two other documents that look favorably on him and his character.

Jan. 31, 2018 MSP report

Rothman met with Dawn in person on January 25, 2018 to go over additional questions, her previous statements, and any new information she may have remembered.

The next MSP document, filed on January 31, 2018, summarizes the investigation's progress during that month.

Included in this report is the Facebook message Patrick Hickey sent to Dawn on November 11, 2015. Rothman asked Dawn if she ever contacted Hickey after receiving that message. She said "no." "In fact, she stated that she blocked him from Facebook and has not had contact with him.

The MSP report includes WTOL reporter Jonathan Walsh's interview with Dawn in 2006 or 2007. (Private investigator Gill had turned over Walsh's summary to the MSP.)

Detective Rothman confirms that a formal complaint was filed against Hickey in 2014 by someone in Washington Local Schools. That likely refers to teacher Becca's complaint about Hickey's "aggressive flirtation." (See Chapter 15.)

Detective Rothman notes that when he first spoke with Dawn,

> ... she verified the statements she had given to both Jonathan Walsh and Chris Gill. She did say that there were some things that were inaccurate (like her and Mr. Hickey having sexual intercourse at the school), however, she did say she was being truthful about having a long term sexual relationship with Patrick Hickey starting when she was 15 and lasting until she graduated. Again at that time the incident was not investigated because Dawn stated that she did not wish to pursue the investigation. To my knowledge the allegations have never been investigated thoroughly by Law Enforcement which contradicts some of Mr. Hickey's previous statements about it being investigated.

PASSING the TRASH

Dawn stated that she believed Patrick Hickey started having interest in her during the 1986-87 school year.... I asked Dawn if she could explain how the relationship started with Mr. Hickey. She stated she started staying after basketball practice doing drills and shooting. She said at one point Mr. Hickey started staying after practice as well. She stated it started ok and then they started playing one on one basketball games. Dawn stated that the one on one games progressed to Mr. Hickey putting his hands on her hips and rubbing up against her. She stated that he would start touching her in different places that she knew were inappropriate, but she stated she liked the attention.

I asked Dawn if Mr. Britsch, her actual coach at the time, ever stayed over to help her with her basketball skills and shooting. She stated she can't remember him ever staying over, but if she asked him he may have. She stated he would have never played one on one, but maybe just rebounded for her.

I asked Dawn if Mr. Hickey was the one that initiated the contact with her during the one on one sessions, and she stated, "the inappropriate contact, yes." She stated at one point there was a transition of just being in contact playing one on one to sexual contact. Dawn stated she started to feel his erect penis up against her at times and knew that the contact was no longer just one on one basketball. Dawn stated a lot of the girls on the basketball team thought Mr. Hickey was very good looking so she thought the contact and attention was a good thing. She again stated he would touch her butt and her hips, but it was done in a way that she knew it was sexual in nature.

When asked how many times this behavior occurred between her and Mr. Hickey Dawn stated numerous times over the three years they were seeing each other.

When asked if she remembered Mr. Hickey saying anything during these times she stated she does not remember him saying much but remembers her being excited about it. I asked Dawn how many times this occurred before they actually had sexual intercourse and she stated maybe only a handful of times.

I asked Dawn other than the touching during after-practice sessions, was there any other sexual contact between her and Mr. Hickey prior to engaging in sexual intercourse. Dawn stated the only thing was the night of the Varsity Boys' Basketball Game in Pittsford (Tuesday February 10th, 1987).

Dawn Speaks with Michigan State Police

Dawn stated in a previous statement that Mr. Hickey was giving her a ride to the Boys' Varsity Basketball Game in Pittsford, Michigan. She stated she could not drive because she was only 15 at the time. Dawn stated Mr. Hickey forgot his checkbook so he had to stop by his house to pick it up.

Dawn stated Mr. Hickey invited her in and when he was in his bedroom she laid down on the Ottoman. She stated she had laid down on her stomach. She stated a short time later Mr. Hickey came out of the bedroom and laid on top of her. She stated she could feel his erect penis rubbing into her. She stated he told her to turn over and she did and they began to kiss. She stated that she could feel his erection "grinding" into her on the outside of her clothing. Dawn state she does remember Mr. Hickey said that he didn't have any condoms so they would have to wait.

NOTE: Dawn stated this occurred at Mr. Hickey's trailer near Devils Lake. The address is ... Manitou Beach, Michigan 49253.

I asked Dawn if she remembered any specific clothing or jewelry that Mr. Hickey may have worn that night and she stated, "no." I asked her if she remembered Mr. Hickey wearing any cologne. Dawn stated she doesn't remember for sure but does remember liking the smell of him, but she stated she can't remember if it was cologne or shower gel or what. Dawn stated she doesn't remember Mr. Hickey ever buying her any gifts or anything during the time they were dating.

Dawn stated that she and Mr. Hickey would write notes back and forth in class and they would sometimes use "code" so no one would find out. Dawn stated that there were a few notes that he wrote in her yearbooks and [in] two of them he used "code." Dawn provided me with her 1987, 1988, and 1989 Addison High School yearbooks....

On page 108 of the 1987 yearbook Mr. Hickey wrote the following:

Dawn, It sure has been fun becoming your friend. Keep practicing hoops & studying and you can accomplish anything [underlined three times] you want. Remember one on one hoops, water fights, 1st period (including top gun flying), shooting hoops in my room, the Pittsford Basketball Game and all the other GREAT TIMES. IWABYBF ME.

Dawn stated that the reference to 1st period and top gun was when she was the office aid and Mr. Hickey had a free hour. She stated she would go sit on his desk and spend time with him. She stated the reference to the Pittsford Basketball Game was the time she spoke about just prior to them having sexual intercourse. She stated the IWABYBF stood for "I will always be your best friend" and again he signed it with "ME".

Mr. Hickey wrote the following on the inside cover of Dawn's 1988 yearbook:

Dawn – Always remember that you have a great deal to offer your many friends. Your personality and warmth are cherished by many people. You will be a success in life, marriage, life, career. I wish you all the best.
Be Good
Mr. Hickey

On page 5 of the 1988 yearbook there is a caption by Patrick Hickey's picture that says, *"what a babe"* and on the last page there is a note from [a friend] that's stated that both her [sic] and Dawn had Mr. Hickey for 7th hour.

On page 19 of the 1989 yearbook Mr. Hickey wrote the following:

Dawn – What can I say? Our friendship will always be a cherished possession. Somewhere out there...... you will always be a success in all that you do... & in all that you want to accomplish. You are very special. Friends Always, Me

Dawn stated that Mr. Hickey would sign letters and her yearbook as "Me" so others would not know that he had signed them. She stated the reference to the song "Somewhere Out There" was because he made her think that they would be together someday.

FIRST SEXUAL INTERCOURSE with MR. HICKEY

I spoke to Dawn about the first time she and Mr. Hickey had sexual intercourse. I asked her to describe to me in as much detail as she could remember.

She stated that it was a few weeks or so after the Pittsford Basketball Game so that would have been after February 10, 1987. Dawn stated she believed the Mr. Hickey picked her up from her apartment which was located at ... in Addison and then drove her to his house which was located at ... Princess St. in Manitou Beach (trailer park by the Devils Lake public access). I asked Dawn if she remembered what kind of car Mr. Hickey drove and she described it as a "beater" olive green colored passenger car.

Dawn stated it was kind of a romantic night but she didn't think it was planned but she stated they both knew what was going to happen. I asked Dawn if she remembered how the night went and she stated it was so long ago she can't remember a lot of detail. She did say that she remembered Mr. Hickey being excited to teach her things. I asked Dawn to explain and she stated that Mr. Hickey would teach her, "how to be on top" and other sexual positions. She stated that she remembered that Mr. Hickey wore a condom. She stated that he would wear a condom every time they had sex. I asked Dawn if she remembered if Mr. Hickey ejaculated the first time they had sexual intercourse and she stated he did because she remembered the condom was full. She stated that night they also engaged in oral sex. She stated he would perform oral sex on her and then she would perform oral sex on him. Dawn stated that she wanted to have sex with him and that she was never forced to have sex or never had sex with Mr. Hickey against her will. She stated at one point she was in love with him.

ADDITIONAL SEXUAL CONTACT / INTERCOURSE:

When asked if she could remember how many times she and Mr. Hickey had sexual intercourse prior to her 16th birthday she stated she could not remember the exact number but maybe around ten. I asked if it was more than one time and she stated, "yes." She stated they had sexual intercourse in her apartment in Addison, his house by Devils Lake. She stated they never had sexual intercourse at the school or out of the State. She stated that was one of the things that was inaccurate in her interview with Chris Gill. She stated in that interview he said they had sexual intercourse at the school and they never did.

When I asked Dawn to describe [for] me the places that she and Mr. Hickey would meet and have sexual intercourse she stated the following places.

… Manitou Beach, Michigan
… Addison, Michigan
… Manitou Beach, Michigan (Round Lake) she stated she was 16 at the time.
… Patrick Hickey's Parents boat (Round Lake) Pontoon Boat, she stated she was 16 at the time.

Dawn stated she remembered one time when they were at the house on Round Lake she remembers him sitting on the couch. She stated she remembered Mr. Hickey telling her that he could make himself "cum" by just thinking about them together and without touching himself. She stated he did it right in front of her. Dawn stated that she was naïve at the time and even though she thought it was strange she just thought that is what people do. I asked Dawn if she could remember how many times she and Mr. Hickey had sexual intercourse after her 16th birthday and she stated numerous times, but could not come up with a specific number.

I asked Dawn if she could remember Mr. Hickey having any moles, scars, or tattoos. She states she can't remember, but he may have had a scar from a surgery but not certain. Dawn stated she was certain the time they had sexual intercourse and oral sex on the pontoon boat was when she was 16 years old. She stated she moved back to the house on Round Lake when she was 16.

Dawn stated that as their relationship progressed Mr. Hickey would tell her that he loved her almost daily. She stated during the time they were having a sexual relationship, Mr. Hickey was dating and engaged to his now wife, Sue. Dawn stated she loved Mr. Hickey and she even vaguely remembers her [herself] and Mr. Hickey having sexual intercourse the night before his wedding in hopes he would call it off. Dawn stated she remembered being invited to the wedding.

She stated she recalls that being the worst day of her life. She stated she loved Mr. Hickey and she remembered having to fight back tears watching him get married. Dawn stated she would have to go into the bathroom to wipe her tears. She stated even to this day that was one of the worst days of her life. She stated after the marriage things didn't change much between them. She stated they would still find time to meet and have sexual intercourse.

I asked Dawn if she had ever had sexual intercourse with anyone else prior to her first time having sexual intercourse with Mr. Hickey. She stated that her first time having sexual [intercourse] was with her boyfriend ... She stated she believed that occurred the summer of 1986/87 and was at her apartment in Addison. Dawn stated she remembered when she told Mr. Hickey that she had already had sex he was disappointed because he said he wanted to be her first.

I asked Dawn if she knew if Mr. Hickey was having sexual intercourse with any other students while she was attending Addison school. She stated she didn't think so but didn't know.

DISCLOSING THE SEXUAL RELATIONSHIP

I asked Dawn if she ever disclosed to anyone that she and Mr. Hickey were having a sexual relationship. She stated that while she was in school she remembered she told her friend ... that they were

362

having a sexual relationship. She stated there were rumors all over the school and she and Mr. Hickey even discussed the rumors from time to time. Dawn stated she was never asked by any staff at Addison High School about those rumors until she graduated and went to college.

Dawn stated she was a freshman at …College in … Michigan when she was called out of class because of a phone call. She stated she went to her coach's office where she spoke to Mr. Britsch her former Addison High School Basketball Coach over the phone. She advised that Mr. Britsch stated that there were rumors that Pat Hickey and ["Julie"] were having a sexual relationship. Dawn stated that Mr. Britsch also stated that there were rumors that she also had a sexual relationship with Patrick Hickey when she was a student at Addison High School.

She stated that is when Mr. Britsch asked her if she had in fact had a sexual relationship with Mr. Hickey when she was a student at Addison High School [and] she initially told him no. She said she believes the same day Patrick Hickey came to her school in … looking for her was the same day he was let go from Addison. She stated she was scared, so several of her teammates took her from the college to her coach's house. Dawn stated her college roommate … actually spoke with Mr. Hickey the day he arrived at the college. Dawn stated she then decided to tell Mr. Britsch the truth. She stated she called him back and told him that she and Mr. Hickey were having a sexual relationship while she was a student at Addison [and] that the relationship had gone on for three years.

Dawn stated she was heartbroken because she had lied to Mr. Britsch and that she had to tell him the truth because he was like a mentor and father figure to her. Dawn stated she remembered telling Mr. Hickey that as long as he never had a relationship with another student like he had with her she would never say anything. She stated after she learned that he was having a sexual relationship with another student she deiced to tell Mr. Britsch.

Dawn stated not only did she disclose the relationship to Mr. Britsch, she also disclosed the relationship to her mother. She stated her mother was very upset and wanted to press charges but Dawn stated she begged and pleaded with her mother not to. She stated she was in college and had a scholarship and didn't want to mess that up so her mother decided not to press charges.

April 11, 2018 MSP report

Between January and April 2018, MSP Detective Rothman would continue to speak to contemporaries and witnesses of Patrick Hickey's time at Addison High School.

In April 2018, Dawn contacted Rothman again when "she remembered a few additional details regarding the sexual relationship" she'd had with Patrick Hickey. She submitted this about her time with him when she was 15 years old:

> [Dawn:] First time – Shortly thereafter [sic] the Pittsford basketball game. I'm pretty sure it was a Sunday evening because my mom always went to a singles dance on Sundays. It was still winter. He picked me up at the apartments in Addison and drove back to his place. I remember him parking away from the apartments as to not be seen in the parking lot. I walked/ran to his car and we left. Once to his trailer, we were both excited but I was very nervous. "What if I wasn't good enough?" "What if I did something wrong? Would he laugh," "Would he not want me again?" those were questions running through my head even though I was still very excited. We eventually made our way to his bedroom. I remember him being very gentle with me being only my second time ever having intercourse and he was bigger than my first time. We kissed and touched each other prior to any penetration. His fingers touched me to see if I was "ready" for him to continue. He put the condom on and gently pushed inside me. I was on the bottom and he was on top of me – missionary position. I remember him being very patient, gentle and loving. Once he was "finished" he removed the condom and went into the bathroom to flush it. Once we put our clothes back on, he drove me back home.

> [Rothman:] It should be noted that Dawn stated she was living in the apartment building in Addison at the time. She stated she and her mother lived there because it was close to the school and she had yet to receive her driver's license. Dawn advised she did not obtain her driver's license until she turned 16 years of age and then they moved to the house on Round Lake. She also makes reference to the Pittsford Game which was in early Feb of 1987. This incident would have been in Feb or March of 1987. Dawn stated she remembered a second time was when she was 15 years old. She sent me the following:

> [Dawn:] Another time, he once again picked me up at the apartments in the same fashion to go back to his place. This time is stuck in my memory because this time he taught me how to be "on

top" during intercourse. He put a condom on of course, then helped guide himself into me as I sat on top of him. I remember his hands on each hip helping to move me back and forth as he moved beneath me. I remember looking down at him at [sic] he had a big sexy smile on his face. I believe that was the moment that I fell in love with him. He made me feel like I was all he ever wanted. He was always very attentive to me to make sure I was ok and enjoyed our time together.

[Rothman:] Dawn stated the sexual relationship continued up until she graduated high school in 1989. She stated she remembered a time when the two of them were alone on the pontoon boat. She stated that is when Mr. Hickey "taught her" how to 69.

It should be noted that the term "69" is referred to a sexual position where both the female and male are both [sic] giving oral sex to the other at the same time, this is usually done while one person is lying on top of the other or the two subjects are laying [sic] side-by-side.

Dawn stated that she also remembered that Patrick Hickey was her basketball coach for her AAU Girls Basketball team in 1988 (Lenawee County Chargers). Dawn was able to provide me a copy of a newspaper article that contains a picture of all the players and Coach Patrick Hickey... Dawn was also able to provide me with additional pictures that list Mr. Hickey as an assistant (unofficial) coach for her varsity team...

Dawn also stated she remembered she was dating [boyfriend] when she first was with Mr. Hickey. She stated that her first time having sexual intercourse was with [boyfriend]... she knows they were still dating even after she had her first sexual experience with Mr. Hickey...

Later in the April 11, 2018 MSP document:

[Detective Rothman:] I asked [Dawn's HS boyfriend] if he remembered why he and Dawn broke up and he said he can't remember why or even when. I asked [boyfriend] if he suspected anything going on between Dawn and Hickey and he stated he had no clue there was anything going on at the time... He stated he is not disputing that something may have happened but is wondering why Dawn wanted to come forward now after all these years ... but again he stated he doesn't care. [He] stated in regards to Mr. Hickey he thinks for one he is a likable guy and it sounds like someone paid a lot of money to dig up dirt on him...

[Boyfriend] stated where there is smoke there is usually fire. He stated he has heard other rumors about Patrick Hickey being with other students. He stated that, "Karma is a bitch and you do get what you deserve."

CHAPTER 23
Michigan State Police Interview Hickey
-- March 2018 --

This chapter is drawn from the Michigan State Police and Lenawee County Court documents from March, April, and May 2018 concerning the case of Patrick Carl Hickey.

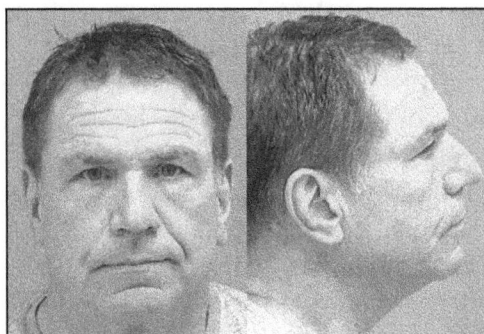

Patrick Carl Hickey's mugshot – March 2018, Michigan State Police

MSP Detective interviews Patrick Hickey, March 14, 2018 -- Highlights

MSP Detective Sgt. Larry Rothman interviewed Patrick Hickey on March 14, 2018. He was indicted just days later, on March 19.

The complete interview (digital images of the MSP report) is available in the Kindle edition of this book. [1] (Some spelling errors have been corrected in the transcription below, others are noted with [sic].)

Of special note in the interview:

Question 2. Are you currently married, separated, divorced?

… Mr. Hickey stated he has been married for the past 30 years … to Sue. It should be noted that I had placed a call to Sue Hickey a week prior and requested she speak to me. She stated she would call me back. A day later I received a phone call from Mr. Hickey's attorney Lorin J. Zaner advising me that Mrs. Hickey will not be speaking with me.

Question 5: What are your hobbies?

Hickey stated one of his hobbies is fitness ... he works out every day ... he and his wife watch Netflix together and he likes working in the yard.

Question 7: On a scale from 1 to 10, how honest are you?

Mr. Hickey stated he was a 9.

Question 8: Rate your life on a scale from 1 to 10.

Mr. Hickey stated his life is a ten.

9. What is going wrong/well?

Mr. Hickey stated his family, a business he is starting, his friends and the very loyal people in his life are the things going well. When asked what is going wrong he stated, "Where I am sitting right now."

Question 10. Do you follow a religion?

Mr. Hickey stated he was raised Catholic but [sic] he believes in Jesus. He stated he went to a nondenominational church for a while. He stated he would just say he was a Christian. He stated he does not currently attend church but the last one he attended was Cedar Creek. It should be noted that I made contact with Cedar Creek and was advised that Mr. Hickey has not been in attendance in some time. They were unable to confirm when Mr. Hickey stopped attending regularly.

Question 17. Describe yourself, who are you in your own words?

Mr. Hickey stated he had a good childhood. He stated he went to Siena Heights College on a running scholarship [and] right into education after that. He stated he taught 6 years at Addison Community School, 6 years at St. Anthony Villa (Toledo, Ohio), 6 years as an administrator at Findlay Community Schools (Findlay, Ohio,), and then the Assistant Superintendent and Superintendent at Washington Local Schools in Ohio for 14 years.

Mr. Hickey went on to say that the last 14 years have been the most successful in his life. He stated that he took a school district that was struggling and made it thrive... they were named the top workplace in Northwest Ohio [and] written up in Fordham magazine in regard to taking kids that were in poverty and increasing their test scores ... He stated he was alumnus of the year at his college [and] Superintendent of the year in Toledo... [He] stated it was the most successful 14 years of his life until two board members got elected and then things went sideways and then they went back to 1988 and it had been a real rough 2 years right on top the most successful time he has had.

Question 18. Who do you represent today? You as a Christian, Husband, Father, School Board Member, Former Superintendent, Former Principal, Former Teacher, Former Coach?

Hickey explained that he represented himself [and that] all of the above titles represented him and it would be impossible for him to take any one of them off.

Question 21. Prior to your current job where were you employed? Why did you leave?

Mr. Hickey stated he left [as WLS Superintendent] because two board members were elected under the dictate to get rid of him. He stated in the last two years of his tenure they were checking his expenses, checking everything he did, voting no on everything he did. He stated it got so suffocating he asked for a buyout and they said no.

He stated then there was an investigation into him and a teacher and he stated he was given a letter of reprimand. He stated after a two week investigation by an independent law firm he was told that he did nothing sexual, nothing romantic, nothing unlawful, nothing financial, and nothing involving a student and he stated that was the end of the investigation. He stated his letter of reprimand was given to him for not turning in the teacher for doing something wrong and he didn't.

He stated after that there was another situation that had nothing to do with him but they came to him with an offer of $300,000 to leave. He stated he discussed it with his wife and they decided to resign at that point.

Question 24. Prior to that job [St. Anthony Villa] where were you employed? When did you leave?

Mr. Hickey then stated he spent 4½ years at Addison.

Question 25. Why do you think we are here today?

Mr. Hickey stated we are here because of some rumors in 1988 that have resurfaced 2 years ago and a very public media campaign that was orchestrated by this Terri Kern [WLS community resident] and she kept this stuff flowing and flowing.

Question 26. What years were you employed at Addison Community Schools in Addison Michigan?

Mr. Hickey stated he was employed at Addison from 1986 to September of 1990. It should be noted that Mr. Hickey was employed until Nov of 1990.

Question 33. Describe what kind of teacher you were while at Addison in 1986?

Mr. Hickey says he was a like a superstar teacher... He stated he was young and a basketball coach and was Lenawee County Basketball Coach of the Year and took the girls to the state final four. He stated he was single for the first two years. He stated he had never taught in a small rural school so the popularity was weird in regards to how popular a young school teacher is in a small school district like that... He stated that kids always wanted to be in his class... his class was fun and he stated he once got an evaluation that the kids were laughing to [sic] much in his class. He stated a lot of kids would come to him, kids that were having trouble at home and he would try to assist them.

Question 34. Describe what kind of coach you were at Addison School?

Mr. Hickey stated he was very extremely [sic] successful. He stated he started as the JV coach and was then promoted to Varsity and took the team to the State Final Four. He stated back then he was coaching both girls' and boys' basketball and AAU basketball in the spring so he was basically coaching basketball year around [sic].

Question 46. In your own words what is the reason you left Addison Schools?

Mr. Hickey stated the reason he left Addison Schools was because of the rampant rumors that he was having sex with students. He stated he was newly married and his wife came to him and told him that it was enough. Mr. Hickey stated his wife told him he could get a job in Toledo. Mr. Hickey said he told his wife that he could get a job in Toledo but wanted to get with Mr. Kersh [Supt.] and Mr. Dieck [HS Principal] to make sure they were going to give him a positive letter of recommendation.

Mr. Hickey stated the rumors were investigated by children's services and he thought the State Police but it appears no one can find a record of it. Mr. Hickey stated he thought that would end the rumors and when it didn't end the rumors he stated that is when they (he and his wife) said they will leave. He stated that was the end of it.

Question 47. Did you resign, get fired, or were you asked to resign?

Mr. Hickey stated he resigned. He stated he went to Mr. Dieck and said to him, "If I resign will you give me a letter of recommendation and will it say I left in good standing with the school district?" Mr. Hickey stated he went to Mr. Kersh with the same request and both of them were granted and he resigned.

Mr. Hickey stated he left. He stated there were rumors that he was escorted out of the building but they were not true. He said he gave them a letter of resignation and he left. I asked Mr. Hickey if he had a copy of the letter still and he said yes, he said he had three of them. He said the letters basically said he left in good standing with the school district. He stated he doesn't remember signing anything. He stated he thinks it was November 5th 1990.

Question 48. Where did you go after to [you] left Addison schools that day?

He stated he went back to his home and started to prepare for a new life.

Question 56. Did you ever give female student[s] rides after hours?

Mr. Hickey stated, "Not that I recall".

Question 60. Did you know a former student named ["Julie"]?

Mr. Hickey said yes... [He] stated the rumor he remembers is that he was having sex with [Julie] and having sex with [Dawn]. Mr. Hickey stated he was friends with [Julie's] family and that is probably where the rumor started...

Question 61. Other than the rumors do you find any of these girls trustworthy?

... He stated that Brooke [Brooks Kelly] and Kris [Elston Hassenzahl] are flat out lying in front of Toledo.

Question 62. You mentioned ["Dawn"] – was she one of your players or a student?

Mr. Hickey stated she was one of his students. He stated that [Dawn] has claimed that he was her coach but he wasn't so yes he remembered her as a player but never coaches [sic] her... "You haven't asked me if she is trustworthy but she has said a number of things that are not true since in [sic] 1988."

I asked Mr. Hickey to tell me what some of those things were. He stated that she said he was her coach and he never was, she said that they had sex when she was 14 and he stated he was a college student when she was 14, she stated she was invited to his wedding which she was not, she said that she had dinner with him and his wife which she did not. Mr. Hickey then looked at some notes he had written down and the stated that she had said that they went to a Pittsford Basketball game that was untrue, she said we had sex in the equipment room which they did not, she said we had sex in the cemetery which they did not, she said that he was escorted out of Addison High School which he was not and then was saying that she had a relationship with his wife. Mr. Hickey stated other than the rumors his wife doesn't not [sic] even remember her.

He then stated that as far as being trustworthy she is the most untrustworthy of the bunch.

[**Questions 63-64**. Detective Rothman names other girls who were at Addison High School, many on the basketball team at the time. Hickey typically replies, "Don't remember her" or "Didn't coach her," etc.]

Question 65. Is there any reason for any of the [many named] above mentioned students or players to think or suggest that you have had any inappropriate/sexual relationships with any former students or players while you were employed at Addison Public Schools?

Mr. Hickey stated he would have no idea why someone would say that.

Question 69. What do you think should happen to someone who is having sex with a student or player if they are a coach or teacher?

Mr. Hickey stated whatever the law say's [sic] should happen and then a long pause and then he stated, "If they are guilty."

[**Questions 71-76**. Hickey denies (while at Addison Schools) touching female students on the butt or chest; denies kissing, sexual contact, or oral sex with female students; denies providing students with alcohol; denies giving students a place to party.]

Question 77. Mr. Hickey during the time you were employed at Addison Schools did you ever engage in sexual intercourse with any female students or players.

No

[**Questions 78-83**. Hickey denies other sexual encounters with current or former female students at Addison.]

Question 84. Mr. Hickey during the time you were employed at Addison Schools did you ever have any inappropriate relationships (sexual) with any female students or players?

No

I advised Mr. Hickey that was the end of all my listed questions. I then asked Mr. Hickey to explain to me how former students, former teachers, and former staff members would come up with these things. Mr. Hickey's attorney then stated he did not want to get into those things. He stated they had some ideas ... Mr. Hickey then stated that when someone puts up 8 websites about him that said he was in rehab, that said his wife had left him, that said he ignored a summons from me. He stated why is that person doing it, he had no idea.

====================

Detective Rothman's further comments after Question 84 are significant. He debunks Hickey's claims that there was a *police investigation* at the time he left Addison in 1990. Rothman wrote:

I advised [Hickey] that these allegations have never been fully investigated until now. Mr. Hickey stated that he remembered that he sat in a room at Addison High School along with [Julie] with the State Police and someone from the Department of Human Services. He stated that was in 1990.

Mr. Hickey stated there was no other contact made by Law Enforcement since then. He said he is not sure if a report was ever filed but he remembers being in Mr. Diek's [Principal Dieck's] office. He stated that was when the State Police wore the big hats... he remembered there were two of them and a large black woman from the Department of Human Services. He stated he was scared out of his mind and it was something he would never forget... he remembered walking out of the room and [Julie] walking in. He said he thinks that was in 1990 and that is when he said this thing has gotten out of control.

I advised Mr. Hickey that I have yet to find a police report that would indicate that anyone from the Michigan State Police or any other Law Enforcement agency in Lenawee County made a police report back in 1990. Mr. Hickey stated he has not been able to locate any reports either. He stated he knows it was after Brooke Brooks' mom made the allegation that he had had sex in the cemetery. Mr. Hickey stated he went to an attorney the next day to file a harassment claim against her.

It should be noted that there was a report filed with the Lenawee County Sheriff's Office on 11-01-1990 stating that the complainant [Hickey] wanted to report that Judith Maude Brooks has made statements to Addison School [where] the complainant works accusing him of having sex with some girls and making threats to have complainant fired... Mr. Hickey stated he may have also called an attorney and believes it may have been Harvey Kaselka.

NOTE: I made contact with F/Lt. Tony Cuevas of the Michigan State Police Monroe Post. Lt. Cuevas utilized the INCC name index which is a pre-AICS name search program that MSP used. He search [sic] Mr. Hickey's name and it returned with no results, meaning he is not listed in any MSP reports prior to 1995. I also made contact [with] Ms. Judy Fox of the FOIA Unit in Lansing. She stated there were similar requests about a year ago but they have been unable to locate any reports. She did say that the INCC name index started around 1991 so it may have started after Mr. Hickey claimed a report was filed. I have since learned that there is no record that Law Enforcement responded to Addison Schools but was advised that someone from the Department of Human Services may have been there. I did make contact with [Julie] and she confirmed that she was talked to by the Department of Human Services but did not want to disclose any further details.

I advised Mr. Hickey that the [MSP] report he talked about in 2016 was not a fully investigated. [sic] I advised him that based on no one coming forward at the time we ended it before a full investigation could be [done]. I did advise Mr. Hickey that someone has come forward now so that is why we have reopened the investigation. I further advised him that what has occurred or is occurring in Toledo is not my concern at the moment and I am investigating the allegations that occurred while he was a teacher and coach in Addison Michigan.

If the Department of Human Services had ever been involved, that would have been concerning the 1990 case with the teen female, Julie, who has not wanted to implicate Hickey in the recent investigations. Note that she "did not want to disclose any further details" to Detective Rothman. It is understandable that she would have denied any sexual relationship if she was, in fact, interviewed during her high school years.

Furthermore, if the DHS was involved in 1990, they surely would have spoken with Dawn who had confessed to Coach Britsch. But she was never contacted by DHS.

Detective Rothman also wrote:

I asked Mr. Hickey if he is telling me that nothing happened, that all the rumors are false and that he never had sexual intercourse with any student or player at Addison. Mr. Hickey said absolutely! I then asked Mr. Hickey again why would people lie to me and why would people come forward now. Mr. Hickey stated he could give me a lot of reasons but then he was advised by his attorney not to answer...

I advised Mr. Hickey that my job is to find facts and then send my report to the prosecutor's office. I advised that it is the job of the prosecutor to see if he violated any laws and what those laws maybe [may be]. I advised him that there are people on one side of the case that love him and think he is great and on the polar opposite I have people saying he is like Larry Nasser. Mr. Hickey stated that is very destressing [sic] after 30 years of education to be compared to Larry Nasser. He stated what he sees is one person who is saying that he had sex with them [sic] and what everybody else is saying is hearsay.

Hickey declined to take a polygraph test at the conclusion of the interview. His attorney then said he doesn't trust polygraphs.

But formerly, Hickey and his attorney had pointed to Hickey "passing" a polygraph test (apparently in December 2015) concerning his time in the Addison Schools.

CHAPTER 24
Hickey Gets a Plea Deal
-- May 2018 --

Hickey has a bit of luck

Patrick Hickey was initially charged on March 21, 2018 with three counts of criminal sexual conduct in the third degree (sexual penetration-intercourse with a victim age 13-15) which would carry a mandatory sentence of 15 years in prison. To that, he had pleaded "**not guilty**."

But his victim Dawn wanted to avoid a trial. So, over the next two months, Hickey got lucky and worked out a plea deal with the Prosecutor and Dawn.

On May 9, 2018, Hickey was arraigned in Lenawee County Circuit Court in Adrian, Michigan. He pleaded "**guilty**" to "**criminal sexual conduct in the fourth degree with a person 13-15 years old**" – in particular, touching the victim's buttocks for his own sexual gratification. [1] In other words, all he admitted to was "groping" Dawn.

Sentencing guidelines for this lesser charge are two years in prison and registration as a sex offender.

Hickey again made page one of *The Toledo Blade*. The print headline read, "*Hickey pleads guilty to sexual conduct; Decades of denial come to an end.*" [2] The Associated Press was spreading the news around the country. [3]

From *The Toledo Blade* (May 9):

> Former Washington Local Schools superintendent and board member Patrick Hickey pleaded guilty Wednesday to a criminal sexual conduct charge and admitted in Lenawee County Circuit Court to groping a student decades ago while a teacher at a Michigan school.
>
> As part of a plea deal, prosecutors agreed to dismiss three charges of criminal sexual conduct in the third degree if Hickey, 55, pleaded to an added sexual conduct charge in the fourth degree. He is scheduled to be sentenced at 8:15 a.m. June 21 [later moved to June 28] and faces a maximum of two years in prison.

Hickey Gets a Plea Deal

During Wednesday's court hearing before Judge Marie Anzalone, Hickey admitted to touching the buttocks of a 15-year-old student for the purpose of sexual gratification decades ago during his tenure as a teacher in Addison Community Schools. [4]

He declined comment after exiting the court room.

Lenawee County Courthouse, Adrian, Michigan

The Monroe News (Michigan) added some detail:

Assistant Lenawee County Prosecutor Angie Borders said after the hearing that Hickey will have to register as a sex offender, but for how long is unclear because Michigan's sex offender registry did not exist when the offense occurred in 1987, though the registry was made to include older cases, and the criminal sexual conduct laws have been changed since then. He could have to register for as long as 25 years.

Fourth-degree criminal sexual conduct involves sexual touching. To satisfy that element of the charge, Hickey admitted to touching the girl's buttocks to achieve sexual gratification...

The prosecutor's office did an excellent job, as did (Michigan State Police) Detective (Larry) Rothman," said Jim Driskill, who was a guidance counselor and itinerant teacher at AHS in 1990 and who was in the courtroom Wednesday. "I'm proud of the victim for coming forward." [5]

PASSING the TRASH

Since he was an Ohio resident, Hickey would be registered for 25 years as a sex offender in Ohio, not Michigan, after his release from jail.

The Monroe News quoted Assistant Prosecutor, Angie Borders:

> Borders said she required an admission that Hickey had an inappropriate sexual relationship with the student, who was a 15 at the time, be part of the plea because criminal punishment of Hickey was not necessarily the victim's goal.

> "This was what the victim wanted. That was my focus," Borders said. The true importance to this victim was that he was exposed. When you're presented with a 30-year-old case with all the factors that were involved — I focused on the victim and making her whole," Borders said. [6]

Dawn would explain at the sentencing (on June 28, 2018) that her main goal was for Hickey to be registered as a sex offender.

> When I met with the prosecuting attorney, Ms. Borders, she asked me what I wanted out of this case as far as punishment for Mr. Hickey. At the time I told her the most important thing was that he was exposed; for him to have to register as a sex offender, and he must plead guilty and fully admit to our relationship.

> People have asked me why I would even entertain a plea deal for him. My answer to that was simple: I didn't want to put my 74-year-old mother, the rest my family and my friends, and of course myself through a long, drawn-out trial.

> With that, however, I am completely insulted with his lack of admission of guilt. His admitting to only touching my butt for his own sexual gratification was, once again, him trying to make people believe he did nothing that bad. Wanting people to potentially feel sorry for him that a woman brought charges against him 30 years later for only touching her butt. That is absolutely ridiculous.

> Your Honor, I'd like to request that the full jail time be added to my wish list of punishments for him. It appears he needs to take the time to take responsibility for his actions and stop blaming other people for his decisions. [7]

Former Addison student Kris Hassenzahl watched the May 9 proceeding.

> For the past few months she has attended Washington Local Schools meetings and told board members Hickey had made inappropriate comments and was "grooming" her when she was a

378

teenager and he was her basketball coach. She said … that Hickey's admission of guilt for something he's denied for decades was "28 years in the making. It's like an open chapter that's finally getting closure not just for me, but for the whole community." [8]

WLS Board President Tom Ilstrup (also Board President at Hickey's 2015 resignation as Superintendent) had no comment on Hickey's guilty plea. Board VP David Hunter said, "My heart goes out to [Hickey's] family, and I hope they are able to put their lives back on track and move forward." [9]

Toledo Blade editorializes on "passing the trash"

Here is the editorial [10] that appeared in *The Toledo Blade* on May 13:

Hickey did it, they hid it

For years, Patrick Hickey vowed he did not do it. It never happened. His foes were lying about him; it was all politics.

"No, it didn't happen," he said on television [11] earlier this year… He swore that the allegation was false and that he had been exonerated many years earlier – though that was not true… His critics were liars, Hickey insisted. His accusers were not to be believed…

Washington Local inherited the problem that was Patrick Hickey thanks to an insidious practice commonly referred to in education as "passing the trash." School districts allow employees accused of misconduct to leave and seek new jobs with new employers who are left in the dark about their troubles because districts do not want negative attention and/or they do not want a lengthy fight.

The victim in the case – after years of remaining silent and hoping to avoid the unwanted attention accusing Hickey would surely bring – told prosecutors she wanted his misdeeds to come to light. She wanted it to be known…

The practice of passing problems on to other school systems without full disclosure is unethical, and in many cases, like this one, morally criminal. There are proposals to make the practice illegal, and to create a searchable national database and require schools to both report teachers and administrators accused of misconduct and check it before hiring anyone. State and federal lawmakers should act on these measures.

How is it right that a woman whose teacher and coach violated her when she was a teenager had to be more courageous than the adults whose job it was to protect students?

More questions

The Blade was told that Addison Schools now have a policy in place to prevent something like this happening in the future.

> Steven Guerra, superintendent of Addison schools, said the matter was handled "in a poor manner" 30 years ago by a prior superintendent, but said the district has done no investigation about its own role… "We are finally happy that after 30 years this terrible situation is going to be resolved and justice is going to prevail," Mr. Guerra said. [12]

What about Hickey's employer just before Washington Local Schools? *The Blade* included this:

> Along with Addison and Washington Local, Hickey worked for about six years in the Findlay school district. In response to *Blade* questions about whether the district plans to investigate whether Hickey may have engaged in inappropriate acts while in the district, Supt. Edward Kurt said in a statement that Findlay schools would cooperate with law enforcement in any investigation. "We have no information of any situations regarding misconduct while under our employment," Mr. Kurt said. [13]

While the *Blade* highlights that Addison Schools "passed the trash," the question remains open: Who in authority within the Washington Local Schools knew there were serious problems with Patrick Hickey? How long did they know? Why was Hickey not terminated in September 2015 for sexual harassment after the teaching couple's complaint – even before the Addison history came out? Was there a conscious cover-up by some of those in power? If so, why?

May 16, 2018 School Board meeting

During the public comments at the May 16 School Board meeting, alumna and district resident Kathy Mayfield rose to speak. "Considering it's been almost three years since the saga began, as teachers we need to reflect on what we've learned." She asked the Board to tell the community what changes are needed to be sure something like this doesn't happen again. How will they ensure staff won't feel harassed, that students will feel safe coming to class, that a leader cannot take advantage of anyone in this district again? (The Board has not publicly answered this question as of this writing.)

Later in May – after his felony guilty plea – the Ohio Board of Education revoked Hickey's educator licenses. *The Blade* reported:

> Because of that guilty plea, an order from the state Superintendent of Public Instruction on Thursday permanently revoked Hickey's educator licenses; unless the conviction is overturned, he cannot appeal the decision.

> "Respondent is not permitted to hold any position in the state of Ohio that requires a license, certificate or permit issued by the State Board of Education," the order reads. [14]

CHAPTER 25
Hickey Sentenced to One Year in County Jail, 25 Years on Ohio Sex Offender Registry, and 5 Years on Probation
-- June 2018 & Beyond –

June 2018: Hickey sentenced to one year in jail

On June 28, 2018, Patrick Carl Hickey was sentenced to one year in the Lenawee County Jail in Adrian, Michigan.

The statements made by victim Dawn, her husband, perpetrator Hickey, and his attorney, and the Judge comprise Chapter 1 in this book.

Patrick Hickey once again made the front page of *The Toledo Blade*. The print edition headline read, *"Hickey gets year in jail for sex with a student."*

The online headline for the *Blade*'s report read, *"Patrick Hickey sentenced to one year in jail for groping student."* [1] *Groping*: That was the lesser charge he agreed to in the plea deal. Hickey can now say he was convicted for just touching a girl's buttocks (rather than sexual intercourse with an underage girl).

However, the Judge made it clear in her statement at the end of the hearing that she believed Hickey was still was not accepting responsibility for his crime. Note that the Judge stated that when Dawn was 15, Hickey had "sexual penetration" with her:

> I read your description of the offense and I was very bothered by your statement that the victim accepted what you were doing and consented to allowing you to do it. She was 14 when you started grooming her and 15 at the time that you had sexual penetration. She was a minor. There's no consent at all for a minor...

As a former teacher herself, the Judge said,

> ... one of the biggest things that I knew is when my students walked in, their parents sent them to school knowing that their children would be cared for and be safe. And that is a vow that you

– almost a vow that you take as a teacher to make sure that you do no harm, and in this case harm was done.

Also male teachers across the United States suffer because of people like you. So my daughter plays basketball, she has a male coach. And as a parent you end up questioning male teachers of female students because of behavior like this. And that is a shame.

The Daily Telegram (Adrian, Michigan) posted a video report including audio of much of Dawn's statement, Hickey's statement, and the Judge passing sentence. [2] WTOL posted a video [3] plus a brief report on the sentencing hearing:

... after giving Hickey chances to admit his guilt and come clean but [given] his continuance to deny any allegations against him, [Dawn] begged the judge for a sentence of jail time so her predator could finally take ownership of what he had done. Hickey also addressed the judge before he was sentenced, saying he was sexually abused by an older brother and that is what caused him to prey on his students. But he said since his time in the Addison Michigan school district in the 1980s, he has gotten help and hasn't victimized anyone else. ... Several of Hickey's victims were in the courtroom, and looked on as he was put in cuffs and punished for his actions. [4]

WTOL video report on Hickey's sentencing hearing [3]

Hickey registered as sex offender in Ohio for 25 years and 5 years on probation

In addition to his sentence of a year in jail, the Judge explained: After his release, Hickey would be on *probation for five years* and *registered as a sex offender for 25 years*. Since he is an Ohio resident, he would be registered on the Ohio Attorney General's sex-offender registry. His other penalties and restrictions are enumerated in Chapter 1.

Google street view of Lenawee County Jail, Adrian, Michigan

Community reactions

The day of Hickey's sentencing, former WLS OAPSE union President Cindy Perry wrote on Facebook:

> I think his name and pictures and anything else that has to do with hickey should be removed, like the flags around [WLS] complex and the butterfly symbol or book; whatever he did. Should not remind us of the sex offender at all. Make the flags at [the school] complex Panther paws and the other logo something else. WLS always stood up on our Panther paws. [5]

Another woman commented:

> Now it's official – Jeremy [Baumhower], Mark [Hughes], Lisa [Canales], Ron and so many others defended a pedophile till the very end... wonder when their apologies to our district will be coming? Glad he is finally being locked up to stop his reign of terror and abuse. My thoughts are with his kids. [6]

Adrian, Michigan newspaper headline: "He was a predator."

A few days after Hickey was incarcerated in the Lenawee County Jail in Adrian, Michigan, a WLS district resident and alumna (and teacher in a nearby district) posted an open letter [7] addressed to Hickey defender and blogger, Jeremy Baumhower. (Though Mr. Baumhower has since passed away, we include this contemporary document because it encapsulates a lot of the anger and sadness in the WLS community at the time.)

An Open Letter to Jeremy Baumhower, the Unapologetic Defender of a Child Predator

By Kathy Mayfield – June 30, 2018

Dear Jeremy,

Patrick Hickey, the former superintendent and school board member you defended for years, is now in jail after admitting to having sex with a child. I'm not sure if you know that. You've been a little quiet lately, and you've got some explaining to do.

My name might be vaguely familiar to you, but you blocked me on Facebook years ago. I had apparently committed an unforgivable offense in commenting on one of your posts about Hickey's well-documented harassment of teachers. For a time, you were effective in hiding the truth from your readers, tirelessly plucking flowers from your garden of weeds.

I can't be happier that those days are over.

And before you wrongly assume, no – I'm not friends with [WLS community resident] Terri Kern, Patricia Carmean, or Jim

Langenderfer. And in the instances I've encountered them at board meetings, we've exchanged little more than brief greetings.

But like them, I learned years ago that Patrick Hickey sexually abused his students. And I'm ashamed to admit that I stayed quiet for so long out of fear that you would point the pitchfork-wielding mob in my direction, or that I would be immortalized in your now ironically-titled book, *Socked: The Unbelievable Tale of How a Bully Used Fake News to Punch a School District.*

You've called Terri Kern – one of Hickey's earliest and most vocal detractors – a bully. She's the central topic of your book, in which you claim that she used anonymous social media accounts to harass you and your family. I don't know whether this is true, but I will admit that her execution of an otherwise noble cause was poor. The same might be said of former board members Patricia Carmean and Jim Langenderfer, who you've also cast as the villains of your now irrelevant tale.

Sure, Ms. Carmean may have watched Hickey leave a gym one day, perhaps seeking to confirm the rumor that he was having an affair with a second teacher. (She did in fact spot the two together.) And yeah, maybe Mr. Langenderfer really did refer to the adultering superintendent as a "son of a bitch" who needed to be removed from power.

But we now know that the actions of these individuals were rooted in the knowledge that Patrick Hickey had sex with children. And to their horror, he still had unfettered access to thousands of them on a daily basis. Maybe their actions weren't so evil after all.

Yours, however, require a second look.

Brooke Kelly, a former student of Hickey's and first hand witness to his sexual abuse, reached out to you personally in the hopes that you would use your platform to tell the truth. You refused. Why? Was it that her story would have dented your book sales? Chipped away at your credibility? Punctured an unsightly hole in your tapestry of falsehoods?

You see, Jeremy, there is a vital component in the definition of "bullying" that you seem to have overlooked. (I'm surprised you didn't learn it from the anti-bullying book tour you organized – you know, the one with the newly "retired" Patrick Hickey as a featured speaker.)

In order for unkind words or actions to be labeled as bullying, there must be an imbalance of power. It's the reason why nobody worries when a chihuahua barks at a Bullmastiff; there's nothing it can do to harm the much-larger canine. Do you see where I'm going with this?

Neither you nor Patrick Hickey were justified in crying "bully." With thousands of followers and supporters, the imbalance of power weighed heavily in your favor. There was little that Hickey's accusers could do to defend themselves against your repeated lies, mischaracterizations, and ridicule.

And I, along with many others, assumed the unfortunate role of the bystander. You had rational people convinced that by speaking up, they would become your next victims. It took careful consideration before I ultimately took the risk and spoke my mind beginning last fall.

Bullies feed off of not only a sense of control, but the attention received from their audience. It had to have felt good knowing that it was you who had whipped the Washington Local community into a frenzy when Hickey's job was originally at risk. It was your so-called whistleblowing that encouraged hundreds to flock to board meetings and demand the resignations of Patricia Carmean and Jim Langenderfer. Once in your corner, people looked to you for the next move.

But did it feel good when Mrs. Carmean found herself having to defend her deceased husband before an angry crowd?

Did it feel good when Mr. Langenderfer admitted to the packed room that he felt physically sick half of the time?

Did it feel good when you discovered that Mrs. Carmean sought a civil protection order against Patrick Hickey? Did you get any kind of high when you posted the entire video of her hearing online and mocked what we now know was legitimate fear of a gaslighting narcissist?

We certainly know you got a kick out of likening two of Hickey's detractors to Selma and Patty of The Simpsons, going as far as to joke that their fixation with taking down a child predator was the result of being sex-deprived. The attention you earned for your wit had to have felt good.

But the truth is, Jeremy, by definition, you were the bully.

You are a convicted domestic abuser, self-admitted adulterer, and now, the unapologetic defender of a child predator. Let's not forget the fact that you accused Hickey's former students of being coached or scripted as they tearfully begged for justice at board meetings. The woman who was raped by Hickey as a child even mentioned you by name in her impact statement. Thirty years later, she was re-victimized not only by her former teacher's vehement denials of wrongdoing, but your casting of him as the doe-eyed victim of attention-seeking women.

You and Patrick Hickey have rightfully earned the distinction of Toledo's worst bullies. Both of you have left Washington Local disheartened and divided — likely for years to come.

That can't feel good.

And now that the true tale of "How a Bully Used Fake News to Punch a School District" has come to a close, I'd like to know: when does that bully plan to apologize for it?

Sincerely,
Kathy Mayfield – Whitmer Class of 2007

Former Addison teacher Jim Driskill (who had spoken before the WLS Board several times) had this letter [8] in *The Toledo Blade* on July 6:

On June 28 in Lenawee County Court, Patrick Carl Hickey was sentenced and a 27-year, 235-day nightmare ended for myself and others from Addison and Washington Local schools, and most importantly the courageous victim who spoke up. I wish to thank *The Blade* and its staff, especially Nolan Rosenkrans, for your important and thorough coverage of this flawed individual, his deviant actions and continuous lies, and exposing his followers.

To the Washington Local Schools Board: Thanks for allowing us from Addison, Michigan to speak. I know that many of you realize that the Addison folks probably kept your district from having Hickey as school board president.

I wish Washington Local the very best. But this wave must continue with the Hickey supporters leaving or renouncing this evil, narcissistic person. I hope all vestiges and all pictures of this convicted sexual predator of children are removed from every location in your fine district.

Jim Driskill – Addison, Michigan

[Blade Editor's note:] Mr. Driskill is an Addison Community School Board member and a member of the Lenawee Co. Court Board of Commissioners.

Early release from jail, April 2019

Patrick Hickey was originally due to be released from Lenawee County Jail in late June 2019. But he was released early, on April 23, getting two months off for "good behavior." When "reached by *The Blade* on Tuesday, Hickey declined to comment." [9]

Patrick Carl Hickey: Sex Offender

Justice has been served.

The Ohio Attorney General placed Patrick Carl Hickey on the state's sex offender registry [10] for 25 years following his release from jail. In addition, he will be on probation for five years.

Ohio Secretary of State: Sex Offender Registry page (partial) for Patrick Carl Hickey.

Should Hickey live to be 80 and have his name removed from the registry, the truth in this chronicle will live on.

It is a very sorry legacy.

The Toledo Blade again editorialized about Hickey [11] on April 28, days after Hickey's release from jail, stating he:

... never should have been hired to work in Toledo-area schools. And no more school officials with such misconduct histories should be allowed to skate from job to job while authorities who know their backgrounds stay silent.

Parents and communities worry about dangerous strangers among us – lingering around the parks and playgrounds or living too close to schools or bus stops. But while we worry about these strangers, schools are too often hiring predators and putting our children in their hands.

At the very least, communities must be able to trust that the adults hired to work in our schools don't have a history of misconduct like Mr. Hickey ... had.

The trash needs to be left at the curb, not passed along.

CHAPTER 26
Resources & Further Reading

Helpful Resources: Educator Misconduct

S.E.S.A.M.E. (Stop Educator Sexual Abuse Misconduct & Exploitation), https://www.sesamenet.org/. Reports and resources.

Professor Charol Shakeshaft, "Know the Warning Signs of Educator Misconduct," *Kappan*, Feb. 2013, https://docs.wixstatic.com/ugd/b75d1b_3bc1e524fc7d4f47b5600c759bbd0ad7.pdf.

Professor Charol Shakeshaft, et al., "A Standard of Care for the Prevention of Sexual Misconduct by School Employees," *Journal of Child Sexual Abuse*, July 2018, https://www.tandfonline.com/doi/abs/10.1080/10538712.2018.1477219.

Professor Charles J. Hobson, *Passing the Trash: A Parent's Guide to Combat Sexual Abuse/Harassment of Their Children in School*, Amazon ed., 2012.

Steve Reilly, "Broken discipline tracking systems let teachers flee troubled pasts; A fragmented system for checking the background of teachers leaves students at risk," *USA Today*, Feb. 14, 2016 (updated Oct. 2017), https://www.usatoday.com/story/news/2016/02/14/broken-discipline-tracking-system-lets-teachers-with-misconduct-records-back-in-classroom/79999634.

ABC Nightline, "Passing the Trash: Teachers Who Cross the Line," April 2017, video. Part 1, https://abcnews.go.com/Nightline/video/passing-trash-part-schools-unload-problematic-teachers-hiding-46743922. Part 2, https://www.youtube.com/watch?v=qjdxm9wT0f0.

ABC WFAA, "Texas law to halt practice of 'passing the trash'," video report, Sept. 2017, https://youtu.be/65FPeI1b8_o.

NASDTEC, National Association of State Directors of Teacher Education and Certification, https://www.nasdtec.org/.

NASDTEC Educator Clearinghouse,
https://www.nasdtec.net/page/Clearinghouse_FAQ. "The Clearinghouse
is a searchable database that provides information regarding individuals
who have had their professional educator certificates/licenses annulled,
denied, suspended, revoked, or otherwise invalidated."

National Sex Offender Public Website, https://www.nsopw.gov/.

Jane Meredith Adams, "Schools failing to protect students from sexual
abuse by school personnel, federal report says," *EdSource*, Feb. 5, 2014,
https://edsource.org/2014/schools-failing-to-protect-students-from-
sexual-abuse-by-school-personnel-federal-report-says/57023.

Vermont Department of Children and Families, "The Grooming Process:
How Abusers Groom Children," no date (accessed 2020),
https://dcf.vermont.gov/prevention/stepup/educate/grooming.

Karen-Ann Broe, Esq., "Educator Sexual Misconduct A Policy and Audit
Guide for Protecting Children," United Educators Insurance, 2007,
https://www.aassa.com/uploaded/Educational_Research/Child_Protectio
n/Educator_Sexual_Misconduct_Policy_and_Audit_Guide.pdf.

Andrea Clemens, *Invisible Target: Breaking the Cycle of Educator Sexual
Abuse*, Amazon Kindle ed., 2015. "A true, detailed account of one girl's
experience of educator sexual abuse at the hands of her middle school
teacher... *Invisible Target* is more than a memoir. With thought-
provoking questions at the close of each chapter, this book serves as a
strong educational tool for students, parents, teachers, and administrators by shedding light on the dynamics of educator sexual abuse so that
school can be a safe haven for every child."

Ohio Dept. of Education & Federal Government

Bennett Haeberle, "Ohio Department of Education can take months,
years to punish teachers," WBNS-10TV (Columbus, Ohio), May 17, 2018,
https://www.10tv.com/article/ohio-department-education-can-take-
months-years-punish-teachers.

Ohio Department of Education, Code of Professional Conduct for Ohio
Educators, http://bit.ly/33NtRlk, and video, 2017,
https://www.youtube.com/watch?v=ETk8lcHJb0Q. *Excerpt:*

Educators behave in a professional manner, realizing that one's actions reflect directly on the status and substance of the profession. Educators maintain a professional relationship with all students at all times, both in and outside the classroom... Educators serve as positive role models.

Ohio Department of Education, Licensure Code of Professional Conduct for Ohio Educators, 2008, http://bit.ly/2L5lIAb. *Excerpt:*

Conduct unbecoming to the profession includes, but is not limited to, the following actions: Committing any violation of state or federal laws, statutes, or rules, although the conduct may not have resulted in a criminal charge, indictment, prosecution or conviction... Being disciplined by another state educational entity or other professional licensing board or entity for unethical conduct... Committing any act of sexual abuse of a student or minor or engaging in inappropriate sexual conduct with a student or minor... Soliciting, encouraging, engaging or consummating an inappropriate relationship with a student or minor... Using inappropriate language, gestures or signs at any school related activity such as racial slurs, biased, lewd or lascivious expressions... Using technology to promote inappropriate communications with students. Educators shall ensure that school property, public funds or fees paid by students or the community are not used for personal gain...

Committee on Education and the Workforce, U.S. House of Representatives, "Federal Agencies Can Better Support State Efforts to Prevent and Respond to Sexual Abuse by School Personnel," Report to the Ranking Member, Jan. 2014, https://www.gao.gov/assets/670/660375.pdf.

U.S. Department of Justice, "K-12 School Employee Sexual Misconduct: Lessons Learned from Title IX Policy Implementation," Sept. 2017 Infographic, http://bit.ly/2QpB3Qw.

U.S. Department of Education, "A Training Guide for Administrators and Educators on Addressing Adult Sexual Misconduct in the School Setting," GAO/Dept of Justice guidelines, March 2017, https://rems.ed.gov/docs/ASMTrainingGuide.pdf. *Excerpts:*

A 2014 report by the U.S. Government Accountability Office (GAO) defines ASM [Adult Sexual Misconduct] as any sexual activity (physical or not) directed to a child with the purpose of developing a romantic or sexual relationship (p. 1–5). The GAO notes that although some types of ASM (such as remarks directed to a student) may not be criminal, these actions often violate other laws, regulations, and professional codes of conduct. These "gray areas" can sometimes be subject to interpretation, which underscores the importance of developing clear policies and procedures on ASM in every school district...

According to the National Education Association, inappropriate physical conduct includes kissing, hair stroking, tickling, and frontal hugging (Simpson, 2006). It is important that school personnel understand what is considered appropriate and inappropriate conduct so that they can protect the children, at school and in its related cyber settings. Furthermore, school personnel will want to take steps to protect themselves while interacting with students before, during, and after school. By modeling appropriate adult behaviors, educators can help teach children protective actions, as well.

ASM [adult sexual misconduct] The GAO (2014) estimates that nearly one in 10 students are subjected to ASM by school personnel during the course of their academic careers. During the course of a seven-month investigation, Associated Press reporters examined the 2001–05 disciplinary records of educators from all 50 states and the District of Columbia (Irvine & Tanner, 2007). The investigation determined that the teaching credentials of 2,570 educators had been revoked, denied, surrendered, or sanctioned as a result of ASM, and that more than 80 percent of victims in the 1,801 cases were students.

The Impact of ASM Child sexual abuse, including ASM in schools, is detrimental to children's physical, psychological, and academic well-being, as well as to their behavioral development (Lalor and McElvaney (2010); Hornor, 2009; Shoop, 2004). This victimization, whether through a single event or chronic exposure, can result in either short-term or lifelong effects that include maladaptive behaviors, mental disorders, developmental delays, social difficulties, and a shorter life expectancy ("Linking Childhood," 2015). The Division of Violence Prevention at the U.S. Centers for Disease Control and Prevention (CDC) views child maltreatment as a serious public health concern ("Child Abuse Prevention," 2015).

[Includes this description of grooming:]

... At the same time [as he is grooming the individual victim], the perpetrator is also testing the adults surrounding the child or school, including those who work at school, individuals in the school community, and the child's family or guardian(s). It is not uncommon for the behaviors to be done publicly so that the perpetrator can gauge reactions; share information (true or false) to manipulate how the behavior is interpreted by the adults; and further control the child victim. For example, a teacher may lead their colleagues to believe the parent has provided consent for them to drive a student home because the parent needs help. In response, the perpetrator receives accolades and gratitude from their colleagues, and has begun the process of grooming peers as well...

To assist in preventing knowingly false allegations, the National Education Association (NEA) has developed suggestions on avoiding compromising situations (Simpson, 2006). These "common sense pointers for avoiding false allegations" are as follows...

Whenever possible, do not be alone with a student, because allegations made when there are no other witnesses hinge on credibility. Authorities often tend to favor the alleged victim in these circumstances.

Maintain a professional demeanor and distance, which means no flirting, teasing, or joking about sex. Do not socialize with students or treat them as "friends." Never give gifts, unless they are given to every student, and do not single out any one student for special attention or flattery. Do not ask students about their social lives or comment on personal appearance. Avoid discussing intimate details of your private life. Do not hire students to babysit or allow them to visit your home.

Avoid physical contact with students. As a general rule, it is best to avoid most forms of physical contact, especially kissing, hair-stroking, tickling, and frontal hugging. Use common sense: A "high five" to acknowledge a job well done is fine; a slap on the bottom is not. Male employees are far more likely to be accused of inappropriate contact with students than female employees...

Never allow a student to obsess over you. While a crush can be flattering, an unfulfilled fantasy can result in a student acting out to gain attention or retaliating for being ignored. If a student expresses a love interest, respond with an unambiguous "no." Don't equivocate or encourage the student by acting pleased by the attention. It is advisable to share this information with another adult...

Context: Changing Attitudes about Sex

By the 1980s and 1990s, many of the younger generation had absorbed the unhealthy ideas of the Sexual Revolution which had gotten underway in post-World War II America. One major impetus was the publication of the pseudo-scientific works of Alfred Kinsey. (See Dr. Judith Reisman's exposés on the shoddy, pseudo-scientific methods used by this entomologist who later changed is focus to human sexuality. http://www.drjudithreisman.com.) Another impetus was the loosening legal standard for pornography.

Young men of Patrick Hickey's generation turned to *Playboy* as legitimate entertainment without a second thought, imbibing an *exploitive attitude towards women and girls*. *Playboy*'s Hugh Hefner referred to himself as Kinsey's pamphleteer – a propagandist for abandoning traditional sexual morés. Young women and girls were similarly sexualized by *Cosmo*, which feminized the *Playboy* attitude in the 1960s. Sexualized movies and popular music continued to transform American society.

It was Kinsey who propagated the myth that children were sexual from birth. His co-author, Wardell B. Pomeroy, Ph.D., published books advocating sexual freedom for teen boys and girls –which would have been current at the time of the scandalous events at Addison High School. He essentially preached, "*If it feels good, do it.*" His books present abortion as an unobjectionable solution for unintended pregnancy. Pomeroy set the standard for the "non-judgmental" instruction on sexuality for teens which would become the norm from the 1970s on.

Wardell B. Pomeroy, Ph.D. (co-author of the Kinsey Reports), *Boys and Sex*, Bantam Doubleday Dell Publishing Group, 1968, 1981. [A few representative excerpts from the 1981 edition:]

> ...more and more people are coming to understand that having sex is a joyful and enriching experience at any age... Parents and churches may teach morality, and boys then may make their own codes... One relationship may end with intercourse; and then the boy goes on to a different kind, or the same kind, of relationship with another girl. This is all part of the process of growing up, of maturing.

Wardell B. Pomeroy, Ph.D. (co-author of the Kinsey Reports), *Girls and Sex*, Bantam Doubleday Dell Publishing Group, 1969, 1981, 1991. [A few representative excerpts from the 1991 edition:]

Never in the history of our country have sexual customs and behavior changed so radically in so short a time, and never has there been so much public acceptance of sexuality... [You are reading] ... books written for your age group by such very popular writers as Judy Blume, containing quite explicit sexual situations... Today more and more women have begun to understand their own sexuality a great deal better, to be more assertive about it ... Parents, especially, ought to stop viewing sexual behavior through the distorted lens of the prejudices and fears they grew up with... teen-age sex should be a learning experience, not a frightening one... sexual behavior for both boys and girls is something that's pleasurable and desirable...

Contemporaneous with the Addison High School scandal

Planned Parenthood has explained that sex education programs changed starting in the 1970s, following recommendations from the World Health Organization. (See http://bit.ly/2KqvQ7i.) It quoted WHO's definition of "sexual health" in 1975:

"Sexual health is the integration of the somatic, emotional, intellectual, and social aspects of sexual being, in ways that are positively enriching and that enhance personality, communication, and love. Fundamental to this concept are **the right to sexual information and the right to pleasure**. [One basic element of sexual health is:] **freedom from fear, shame, guilt, false beliefs, and other psychological factors inhibiting sexual response and impairing sexual relationship**... Thus the notion of sexual health implies a **positive approach to human sexuality**, and the purpose of sexual health care should be the enhancement of life and personal relationships and not merely counseling and care related to procreation or sexually transmitted diseases." (World Health Organization, 1975)

WHO's early definition is at the core of our understanding of sexual health today and is a departure from prevailing notions about sexual health – and **sex education** – that predominated in the 19th and 20th centuries. Until the 1960s and 1970s, the goals of social hygiene and moral purity activists eclipsed broader sexual health concerns in the public health arena. **Their narrow goals** were to prevent sexually transmitted infections, stamp out masturbation and prostitution, and **limit sexual expression to marriage**. [Emphasis added.]

James Patterson and Peter Kim, *The Day America Told the Truth*, 1991. The authors interviewed 2,000 Americans. Some of their findings:

Overwhelmingly, the American attitude toward sex (anything but sex with children) has become: Just do it. We are living in a time of tremendous sexual experimentation, even sexual revolution. We feel far less guilty about sexual matters than we've ever felt before.

There is absolutely no moral consensus at all in the 1990s. Everyone is making up their own personal moral codes – their own Ten Commandments.

America's Number One Rationalization: "If everybody's doing it, why shouldn't I?"

A letdown in moral values is now considered the number one problem facing our country. Eighty percent of us believe that morals and ethics should be taught in our schools again.

Young American males are our biggest national tragedy. Males between the ages of eighteen and twenty-five are ... responsible for most child abuse.

Lying has become an integral part of the American culture, a trait of the American character.

The ideal of childhood is ended. A startling percentage of American children actually lose their virginity before the age of thirteen.

More background

Professor William Kilpatrick, *Why Johnny Can't Tell Right from Wrong*, Simon & Schuster, 1995. The Boston College Professor of Education addressed the "crisis in moral education."

Social critic Mary Eberstadt, author of several books on the sexual revolution, explained in a recent interview:

> ... the sexual revolution has changed the human ecosystem and under that change, women are particularly more menaced than before... My question is, "Why are so many young women in harm's way? Why do these terrible things keep happening to them?" I think it gets back to, again, the fact that many women and many men are not socialized the way humanity has grown accustomed to being socialized. That is to say without a robust family and extended family, without nonsexual knowledge of the opposite sex, people miss a lot of things about relations between the sexes, and I think that kind of incoherence comes through very strongly in these Rashomon-like stories that emanate from #MeToo. So, it seems to me a classic example of a breakdown in social

learning by a social animal… For 60 years the sexual revolution has been a great big party, and now we're at the point in the story where it's two in the morning and nobody wants to call the cops. (https://www.dailysignal.com/2019/09/04/how-the-sexual-revolution-gave-us-identity-politics/)

Michael Brown, PhD, "What Alfred Kinsey and Hugh Hefner Had in Common," 2017. *Excerpt*:

If Hugh Hefner was the poster boy of the sexual revolution, Alfred Kinsey was the father of the revolution. But that is not the only thing that joins these men together. Both of them were overt rebels against "puritanical" Christianity, devoting their lives to "liberate" humanity from what they perceived to be the bondage of a sterile, restrictive morality…. [Kinsey] is the man celebrated as the "father of the sexual revolution." In his own words, "there are only three kinds of sexual abnormalities: abstinence, celibacy and delayed marriage." (TownHall.com, Oct. 9, 2017)

Robert H. Knight, "How Alfred C. Kinsey's Sex Studies Have Harmed Women and Children," 2003. *Excerpt*:

… Kinsey's studies have had an enormous impact on the law and the culture, despite later evidence that the research was fatally flawed and even involved cover-ups of child rape… [His] studies have had a profoundly negative impact on American women and children, weakening legal protection from sexual abuse and falsely portraying "sexual liberation" as an unalloyed good, despite astronomic increases in divorce, abortion, sexually transmitted diseases and physical abuse of women and children.

With his benign view of child sexual abuse, Kinsey became an activist on behalf of child molesters. In 1949, for example, he testified before the California General Assembly's Subcommittee on Sex Crimes, urging them to liberalize sex offense statutes. He argued specifically for granting immediate paroles to suspected child molesters, and warned that societal "hysteria" does more harm to children than the actual molestations… (Concerned Women for America, Nov. 2003).

SOURCES

Note on quotes and images

For quotes taken from the Michigan State Police investigation documents, names were changed. In the images of MSP documents, names were redacted (unless they were witnesses who spoke publicly).

Photos and screengrabs: Faces of adults and older students taken from WLS Board meeting videos, videos produced for WLS, and WLS online newsletters were left unredacted. Images used are either from videos of *public forums* where there is no expectation of privacy; are posted on the district's public website (still posted in 2020); or are from videos made for the WLS district (still posted at YouTube in 2020). Anyone concerned about children's faces being shown should address the school system. Other photos taken from public Facebook and Twitter pages are by their nature *public* and carry no expectation of privacy. In those cases, too, we redacted the faces of younger children.

In testimonies taken from WLS School Board meetings, we have included last names only for those persons who were larger players, and for others gave either no name or first name only. In any case, WLS Board meetings are a public forum where the speakers were required to give their full names and addresses, and there is no expectation of privacy.

Quotes from source documents and our transcriptions from oral testimony generally leave intact any errors in grammar, punctuation, spelling, word usage, etc. as they occurred in the source. In some cases, we noted the error with [sic].

Patrick Hickey and Washington Local Schools

Michigan State Police, investigations of Patrick C. Hickey, official filings, 2016, 2018 (public record).

Lenawee County Court, official transcripts of Patrick Hickey's arraignment and sentencing hearing, 2018 (public record).

Sources

On-the-record conversations with Jim Langenderfer (former WLS Board member), Patricia Carmean (former WLS Board member and teacher), private investigator Chris Gill, and several WLS teachers.

Washington Local Schools (WLS), Board of Education, Toledo, Ohio (public). See especially minutes and videos of Board meetings and "Across the Board" online newsletters. All WLS videos and web pages referenced were still posted in 2020. https://www.wls4kids.org/.

Washington Local Schools, Policy Manual and 2016 video.

Washington Local Schools, Human Resources video, Nov. 2016, bit.ly/33T4myTbit.ly/.

Videos made for Washington Local Schools by Punsalan Productions, https://www.youtube.com/user/3HMProductions/videos.

Patrick Hickey's emails on WLS system, retrieved in early 2019 via public records request.

Patrick Hickey, Facebook.com/Patrick.Hickey.77770 (public; accessed 2018 and 2019; no longer online).

#IStandWithMrHickey (https://twitter.com/hashtag/Istandwithmrhickey) and #IStandWithHickey (https://twitter.com/hashtag/istandwithhickey), Sept. 2015 (still online 2020).

Facebook.com/WLSpolitics, accessed early 2019.

Jeremy Baumhower, iHeartGlassCity blog; IHeartGlassCity Facebook; and *Socked: The Unbelievable Tale of How a Bully Used Fake News to Punch a School District (and Me)*, eBook, 2017 (no longer available at Apple but still available at Kobo).

The following media sources are quoted under Fair Use policy of U.S. copyright law:

The Toledo Blade, Toledo, Ohio
The Daily Telegram, Adrian, Michigan
The Monroe News, Monroe, Michigan
Toledo City Paper, Toledo, Ohio
WTOL 11 CBS, Toledo, Ohio
13abc News, Toledo, Ohio

PASSING the TRASH

NBC 24 News, Toledo, Ohio
Fred LeFebvre, WSPD 1370, Toledo, Ohio
Jerry Schaffer, Q105.5, Toledo, Ohio
Belt Magazine, Cleveland, Ohio
SwampBubbles.com (via web archive)
Punsalan Productions videos

ENDNOTES

CHAPTER 1 – Patrick Hickey's Sentencing Hearing
1. Lenawee County Circuit Court, Adrian, Michigan. Video reports: *The Daily Telegram* (Adrian, Michigan), https://youtu.be/qwYS4Gor2DM. *WTOL 11*, Toledo, Ohio, http://bit.ly/2Q8eMGt.

CHAPTER 2 – No-Nonsense Langenderfer
1. WLS online newsletter, Jan. 8, 2014, https://www.wls4kids.org/view/402.pdf.
2. WLS Board meeting, video, April 23, 2015, http://bit.ly/358Mz6h.
3. WLS online newsletter, Apr. 1, 2015, https://www.wls4kids.org/view/11018.pdf.

CHAPTER 3 – Hickey at Addison High School, 1986-1990
1. Letter to the Editor, "Some did not stay silent about Hickey," *Toledo Blade*, May 1, 2019, https://www.toledoblade.com/opinion/letters-to-the-editor/2019/05/02/some-did-not-stay-silent-about-patrick-hickey-addison-whitmer-schools/stories/20190501135.
2. Jeremy Baumhower, *Socked: The Unbelievable Tale of How a Bully Used Fake News to Punch a School District (and Me)* (eBook, 2017), no longer available at Apple, still live at Kobo in 2020.

CHAPTER 7 – The Intervening Years, 1990-2002
1. Sandra Svoboda, "St. Anthony Villa to shut doors," *Toledo Blade*, May 31, 2001, https://www.toledoblade.com/Print-Furniture/2001/05/31/St-Anthony-Villa-to-shut-doors/stories/200105310041.
2. "School chief's pay in Addison suspended during inquiry," *Toledo Blade*, May 15, 2002, https://www.toledoblade.com/local/education/2002/05/15/School-chief-s-pay-in-Addison-suspended-during-inquiry/stories/200205150023.
3. "Hickey pleads guilty to sexual conduct charge," *Toledo Blade*, May 9, 2018, https://www.toledoblade.com/Courts/2018/05/09/Hickey-pleads-guilty-in/stories.

CHAPTER 8 – Hickey Hired by WLS; 2002 & 2007 Job Applications
1. Ignazio Messina, "9 superintendent candidates on list for Washington Local," *Toledo Blade*, June 6, 2007, https://www.toledoblade.com/local/education/2007/06/06/9-superintendent-candidates-on-list-for-Washington-Local/stories/200706060036.
2. Ignazio Messina, "Hickey gets unanimous nod to lead school district," *Toledo Blade*, July 6, 2007, https://www.toledoblade.com/local/Education/2007/07/06/Hickey-gets-unanimous-nod-to-lead-school-district/stories/200707060090.

CHAPTER 10 – The Cult of Hickey
1. Ohio Dept. of Education, http://education.ohio.gov.
2. Ohio Dept. of Education, http://bit.ly/2MKtbXc.
3. WLS online newsletter, Sept. 18, 2013, https://www.wls4kids.org/files/user/2/file/board/2013/Across-the-Board-9_18_13.pdf.
4. Jetta Fraser, "Infinite Opportunity Olympic Games," *Toledo Blade*, May 5, 2012, https://www.toledoblade.com/gallery/Infinite-Opportunity-Olympic-Games.

5. Punsalan Productions video, " 'I AM Washington Local' 2014 Commercial Campaign,"
Aug. 20, 2014, https://youtu.be/eGqKCGPp6hg.
6. *Toledo Blade*, "Top Workplaces 1-26-14,"
https://issuu.com/toledoblade/docs/top_workplaces_1-26-14, pp. 18-19 and photo on cover
of Hickey with WLS union presidents Christopher Hodnicki and Cindy Perry.
7. Punsalan Productions, " 'Happy' Washington Local Schools Voted TOP WORKPLACE
in NW Ohio - OFFICIAL VIDEO," Feb. 19, 2014, https://youtu.be/fhLnlSHNVA0.
8. WLS Board meeting, podcast, Feb. 19, 2014,
https://www.wls4kids.org/District/Department/12-Board-Information/Podcasts/3190-
Board-Meeting-2014-02-19.html.
9. WLS, State Report Cards by School Year,
https://www.wls4kids.org/District/Department/52-State-Report-Cards.
10. Chris Myers, "The question is not if Washington Local violated state law during its
Issue 2 levy campaign in 2014, but to what extent," *SwampBubbles.com*, Oct. 14, 2015,
http://bit.ly/2stbqof.
11. WLS online newsletter, Dec. 16, 2009, https://www.wls4kids.org/view/335.pdf.
12. State Report Card for WLS, 2015-2016, http://bit.ly/2SyPX83.
13. WLS online newsletter, Nov. 16, 2011, bottom of p. 3,
https://www.wls4kids.org/view/375.pdf.
14. "Narcissism," *Psychology Today*, no date,
https://www.psychologytoday.com/us/basics/narcissism.
15. "Narcissism," *Wikipedia*, https://en.wikipedia.org/wiki/Narcissism.
16. "Narcissistic Personality Disorder," *Psychology Today*, no date,
https://www.psychologytoday.com/us/conditions/narcissistic-personality-disorder.
17. "Narcissism," *Wikipedia*,
https://en.wikipedia.org/wiki/Narcissism#Seven_deadly_sins_of_narcissism.
18. "Narcissism," *Wikipedia*, https://en.wikipedia.org/wiki/Narcissism#Sexual_narcissism.
19. Peg Streep, "The Communal Narcissist: Another Wolf Wearing a Sheep Outfit,"
Psychology Today, May 24, 2016, https://www.psychologytoday.com/us/blog/tech-
support/201605/the-communal-narcissist-another-wolf-wearing-sheep-outfit.
20. Ibid.
21. "Collective Narcissism," *Wikipedia*, https://en.wikipedia.org/wiki/Collective_narcissism.
22. "Collective Narcissism," *Wikipedia*,
https://en.wikipedia.org/wiki/Collective_narcissism#The_charismatic_leader-
follower_relationship.
23. Christian Jarrett, "There's such a thing as collective narcissism," British Psychological
Society, *Research Digest*, Dec. 9, 2016, https://digest.bps.org.uk/2016/12/09/theres-such-a-
thing-as-collective-narcissism-and-it-might-explain-a-lot-thats-going-on-at-the-moment.
24. *WLS Board meeting, video*, Sept. 16, 2015, http://bit.ly/3514fkx.
25. Ch. 10, Note 6.
26. Ch. 10, Note 21.
27. Twitter, https://twitter.com/hashtag/IStandWithMrHickey. Still posted in 2020.

CHAPTER 11 – Violating Appropriate Boundaries
1. "The RCA Experience" slideshow (posted by WLS teachers), Nov. 2013 (WLS
professional development trip to Ron Clark Academy), https://bit.ly/2SuXQZ4.
2. Jeremy Baumhower, *Socked: The Unbelievable Tale of How a Bully Used Fake News to Punch a
School District (and Me)* (eBook, 2017), no longer available at Apple, still live at Kobo.

Endnotes

3. Charol Shakeshaft, "Know the Warning Signs of Educator Misconduct," *Kappan*, Feb. 2013, https://docs.wixstatic.com/ugd/b75d1b_3bc1e524fc7d4f47b5600c759bbd0ad7.pdf.

4. U.S. Department of Education, "A Training Guide for Administrators and Educators on Addressing Adult Sexual Misconduct in the School Setting," GAO/Dept of Justice guidelines, March 2017, https://rems.ed.gov/docs/ASMTrainingGuide.pdf.

5. "Patricia Carmean's C.P.O. petition hearing against Patrick Hickey 4/20/17 (1 of 2)," posted by Jeremy Baumhower, Apr. 24, 2017, https://youtu.be/RTORgtQ0fKM.

6. WLS Board meeting, video, Sept. 16, 2015, http://bit.ly/2MAtJyC.

7. WLS online newsletter, March 21, 2012, https://www.wls4kids.org/view/380.pdf.

8. Retrieved by private investigator Chris Gill.

9. WLS online newsletter, June 16, 2010, https://www.wls4kids.org/view/346.pdf.

10. WLS Board Policies, https://go.boarddocs.com/oh/washlsd/Board.nsf/Public?open&id=policies.

11. WLS Human Resources video, Nov. 17, 2016, http://bit.ly/33T4myT.

12. Ch. 11, Note 10.

13. WLS Teachers' complaint vs. Supt. Hickey, *Toledo Blade*, Sept. 23, 2015, https://www.toledoblade.com/attachment/2015/09/23/Formal-complaint-and-e-mail-exchanges.PDF.

14. WLS online newsletter, Mar. 20, 2013, https://www.wls4kids.org/view/391.pdf.

CHAPTER 12 – WLS Core Values, Hypocrisy, Scandal

1. WLS online newsletter, p. 4, Aug. 11/18. 2010, https://www.wls4kids.org/view/348.pdf.

2. WLS Board meeting, podcast, Oct. 16, 2013, https://www.wls4kids.org/files/user/2/file/board/2013/Board-Comments-and-Mission-Statement.mp3 (at 3:38). Mission Statement, https://www.wls4kids.org/files/user/2/file/board/2013/Mission-Statement.pdf.

3. *Toledo Blade*, "Top Workplaces 1-26-14," pp. 18-19, https://issuu.com/toledoblade/docs/top_workplaces_1-26-14.

4 WLS online newsletter, Dec. 15, 2010, https://www.wls4kids.org/view/362.pdf.

5. Nolan Rosenkrans, "Educator's history at Whitmer leads to his dismissal in Monroe; Teacher and coach allegedly had inappropriate relationships," *Toledo Blade*, Feb. 25, 2013, https://www.toledoblade.com/local/education/2013/02/25/Educator-s-history-at-Whitmer-leads-to-his-dismissal-in-Monroe/stories/20130208193.

6. Jonathan Walsh, *WTOL 11*, "2 Whitmer teachers resign amid allegations of sexual misconduct," Oct. 9, 2008, https://www.wtol.com/article/news/2-whitmer-teachers-resign-amid-allegations-of-sexual-misconduct/512-270829c3-e0e9-434e-8550-0d3fd30e5f7f.

7. "2 at Whitmer being investigated, on leave," *Toledo Blade*, Oct. 3, 2008, https://www.toledoblade.com/local/education/2008/10/03/2-at-Whitmer-being-investigated-on-leave/stories/200810030061.

8. "Whitmer fined $50,000 and wins by OHSAA for violating bylaw," *USA Today High School Sports*, Dec. 22, 2012, https://usatodayhss.com/2012/whitmer-fined-50000-and-wins-by-ohsaa-for-violating-bylaw-2. (It was in commenting on this scandal that Hickey wrote: "People have been repeating rumors and mistruths. Mr. Hickey shared with the football team the words he has on a plaque in his office: '*Mediocre minds will violently oppose great spirits.*' When you are striving to be great, you will be attacked, and the district has been attacked for 100 days." WLS online newsletter, Nov. 16, 2011, bottom of p. 3, https://www.wls4kids.org/view/375.pdf).

9. Ron Clark Academy, Atlanta, GA, http://www.ronclarkacademy.com/Who-we-are & http://www.ronclarkacademy.com/Training.

10. D. Aileen Dodd, "Ron Clark Academy success comes at a price few schools can afford," *Atlanta Journal-Constitution*, July 1, 2010, https://www.ajc.com/news/local/ron-clark-academy-success-comes-price-few-schools-can-afford/BvFkypZGWwo0BgTYNoVyUI.

11. Nolan Rosenkrans, "5 suburban school districts to elect school board members," *Toledo Blade*, Nov. 3, 2103, https://www.toledoblade.com/local/politics/2013/11/03/5-suburban-Toledo-districts-to-elect-school-board-members/stories/20131101187.

12. WLS Board meeting, video, April 22, 2015, http://bit.ly/358Mz6h.

13. "The RCA Experience" slideshow (posted by WLS teachers), Nov. 2013, https://bit.ly/2SuXQZ4.

14. WLS Board meeting, video, April 22, 2015, http://bit.ly/358Mz6h. April 22, 2019 Board meeting, Minutes, https://www.wls4kids.org/files/user/21/file/Board_Minutes_2015-04-22.pdf. April 29, 2019 Board meeting, Minutes, https://www.wls4kids.org/files/user/21/file/Board_Minutes_2015-04-29.pdf.

15. "Washington JH renovation zone," 2014, https://vimeo.com/90346035.

16. Washington Junior High, "Bathroom reveal 1," 2013, https://youtu.be/vzr9vylDk90. "Washington JH renovation zone," 2014, https://vimeo.com/90346035.

17. WLS online newsletter, April 16, 2014, https://www.wls4kids.org/view/453.pdf.

18. WLS online newsletter, Jan. 18, 2012, https://www.wls4kids.org/view/378.pdf.

19. Janet Romaker, "Zuber resigns from Washington local board," *Toledo Blade*, Apr. 17, 2014, https://www.toledoblade.com/local/education/2014/04/17/photo-available-on-school-Web-site/stories/20140417113.

20. Chip Towns, "District operates as extended family; No. 1 Large Business: Washington Local Schools," *Toledo Blade*, Jan. 25, 2014, https://www.toledoblade.com/business/2014/01/26/Washington-Local-School-District-operates-as-extended-family.html.

21. Punsalan Productions, "'Happy' Washington Local Schools Voted TOP WORKPLACE in NW Ohio – OFFICIAL VIDEO," Feb. 19, 2014, https://youtu.be/fhLnlSHNVA0.

22. Punsalan Productions, "Happy Mullan – Outtake #2," Mar. 14, 2014, https://youtu.be/M72YdmllH0E.

23. Jennifer Lopez, "Booty," 2014, https://youtu.be/nxtIRArhVD4.

24. T-shirt from a school presentation on "teen dating violence" in March 2012. See https://www.wls4kids.org/view/380.pdf.

25. WLS Board Policies, https://go.boarddocs.com/oh/washlsd/Board.nsf/Public?open&id=policies.

26. Carl Ryan, "Ex-Bedford schools officer now top cop in Washington Local district; School officials: Randy Sehl only person for job," *Toledo Blade*, Nov. 18, 2013, https://www.toledoblade.com/local/police-fire/2013/11/18/Ex-Bedford-schools-officer-now-top-cop-in-Toledo-district/stories/20131117202.

27. Ray Kisonas, "Charges not being filed against Randy Sehl," *Monroe News*, Feb. 10, 2015, http://radionecrosis3.rssing.com/chan-3392934/all_p650.html.

28. "Washington Local Schools' security director steps down," Feb. 7, 2015, *Toledo Blade*, https://www.toledoblade.com/Education/2015/02/07/Washington-Local-Schools-security-director.html. Mike Sigov, "Accused deputy is placed on leave," Jan. 22, 2015, *Toledo Blade*, https://www.toledoblade.com/Police-Fire/2015/01/22/Accused-deputy-is-placed-on-leave.html.

29. Ch. 12, Note 21.

Endnotes

30. William Kilpatrick, *Why Johnny Can't Tell Right from Wrong* (New York: Simon & Schuster, 1995), 173-174.

31. Punsalan Productions, "Uptown Funk: Whitmer Teacher Flash Mob — Homecoming 2017," Oct. 13, 2017, https://youtu.be/mRCp8Gg4wmo.

32. Kimberly White, "Gymnasium Goes Nuts When Teachers Storm Court With Epic 'Uptown Funk' Flash Mob," *InspireMore*, Feb. 28, 2018, https://www.inspiremore.com/uptown-funk-homecoming.

33. "Mark Ronson - Uptown Funk (Official Video) ft. Bruno Mars," Nov. 19, 2014, https://youtu.be/OPf0YbXqDm0. Scroll down for the sexually suggestive (and sometimes intentionally inscrutable) lyrics.

34. Vanessa McCray, "Seven Washington Local employees on paid leave identified," *Toledo Blade*, May 25, 2017, https://www.toledoblade.com/Education/2017/05/25/Five-teachers-two-students-placed-on-paid-leave-by-Washington-Local.html.

35. Vanessa McCray, "5 Washington Local teachers resign amid district probe; School board president confirms 'all seven did drink'," *Toledo Blade*, May 26, 2017, https://www.toledoblade.com/Education/2017/05/26/5-Washington-Local-teachers-resign-amid-district-probe.html.

36. "Washington Local teacher under investigation resigns," *Toledo Blade*, July 10, 2018, https://www.toledoblade.com/Education/2018/07/09/Washington-Local-teacher-Michael-Punsalan-under-investigation-resigns-npr.html.

37. Punsalan Productions, "Whitmer Film Project™: Teachers Dancing Behind Students Vol.178," Mar. 7, 2016, https://youtu.be/vk2qyXDpn4k.

38. YouTube, "Teachers Dancing Behind Students," https://binged.it/2P08TJF.

39. Punsalan Productions, "'The Breakfast Club' Library Dance Scene Parody Whitmer High School," Dec. 19, 2017, https://youtu.be/LGH-dUeacHA.

40. Punsalan Productions, " 'Love On Hold: The Musical' by The Whitmer Film Project - Tree City Film Festival 2013 Winner," Apr. 13, 2013, https://youtu.be/KtNutqNDuk4.

41. Punsalan Productions, " 'Making Our Mark' by The Whitmer Film Project - Tree City Film Festival 2014," Apr. 26, 2014, https://youtu.be/XH7yJy70ZJs.

CHAPTER 13 – WLS Teachers File Complaint vs. Hickey; Scandalous Emails Published

1. Nolan Rosenkrans, "Educator's history at Whitmer leads to his dismissal in Monroe; Teacher and coach allegedly had inappropriate relationships," *Toledo Blade*, Feb. 25, 2013, https://www.toledoblade.com/local/education/2013/02/25/Educator-s-history-at-Whitmer-leads-to-his-dismissal-in-Monroe/stories/20130208193.

2. WLS Board Policy 3362, https://www.boarddocs.com/oh/washlsd/Board.nsf/Public?open&id=policies.

3. The information as released by WLS to *The Blade* is available online at https://www.toledoblade.com/attachment/2015/09/23/Formal-complaint-and-e-mail-exchanges.PDF.

4. It is difficult to follow the chronology in the original documents as published in *The Blade* (ibid.).

CHAPTER 14 – The Big Blow-Up: Community Anger & Hickey's Reprimand

1. Ohio Dept. of Education, http://bit.ly/2F2DrFN.

2. Available via Internet Archive, https://web.archive.org/web/*/http:/iheartglasscity.com and https://glasscityhalffull.wordpress.com (accessed Jan. 2020).

3. Jeremy Baumhower, "Making or Breaking the Coup: The Future of 7,200 Children is up for Grabs #ElectionDay2015 #WLS #ABC ," *IHeartGlassCity*, Nov. 2, 2015, http://bit.ly/369C0RT.

4. Jeremy Baumhower, *Socked: The Unbelievable Tale of How a Bully Used Fake News to Punch a School District (and Me)* (Apple iBook, 2017), loc. 44 & 50. The book is still available at Kobo in 2020.

5. Ch. 14, Note 2.

6. *WLS Board meeting, video, Aug. 5, 2015*, https://vimeo.com/138306738.

7. ToledoTalk.com, *"WLS BOE wants to get rid of superintendent Hickey?,"* Sept. 12, 2015, http://bit.ly/2Sx1apI.

8. "Whitmer fined $50,000 and wins by OHSAA for violating bylaw," *USA Today High School Sports*, Dec. 22, 2012, https://usatodayhss.com/2012/whitmer-fined-50000-and-wins-by-ohsaa-for-violating-bylaw-2.

9. *WLS Board meeting, podcast, Sept. 3, 2015*, https://www.wls4kids.org/District/Department/12-Board-Information/Podcasts/7503-Board-Meeting-2015-09-03.html.

10. WLS Board meeting, Minutes, Sept. 3, 2015, https://www.wls4kids.org/files/user/21/file/Board%20Minutes/Board_Minutes_2015-09-03.pdf.

11. Ilstrup-Hickey emails retrieved via public records request.

12. Jeremy Baumhower, "Making or Breaking the Coup: The Future of 7,200 Children is up for Grabs #ElectionDay2015 #WLS #ABC ," *IHeartGlassCity*, Nov. 2, 2015, http://bit.ly/369C0RT.

13. #IStandWithMrHickey, https://twitter.com/hashtag/istandwithmrhickey?lang=en.

14. "Sponsorship continues to draw controversy at Washington Local; Offer of $270,000 for advertising opportunities withdrawn," *Toledo Blade*, Sept. 12, 2015, https://www.toledoblade.com/Education/2015/09/12/Sponsorship-continues-to-draw-controversy-at-Washington-Local.html.

15. WLS Board meeting, video, Sept. 12, 2015, http://bit.ly/39o5IEQ. (The title caption mistakenly reads "September 9" instead of September 12.)

16. #TeamHickey, https://twitter.com/hashtag/teamhickey. #IStandWithHickey, https://twitter.com/hashtag/IStandWithHickey.

17. Ch. 14, Note 15.

18. Ch. 14, Note 14.

19. "Hundreds of residents defend Washington Local superintendent," *13abc News*, Sept. 12, 2015, https://www.13abc.com/home/headlines/Hundreds-of-residents-defend-Washington-local-superintendent-327094351.html.

20. "Parents support superintendent at Washington Local board meeting," *WTOL 11*, Sept. 13, 2015, http://www.wtol.com/story/30017329/washington-local-web-story.

21. WLS Board meeting, video, Sept. 15, 2015, http://bit.ly/3514fkx

22. Twitter, dead link, https://twitter.com/malakabdo96/status/643898401923465216 (accessed late 2019).

23. Nolan Rosenkrans, "Washington Local board gets message of support for Hickey," *Toledo Blade*, Sept. 16, 2015, https://www.toledoblade.com/Education/2015/09/16/Washington-Local-board-gets-message-of-support-for-Hickey.

24. "Hundreds show support for Washington Local Schools superintendent at meeting Tuesday," *WTOL 11*, Sept. 16, 2015, http://www.wtol.com/story/30040132/hundreds-show-support-for-washington-local-schools-superintendent-at-meeting-tuesday.

Endnotes

25. Ch. 14, Note 23.

26. WLS Board meeting, Sept. 16, 2015, video, https://vimeo.com/141583460. Minutes, https://www.wls4kids.org/files/user/21/file/Board%20Minutes/Board_Minutes_2015-09-16.pdf.

27. Christine Long, "WLS Superintendent of community support: 'Their faith is well placed in me'," *13abc News*, Sept. 16, 2014, https://www.13abc.com/home/headlines/WLS-Superintendent-of-community-support-Their-faith-is-well-placed-in-me-327974321.html.

28. WLS Board meeting, Minutes, Sept. 16, 2015, https://www.wls4kids.org/files/user/21/file/Board%20Minutes/Board_Minutes_2015-09-16.pdf.

29. Nolan Rosenkrans and Sarah Elms, "Washington Local Schools considered firing Hickey before resignation in 2015 ," *Toledo Blade*, Oct. 17, 2017, https://www.toledoblade.com/Education/2017/10/17/Washington-Local-Schools-considered-firing-former-superintendent-Patrick-Hickey-in-2015.html.

30. WLS Board Policies, https://www.boarddocs.com/oh/washlsd/Board.nsf/Public?open&id=policies.

31. Hickey reads his statement at 4 mins, 15 secs in the WLS video, https://vimeo.com/141583460.

32. WLS online newsletter, Sept. 16, 2015, https://www.wls4kids.org/view/13303.pdf.

33. WLS Board meeting, Sept. 16, 2015, video, https://vimeo.com/141583460.

34. Kristian Brown, "WLS Superintendent back on the job," *13abc News*, Sept. 17, 2015, http://bit.ly/39qtPm6.

35. Photos of hugs: #TeamHickey, https://twitter.com/hashtag/teamhickey. Jim Nelson, "Patrick Hickey steps down as WLS superintendent," *NBC 24 News*, Dec. 11, 2015, https://nbc24.com/news/local/patrick-hickey-steps-down-as-wls-superintendent. For *13abc News*, see Ch. 14, Note 27.

36. Ibid.

37. Nolan Rosenkrans, "Reprimand tells Hickey not to get 'too personal'," *Toledo Blade*, Sept. 18, 2015, https://www.toledoblade.com/Education/2015/09/18/Reprimand-tells-Hickey-not-to-get-too-personal.html.

38. Nolan Rosenkrans, "Staff member claims unwanted contact by Hickey; Complaint, emails reveal concerns," *Toledo Blade*, Sept. 23, 2015, https://www.toledoblade.com/Education/2015/09/23/Staff-member-claims-unwanted-contact-by-Hickey.html.

39. "Mr. Hickey's written reprimand," *Toledo Blade*, Sept. 23, 2015, https://www.toledoblade.com/attachment/2015/09/23/Mr-Hickey-s-written-reprimand.pdf.

40. "Statement from Mr. Hickey," *Toledo Blade*, Sept. 23, 2015, https://www.toledoblade.com/attachment/2015/09/23/Statement-from-Mr-Hickey.pdf.

41. "Full report of WLS superintendent's unprofessional behavior released," *WTOL 11*, Sept. 23, 2015, report, http://www.wtol.com/story/30101433/full-report-of-wls-superintendents-unprofessional-behavior-released. PDF, http://ftpcontent4.worldnow.com/wtol/pdf/WLSrecordsonSuperintendentHickey.pdf.

42. Ch. 14, Note 7.

43. "Patricia Carmean's C.P.O. petition hearing against Patrick Hickey 4/20/17 (1 of 2)," posted by Jeremy Baumhower, Apr. 24, 2017, https://youtu.be/RTORgtQ0fKM.

44. Retrieved 2019 via public records request for Hickey's emails on WLS system.

CHAPTER 16 – Investigations Begin; Hickey on Administrative Leave

1. WLS online newsletter, Oct. 21, 2015, https://www.wls4kids.org/view/14995.pdf.

2. Email retrieved by the author via public records request.

3. "WLS superintendent, parent to file ethic complaints against school board," *WTOL 11*, Dec. 11, 2015, https://www.wtol.com/article/news/wls-superintendent-parent-to-file-ethic-complaints-against-school-board/512-bf6547fc-41f2-488d-9423-ea18dec3f49e.

4. Nolan Rosenkrans, "Hickey faces new claims he harassed; Board member files complaint," *Toledo Blade*, Nov. 6, 2015, https://www.toledoblade.com/local/education/2015/11/06/Hickey-faces-new-claims-he-harassed/stories/20151106087.

5. Ch. 16, Note 4; conversation with Carmean. Video, "Patricia Carmean's C.P.O. petition hearing against Patrick Hickey 4/20/17 (1 of 2)," posted by Jeremy Baumhower, Apr. 24, 2017, https://youtu.be/RTORgtQ0fKM.

6. Email retrieved via public records request.

7. Ch. 16, Note 4.

8. Emails from Hickey retrieved by the author via public records request.

9. Retrieved via public records request.

10. Email given to author by Patricia Carmean.

11. Retrieved via public records request.

12. Ch. 16, Note 4.

13. Jeremy Baumhower, "Making or Breaking the Coup: The Future of 7,200 Children is up for Grabs #ElectionDay2015 #WLS #ABC ," *IHeartGlassCity*, Nov. 2, 2015, http://bit.ly/369C0RT.

14. For digital images of the MSP investigation reports, see the Kindle edition of this book, https://www.amazon.com/PASSING-TRASH-Covering-Educators-Superintendent-ebook/dp/B0817MK4ZP.

15. Ch. 16, Note 4.

16. Nolan Rosenkrans, "Video shows Hickey by class door; Paid leave, probe sparked by ex-superintendent taking photos at night," *Toledo Blade*, Dec. 30, 2015, https://www.toledoblade.com/Education/2015/12/30/Video-shows-Hickey-by-class-door.html.

17. According to Langenderfer.

18. Ch. 16, Note 16.

19. Ibid.

20. Ibid.

21. Nolan Rosenkrans, "New plan promised for troubled Washington Local; District chief has come under fire," *Toledo Blade*, Nov. 18, 2015, https://www.toledoblade.com/Education/2015/11/18/New-plan-promised-for-troubled-Washington-Local.html.

22. WLS Board meeting, video, Nov. 18, 2015, http://bit.ly/2QI1qjh.

23. WLS online newsletter, Nov. 18, 2015, https://www.wls4kids.org/view/15544.pdf.

24. Nolan Rosenkrans, "Washington Local leader placed on paid suspension, *Toledo Blade*, Nov. 19, 2015, https://www.toledoblade.com/local/education/2015/11/19/Washington-Local-leader-placed-on-paid-suspension/stories/20151118255.

25. Joey Horan, "Toledo's #MeToo Moment: A popular school board member with a well-known history as a sexual predator finally gets taken down," *Belt Magazine*, Mar. 22, 2018, http://beltmag.com/patrick-hickey-finally-goes-down.

26. Retrieved via public records request to Michigan State Police.

27. Ibid.

Endnotes

CHAPTER 17 – Hickey Resigns; The 37 Charges

1. WLS Board meeting, Dec. 2, 2015, Podcast, https://www.wls4kids.org/District/Department/12-Board-Information/Podcasts/8003-2015-12-02.html. Minutes, https://www.wls4kids.org/files/user/21/file/2015_December_2_Board_Meeting_Minutes.pdf.

2. Vanessa McCray, "Washington Local Schools superintendent Patrick Hickey resigns," *Toledo Blade*, Dec. 11, 2015, https://www.toledoblade.com/Education/2015/12/11/Washington-Local-Schools-superintendent-Patrick-Hickey-resigns.html.

3. Nolan Rosenkrans and Sarah Elms, "Washington Local Schools considered firing Hickey before resignation in 2015," *Toledo Blade*, Oct. 17, 2017, https://www.toledoblade.com/Education/2017/10/17/Washington-Local-Schools-considered-firing-former-superintendent-Patrick-Hickey-in-2015.html.

4. Jeremy Baumhower, "The Email Washington Local Schools' Superintendent Dr. Susan Hayward Doesn't Want You to Read," *IHeartGlassCity*, Feb. 2, 2018, https://glasscityhalffull.wordpress.com/2018/02/02/the-email-washington-local-schools-superintendent-dr-susan-hayward-doesnt-want-you-to-read.

5. WLS Board meeting, Minutes, Feb. 13, 2016, https://www.wls4kids.org/files/user/21/file/Board%20Minutes/Board_Minutes_2016_02_13.pdf.

6. WLS Board meeting, Feb. 13, 2016, video, http://bit.ly/2SDqWZA. Agenda, https://www.wls4kids.org/files/user/21/file/2015%20December%2011%20special%20meeting.pdf. Minutes, https://www.wls4kids.org/files/user/21/file/2015%20Dec%2011.pdf.

7. *NBC 24 News*, video, Dec. 11, 2015, https://nbc24.com/news/local/patrick-hickey-steps-down-as-wls-superintendent.

8. *WTOL 11*, "Former WLS superintendent talks to WTOL about decision to resign," Dec. 11, 2015, http://www.wtol.com/story/30728524/wls-board-approves-resignation-of-superintendent. *WTOL 11*, "WLS superintendent, parent to file ethic complaints against school board," Dec. 11, 2015, http://www.wtol.com/story/30725082/wls-superintendent-parent-to-file-ethic-complaints-against-school-board.

9. *WTOL 11*, "WLS releases details of former supt. Hickey's separation agreement," Dec. 15, 2015, http://www.wtol.com/story/30755556/washington-local-schools-releases-details-of-former-supthickeys-separation-agreement.

10. *WTOL 11*, "Former WLS superintendent talks to WTOL about decision to resign," Dec. 11, 2015, http://www.wtol.com/story/30728524/wls-board-approves-resignation-of-superintendent.

11. Vanessa McCray, "Superintendent Hickey steps down; Board accepts resignation, ending controversy," *Toledo Blade*, Dec. 12, 2015, https://www.toledoblade.com/Education/2015/12/12/Superintendent-Hickey-steps-down-1.html.

12. Jim Nelson, "Patrick Hickey steps down as WLS superintendent," *NBC 24 News*, Dec. 11, 2015, https://nbc24.com/news/local/patrick-hickey-steps-down-as-wls-superintendent.

13. Chris Myers, "Patrick Hickey Resigns, *SwampBubbles.com*, Dec. 11, 2015, http://bit.ly/359J5R0.

14. Photographic images of the leaked document, *Toledo Blade*, http://toledobladedata.com/pdfs/hickey.pdf.

15. Ch. 17, Note 3.

16. Nolan Rosenkrans, "Patrick Hickey threatens lawsuit over leaked documents," *Toledo Blade*, Jan. 14, 2018, https://www.toledoblade.com/local/2018/01/13/Patrick-Hickey-threatens-lawsuit-over-leaked-documents.html.
17. Ch. 17, Note 3.
18. WLS Board meeting, Dec. 16, 2015, Minutes, https://www.wls4kids.org/files/user/21/file/2015_December_16_Board_Minutes1.pdf. Video, http://bit.ly/2QvP8dC.
19. See *SwampBubbles.com*, Dec. 21, 2015, http://bit.ly/2rF6lZJ.
20. Nolan Rosenkrans, "Video shows Hickey by class door," *Toledo Blade*, Dec. 30, 2015, https://www.toledoblade.com/Education/2015/12/30/Video-shows-Hickey-by-class-door.html.

CHAPTER 18 – More Investigations, More Hickey Drama

1. For digital images of the MSP investigation reports, see the Kindle edition of this book, https://www.amazon.com/PASSING-TRASH-Covering-Educators-Superintendent-ebook/dp/B0817MK4ZP.
2. Ibid.
3. 2016 School Board photo, https://www.wls4kids.org/view/15979.pdf.
4. Jim Nelson, "Former WLS superintendent Hickey banned from school events," *NBC 24 News*, Feb. 13, 2016, https://nbc24.com/news/local/former-wls-superintendent-hickey-banned-from-school-events.
5. Ibid.
6. Jeremy Baumhower, *Socked: The Unbelievable Tale of How a Bully Used Fake News to Punch a School District (and Me)* (eBook, 2017), no longer available at Apple but live at Kobo.
7. WLS Board, Notice of Emergency Meeting on Feb. 13, 2016, https://www.wls4kids.org/files/user/22/file/News%202016_Emergency%20Board%20Meeting%20--%20February%2013.pdf. Minutes, https://www.wls4kids.org/files/user/21/file/Board%20Minutes/Board_Minutes_2016_02_13.pdf.
8. WLS Board meeting, Minutes, Feb. 15, 2016, https://www.wls4kids.org/files/user/21/file/Board%20Minutes/Board_Minutes_2016_02_15.pdf.
9. Amy Montgomery, "Washington Local school board upholds decision to ban former Supt. from property," *13abc News*, Feb. 15, 2016, https://www.13abc.com/home/headlines/Former-Washington-Local-Superintendent-banned-from-school-property-368721071.html.
10. Vanessa McCray, "Board OK's Hickey's ban from schools, *Toledo Blade*, Feb. 16, 2016, https://www.toledoblade.com/Education/2016/02/16/Board-OKs-Hickey-s-ban-from-schools.html.
11. WLS Board meeting, audio, Feb. 15, 2016, https://www.wls4kids.org/District/Department/12-Board-Information/Podcasts/8146-2016-02-15.html.
12. WLS Board meeting, Minutes, Feb. 17, 2016, https://www.wls4kids.org/files/user/21/file/Board%20Minutes/Board_Minutes_2016-02-17.pdf. Video, http://bit.ly/2SIC334.
13. On the record statement to the author.
14. WLS Board meeting, video, Feb. 17, 2016, http://bit.ly/2SIC334.

Endnotes

15. WLS Board meeting, podcast, June 11, 2016,
https://www.wls4kids.org/District/Department/12-Board-Information/Podcasts/8415-2016-
06-11.html.
16. Petition at https://www.change.org/p/washington-local-board-of-education-let-mr-
patrick-hickey-speak-at-the-class-of-2016-graduation.
17. On the record statement to the author.
18. Ibid.
19. Documents included in Michigan State Police report on Hickey investigation, retrieved
via public records request.
20. On the record statement to the author.
21. Ibid.
22. On the slow work at the Ohio DOE, see Bennett Haeberle, "Ohio Department of
Education can take months, years to punish teachers," WBNS-10TV (Columbus, Ohio),
May 17, 2018, https://www.10tv.com/article/ohio-department-education-can-take-months-
years-punish-teachers.
23. State report card,
https://www.wls4kids.org/files/user/22/file/Report%20Card%20Board%20Meeting%20Pow
erPoint%209_21_2016.pdf.
24. Retrieved via public records request.
25. PatrickHickey425.

CHAPTER 19 – Hickey Roils the District; Elected to School Board
1. Ignazio Messina, "Washington Local superintendent to retire," *Toledo Blade*, March 22,
2017, https://www.toledoblade.com/local/education/2007/03/22/Washington-Local-
superintendent-to-retire/stories/200703220081. Obituary,
https://www.legacy.com/obituaries/toledoblade/obituary.aspx?n=michael-w-
carmean&pid=124592629.
2. On the record statement to the author.
3. Carmean's preliminary hearing on Apr. 20, 2017, video (part 2), posted by Jeremy
Baumhower on Apr. 24, 2017,   https://www.youtube.com/watch?v=gdtvIkc56wI.
4. Nolan Rosenkrans, "Hickey target of protection order," *Toledo Blade*, April 21, 2017,
https://www.toledoblade.com/Education/2017/04/21/Former-Washington-Local-
superintendent-Patrick-Hickey-target-of-protection-order.html.
5. Nolan Rosenkrans, "Washington Local board rivals appear before magistrate," *Toledo
Blade*, May 3, 2017, https://www.toledoblade.com/Courts/2017/05/04/Washington-Local-
board-rivals-appear-before-magistrate/stories/feed/feed/index.rss.
6. Denny Shaffer show, Q105.5, April 18, 2017, https://audioboom.com/posts/5829843-4-18-
17-7am-seg-1-patrick-hickey.
7. ProPublica profile, https://projects.propublica.org/nonprofits/organizations/271911976.
8. Denny Shaffer show, Q105.5, April 18, 2017, Segment 2,
https://audioboom.com/posts/5829844-4-18-17-7am-seg-2-reactions-to-the-hickey-
interview?playlist_direction=forward.
9. "Office-seeking as grudge sport," *Toledo Blade*, May 13, 2017,
https://www.toledoblade.com/opinion/editorials/2017/05/13/Office-seeking-as-grudge-
sport/stories/feed/feed/index.rss.
10. Johnny Hildo, "Keeping Score in City Politics," *Toledo City Paper*, June 1, 2017,
https://toledocitypaper.com/politics/keeping-score-in-city-politics.
11. Email provided to author by Mr. Hodnicki.

12. Sarah Elms, "Former Washington Local Schools superintendent among field of nine for election," *Toledo Blade*, Sept. 29, 2017, https://www.toledoblade.com/Education/2017/09/29/Former-Washington-Local-Schools-superintendent-among-field-of-nine-for-election.html.

13. Ibid.

14. Nolan Rosenkrans and Sarah Elms, "Washington Local Schools considered firing Hickey before resignation in 2015, *Toledo Blade*, Oct. 17, 2017, https://www.toledoblade.com/local/education/2017/10/17/Washington-Local-Schools-considered-firing-former-superintendent-Patrick-Hickey-in-2015/stories/20171017118.

15. Fred LeFebvre show, WSPD radio, Oct. 16, 2017, https://wspd.iheart.com/featured/fred/content/2017-10-16-monday-60-minute-poll-friending-girls-on-facebook.

16. Ch. 19, Note 14.

17. Kaylie Spotts, "Former superintendent running for Board of Education raising some questions," *NBC 24 News*, Oct. 17, 2017, https://nbc24.com/news/local/former-superintendent-running-for-board-of-education-raising-some-questions.

18. As Hickey said this, there was an open investigation by the Ohio Department of Education which had subpoenaed his Addison School personnel records plus WLS Board members and teachers for their information concerning him.

19. A second reprimand happened when he was put on administrative leave and banned from school properties (unless involving his children) in November 2015 (while still Supt.). His forced resignation in December 2015 was a third reprimand. A fourth reprimand was in February 2016 when he was totally banned from school properties (even his own children's events) after erratic behavior at a high school basketball game.

20. This is contradicted in the Dec. 2015 document with "37 Charges." The Board leadership apparently let him off easy in order to avoid a larger scandal and a likely legal challenge from Hickey.

21. Anything inappropriate that happened was all Anna's fault, he implies.

22. Supt. Kersh's letter on file did *not* say Hickey left Addison "in good standing." It stated he "resigned from Addison Community Schools on November 5, 1990. He did so without prejudice of any sort." Hickey later tried but failed to get Kersh to add the phrase "in good standing."

23. There is no record of any police investigation, according to the recent Michigan State Police reports. Nor has any investigator been able to find record of any child welfare agency investigation.

24. Private investigators could not verify Hickey's job titles at St. Anthony Villa. Jim Driskill challenged Hickey's claims.

25. Former Superintendent Michael Carmean did *not* promote Hickey to Asst. Superintendent, the WLS Board did (with input from the Ohio School Board Association).

26. Hickey did not truthfully list the exact dates of his former employment at Addison Schools, nor did he account for his "missing year" after leaving Addison. The School Board's list of "37 Charges" noted that.

27. Some of Hickey's expenditures and reimbursements were challenged by the Board and Treasurer, and he was forced to reimburse WLS.

28. The fight between the two women teachers was related to their intimate relationships with Hickey. It took place in the high school cafeteria in front of hundreds of students was not an insignificant event. It drew children into the sexual gossip surrounding their Superintendent and teachers.

Endnotes

29. Left unanswered is why Hickey was roaming the halls in a locked school building at night to begin with, and why in particular he would be scrutinizing the classroom door of the teacher who brought the complaint against him (Anna).

30. The School Board leadership believed they had cause for terminating Hickey, but apparently wanted to avoid a larger scandal and prolonged legal challenges from him. See Ch. 19, Note 14.

31. Marcus Espinoza, "Local billboard causing controversy," *NBC 24 News*, Nov. 1, 2017, https://nbc24.com/news/local/local-billboard-causing-controversy.

32. Fred LeFebvre show, WSPD Radio, Nov. 2, 2017, https://www.spreaker.com/user/9809225/brooke-brooks-interview.

33. Nolan Rosenkrans, "Woman claims sex with Hickey as a teen; School board candidate was her teacher then," *Toledo Blade*, Nov. 6, 2017, https://www.toledoblade.com/local/2017/11/04/Woman-admits-to-affair-with-Washington-Local-board-candidate-Patrick-Hickey-as-a-teenager/stories/20171103192.

34. Michigan State Police report (from Feb. 12, 2016), *Toledo Blade*, Nov. 3, 2017: https://www.toledoblade.com/attachment/2017/11/03/REPORT.pdf. For digital images of these and other Michigan State Police reports on the Hickey investigation, see the Kindle edition of this book, https://www.amazon.com/PASSING-TRASH-Covering-Educators-Superintendent-ebook/dp/B0817MK4ZP.

35. Melissa Voetsch, "Hickey gets ready for return to the Washington Local School District," Nov. 8, 2017, *13abc News*, https://www.13abc.com/content/news/Hickey-gets-ready-for-return-to-the-Washington-Local-School-District--456217613.html.

36. Emails between Hickey, WLS Supt. Hayward, Board members, and WLS staff: PDF at *Toledo Blade*, Nov. 2017, http://toledobladedata.com/pdfs/hickeyemails.pdf.

37. WLS Board meeting, video, Nov. 8, 2017, http://bit.ly/39rfiGT.

38. Blair Caldwell, "Hickey elected to school board despite a ban from school property," *WTOL 11*, Nov. 9, 2017, http://www.wtol.com/story/36800409/hickey-elected-to-school-board-despite-a-ban-from-school-property.

39. Petition at https://www.change.org/p/residents-for-a-safe-wls-keep-patrick-hickey-s-wls-ban-in-place.

40. Associated Press, "Ex-school leader elected to board still banned from district," *Washington Times*, Jan. 4, 2018, https://www.washingtontimes.com/news/2018/jan/4/ex-school-leader-elected-to-board-still-banned-fro/

41. Nolan Rosenkrans, "Hickey's election to Washington Local board prompts legal threats," *Toledo Blade*, Nov. 17, 2017, https://www.toledoblade.com/local/2017/11/16/Hickey-s-election-to-Washington-Local-board-prompts-legal-threats-behind-the-scenes/stories. Emails at http://toledobladedata.com/pdfs/hickeyemails.pdf

42. Nolan Rosenkrans, "Washington Local lawyers told Hickey to pay back public funds," *Toledo Blade*, Dec. 20, 2017, https://www.toledoblade.com/Education/2017/12/19/Washington-Local-lawyers-told-Hickey-to-pay-back-public-funds.html

43. For example, WLS online newsletter on Jeanne Hickey Memorial Fund, May 15, 2013, p. 12, https://www.wls4kids.org/view/393.pdf. ProPublica profile, https://projects.propublica.org/nonprofits/organizations/271911976.

44. WLS Board meeting, video, Dec. 20, 2017, https://vimeo.com/249827585.

45. Sarah Elms, "Outgoing Washington Local board maintains ban on Hickey," *Toledo Blade*, Dec. 21, 2017, https://www.toledoblade.com/local/education/2017/12/20/Divided-

Washington-Local-Schools-board-refuses-to-ease-ban-on-former-superintendent-now-elected-to-board/stories/20171220157.
46. Ch. 19, Note 44.
47. Nolan Rosenkrans, "Patrick Hickey, Washington Local schools spar over 2K reimbursement," *Toledo Blade*, Dec. 23, 2017, https://www.toledoblade.com/Education/2017/12/22/Patrick-Hickey-Washington-Local-Schools-spar-over-2k-reimbursement.html.
48. WLS Board meeting, video, Dec. 20, 2017, https://vimeo.com/249827585.
49. Jay Hannah, "Patrick Hickey remains banned from school grounds after Washington Local waiver vote fails," *NBC 24 News*, Dec. 20, 2017, https://nbc24.com/news/local/patrick-hickey-remains-banned-from-school-grounds-after-washington-local-waiver-vote-fails.
50. Ibid.
51. Ch. 19, Note 45.
52. Editorial, "No shushing Hickey critics," *Toledo Blade*, Jan. 1, 2018, https://www.toledoblade.com/Editorials/2018/01/01/No-shushing-Hickey-critics.html.
53. Joey Horan, "Toledo's #MeToo Moment: A popular school board member with a well-known history as a sexual predator finally gets taken down," *Belt Magazine*, Mar. 22, 2018, http://beltmag.com/patrick-hickey-finally-goes-down.
54. Ch. 19, Note 47.
55. Ignazio Messina, "Toledo's top stories 2017," *Toledo Blade*, Dec. 29, 2017, https://www.toledoblade.com/local/2017/12/29/Toledo-s-top-stories-2017.html.

CHAPTER 20 – Chaos as Hickey Seated on Board; MSP Reopen Investigation
1. *ToledoTalk.com*, dead link, http://toledotalk.com/cgi-bin/tt.pl/articleall/214401/Hickey_For_Kids_Campaign_Signs.
2. Emails retrieved via public records request.
3. Editorial, "No shushing Hickey critics," *Toledo Blade*, Jan. 1, 2018, https://www.toledoblade.com/Editorials/2018/01/01/No-shushing-Hickey-critics.html.
4. Fred LeFebvre, WSPD Radio, https://wspd.iheart.com/featured/fred/content/2018-01-02-troubled-wls-board.
5. Ibid.
6. Dead link: https://www.facebook.com/patrick.hickey.77770/videos/10155765012562419/
7. Author's transcription from the video.
8. Nolan Rosenkrans, "Patrick Hickey swears in himself as Washington Local board member on Facebook Live," *Toledo Blade*, Jan. 3, 2018, https://www.toledoblade.com/Education/2018/01/03/Washington-Local-board-to-meet-discuss-Hickey-ban.html. Twitter, https://twitter.com/NolanRosenkrans.
9. Nolan Rosenkrans, "Washington Local keeps ban of board member in effect," *Toledo Blade*, Jan. 4, 2018, https://www.toledoblade.com/local/education/2018/01/03/Washington-Local-board-meetings-will-move-off-campus/stories/20180103135.
10. WLS online newsletter, Jan. 3, 2018, https://www.wls4kids.org/files/user/22/file/Across%20the%20Board%201_3_18%20Organizational%20Meeting.pdf.
11. WLS Board meeting, video, Jan. 3, 2018, http://bit.ly/2QafxPg.
12. Audio of the Addison group's statements on Jan. 3, 2018 were posted on YouTube, https://youtu.be/LPuGWgLyeaU, complete with an aerial photo of the local cemetery. The subtitle on one frame reads, "Very shortly thereafter the vehicle starts bouncing."

Endnotes

13. Nolan Rosenkrans, "Patrick Hickey threatens lawsuit over leaked documents," *Toledo Blade*, Jan. 14, 2018, https://www.toledoblade.com/local/2018/01/13/Patrick-Hickey-threatens-lawsuit-over-leaked-documents.html.
14. Sarah Elms, "Location not yet determined for Washington Local Schools meetings," *Toledo Blade*, Jan. 6, 2018, https://www.toledoblade.com/Education/2018/01/06/Location-not-yet-determined-for-Washington-Local-Schools-meetings.html.
15. Ch. 20, Note 13.
16. Editorial, "With Hickey: watch and wait," *Toledo Blade*, Jan. 11, 2018, https://www.toledoblade.com/Editorials/2018/01/11/With-Hickey-watch-and-wait.html.
17. WLS Board meeting, video, Jan. 16, 2018, http://bit.ly/2Zybxet.
18. WLS Board meeting, Jan. 18, 2018, Agenda, https://www.wls4kids.org/files/user/216/file/WLS%20Board%20Agenda%201_18_2018(1).pdf. Video, https://vimeo.com/253988753.
19. WTOL has removed the video. Brief excerpt at WLSPolitics, https://www.facebook.com/WLSpolitics/posts/1712387412114917.
20. *WTOL 11*, "Patrick Hickey pleads guilty to criminal sexual conduct," May 9, 2018, http://www.wtol.com/story/38148345/patrick-hickey-pleads-guilty-to-criminal-sexual-conduct.
21. *13abc News*, "Washington Local School Board calls for Patrick Hickey to resign," Jan. 25, 2018, https://www.13abc.com/content/news/An-investigation-involving-Patrick-Hickey-is-underway-in-Lenawee-Co-471141613.html.
22. Sarah Elms, "Michigan State Police investigating Patrick Hickey," *Toledo Blade*, Jan. 26, 2018, https://www.toledobladFe.com/Education/2018/01/25/Michigan-State-Police-investigating-Patrick-Hickey.html
23. WLS Politics, https://www.facebook.com/WLSpolitics.
24. David Panian, "Relationship between former Addison teacher, student investigated," *Daily Telegram*, Jan. 27, 2018, https://www.lenconnect.com/news/20180127/relationship-between-former-addison-teacher-student-investigated.
25. Jeremy Baumhower, *IHeartGlassCity*, Feb. 2, 2018, https://glasscityhalffull.wordpress.com/2018/02/02/the-email-washington-local-schools-superintendent-dr-susan-hayward-doesnt-want-you-to-read.
26. Fred LeFebvre show, WSPD Radio, Jan. 29, 2018, https://wspd.iheart.com/featured/fred/content/2018-01-29-kristina-hassenzahl-student-asst-to-hickey.

CHAPTER 21 – MSP Build Their Case; Hickey Arraigned

1. WLS Board meeting, video, Feb. 1, 2018, http://bit.ly/2Qt4PlS.
2. WTVG, "Washington Local School Board calls for Patrick Hickey to resign," *13abc News*, Feb. 1, 2018, https://www.13abc.com/content/news/An-investigation-involving-Patrick-Hickey-is-underway-in-Lenawee-Co-471141613.html.
3. For example, in *US News*, "Ex-School Leader Elected to Board Still Banned From District," Jan. 4, 2018, https://www.usnews.com/news/best-states/ohio/articles/2018-01-04/ex-school-leader-elected-to-board-still-banned-from-district. In *Washington Times*, "School board says member under investigation should resign," Feb. 2, 2018, https://www.washingtontimes.com/news/2018/feb/2/school-board-says-member-under-investigation-shoul.
4. WLS Board meeting, video, Feb. 20, 2018, http://bit.ly/37qM7lL. On the student violence at the school, see *Toledo Blade*, "Police: Teenage boy stabs Washington Local security officer,"

Feb. 21, 2018, https://www.toledoblade.com/Police-Fire/2018/02/20/Teenage-boy-reportedly-stabs-Washington-local-Schools-security-officer.html.

5. WLS Board meeting, podcast, Feb. 21, 2018, https://www.wls4kids.org/District/Department/12-Board-Information/Podcasts/9856-2018-02-21.html.

6. Ibid.

7. WLS Board meeting, video, Mar. 1, 2018, http://bit.ly/39pJthQ.

8. WLS Board meeting, podcast, Mar. 17, 2018, https://www.wls4kids.org/District/Department/12-Board-Information/Podcasts/9894-2018-03-27.html.

9. KC Baker, "Ohio School Board Member Accused of Sex With 15-Year-Old Student Decades Ago — Which He Denies." *People*, Mar. 21, 2018, https://people.com/crime/ohio-school-board-member-superintendent-accused-sex-female-student.

10. Nolan Rosenkrans, "Defense attorney says Patrick Hickey charged with criminal sexual conduct," *Toledo Blade*, Mar. 20, 2018, https://www.toledoblade.com/Police-Fire/2018/03/19/Lenawee-County-prosecutors-reviewing-Hickey-sex-abuse-case.html.

11. *WTOL 11*, "Patrick Hickey announces resignation after being charged with three counts of criminal sexual conduct," Mar. 19, 2018, http://www.wtol.com/story/37759913/patrick-hickey-announces-resignation-after-being-charged-with-three-counts-of-criminal-sexual-conduct.

12. Fred LeFebvre show, WSPD radio, https://www.spreaker.com/user/9809225/brook-brooks.

13. Amy Montgomery, "Washington Local community speaks about criminal charges against Patrick Hickey," *13abc News*, Mar. 20, 2018, https://www.13abc.com/content/news/Washington-Local-community-speaks-about-criminal-charges-against-Patrick-Hickey-477464763.html.

14. Jetta Fraser photo, *Toledo Blade*, Mar. 21, 2018, https://www.toledoblade.com/Courts/2018/03/21/WLS-board-member-Patrick-Hickey-pleads-not-guilty-to-criminal-sexual-conduct.html.

15. *Daily Telegram*, Mar. 21, 2018, video, https://youtu.be/OYJ8rK5PjAg.

16. MLive.com, https://www.mlive.com/news/jackson/index.ssf/2018/03/teacher_charged_with_felonies.html.

17. Javonte Anderson, "Washington Local school board accepts Patrick Hickey's resignation," *Toledo Blade*, Mar. 21, 2018, https://www.toledoblade.com/Education/2018/03/21/Washington-Local-school-board-accepts-Patrick-Hickey-s-resignation.html.

18. McKenzie Kuehnlein, "Patrick Hickey arraigned on criminal sexual conduct charges," *13abc News*, Mar. 21, 2018, https://www.13abc.com/content/news/Patrick-Hickey-faces-a-judge-477510753.html.

19. Ch. 21, Note 17.

20. WLS Board meeting, video, Mar. 21, 2018, http://bit.ly/2MGD348.

21. Editorial, "No more Hickey circus at WLS," *Toledo Blade*, Mar. 21, 2018, https://www.toledoblade.com/Editorials/2018/03/21/No-more-Patrick-Hickey-circus-at-Washington-Local-Schools-WLS.html.

Endnotes

CHAPTER 22 – Dawn Speaks with MSP

1. For digital images of the MSP investigation reports, see the Kindle edition of this book, https://www.amazon.com/PASSING-TRASH-Covering-Educators-Superintendent-ebook/dp/B0817MK4ZP.

CHAPTER 23 – MSP Interview Hickey

1. Ch. 22, Note 1.

CHAPTER 24 – Hickey Gets Plea Deal

1. For digital images of the court documents, see the Kindle edition of this book, https://www.amazon.com/PASSING-TRASH-Covering-Educators-Superintendent-ebook/dp/B0817MK4ZP

2. "Hickey pleads guilty to sexual conduct charge," *Toledo Blade*, May 9, 2018, https://www.toledoblade.com/local/courts/2018/05/09/Hickey-pleads-guilty-in/stories/20180509137.

3. For example, *The Detroit News*, "Ex-school official pleads guilty to sexual misconduct," May 9, 2018, https://www.detroitnews.com/story/news/local/michigan/2018/05/09/school-official-banned-sexual-misconduct/34727153.

4. Ch. 24, Note 2.

5. David Panian, "Hickey pleads guilty in Michigan charges," *The Monroe News*, May 10, 2018, http://www.monroenews.com/news/20180510/hickey-pleads-guilty-in-michigan-charges.

6. Ibid.

7. See Chapter 1 for Dawn's full statement.

8. Ch. 24, Note 2.

9. Ibid.

10. Editorial, "Hickey did it, they hid it," *Toledo Blade*, May 13, 2018, https://www.toledoblade.com/opinion/editorials/2018/05/13/Patrick-Hickey-did-it-they-hid-it/stories/20180513041.

11. Melissa Voetsch, "Hickey gets ready for return to the Washington Local School District," *13abc News*, Nov. 8, 2017, https://www.13abc.com/content/news/Hickey-gets-ready-for-return-to-the-Washington-Local-School-District--456217613.html.

12. Ch. 24, Note 2.

13. Ibid.

14. "Hickey loses educator licenses after felony sex crime conviction," *Toledo Blade*, May 18, 2018, https://www.toledoblade.com/Education/2018/05/18/Hickey-loses-educator-licenses-after-felony-sex-crime-conviction.html.

CHAPTER 25 – Hickey Sentenced, Jailed; on Sex Offender Registry

1. Eve Sneider, "Patrick Hickey sentenced to one year in jail for groping student," *Toledo Blade*, June 29, 2018, https://www.toledoblade.com/local/courts/2018/06/28/Patrick-Hickey-sentenced-to-one-year-in-jail-for-groping-student/stories/20180628155.

2. "Patrick Hickey sentencing - June 28, 2018," *Daily Telegram*, video, https://youtu.be/qwYS4Gor2DM.

3. WTOL video on sentencing hearing, July 8, 2018, http://bit.ly/2Q8eMGt. (Accessed Jan. 2020.)

4. Michelle Shiels, "Patrick Hickey sentenced to 1 year in jail, 5 years probation," *WTOL 11*, http://www.wtol.com/story/38531454/patrick-hickey-sentenced-to-1-year-in-jail-5-years-probation.
5. WLS Politics, https://www.facebook.com/WLSpolitics/posts/1712387412114917.
6. Ibid.
7. Mayfield's letter is no longer online. (Dead link: https://medium.com/@kathymayfield/an-open-letter-to-jeremy-baumhower-the-unapologetic-defender-of-a-child-predator-33f6469a73bc.) *Toledo Blade* reporter Nolan Rosenkrans referenced her letter on Twitter, July 2, 2018, http://bit.ly/2Q3QNI6.
8. Letter to the Editor, *Toledo Blade*, July 6, 2018, https://www.toledoblade.com/opinion/letters-to-the-editor/2018/07/06/To-the-editor-It-is-not-over-for-WLS-just-yet/stories/20180706141.
9. Kate Snyder, "Ex-Washington Local superintendent Patrick Hickey released from jail," *Toledo Blade*, Apr. 23, 2019, https://www.toledoblade.com/local/courts/2019/04/23/former-washington-local-superintendent-patrick-hickey-released-from-jail/stories/20190423113.
10. Ohio Attorney General, Sex Offender Registry, http://www.icrimewatch.net/offenderdetails.php?OfndrID=6670289&AgencyID=55149.
11. Editorial, "Silence and trash in our schools: Communities must be able to trust that those working don't have a history of misconduct," *Toledo Blade*, Apr. 27, 2019, https://www.toledoblade.com/opinion/editorials/2019/04/28/patrick-hickey-washington-local-pat-murtha-rossford-high-school/stories/201

www.ingramcontent.com/pod-product-compliance
Lightning Source LLC
Chambersburg PA
CBHW052118270326
41930CB00012B/2676